Download Disability Listings on Nolo.com

You can download the disability listings that come with this book at:

 www.nolo.com/back-of-book/QSS.html

We'll also post updates whenever there's an important change to the law affecting this book—as well as articles and other related materials.

More Resources from Nolo.com

 Legal Forms, Books, & Software
Hundreds of do-it-yourself products—all written in plain English, approved, and updated by our in-house legal editors.

 Legal Articles
Get informed with thousands of free articles on everyday legal topics. Our articles are accurate, up to date, and reader friendly.

Find a Lawyer
Want to talk to a lawyer? Use Nolo to find a lawyer who can help you with your case.

⚖ NOLO The Trusted Name
(but don't take our word for it)

"In Nolo you can trust."

THE NEW YORK TIMES

"Nolo is always there in a jam as the nation's premier publisher of do-it-yourself legal books."

NEWSWEEK

"Nolo publications…guide people simply through the how, when, where and why of the law."

THE WASHINGTON POST

"[Nolo's]…material is developed by experienced attorneys who have a knack for making complicated material accessible."

LIBRARY JOURNAL

"When it comes to self-help legal stuff, nobody does a better job than Nolo…"

USA TODAY

"The most prominent U.S. publisher of self-help legal aids."

TIME MAGAZINE

"Nolo is a pioneer in both consumer and business self-help books and software."

LOS ANGELES TIMES

10th Edition

Nolo's Guide to Social Security Disability

Getting & Keeping Your Benefits

David A. Morton III, M.D.

TENTH EDITION	MARCH 2020
Editor	BETHANY LAURENCE
Cover & Book Design	SUSAN PUTNEY
Proofreading	LINDA FOUST
Indexes	UNGER INDEXING
	RICHARD GENOVA
Printing	BANG PRINTING

Names: Morton, David A., 1945- author.

Title: Nolo's guide to social security disability : getting & keeping your
benefits / David A. Morton III, M.D.

Description: 10th edition. | Berkeley : Nolo Law for All, 2020. | Includes
index.

Identifiers: LCCN 2019041468 (print) | LCCN 2019041469 (ebook) | ISBN
9781413327274 (paperback) | ISBN 9781413327281 (ebook)

Subjects: LCSH: Disability insurance--United States--Handbooks, manuals,
etc. | Social security--United States--Handbooks, manuals, etc.

Classification: LCC HD7105.25.U6 M675 2020 (print) | LCC HD7105.25.U6
(ebook) | DDC 368.38/600973--dc23

LC record available at https://lccn.loc.gov/2019041468

LC ebook record available at https://lccn.loc.gov/2019041469

This book covers only United States law, unless it specifically states otherwise.

Please note

We believe accurate, plain-English legal information should help you solve many of
your own legal problems. But this text is not a substitute for personalized advice
from a knowledgeable lawyer. If you want the help of a trained professional—and
we'll always point out situations in which we think that's a good idea—consult an
attorney licensed to practice in your state.

Dedication

To my mother, Mary E. Morton, and to my wife, Mary L. Morton.

Acknowledgments

I would like to thank Nolo founder Ralph "Jake" Warner for seeing the need for a book on Social Security disability that can be read and used by ordinary people. I would also like to thank former Nolo editors Robin Leonard, Steve Elias, and Spencer Sherman for helping to take difficult and complex areas of law and make them accessible to the general public. Thank you also to Nolo editors Ilona Bray, Cathy Caputo, Janet Portman, and Bethany Laurence.

About the Author

David A. Morton has degrees in psychology (B.A.) and medicine (M.D.). For 14 years, he was a consultant for disability determination to the Social Security Administration in Arkansas. He was chief medical consultant for eight years of that time. In that capacity, he hired, trained, supervised, and evaluated the work of medical doctors and clinical psychologists in determining mental disability claims. He also supervised medical disability determinations of physical disorders and personally made determinations of both physical and mental disorders in adults and children in every specialty of disability medicine. Since 1983, Dr. Morton has authored several books on Social Security disability used by attorneys and federal judges.

Table of Contents

Appendixes

Medical Listing Table of Contents

Download the Medical Listings at **www.nolo.com/back-of-book/QSS.html**

Introduction: Your Social Security Disability Companion

This book is about Social Security disability benefits, which are provided through a U.S. government system run by the Social Security Administration (SSA). These disability programs provide cash support for individuals with mental or physical disorders (and their dependents, in some cases) who cannot work because of the severity of their condition. This book is useful for anyone who:

- is injured or ill and wants to know if they are eligible for disability benefits
- wants to apply for disability benefits
- is already receiving disability benefits and wants to know how to protect the benefits during periodic government reviews of their condition
- wants to appeal a decision denying disability benefits, or
- is helping an adult or child apply for or keep current benefits.

The SSA uses two systems to distribute disability payments:

- Social Security Disability Insurance (SSDI), for workers who have paid into the Social Security trust fund (and their dependents), and
- Supplemental Security Income (SSI), for disabled individuals with limited incomes and assets.

It's easy to become overwhelmed at the thought of applying for disability benefits. The SSA is one of the world's largest bureaucracies; its regulations, rules, operating policies, and guidelines fill reams of paper. For example, one chapter of the SSA's operating manual is about 20,000 pages long. And much of this information changes over time.

Still, it is very possible to apply for, receive, and maintain disability benefits with the help you will find here. We recognize, however, that people applying for disability benefits are most often ill or injured in a way that makes it difficult to accomplish the tasks of daily life, let alone pursue a claim for support from the government. So you may need help beyond this book. We have included an entire chapter on what to do if you need legal assistance (Chapter 15). Also, throughout the book, we've noted situations in which, you may need the advice and support of a family member, trusted friend, paid representative, or attorney.

Medical and Legal Questions

When deciding on your disability claim, the government considers both legal and medical issues. Social Security officials review your claim to decide whether you are legally entitled to the benefits you request. They also request and review medical opinions on your condition to see if it is severe enough to make you disabled. The government considers you disabled only if you are not able to work in your current or most recent job and you do not have the education, experience, or ability to do any other job. For example, a physically disabled

60-year-old doctor may have the ability to work in some other capacity in the medical industry and could be denied benefits for that reason. But the same doctor could not work as a field laborer picking fruit all day because he would not have the physical ability necessary for the job.

Chapters 1 through 15 lead you through the legal and practical issues of applying for disability payments, appealing if you are denied, and making sure that you retain benefits as long as you need them. For most applicants, it will be useful to read all of these chapters in the order presented. But if you have a particular issue to research (for example, you want to file an appeal), you can start with any chapter and you will be directed to important information in other parts of the book as needed. Also note that we occasionally give you references to the Social Security portions of the Code of Federal Regulations (CFR) or to the federal law, U.S. Code (U.S.C.).

Medical Listings

Information about the requirements and functionally disabling aspects of more than 200 specific medical problems that make individuals eligible for disability payments is available on Nolo's website (free for readers of this book) at:

www.nolo.com/back-of-book/QSS.html
These are descriptions of what the SSA calls the Listing of Impairments.

Go to Nolo's website and start with the table of contents for these listings—once you find the section that matches or most closely approximates your disability, you will find all the medical information you need to determine if your disability meets the requirements to obtain benefits. For example, if you suffer from kidney disease, you would open Part 6 and read through the listings there until you found a disorder that matches or is similar to your illness.

Each section of the medical listings begins with a list of medical definitions in plain English related to the disorders discussed in that section. Next, you'll find general background information about the disorders discussed in that section. Finally, each section lists specific medical disorders taken from the official Listing of Impairments the SSA uses in disability claims. The number before each listing is the official number the SSA uses to identify the disability. Following the numbers is a brief discussion of the meaning and how to interpret each listing.

These medical listings contain every listing the SSA has approved for disability claims. We have revised the SSA's wording of the listings to make them more under-standable. Rest assured, however, that we made no changes that would compromise their legal meaning.

Also included in each listing are com-ments about what the SSA calls "residual functional capacity" (RFC). This is a type of rating given to a disability claimant who

How Claims Are Decided

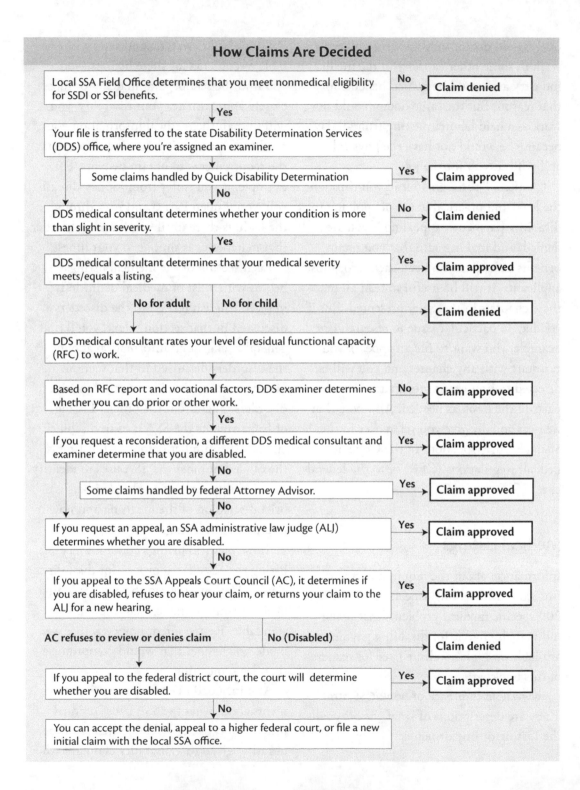

Local SSA Field Office determines that you meet nonmedical eligibility for SSDI or SSI benefits.	**No** → Claim denied
Your file is transferred to the state Disability Determination Services (DDS) office, where you're assigned an examiner.	
Some claims handled by Quick Disability Determination	**Yes** → Claim approved
DDS medical consultant determines whether your condition is more than slight in severity.	**No** → Claim denied
DDS medical consultant determines that your medical severity meets/equals a listing.	**Yes** → Claim approved
No for adult / **No for child**	→ Claim denied
DDS medical consultant rates your level of residual functional capacity (RFC) to work.	
Based on RFC report and vocational factors, DDS examiner determines whether you can do prior or other work.	**No** → Claim approved
If you request a reconsideration, a different DDS medical consultant and examiner determine that you are disabled.	**Yes** → Claim approved
Some claims handled by federal Attorney Advisor.	**Yes** → Claim approved
If you request an appeal, an SSA administrative law judge (ALJ) determines whether you are disabled.	**Yes** → Claim approved
If you appeal to the SSA Appeals Court Council (AC), it determines if you are disabled, refuses to hear your claim, or returns your claim to the ALJ for a new hearing.	**Yes** → Claim approved
AC refuses to review or denies claim / **No (Disabled)**	→ Claim denied
If you appeal to the federal district court, the court will determine whether you are disabled.	**Yes** → Claim approved
You can accept the denial, appeal to a higher federal court, or file a new initial claim with the local SSA office.	

Flow arrows between boxes are labeled: Yes, No, No, Yes, Yes, No, Yes, No, Yes, No, No, Yes.

does not meet the requirements of a Listing of Impairment. The RFC says what kind of work a claimant could do, even considering his or her impairments. If no work is available anywhere in the United States that fits into a claimant's RFC, the claimant may be approved for disability payments even though the claimant's condition does not exactly fit the listing.

Quick Disability Determination (QDD)

In 2006, the SSA tried to improve the disability system by implementing the "disability service improvement process" (DSIP)—sometimes simply called "disability service improvement" (DSI). Most of the DSIP changes affected the way initial disability determinations and appeals are handled. Implementation of this experiment proved unworkable. In 2010, the SSA canceled DSIP, with one exception: The Quick Disability Determination (QDD) process was retained. QDD is a quicker disability determination process for those who are obviously disabled (with, for example, metastatic cancer, severe blindness, profound intellectual disability (formerly called mental retardation),

severe kidney failure requiring dialysis, and the inability to walk—to name a few possibilities). Favorable decisions will be made in such cases within 20 days after the claim is received by the state disability determination agency (DDS). The average time is about 12 days. See Chapter 6 for more information about QDD.

CAUTION
Throughout this book you will see samples of Social Security Administration forms. These are to help you fill out the actual forms. But the SSA requires that you obtain the forms from a Social Security office either in person, by mail, or from the SSA website (www.ssa.gov). Throughout the book we tell you where to locate the forms you need.

Get Updates and More Online

When there are important changes to the information in this book, we'll post updates online, on a page dedicated to this book: **www.nolo.com/back-of-book/QSS.html** You'll find other useful information there, too, including the Medical Listings, author blogs, podcasts, and videos.

What Is Social Security Disability?

The Social Security Administration (SSA) decides who is eligible for disability payments under rules established in the Social Security Act by the U.S. Congress. In this chapter, we describe the two main SSA programs that administer disability payments. We briefly explain the requirements that any claimant must meet to receive benefits. We also provide a number of tips on how to deal with the SSA bureaucracy, and include answers to some of the most frequently asked questions about Social Security disability.

A. Two Different Programs

Once you qualify as disabled under the Social Security Act, the SSA makes disability payments under one of two programs:

- Social Security Disability Insurance (SSDI), for workers who have paid into the Social Security trust fund (and their dependents), or
- Supplemental Security Income (SSI), for disabled individuals with limited incomes and assets.

SSDI claims are also referred to as "Title 2 claims" because they are authorized under Title 2 of the Social Security Act. SSI claims may be referred to as "Title 16 claims" because they are authorized under Title 16 of the Social Security Act. A person claiming a disability is called a "claimant." Some claimants apply under both Title 2 and Title 16; these are known as "concurrent claims."

When the SSA receives your application, it will determine whether you are eligible for disability benefits under SSDI and/or SSI, even if you have not specifically requested both. This means that if you apply only for SSDI benefits, the SSA will automatically process your claim for any SSI disability benefits to which you might be entitled. If your SSDI claim is turned down, you don't have to file another claim for possible SSI benefits.

1. Social Security Disability Insurance

SSDI provides payments to workers who have made contributions to the Social Security trust fund through the Social Security tax on their earnings. SSDI is also available to certain dependents of workers. If you are found eligible for SSDI, you might be entitled to retroactive (past) benefits if you can show that you were disabled before the date of your application. (See Chapter 10 for more details on when benefits begin.)

a. Who Qualifies?

To qualify for SSDI, you must fall into one of the following categories.

i. You are a disabled insured worker under age 66

You must have worked both long enough and recently enough to qualify. It may not be sufficient that you worked for many years and paid Social Security taxes. When you worked is also important. The law requires

Comparing SSDI and SSI		
	SSDI (Title 2)	**SSI (Title 16)**
Must have paid Social Security tax to qualify?	Yes	No
Disability benefits for children?	Only adult children at least 18 years of age and disabled before age 22	Children of any age
Waiting period before benefits begin?	Adults: Five months Children: None	No
Health insurance comes with disability award?	Yes, Medicare starts 24 months after waiting period.	Yes, Medicaid starts immediately in most states.
Can be presumed disabled before actual approval of benefits?	No	Yes, up to six months before decision. Claimant does not have to return payments if found not disabled.
Retroactive benefits?	Yes, up to 12 months	No
Minimum duration of disability?	12 months	12 months. (Blind claimants are exempt from duration requirement.)
What financial factors may prevent eligibility for benefits?	Substantial gainful activity: Work earning more than $1,260/month ($2.110/month if blind) in 2020	a. Substantial gainful activity b. Nonwork income and other resources equivalent to income
Benefits to noncitizens in United States?	Yes	Generally not, but some exceptions
Possible freeze on earnings?	Yes	No
Benefits for past period of disability ("closed period"), even if not currently disabled?	Yes	Yes
Auxiliary benefits to others available on the work earnings of a relative or spouse?	Yes	No
Benefits continued during a period of trial work?	Yes	Yes
Quick reentitlement to benefits if work effort fails after termination of benefits?	Yes	Yes
Benefits outside of United States?	Yes, both U.S. citizens and noncitizens	Generally not for U.S. citizens; never for noncitizens

that you earn a certain number of work credits in a specified time before you are eligible for benefits. You can earn up to four credits per year, each credit representing three months. The amount of earnings required for a credit increases each year as general wage levels rise.

The number of work credits needed for disability benefits depends on your age when you become disabled. Most people need at least 20 credits earned over ten years, ending with the year they become disabled. Younger workers may qualify with fewer credits.

In effect, you count backwards from the year that you became disabled to see whether you have the appropriate number of credits. That means that credits from many years before you became disabled are automatically wiped out, or expire. This can lead to a dangerous situation for people who haven't worked for many years before becoming disabled. Their credits might dip below the required amount, and they can lose eligibility for SSDI. The date after which they lose their eligibility is called the "date last insured" (DLI)—often a subject of dispute in Social Security cases. If you think your DLI is too far in the past to qualify you for SSDI, talk to your local SSA Field Office to make sure—in certain rare circumstances, you may still qualify.

The rules follow; if you are:

- **Before age 24.** You'll need at least six credits earned in the three-year period ending when your disability started.

- **Age 24 to 31.** You need credits for having worked half the time between age 21 and the time you become disabled. For example, if you become disabled at age 27, you would need credit for three years of work (12 credits) during the six years between ages 21 and 27.

- **Age 31 or older.** In general, you will need the number of work credits shown in the chart below. Unless you are blind (see Part 2 of the Medical Listings on Nolo.com for definitions of legal blindness), at least 20 of the credits must have been earned in the ten years immediately before you became disabled.

Born after 1929 and became disabled at age:	Credits needed
31 through 42	20
44	22
46	24
48	26
50	28
52	30
54	32
56	34
58	36
60	38
62 or older	40

TIP

You can find out how many credits you have by contacting your local SSA office or, if you have access to the Internet, by filling out a form at www.ssa.gov/mystatement.

ii. You are the family member of an eligible worker

The SSA pays "auxiliary benefits" (also known as dependents benefits) to people who qualify based on certain family members' entitlement to Social Security retirement or disability benefits. Benefits are paid based on the earnings records of the insured worker who paid Social Security taxes. If you qualify for auxiliary benefits, you do not necessarily have to be disabled; nor do you need the work credits described above.

Spouse's and divorced spouse's benefits. To qualify for auxiliary benefits as a spouse or divorced spouse, one of the following must apply (42 U.S.C. § 402(b), (c), (e), (f); 20 CFR §§ 404.330–349):

- Older spouse of disabled worker. You are at least 62 years old, have been the spouse of a disabled worker for at least one year, and you are not entitled to a retirement or disability insurance benefit that is half or more of your spouse's benefit.
- Divorced spouse of disabled worker. You are the divorced spouse of a disabled worker who is entitled to benefits, you are 62 years old or older, and you were married to the worker for at least ten years.

- Divorced spouse of insured worker. You are the divorced spouse of a worker insured under SSDI who has not filed a claim for benefits, you are age 62 or older, your former spouse is aged 62 or older, you were married for at least ten years, and you have been divorced for at least two years.
- Disabled widow or widower. You are a disabled widow or widower, at least 50 years of age but younger than 60 years old, and you are the surviving spouse or divorced surviving spouse of a worker who received Social Security disability or retirement benefits.
- Older widow or widower. You are the surviving spouse (including a surviving divorced spouse) of a deceased insured worker, and you are age 60 or older.
- Parent of minor and surviving spouse. You are the surviving spouse (including a surviving divorced spouse) of a deceased insured worker, and you care for a child of the deceased entitled to benefits who either is younger than 16 or has been disabled since before age 22. (These benefits are known as "mother's or father's benefits.")

Child's benefits. A dependent, unmarried child is entitled to child's insurance benefits on the Social Security record of an insured parent, or deceased parent who was insured at death, if any of the following apply (42 U.S.C. § 402(d); 20 CFR §§ 404.350–369):

- The child is younger than 18.

- The child is age 18 or 19 and a full-time student.
- The child is an adult and has been disabled since before age 22.

(See Chapter 3 for a more detailed discussion of benefits for children.)

Parent's benefits. You might qualify for parent's benefits if all of the following are true (42 U.S.C. § 402(h); 20 CFR §§ 404.370–374):

- Your child was an insured worker who died.
- You are at least 62 years old.
- You are divorced, widowed, or unmarried and have not married since your child's death.
- You were receiving at least one-half of your support from your child at the time of death.
- You can provide evidence of this support within two years of the death (you may be exempt from providing evidence if unusual circumstances, such as extended illness, mental or physical incapacity, or language barrier, show that you could not have reasonably known of the two-year rule).

Lump-sum death benefits. A lump-sum death payment of several hundred dollars may be paid to the surviving spouse of an insured worker if the survivor was living in the same household as the deceased at the time of death. You must apply for this benefit within two years of the insured worker's death. (42 U.S.C. § 402(i); 20 CFR §§ 404.390–395.)

b. Citizenship or Residency Requirements

If you qualify for SSDI based on the criteria listed above, you may receive SSDI payments if you are a U.S. citizen or permanent resident, living in the United States or abroad. If you are neither a citizen nor a permanent resident, you still may be entitled to receive SSDI if you can show that you are lawfully present in the United States and meet certain other criteria. (8 U.S.C. § 1611(b)(2).)

If you are a citizen when you apply for SSDI, you will have to show proof of your citizenship. Acceptable forms of proof include a birth certificate showing birth within the United States (including Washington, D.C.), Puerto Rico after January 14, 1941, Guam, U.S. Virgin Islands after 1917, American Samoa, Swain's Island, or Northern Mariana Islands. Any of the following documents will also satisfy the proof of citizenship requirement:

- Forms N-550 and N-570, *Certificate of Naturalization,* issued by U.S. Citizenship and Immigration Services (USCIS) or its predecessor, the Immigration and Naturalization Service (INS)
- U.S. passport issued by the U.S. State Department
- Form I-197, *U.S. Citizen Identification Card,* issued by USCIS or the INS
- Form FS-240, *Report of Birth Abroad of a Citizen of the U.S.,* issued by the U.S. State Department)

- Form FS-545, *Certification of Birth,* issued by a foreign service post
- Forms N-560 and N-561, *Certificate of Citizenship,* issued by USCIS or the INS
- Form DS-1350, *Certification of Report of Birth,* issued by the U.S. State Department
- American Indian Card I-872 (DHS for Kickapoo Indian Tribe), or
- Northern Mariana Card I-873 (INS card for birth in the Northern Mariana Islands before 1986, obsolete but still valid).

If you are a permanent resident or resident alien, you will have to show that you are lawfully in the United States under one of the following conditions:

- lawful admission for permanent residence
- admission as a refugee or conditional entrance as a refugee
- asylum status or pending application for political asylum
- parole status
- deportation withheld or pending application for withholding of deportation
- member of a class of aliens permitted to remain in the United States for humanitarian or other public policy reasons, or
- you have been battered or subjected to cruelty by a family member while in the United States.

Most foreign workers in the United States are covered under the U.S. Social Security program and can potentially qualify for disability benefits. If, however, you are neither a citizen nor a permanent resident, you still may be covered under Social Security Disability. Federal law generally requires that all workers should pay Social Security taxes and, therefore, be covered under SSDI for services performed in the United States. This is true even for workers who are nonresident aliens or employees who work here for short periods.

There are a few exceptions, however. Some nonimmigrant foreign students and exchange visitors temporarily working in the United States may be exempt from paying Social Security taxes and, therefore, would not qualify for disability benefits under SSDI if they become disabled.

Noncitizen or permanent residents of the United States who are entitled to SSDI may be paid benefits while they reside abroad, depending upon their citizenship status and the countries in which they live. However, with some exceptions, an alien beneficiary who leaves the United States must either return to the United States at least every 30 days or for 30 consecutive days during each six-month period in order to continue to draw benefits.

One exception is made for alien beneficiaries who are on active military duty for the United States. Another exception exists for alien beneficiaries who live in and are citizens of Germany, Greece, Ireland, Israel,

Italy, or Japan. (The United States has treaty obligations with these nations to continue paying benefits regardless of how long beneficiaries are outside the United States.) Citizens of the Netherlands may receive partial benefits. (See Chapter 13 for more information about receiving benefits outside of the United States.)

International Social Security Agreements

The United States has entered into several International Social Security agreements called totalization agreements, which have two major purposes. First, they eliminate dual Social Security taxation, the situation that occurs when a worker from one country works in another country and is required to pay Social Security taxes to both countries on the same earnings. Second, the agreements help fill gaps in benefit protection for workers who have divided their careers between the United States and another country. The United States has totalization agreements with Australia, Austria, Belgium, Canada, Chile, Finland, France, Germany, Greece, Ireland, Italy, Luxembourg, Netherlands, Norway, Poland, Portugal, South Korea, Spain, Sweden, Switzerland, and the United Kingdom. (42 U.S.C. § 433.) (See Chapter 13 for a more complete list and discussion of international agreements.)

 CAUTION
Be aware of restricted countries. There are a few countries where residents cannot receive benefits even if they otherwise qualify. These include Cuba and North Korea.

c. SSDI Payments

If you are eligible for Social Security Disability Insurance (SSDI) benefits, the amount you receive each month will be based on your average lifetime earnings. It is not based on how severe your disability is or how much income you have. However, if you are receiving disability payments from other sources, as discussed below, your payment may be reduced.

If your income has declined between the period when you worked and when you stopped working full time because of your disability, the SSA recognizes that it is usually to your advantage to have your earning record "frozen" to reflect the higher income, before you were disabled. Therefore, the SSA will exclude from its benefit calculations low-income quarters of earnings resulting from a period of disability, unless it's to your financial advantage to include those quarters. (42 U.S.C. §§ 423(a), 426(b)(f); 20 CFR § 404.320.)

(SSDI payments are discussed in more detail in Chapter 13.)

2. Supplemental Security Income (SSI)

The SSI program provides payments to adults or children who are disabled and have limited income and resources. If your income and resources are too high, you will be turned down for SSI benefits no matter how severe your medical disorders. You will be turned down even if you have not paid enough in Social Security taxes to qualify for SSDI.

The SSI limits on income and resources are one of the most complicated areas handled by the SSA. Although important points are covered here, only SSA representatives can accurately determine your income and resources for purposes of qualifying for SSI.

a. Income Limits

To qualify for SSI, your monthly income (as counted by the SSA) cannot exceed something called the "federal benefit rate" (FBR). The FBR is set by law. It increases annually as dictated by cost-of-living adjustments. For 2020, the FBR is $783 per month for individuals and $1,175 for couples.

If only one member of a couple is eligible, both spouses' income is still considered, with some deductions allowed. If a child younger than 18 is living with parents, then the parents' income is considered, with some deductions allowed.

The federal benefit rate sets both the SSI income limit and the maximum federal SSI payment. However, the FBR payment may be supplemented with an extra payment by every state except Arizona, Mississippi, North Dakota, West Virginia, and the Northern Marianna Islands territory. This means that in all other states, the allowed SSI income level (and the SSI payments) may be higher than the federal maximums. And in California, Iowa, Massachusetts, and Nevada, the state supplements are higher for blind recipients than for others. Also, the amount of the state supplement depends on whether you are single or married and on your particular living arrangements. Although the amount of the state supplement varies widely, it can be as much as several hundred dollars (or as little as $10).

The SSA does not count the following income and benefits when calculating your income level:

- $20 per month of income except wages
- $65 per month of wages and one-half of wages over $65
- food stamps, and
- home energy or housing assistance.

(See Chapter 13 for more detailed information on income limitations.)

b. Resource Limits

To qualify for SSI, your resources (assets) must also not exceed certain limits. A "resource" is cash or another asset that can be converted to cash and used for your support. If you or your spouse has the right, authority, or power to sell property and keep the proceeds, it will be considered a resource.

Resources are categorized as either liquid or nonliquid. "Liquid resources" include cash and other assets that could be converted to cash within 20 working days. The most common types of liquid resources are savings and checking accounts, stocks, bonds, mutual funds, promissory notes, and certain types of life insurance. "Nonliquid resources" cannot be converted to cash within 20 working days. They include both real property (land) and personal property. The SSA may consider some resources to be both liquid and nonliquid (such as an automobile or life insurance policy).

Conditional Payments

It's possible that you don't qualify for SSI benefits due to your resource levels but might be entitled to conditional payments —in essence, a loan. This happens when you are disabled, and your resources are above the SSI resource limits but include nonliquid assets that may take months for you to convert into cash in order to use as support. In that situation, the SSA will make conditional payments until you sell your assets and can support yourself. You will not receive SSI—and at the end of the conditional payment period, you must refund to the SSA the amount you received.

The SSI resource limits are set by law. They are not subject to regular cost-of-living adjustments, but they have increased slowly over the years. For 2020, you will not be eligible for SSI disability payments if your assets exceed:

- $2,000 for a single person, or
- $3,000 for a married couple (even if only one member is eligible for SSI).

When counting up your assets, the SSA must exclude certain assets, including the following:

- your home (including adjacent land and related buildings), regardless of value. The home must be owned by you or your spouse and used as your principal residence.
- restricted allotted Indian lands
- household goods and personal effects up to $2,000 in value
- one wedding ring and one engagement ring of any value
- necessary health aids, such as a wheel- chair or prosthetic device
- one automobile, regardless of value, if used to provide necessary transport- ation; if not used for that purpose, then one automobile up to $4,500 in value
- money in an ABLE account, up to $100,000 (see ABLE acounts, below.)

ABLE Accounts

The Achieving a Better Life Experience (ABLE) Act allows for the creation of special savings accounts for individuals with disabilities, in which funds of up to $100,000 don't count as assets for the purpose of SSI (or Medicaid). To qualify to use an ABLE account, an individual must have a disabling condition that began before age 26. The funds in the account can be spent only on "qualified disability-related expenses," which include:

- health care, including assistive technology and personal support services (such as home health aides)
- housing
- transportation
- employment training
- education expenses
- financial management, and
- basic living expenses.

Not all states have started to offer ABLE accounts, but some states' ABLE programs are available to other states' residents.

- grants, scholarships, fellowships, or gifts used to pay tuition, fees, or other necessary educational expenses at an educational institution (including vocational or technical institution) for nine months beginning the month after the month the educational assistance was received

- nonbusiness property needed for support, up to a reasonable value
- resources of a blind or disabled person needed to fulfill an approved "plan for achieving self-support" (PASS). (See Chapter 13 for more information.)
- life insurance with a face value of $1,500 or less
- burial plots and certain burial funds up to $1,500
- disaster relief, and
- housing assistance paid under the U.S. Housing Act, the National Housing Act, or the Housing and Urban Development Act.

c. Citizenship and Residency Requirements

SSI disability payments are usually available only to U.S. citizens. There are several exceptions, however, under which noncitizens might be eligible, including the following:

- During the first seven years after you were admitted to the United States, you are either legally residing in the United States as a refugee, have been granted asylum, satisfy certain conditions of withheld deportation, have been granted status as a Cuban or Haitian entrant, or, under some conditions, entered as an Amerasian immigrant. (8 U.S.C. § 1612(a)(2)(A)(i)(I-V).)
- You legally entered the United States.

- You were honorably discharged from the U.S. military; you are on active duty in the U.S. military; or you are the spouse of a veteran or person on active duty, the unmarried dependent child of a veteran or person on active duty, or the surviving spouse of a deceased veteran or person who was on active duty and you have not remarried. (8 U.S.C. § 1612(a)(2)(C)(i-iii).)
- You were lawfully residing in the United States and receiving SSI benefits on August 22, 1996. (8 U.S.C. § 1612(a)(2)(E).)
- You were lawfully residing in the United States on August 22, 1996 and you are blind or otherwise became disabled at any time. (8 U.S.C. § 1612(a)(2)(F).)
- You are lawfully residing in the United States and are a Native American born in Canada. (8 U.S.C. § 1612(a)(2)(G).)
- You have been battered or subjected to cruelty in the United States by a family member. (See Public Law 104-193, the Personal Responsibility and Work Opportunity Reconciliation Act of 1996, as amended by P.L.104-208, the Illegal Immigration Reform and Immigrant Responsibility Act of 1996, and P.L. 105-33, the Balanced Budget Act of 1997.)

SEE AN EXPERT

Exceptions to the residency require-ments often involve complex legal issues, and you are probably best off consulting an attorney if you think an exception might apply to you.

d. Receiving Benefits When Outside of the United States. SSI payments are generally only available to people residing in the 50 states, District of Columbia, or Northern Mariana Islands. If you receive SSI disability benefits and move, for example, to Mexico or Puerto Rico, you will lose those benefits. There are a few exceptions for some U.S. citizen children and students:

- A blind or disabled child may be eligible for SSI benefits while out-side the United States if the child is a U.S. citizen, lives with a parent who is a member of the U.S. Armed Forces assigned to permanent duty outside the United States, and was eligible to receive SSI benefits in the month before the parent reported for duty abroad.
- A student of any age may be eligible for SSI benefits while temporarily outside the United States for the purpose of engaging in studies not available in the United States, sponsored by an educational institution in the United States, and designed to enhance the student's ability to engage in gainful employment. The student must have been eligible to receive SSI benefits in the month preceding the first full month abroad.

B. Defining Disabled

For adults applying for disability, being disabled means that you are unable to engage in any substantial gainful activity because of a medically determinable physical or mental impairment. The disability must have lasted or be expected to last for a continuous period of at least 12 months, or be expected to result in death.

For children applying for SSI, being disabled means the child has a medically determinable physical or mental impairment that causes marked and severe functional limitations. The limitations must have lasted or be expected to last for a continuous period of at least 12 months or be expected to result in death.

Let's break these concepts down further.

1. Inability to Engage in Substantial Gainful Activity

Inability to engage in "substantial gainful activity" (SGA) means that if you work, you do not earn more than a certain amount of money. For nonblind people, the 2020 amount is $1,260 per month. For blind people, the amount is $2,110 per month in 2020. The SGA amount is usually adjusted annually. (If you ever need to find out the SGA income limit for a given year, simply call a local SSA office or check the SSA's website. See Section C, below.)

Even if you have an impairment that meets the requirements for disability, you won't qualify for SSDI or SSI if you earn more than the SGA level. In this situation, if you stop working and apply for disability payments, you must be able to show that your medical condition became worse or that special help you required to do your job

was no longer available. You may be eligible for what's called an "unsuccessful work attempt" (UWA), if you make it clear that you had to stop working because of your medical problems. If you say you stopped working without a medical reason, the work won't count as a UWA and you won't be granted benefits.

SGA refers only to money you obtain from working, not money you obtain from other sources, such as investments or gifts.

2. Medically Determinable Impairment

A medically determinable physical or mental impairment is a disorder (abnormal condition) that results from anatomical (body structure), physiological (body function), or psychological (mental) abnormalities that can be proved by medically acceptable clinical and laboratory diagnostic techniques. The Social Security Act requires that a physical or mental impairment be established by medical evidence consisting of signs (objective findings by a medical provider), symptoms (subjective complaints by you), and laboratory findings.

In other words, the SSA must be able to determine that you have something wrong with you, either physically or mentally. To make such a decision, the government can ask to examine your treating doctor's records and your hospital records, order X-rays or other tests as needed, or have you examined by a doctor of its choosing if your records are incomplete or too old. Symptoms such as pain are important but alone cannot get you benefits. They must be linked to some physical or mental problem. In addition, your statement alone that you have symptoms is not sufficient. A doctor must show that you have a physical or mental condition that could cause the symptoms you say you have.

Pain and Other Symptoms

Your pain and symptoms are important parts of your disability claim. SSA staff frequently hand out forms that allow you to describe your pain and symptoms in your own words. For example, you might be asked to say where you have pain, what it feels like, what activities cause it or make it worse, and how long it lasts. In addition, you might be asked what medications you are taking and what side effects they may be causing. In fact, you should be asked these questions at some point during the claims process because federal law requires that the SSA consider your allegations of pain and other symptoms in reaching a decision. (Pain and other symptoms are discussed more fully in Chapter 5.)

MEDICAL LISTINGS

Remember: The medical listings are on Nolo's website. (See Appendix D for the link.) Parts 1 through 14 contain the Listing of Impairments, which is the medical information the SSA uses to determine whether your impairment meets the requirements to obtain disability benefits.

3. Duration of Disability

Your impairment must be severe enough to disable you (according to the SSA's medical criteria) for at least 12 continuous months or to result in your death. The 12-month duration requirement does not mean that you must have been severely ill for a year before applying for benefits, just that it is expected to last at least one year. The SSA often presumes that an impairment will last a year when it has not improved after three months.

If an impairment is obviously long-lasting and very severe, the SSA can make an immediate determination. For example, if your spinal cord was cut in half in an automobile accident, you will, at the very least, be unable to walk for the rest of your life. There would no reason for the SSA to wait before approving your claim, assuming you otherwise qualify.

The SSA includes the possibility of death in the definition of disability because death is the most extreme disability possible. Nothing in the Social Security Act specifies how to measure the possibility of death. But the SSA does provide some guidance. If you meet the criteria of any of the cancer listings, the SSA presumes you cannot work, based more on a poor prognosis than on an inability to do work. These cancer prognoses include a median life expectancy of 36 months. (See Part 13 of the Medical Listings on Nolo's website for more on cancer listings and the definition of median life expectancy.) Sometimes, the SSA uses the same survival probabilities in deciding noncancer disabilities that might result in death. These estimates can be difficult to make and require medical knowledge.

Many people apply for disability after acute injuries or impairments that won't produce any long-term effect severe enough to qualify for benefits. If you have any question in your mind about how long your impairment will last, apply for benefits. This is especially true if you are older than 50 years old. Older people do not need as severe an impairment as people younger than 50 to be allowed benefits. You can also ask your doctor's opinion about how long your illness will last. But it will be up to the SSA to decide whether you meet the minimum duration requirement of 12 months. In some cases, the SSA might think your impairment will last long enough, even if your doctor does not.

There is one exception to the duration of disability requirement: SSI claims based on blindness have no duration requirement.

C. Contacting the Social Security Administration

Local Social Security offices are where you can apply for:

- Social Security benefits
- SSI, hospital insurance protection, and
- a Social Security number.

You can also:

- check on your earnings record
- enroll for medical insurance

- receive assistance in applying for food stamps
- get information about your rights and obligations under the law, and
- obtain forms you need to apply for or maintain benefits or appeal SSA decisions.

There is no charge for these services. Employees of the SSA are public servants paid by your tax dollars. They are obligated to be helpful and courteous. If you encounter someone who is not helpful and courteous, ask to talk to a supervisor. Usually, this will cause an immediate change in attitude, because complaints might affect the employee's job performance ratings and ultimately, that person's promotions or income.

If it is necessary, insist on speaking to the supervisor. Supervisors are usually very interested in working out problems. A request to talk to the supervisor's supervisor is rarely necessary. If you feel you have been treated really badly, you can contact your local U.S. congressperson or senator. They will send a "Congressional inquiry" to the SSA. The SSA is very sensitive to public relations, and inquiries by Congress often get results if the complaint has merit.

Local Social Security offices exist in large cities of every state, and in bureaucratic language are known as "Field Offices." Social Security office staff make regular visits to outlying areas to serve people who live a distance from the city in which the local office is situated. These visits are made to locations called "contact stations." You can obtain a schedule of these visits from your local Social Security office. Some contact stations are visited twice a week, while others may be visited only once or twice a month.

The SSA is headed by a commissioner. The commissioner, administrative offices, and computer operations are located in Baltimore. The SSA discourages visits to this central office regarding individual claims because service can be provided by local offices.

If you are denied SSDI or SSI, you can appeal that decision. (Appealing is discussed in Chapter 12.) The Office of Hearings Operations (OHO) formerly known as the Office of Disability Adjudication and Review administers the entire hearings and appeals program for the SSA. Administrative law judges, located in or traveling to major cities throughout the United States and its territories, hold hearings and issue decisions when a claimant appeals a determination. The Appeals Council, located in Falls Church, Virginia, can review hearing decisions.

You can reach a live service representative by calling the SSA hotline at 800-772-1213, Monday through Friday (except holidays), from 7 a.m. to 7 p.m. If you are deaf or hard of hearing, TTY service representatives are available at the same times at 800-325-0778. All calls are confidential. After hours, you can obtain prerecorded information on a variety of topics.

SSA representatives can direct you to the Social Security office nearest you, as well as answer numerous other questions. Once you have made contact with your local SSA Field Office, you will deal with it rather than using the hotline.

The SSA's phone lines are busiest early in the week and early in the month; if your business can wait, call at other times.

Have the following items handy when you call:

- your Social Security number
- a list of questions you want to ask
- any recent correspondence you received from the SSA, and
- a pencil and paper to write down information and answers to your questions. Always write down the date you called.

On the Internet, information about Social Security is at www.ssa.gov.

D. Frequently Asked Questions About Social Security Disability

Following are some frequently asked questions about SSDI and SSI.

1. How is the disability determination made?

The SSA disability evaluation is a five-step evaluation process. For adults, this process requires step-by-step review of your current work activity, the severity of your impairment, your remaining physical and mental abilities, your past work, and your age, education, and work experience.

For children applying for SSI, the process requires sequential review of the child's current work activity (if any), the severity of the impairment, and an assessment of whether the impairment results in marked and severe functional limitations.

The sequential evaluation process is discussed in Chapter 7.

2. When do disability benefits start?

SSDI payments cannot be made until five months after the date of the onset (beginning) of disability. SSDI claimants may be entitled to retroactive (past) benefits, if the SSA finds they were disabled before their application date. Cash benefit payments cannot be paid retroactively to cover more than 12 months before the application date—no matter how severe your disability.

There are exceptions to the five-month waiting period requirement. These exceptions, along with more detailed information about the onset of disability, can be found in Chapter 10.

Under SSI, disability payments may begin as early as the first day of the month after an individual files an application, but no earlier. If your claim isn't approved until months after you apply, you'll be entitled to back payments to that date. In addition, under the SSI program, you may be found "presumptively disabled" and receive cash payments for up to six months while the formal disability determination is made. The presumptive payment is designed to allow a needy person to meet his or her basic living expenses during the time it takes to process the application. A claimant who is denied SSI benefits is not required to refund the payments. (Presumptive disability is covered in Chapter 4.)

3. What if I disagree with the determination?

If you disagree with the SSA's initial determination, you can appeal the decision. The first appeal of a denial is called a "reconsideration," which is a review of your case by a Disability Determination Services (DDS) team that was not involved in the original determination. If your case is denied at the reconsideration stage, you can request a hearing before an administrative law judge. If you are dissatisfied with that decision and wish to continue pursuing the case, you can request a review by the Appeals Council and then file a civil lawsuit in federal district court and eventually appeal all the way to the U.S. Supreme Court. (Appeals are covered in Chapter 12.)

4. Can I receive disability benefits or payments while getting Medicare or Medicaid coverage?

Yes. Medicaid and Medicare are our country's two major government-run health insurance programs. Generally, people on SSI and other people with low incomes qualify for Medicaid, while Medicare coverage is earned by working in jobs covered by Social Security, the Railroad Retirement Act, or for the federal government. Many people qualify for both. In most states, you do not have to do anything special or additional to obtain Medicare or Medicaid coverage once you have qualified for disability. If and when you qualify for such coverage, the federal government will send you any forms you need to fill out. This is not true for Medicaid in all states, however. (See SSI and Medicaid, below.)

SSDI and Medicare. SSDI claimants granted disability benefits qualify for Medicare coverage. However, the coverage doesn't start for two years from the date of entitlement to disability benefits—and that means two years starting after the initial five-month waiting period. Therefore, you may be left without medical insurance coverage for several years if you don't have some other type of coverage or are not poor enough to qualify for SSI Medicaid coverage. There are three exceptions to the two-year rule:

- If you have end-stage renal disease with kidney failure and you require dialysis or a kidney transplant, coverage by Medicare can begin the third month after the month in which dialysis began.
- If you are terminally ill with a life expectancy of six months or less and receive hospice care, coverage by Medicare can begin immediately.
- Individuals with amyotrophic lateral sclerosis (ALS) qualify for Medicare as soon as they begin collecting disability benefits.

If you get Medicare and have low income and few resources, your state may pay your Medicare premiums and, in some cases, other out-of-pocket Medicare expenses such as deductibles and coinsurance. Contact your local welfare office or Medicaid agency, search for "Medicare Savings Programs" on www.medicare.gov, or get Nolo's book Social Security, Medicare & Government Pensions.

SSI and Medicaid. In most states, SSI recipients who are granted disability benefits automatically qualify for Medicaid coverage. Where SSI recipients automatically qualify, Medicaid coverage starts immediately. In a few states, eligibility for Medicaid is not automatic when you receive SSI, and you will need to apply for Medicaid separately. Your local SSA office can tell you if you need to file a separate application for Medicaid. You can call your state medical assistance office for help applying; call the Centers for Medicare and Medicaid Services at 800-633-4227 to get the telephone number of your state medical assistance office.

5. Can I work and still receive disability benefits?

Social Security rules make it possible for people to test their ability to work without losing their rights to cash benefits and Medicare or Medicaid. These are called "work incentives." The rules are different for SSDI and SSI, but under both programs, you can receive:

- continued cash benefits
- continued help with medical bills
- help with work expenses, or
- vocational training.

For more information about work incentives, see Chapter 13, Section D.

6. How can I receive vocational training services?

Claimants for SSDI or SSI may be referred to a state vocational rehabilitation agency for rehabilitation services. The referral may be made by the DDS (see Chapter 6), the SSA, a treating source, or personal request. The services may be medical or nonmedical and may include counseling, teaching of new employment skills, training in the use of prostheses, and job placement. In determining whether vocational rehabilitation services would benefit you in returning to work, medical evidence from your treating doctor may be very important. (Vocational rehabilitation is discussed more in Chapter 9.)

7. Do I have to be disabled for a year before I can get benefits?

You do not have to wait a year after the onset of the disability before you can get benefits. File as soon as you can after becoming disabled.

8. Is there a time limit on how long I can receive Social Security disability benefits?

No. You will continue to receive a disability benefit as long as your condition keeps you from working. But your case will be reviewed periodically to see if there has been any improvement in your condition and whether you are still eligible for benefits (see Chapter 14). If you are still eligible when you reach 66, your disability benefits will be automatically converted to retirement benefits.

9. If I reapply for benefits after going off disability because my back had gotten better, will my wait be as long as it was the first time?

Maybe not. It depends on what the new medical reports say and whether additional evidence is required. A worker who becomes disabled a second time within five years after benefits stop can have his or her checks start again, beginning with the first full month of disability, if the new claim is approved. (For SSDI, the five-month waiting period can be waived.)

10. My brother is receiving SSDI disability benefits. Is his daughter by a woman to whom he has never been married entitled to some benefits as well?

Yes. Even though your brother was not married to the second child's mother, Social Security pays benefits to all of his children. Each child is entitled to equal benefits.

Applying for Disability Benefits

This chapter explains how to apply for disability benefits.

A. Preparing to Apply

You can play an active and important role in ensuring that your claim is processed accurately and quickly. The best advice is to keep thorough records that document the symptoms of your illness or injury and how it affects your daily activities before you apply. Then, provide this information to the Social Security Administration when you file your claim.

1. Document Your Symptoms Early and Often

Use a calendar to jot down brief notes about how you feel each day. Record any of your usual activities that you could not do. Be specific. Remember to include any psychological (emotional or mental) difficulties.

2. Help Your Doctor Help You

Not all doctors are aware of the kind of information the SSA needs to document a disability. Ask your doctor to track the course of your symptoms in detail over time and to keep a thorough record of any evidence of fatigue, depression, forgetfulness, dizziness, and other hard-to-document symptoms. Note that the SSA will accept medical opinions as to your limitations only from doctors who are *acceptable medical sources*. (Acceptable

medical sources are covered in Chapter 5.) If you don't have a doctor, the SSA will have you examined at its expense.

3. Record How Your Condition Affected You on the Job

If you were working but lost your job because of your illness or injury, make notes that describe what it is about your condition that forced you to stop working.

B. Applying for Disability Benefits

You can apply for disability benefits at a local Field Office or contact station. You do not have to call or make an appointment to visit a Field Office or contact station, but it is advisable that you do. Otherwise, you might have to wait or come back another time. You can also apply for benefits online or over the phone. See "Applying Over the Phone" and "Applying Online," below, for details.

If you apply at an SSA office, when you arrive, tell the desk or counter clerk that you want to apply for disability benefits. You'll be scheduled to meet an interviewer, who will inform you of your rights and responsibilities, assist you in completing your application, and obtain information and evidence from you that is needed to determine your eligibility. Note the name of the specific person assigned to help you in case you need to contact someone later for help. Bring reading materials with you. You may have a bit of a wait before you see the interviewer.

TIP

The Social Security Administration has a helpful website filled with useful information and up-to-date rules and regulations for disability claimants at www.ssa.gov. Another useful website, www.disabilitysecrets.com, is one of Nolo's partners.

Applying Over the Phone

If you prefer, you can call the SSA at 800-772-1213 to file an application. This is especially convenient if you live some distance from the nearest Field Office or contact station (you can find the location of the nearest SSA facility by calling the 800 number listed above). If you need help, a family member, caseworker, or other representative can contact the SSA for you. You do not have to give that person a power of attorney—the authority to sign legal documents and make legal decisions for you—to help you obtain an application form and file a claim.

If you cannot go to the Social Security office because of poor health, or if there is no Social Security office nearby, you can get full information and application forms by making an appointment for a telephone interview. Even if you cannot get to the Field Office to file an application (due to illness, lack of transportation, or whatever other reason), an SSA representative can do the interview over the telephone.

You can speed up the processing of your claim by being as prepared as possible before contacting the SSA Field Office. Remember that the SSA is a huge and complex bureaucracy that needs a lot of information about you. If you do some basic preparation, the whole process can proceed smoothly. On the other hand, do not wait until you have every conceivable detail ready for review before you contact the Field Office.

You are responsible for submitting the necessary evidence to support your claim of disability (see Chapter 5). The Social Security office will assist you by telling you what evidence is required to establish your claim and how you can obtain that evidence. If you can't get the necessary evidence, the Social Security office will offer special assistance, based upon your needs, to ensure the proper resolution of the claim.

Never assume that the claims representative can read your mind if you have a special problem regarding your application. If you have some concern, mention it. SSA claims representatives are instructed to help you if they can reasonably solve a problem that is related to your application.

For example, if a claimant cannot read or write, the claims representative will provide assistance in completing the forms. In addition, the SSA Field Office will provide an interpreter if you need language assistance. The SSA uses whatever qualified interpreters or interpreter services are most appropriate to the situation and are most reliable and readily available.

Applying Online

You can apply for SSDI benefits online at www.ssa.gov. Before you fill out the online application, use the "Benefit Eligibility Screening Tool" (BEST) at https://ssabest. benefits.gov. This tool helps you identify all the different Social Security programs for which you may be eligible, and you should use it before you start the application process. The SSA's website also has a number of useful links to planners, calculators, and additional information about the disability program.

When you are ready to apply, go to www. socialsecurity.gov/applyfordisability to get started. The SSA will guide you through the three-step process, in which you'll:

- review the Adult Disability Starter Kit, which answers common questions about applying for benefits and includes a worksheet to help you gather the information you'll need
- fill out the online application for Social Security benefits, and

- fill out the online Adult Disability Report.

One of the nice things about an online application is that you can work at your own speed. If you don't have some needed information, for example, you can stop your application and return to it later where you stopped. The SSA will issue a confirmation number you can use to reaccess your application information. Your application is confidential.

If you decide you need help applying online or simply decide to apply in a different way, it is no problem. The SSA displays contact telephone numbers right on the application page. Representatives are available Monday through Friday. For many people, however, an online application is a very attractive alternative to going to a Social Security Field Office in person or applying over the telephone.

Furthermore, the SSA maintains cooperative relationships with many groups and organizations that provide assistance with the application process. Each SSA office maintains a list of the agencies (both public and private) in the community and the types of services provided by each. If you inquire, you can immediately be referred to an agency providing the needed services.

1. Your Application

If you are applying for adult disability offline, the SSA will send you Form SSA-3368-BK, *Adult Disability Report*, to begin the process. We include a sample filled-in form below. (If you are applying for a child, you will receive Form SSA-3820-BK, *Child Disability Report*. See Chapter 3 for a sample of that form.)

When you arrive at the Social Security Field Office for an interview, the official will ask you many questions. Your answers will be put on either Form SSA-16-BK, *Application for Disability Insurance Benefit* or Form SSA-8000-BK, *Application for SSI*.

Take a look at the appropriate samples below before you head out to the Social Security office or have your interview. That way you can gather in advance as much information and paperwork as possible. Don't worry if you can't answer every question or find all documents; the claims representative or interviewer will help you. Realize, however, that if you don't have key information with you at the time of your interview (see just below), you might have to get it and send it in to the SSA office. This could delay the processing of your application. You should be aware that various SSA forms for filing online, such as the SSA-3368-BK adult application form, will look different than the paper forms. However, the information required is the same.

CAUTION

You must use forms provided by the SSA. You can obtain them at your local SSA Field Office or by calling the SSA hotline at 800-772-1213, Monday through Friday (except holidays), from 7 a.m. to 7 p.m. If you are deaf or hard of hearing, TTY service representatives are available at the same times at 800-325-0778. You can also download many necessary forms from the Social Security Administration website at www.ssa.gov.

2. What the SSA Needs to Process Your Claim

The SSA needs several types of information to process your disability claim.

a. Social Security Number and Birth Certificate

The SSA needs your Social Security number and birth certificate or other proof of your age. You will also need to provide the Social Security numbers and birth certificates for family members—such as a disabled adult child—who are applying for benefits on your earnings record.

If you submit an original record of some kind, the SSA will return it to you after making a copy. If you cannot or do not want to submit an original record, you can offer a copy, if it is properly certified. You can obtain a properly certified copy from any of the following:

- the official custodian of the record
- an SSA employee authorized to certify copies, who can certify that the copy is an exact reproduction of an original
- a U.S. consular officer or employee of the State Department authorized to certify evidence received outside the United States, or
- an employee of a state agency or state welfare office authorized to certify copies of original records in the agency's or office's files.

Form SSA-3368-BK, *Disability Report—Adult* (SSI) (Page 1)

SOCIAL SECURITY ADMINISTRATION	Form Approved OMB No. 0960-0579

DISABILITY REPORT ADULT	For SSA Use Only- Do not write in this box. Related SSN _____ Number Holder _____

Anyone who makes or causes to be made a false statement or representation of material fact for use in determining a payment under the Social Security Act, or knowingly conceals or fails to disclose an event with an intent to affect an initial or continued right to payment, commits a crime punishable under Federal law by fine, imprisonment, or both, and may be subject to administrative sanctions.

If you are filling out this report for someone else, please provide information about him or her. When a question refers to "you" or "your," it refers to the person who is applying for disability benefits.

SECTION 1 - INFORMATION ABOUT THE DISABLED PERSON

1.A. Name (First, Middle Initial, Last) William I. Hamilton	1.B. Social Security Number 999-99-9999

1.C. Mailing Address (Street or PO Box) Include apartment number or unit if applicable.

P.O. Box 24007

City	State/Province	ZIP/Postal Code	Country (If not USA)
Chicago	IL	60681	

1.D. Email Address

WIH@yahoo.com

1.E. Daytime Phone Number, including area code, and the IDD and country codes if you live outside the USA or Canada.   Phone number 515-123-4567

☐ Check this box if you do not have a phone or a number where we can leave a message .

1.F. Alternate Phone Number - another number where we may reach you, if any.

Alternate phone number 515-123-5678

1.G. Can you speak and understand English?	☑ Yes ☐ No

If no, what language do you prefer? _____

If you cannot speak and understand English, we will provide an interpreter, free of charge.

1.H. Can you read and understand English?	☑ Yes ☐ No
1.I. Can you write more than your name in English?	☑ Yes ☐ No

1.J. Have you used any other names on your medical or educational records? Examples are maiden name, other married name, or nickname.   ☐ Yes ☑ No

If yes, please list them here: _____

SECTION 2 - CONTACTS

Give the name of someone **(other than your doctors)** we can contact who knows about your medical conditions, and can help you with your claim.

2.A. Name (First, Middle Initial, Last) Payne, Mildred	2.B. Relationship to you Cousin

2.C. Daytime Phone Number (as described in 1.E. above)

515-123-6789

2.D. Mailing Address (Street or PO Box) Include apartment number or unit if applicable.

456 Center Street, #112

City	State/Province	ZIP/Postal Code	Country (If not USA)
Chicago	IL	60692	

2.E. Can this person speak and understand English?	☑ Yes ☐ No

If no, what language is preferred? _____

Form **SSA-3368-BK** (10-2015) UF (10-2015)   Page 1
Destroy Prior Editions

Form SSA-3368-BK, *Disability Report—Adult* (Page 2)

SECTION 2 - CONTACTS (continued)

2.F. Who is completing this report?

- ☑ The person who is applying for disability. (Go to Section 3 - Medical Conditions)
- ☐ The person listed in 2.A. (Go to Section 3 - Medical Conditions)
- ☐ Someone else (Complete the rest of Section 2 below)

2.G. Name (First, Middle Initial, Last)	2.H. Relationship to Person Applying

2.I. Daytime Phone Number

2.J. Mailing Address (Street or PO Box) Include apartment number or unit if applicable.

City	State/Province	ZIP/Postal Code	Country (If not USA)

SECTION 3 - MEDICAL CONDITIONS

3.A. List all of the physical or mental conditions (including emotional or learning problems) that limit your ability to work. If you have cancer, please include the stage and type. List each condition separately.

1. Arthritis right shoulder
2. Liver problems (cirrhosis)
3. Cataracts
4. Nervous
5. Back pain

If you need more space, go to Section 11-Remarks on the last page

3.B. What is your height without shoes? __5__ __10__ OR _____
feet / inches / centimeters (if outside USA)

3.C. What is your weight without shoes? __176__ OR _____
pounds / kilograms (if outside USA)

3.D. Do your conditions cause you pain or other symptoms? ☑ Yes ☐ No

SECTION 4 - WORK ACTIVITY

4.A. Are you currently working?

- ☐ No, I have never worked (Go to question **4.B.** below)
- ☑ No, I have stopped working (Go to question **4.C.** below)
- ☐ Yes, I am currently working (Go to question **4.F.** on page 3)

IF YOU HAVE NEVER WORKED:
4.B. When do you believe your condition(s) became severe enough to keep you from working (even though you have never worked)? (month/day/year) _____ (Go to Section 5 on page 3)

IF YOU HAVE STOPPED WORKING:
4.C. When did you stop working? (month/day/year) __10/12/2015__
Why did you stop working?

- ☑ Because of my condition(s).

- ☐ Because of other reasons. Please explain why you stopped working (for example: laid off, early retirement, seasonal work ended, business closed)

_____

Even though you stopped working for other reasons, when do you believe your condition(s) became severe enough to keep you from working? (month/day/year) _____

4.D. Did your condition(s) cause you to make changes in your work activity? (for example: job duties, hours, or rate of pay)

- ☐ No (Go to Section 5 - Education and Training on page 3)
- ☑ Yes When did you make changes? (month/day/year) __5/8/2015__

Form SSA-3368-BK, *Disability Report—Adult* (Page 3)

SECTION 4 - WORK ACTIVITY (continued)

4.E. Since the date in 4.D. above, have you had gross earnings greater than $1,090 in any month? Do not count sick leave, vacation, or disability pay. (We may contact you for more information.)

☐ No (Go to Section 5) ☑ Yes (Go to Section 5)

IF YOU ARE CURRENTLY WORKING:

4.F. Has your condition(s) caused you to make changes in your work activity? (for example: job duties or hours)

☐ No   When did your condition(s) first start bothering you? (month/day/year) _____

☐ Yes   When did you make changes? (month/day/year) _____

4.G. Since your condition(s) first bothered you, have you had gross earnings greater than $1,090 in any month? Do not count sick leave, vacation, or disability pay. (We may contact you for more information.)

☐ No   ☐ Yes

SECTION 5 - EDUCATION AND TRAINING

5.A. Check the highest grade of school completed.   College:

0	1	2	3	4	5	6	7	8	9	10	11	12	GED	1	2	3	4 or more
☐	☐	☐	☐	☐	☐	☐	☐	☐	☐	☐	☐	☑	☐	☐	☐	☐	☐

Date completed: ___June 1990___

5.B. Did you attend special education classes?   ☐ Yes   ☑ No (Go to 5.C.)

Name of School _____

City _____ State/Province _____ Country (If not USA) _____

Dates attended special education classes: from _____   to _____

5.C. Have you completed any type of specialized job training, trade, or vocational school?

☑ Yes   ☐ No

If "Yes," what type? ___Electrician Helper___   Date completed: ___1993___

If you need to list other education or training use Section 11 - Remarks on the last page.

SECTION 6 - JOB HISTORY

6.A. List the jobs (up to 5) that you have had in the 15 years before you became unable to work because of your physical or mental conditions. List your most recent job first.

☐ Check here and go to Section 7 on page 5 if you did not work at all in the 15 years before you became unable to work.

	Job Title	Type of Business	Dates Worked From MM/YY	Dates Worked To MM/YY	Hours Per Day	Days Per Week	Rate of Pay Amount	Rate of Pay Frequency
1.	Electrician Helper	Utility	9/1996	10/2015	8	6	$25	hr
2.								
3.								
4.								
5.								

Form SSA-3368-BK, *Disability Report—Adult* (Page 4)

SECTION 6 - JOB HISTORY (continued)

Check the box below that applies to you.

☑ I had **only one job** in the last 15 years before I became unable to work. Answer the questions below.

☐ I had **more than one job** in the last 15 years before I became unable to work. Do **not** answer the questions on this page; go to Section 7 on page 5. (We may contact you for more information.)

Do not complete this page if you had **more than one job** in the last 15 years before you became unable to work.

6.B. Describe this job. What did you do all day?

Numerous duties, including assisting in installation and repair of electric power equipment, underground cable and related activities

(If you need more space, use Section 11 - Remarks on the last page.)

6.C. In this job, did you:

Use machines, tools or equipment?	☑ Yes ☐ No
Use technical knowledge or skills?	☑ Yes ☐ No
Do any writing, complete reports, or perform any duties like this?	☐ Yes ☑ No

6.D. In this job, how many total hours each day did you do each of the tasks listed:

Task	Hours	Task	Hours	Task	Hours
Walk	6–8	Stoop *(Bend down & forward at waist.)*	3	Handle large objects	6–8
Stand	6–8	Kneel *(Bend legs to rest on knees.)*	2–3	Write, type, or handle small objects	6–8
Sit	0–1	Crouch *(Bend legs & back down & forward.)*	2–3	Reach	6–8
Climb	3	Crawl *(Move on hands & knees.)*	1–2		

6.E. Lifting and carrying *(Explain in the box below, what you lifted, how far you carried it, and how often you did this in your job.)*

Heavy machine parts, electrical cable, worked with heavy equipment like transformers, rigged scaffolding & hoists. Carried heavy objects 50–1,000 ft most of day

6.F. Check **heaviest** weight lifted:

☐ Less than 10 lbs.　☐ 10 lbs.　☐ 20 lbs.　☐ 50 lbs.　☑ 100 lbs. or more　☐ Other _____

6.G. Check weight **frequently** lifted: *(by frequently, we mean from 1/3 to 2/3 of the workday.)*

☐ Less than 10 lbs.　☐ 10 lbs.　☑ 25 lbs.　☐ 50 lbs. or more　☐ Other _____

6.H. Did you supervise other people in this job?　☐ Yes (Complete items below.)　☑ No (if No, go to **6.I.**)

How many people did you supervise? _____
What part of your time did you spend supervising people? _____

Did you hire and fire employees? ☐ Yes ☑ No

6.I. Were you a lead worker?　☐ Yes ☑ No

Form SSA-3368-BK, *Disability Report—Adult* (Page 5)

SECTION 7 - MEDICINES

7. Are you taking any medicines (prescription or non-prescription)?

☑ Yes (Give the information requested below. You may need to look at your medicine containers.)

☐ No (Go to Section 8-Medical Treatment.)

Name of Medicine	If prescribed, give name of doctor	Reason for medicine
Aldactone	Dr. Simmons	Remove excess fluid in abdomen
Xanax	Dr. Hill	nervousness
Ibuprofen	Dr. Bates	back pain

If you need to list other medicines, go to Section 11 - Remarks on the last page.

SECTION 8 - MEDICAL TREATMENT

Have you seen a doctor or other health care professional or received treatment at a hospital or clinic, or **do you have a future appointment scheduled?**

8.A. For any **physical** condition(s)?

☑ Yes ☐ No

8.B. For any **mental** condition(s) **(including emotional or learning problems)?**

☑ Yes ☐ No

If you answered "No" to both 8.A. and 8.B., go to Section 9 - Other Medical Information on page 11.

Form SSA-3368-BK, *Disability Report—Adult* (Page 6)

SECTION 8 - MEDICAL TREATMENT (continued)

Tell us who may have medical records about any of your **physical and/or mental** condition(s) (including emotional or learning problems). This includes doctors' offices, hospitals **(including emergency room visits)**, clinics, and other health care facilities. Tell us about your next appointment, if you have one scheduled.

8.C. Name of Facility or Office	Name of health care professional who treated you
Midwest Orthopedics	David Bates, M.D.

ALL OF THE QUESTIONS ON THIS PAGE REFER TO THE HEALTH CARE PROVIDER ABOVE.

Phone Number	Patient ID# (if known)
312-555-1234	none

Mailing Address

2325 Front Street

City	State/Province	ZIP/Postal Code	Country (If not USA)
Chicago	IL	unknown	

Dates of Treatment

1. Office, Clinic or Outpatient visits	2. Emergency Room visits List the most recent date first	3. Overnight hospital stays List the most recent date first	
First Visit May 2013	A. none	A. Date in	Date out
Last Visit November 2015	B.	B. Date in	Date out
Next scheduled appointment (if any) June 12, 2016	C.	C. Date in	Date out

What medical conditions were treated or evaluated?

Low back pain caused by arthritis and disk disease. Arthritis shoulder

What treatment did you receive for the above conditions? (Do not describe medicines or tests in this box.)

Physical therapy, light exercise, training proper posture

Check the boxes below for any tests this provider performed or sent you to, or has scheduled you to take. Please give the dates for past and future tests. If you need to list more tests, use Section 11-Remarks on the last page.

☐ Check this box if no tests by this provider or at this facility.

Kind of Test	Dates of Tests	Kind of Test	Dates of Tests
☐ EKG (heart test)		☐ EEG (brain wave test)	
☐ Treadmill (exercise test)		☐ HIV Test	
☐ Cardiac Catheterization		☐ Blood Test (not HIV)	
☐ Biopsy (list body part)		☑ X-Ray (list body part) Back, shoulder	2013
☐ Hearing Test		☐ MRI/CT Scan (list body part)	
☐ Speech/Language Test			
☐ Vision Test		☐ Other (please describe)	
☐ Breathing Test			

If you do not have any more doctors or hospitals to describe, go to Section 9 on page 11.

Form SSA-3368-BK, *Disability Report—Adult* (Page 7)

SECTION 8 - MEDICAL TREATMENT (continued)

Tell us who may have medical records about any of your **physical and/or mental** condition(s) (including emotional or learning problems). This includes doctors' offices, hospitals **(including emergency room visits)**, clinics, and other health care facilities. Tell us about your next appointment, if you have one scheduled.

8.D. Name of Facility or Office	Name of health care professional who treated you
The Gastroenterology Clinic	John Simmons, M.D.

ALL OF THE QUESTIONS ON THIS PAGE REFER TO THE HEALTH CARE PROVIDER ABOVE.

Phone Number	Patient ID# (if known)
312-555-9999	512488

Mailing Address

17 Outer Loop Drive

City	State/Province	ZIP/Postal Code	Country (If not USA)
Chicago	IL	60686	

Dates of Treatment

1. Office, Clinic or Outpatient visits	2. Emergency Room visits List the most recent date first	3. Overnight hospital stays List the most recent date first	
First Visit January 2012	A. none	A. Date in 11-2012	Date out 12-2012
Last Visit August 2015	B.	B. Date in	Date out
Next scheduled appointment (if any) February 2016	C.	C. Date in	Date out

What medical conditions were treated or evaluated?

Liver problem--cirrhosis

What treatment did you receive for the above conditions? (Do not describe medicines or tests in this box.)

Surgical shunt to decrease fluid pressure in liver; abdominal fluid drained

Tell us about any tests this provider performed or sent you to, or has scheduled you to take. Please give the dates for past and future tests. If you need to list more tests, use Section 11 - Remarks on the last page.

☐ Check this box if no tests by this provider or at this facility.

Kind of Test	Dates of Tests	Kind of Test	Dates of Tests
☑ EKG (heart test)	2012	☐ EEG (brain wave test)	
☐ Treadmill (exercise test)		☐ HIV Test	
☐ Cardiac Catheterization		☐ Blood Test (not HIV)	
☑ Biopsy (list body part) Liver	2012	☐ X-Ray (list body part)	
☐ Hearing Test		☑ MRI/CT Scan (list body part) Abdomen	2012
☐ Speech/Language Test			
☐ Vision Test		☐ Other (please describe)	
☐ Breathing Test			

If you do not have any more doctors or hospitals to describe, go to Section 9 on page 11.

Form SSA-3368-BK, *Disability Report—Adult* (Page 8)

SECTION 8 - MEDICAL TREATMENT (continued)

Tell us who may have medical records about any of your **physical and/or mental** condition(s) (including emotional or learning problems). This includes doctors' offices, hospitals **(including emergency room visits)**, clinics, and other health care facilities. Tell us about your next appointment, if you have one scheduled.

8.E. Name of Facility or Office	Name of health care professional who treated you
Mental Health Associates, Inc.	Henry Hill, M.D.

ALL OF THE QUESTIONS ON THIS PAGE REFER TO THE HEALTH CARE PROVIDER ABOVE.

Phone Number	Patient ID# (if known)
312-555-6789	

Mailing Address

4800 State Building, Ste. 43

City	State/Province	ZIP/Postal Code	Country (If not USA)
Chicago	IL	60686	

Dates of Treatment

1. Office, Clinic or Outpatient visits	2. Emergency Room visits List the most recent date first	3. Overnight hospital stays List the most recent date first	
First Visit June 2012	A.	A. Date in	Date out
Last Visit December 2013	B.	B. Date in	Date out
Next scheduled appointment (if any) June 2016	C.	C. Date in	Date out

What medical conditions were treated or evaluated?

Nervousness

What treatment did you receive for the above conditions? (Do not describe medicines or tests in this box.)

Talk about how to handle nervousness. Took pill for nerves a few months, not now.

Tell us about any tests this provider performed or sent you to, or has scheduled you to take. Please give the dates for past and future tests. If you need to list more tests, use Section 11 - Remarks on the last page.

☐ Check this box if no tests by this provider or at this facility.

Kind of Test	Dates of Tests	Kind of Test	Dates of Tests
☐ EKG (heart test)		☐ EEG (brain wave test)	
☐ Treadmill (exercise test)		☐ HIV Test	
☐ Cardiac Catheterization		☐ Blood Test (not HIV)	
☐ Biopsy (list body part)		☐ X-Ray (list body part)	
☐ Hearing Test		☐ MRI/CT Scan (list body part)	
☐ Speech/Language Test			
☐ Vision Test		☑ Other (please describe) mental tests	2012
☐ Breathing Test			

If you do not have any more doctors or hospitals to describe, go to Section 9 on page 11.

Form **SSA-3368-BK** (10-2015) UF (10-2015)   Page 8

Form SSA-3368-BK, *Disability Report—Adult* (Page 9)

SECTION 8 - MEDICAL TREATMENT (continued)

Tell us who may have medical records about any of your **physical and/or mental** condition(s) (including emotional or learning problems). This includes doctors' offices, hospitals **(including emergency room visits)**, clinics, and other health care facilities. Tell us about your next appointment, if you have one scheduled.

8.F. Name of Facility or Office	Name of health care professional who treated you

ALL OF THE QUESTIONS ON THIS PAGE REFER TO THE HEALTH CARE PROVIDER ABOVE.

Phone Number	Patient ID# (if known)

Mailing Address

City	State/Province	ZIP/Postal Code	Country (If not USA)

Dates of Treatment

1. Office, Clinic or Outpatient visits	2. Emergency Room visits List the most recent date first	3. Overnight hospital stays List the most recent date first	
First Visit	A.	A. Date in	Date out
Last Visit	B.	B. Date in	Date out
Next scheduled appointment (if any)	C.	C. Date in	Date out

What medical conditions were treated or evaluated?

What treatment did you receive for the above conditions? (Do not describe medicines or tests in this box.)

Tell us about any tests this provider performed or sent you to, or has scheduled you to take. Please give the dates for past and future tests. If you need to list more tests, use Section 11 - Remarks on the last page.

☐ Check this box if no tests by this provider or at this facility.

Kind of Test	Dates of Tests	Kind of Test	Dates of Tests
☐ EKG (heart test)		☐ EEG (brain wave test)	
☐ Treadmill (exercise test)		☐ HIV Test	
☐ Cardiac Catheterization		☐ Blood Test (not HIV)	
☐ Biopsy (list body part)		☐ X-Ray (list body part)	
☐ Hearing Test		☐ MRI/CT Scan (list body part)	
☐ Speech/Language Test			
☐ Vision Test		☐ Other (please describe)	
☐ Breathing Test			

If you do not have any more doctors or hospitals to describe, go to Section 9 on page 11.

Form SSA-3368-BK, *Disability Report—Adult* (Page 10)

SECTION 8 - MEDICAL TREATMENT (continued)

Tell us who may have medical records about any of your **physical and/or mental** condition(s) (including emotional or learning problems). This includes doctors' offices, hospitals **(Including emergency room visits)**, clinics, and other health care facilities. Tell us about your next appointment, if you have one scheduled.

8.G. Name of Facility or Office	Name of health care professional who treated you

ALL OF THE QUESTIONS ON THIS PAGE REFER TO THE HEALTH CARE PROVIDER ABOVE.

Phone Number	Patient ID# (if known)

Mailing Address

City	State/Province	ZIP/Postal Code	Country (If not USA)

Dates of Treatment

1. Office, Clinic or Outpatient visits	2. Emergency Room visits List the most recent date first	3. Overnight hospital stays List the most recent date first	
First Visit	A.	A. Date in	Date out
Last Visit	B.	B. Date in	Date out
Next scheduled appointment (if any)	C.	C. Date in	Date out

What medical conditions were treated or evaluated?

What treatment did you receive for the above conditions? (Do not describe medicines or tests in this box.)

Tell us about any tests this provider performed or sent you to, or has scheduled you to take. Please give the dates for past and future tests. If you need to list more tests, use Section 11 - Remarks on the last page.

☐ Check this box if no tests by this provider or at this facility.

Kind of Test	Dates of Tests	Kind of Test	Dates of Tests
☐ EKG (heart test)		☐ EEG (brain wave test)	
☐ Treadmill (exercise test)		☐ HIV Test	
☐ Cardiac Catheterization		☐ Blood Test (not HIV)	
☐ Biopsy (list body part)		☐ X-Ray (list body part)	
☐ Hearing Test		☐ MRI/CT Scan (list body part)	
☐ Speech/Language Test			
☐ Vision Test		☐ Other (please describe)	
☐ Breathing Test			

If you have been treated by more than five doctors or hospitals, use Section 11 - Remarks on the last page and give the same detailed information as above for each healthcare provider.

Form **SSA-3368-BK** (10-2015) UF (10-2015)   Page 10

Form SSA-3368-BK, *Disability Report—Adult* (Page 11)

SECTION 9 - OTHER MEDICAL INFORMATION

9. Does **anyone else** have medical information about your physical and/or mental condition(s) (including emotional and learning problems), or are you scheduled to see anyone else? (This may include places such as workers' compensation, vocational rehabilitation, insurance companies who have paid you disability benefits, prisons, attorneys, social service agencies and welfare.)

☐ Yes (Please complete the information below.)

☑ No (If you are receiving Supplemental Security Income (SSI) and have been asked to complete this report, go to Section 10 - Vocational Rehabilitation; if not, go to Section 11 on the last page.)

Name of Organization	Phone Number

Mailing Address

City	State/Province	ZIP/Postal Code	Country (If not USA)

Name of Contact Person	Claim or ID number (if any)

Date of First Contact	Date of Last Contact	Date of Next Contact (if any)

Reasons for Contacts

If you need to list other people or organizations use Section 11 - Remarks on the last page and give the same detailed information as above for each one you list.

COMPLETE THIS SECTION ONLY IF YOU ARE ALREADY RECEIVING SSI.

SECTION 10 - VOCATIONAL REHABILITATION, EMPLOYMENT, OR OTHER SUPPORT SERVICES

10.A. Have you participated, or are you participating in:

- An individual work plan with an employment network under the Ticket to Work Program;
- An individualized plan for employment with a vocational rehabilitation agency or any other organization;
- A Plan to Achieve Self-Support (PASS);
- An Individualized Education Program (IEP) through a school (if a student age 18-21); or
- Any program providing vocational rehabilitation, employment services, or other support services to help you go to work?

☐ Yes (Complete the following information)   ☐ No (Go to Section 11)

10.B. Name of Organization or School

Name of Counselor, Instructor, or Job Coach	Phone Number

Mailing Address

City	State/Province	ZIP/Postal Code	Country (If not USA)

10.C. When did you start participating in the plan or program?

Form SSA-3368-BK, *Disability Report—Adult* (Page 12)

SECTION 10 - VOCATIONAL REHABILITATION, EMPLOYMENT, OR OTHER SUPPORT SERVICES
(continued)

10.D. Are you still participating in the plan or program?

☐ **Yes,** I am scheduled to complete the plan or program on: _____

☐ **No.** I completed the plan or program on: _____

☐ **No.** I stopped participating in the plan or program before completing it because:

10.E. List the types of services, tests, or evaluations that you received (for example: intelligence or psychological testing, vision or hearing test, physical exam, work evaluations, or classes).

If you need to list another plan or program use Section 11 -
Remarks and give the same detailed information as above.

SECTION 11 - REMARKS

Please write any additional information you did not give in earlier parts of this report. If you did not have enough space in the sections of this report to write the requested information, please use this space to tell us the additional information requested in those sections. Be sure to show the section to which you are referring.

Although Dr. Bates originally gave me pain medicine for my back and shoulder, it had to be stopped, because it worsened my liver problem. So I have little relief of my back and shoulder pain. I can't bend over because of fluid in my abdomen and back pain. Lifting over 10 lbs. hurts my back and shoulder, and I can't reach overhead with my right arm any more. I feel weak all the time and cannot do much even around the house: mostly, I sit in a chair and read or watch TV. I try to help with some of the housework but get tired in a few minutes. My wife now takes care of the car and all the shopping. Sometimes, my daughter comes over and helps.

All of our savings are about gone. I lost my health insurance when I could no longer work, so my wife lost hers too. I can't afford to get treatment for my cataracts, and my vision is getting worse.

My psychiatrist, Dr. Hill, says that my nervousness will improve if my financial situation gets better. I'd like to learn some other type of work, if I can get help for my medical problems. But I just can't do the heavy work I did before.

Date Report Completed _____ 10/11/15 _____
month, day, year

Form SSA-16, *Application for Disability Insurance Benefits* (Page 1)

Form **SSA-16** (06-2018) UF
Discontinue prior editions
Social Security Administration

OMB No. 0960-0618
(Do not write in this space)

APPLICATION FOR DISABILITY INSURANCE BENEFITS

I apply for a period of disability and/or all insurance benefits for which I am eligible under Title II and Part A of Title XVIII of the Social Security Act, as presently amended.

1.	**PRINT your name**	FIRST NAME, MIDDLE INITIAL, LAST NAME John D. Doe
2.	Enter your Social Security Number	123-45-6789
3.	Check (X) whether you are	☐ Female ☒ Male

Answer question 4 if English is not your preferred language. Otherwise, go to item 5.

4.	Enter the language you prefer to: speak	write
5.	(a) Enter your date of birth	6/12/72
	(b) Enter name of city and state or foreign country where you were born.	Sacramento, CA
	(c) Was a public record of your birth made before you were age 5?	☒ Yes ☐ No ☐ Unknown
	(d) Was a religious record of your birth made before you were age 5?	☐ Yes ☐ No ☒ Unknown
6.	(a) Are you a U.S. citizen?	☒ Yes ☐ No (If "Yes," go to item 7) (If "No," answer (b))
	(b) Are you an alien lawfully present in the U.S.?	☐ Yes ☐ No (If "Yes," answer (c)) (If "No," go to item 7)
	(c) When were you lawfully admitted to the U.S.?	
7.	(a) Enter your name at birth if different from item (1)	
	(b) Have you used any other names?	☐ Yes ☒ No (If "Yes," answer (c)) (If "No," go to item 8)
	(c) Other name(s) used.	
8.	(a) Have you used any other Social Security number(s)?	☐ Yes ☒ No (If "Yes," answer (b)) (If "No" go to item 9)
	(b) Enter Social Security number(s) used.	
9.	When do you believe your condition(s) became severe enough to keep you from working (even if you have never worked)?	
10.	(a) Have you (or has someone on your behalf) ever filed an application for Social Security benefits, a period of disability under Social Security, Supplemental Security Income, or hospital or medical insurance under Medicare?	☐ Yes ☒ No ☐ Unknown (If "Yes," answer (b) and (c)) (If "No," or "Unknown," go to item 11)
	(b) Enter name of person on whose Social Security record you filed the other application.	
	(c) Enter Social Security Number of person named in (b). *If unknown, check this block.* ☐ Unknown	

Form SSA-16, *Application for Disability Insurance Benefits* (Page 2)

Form **SSA-16** (06-2018) UF

11.	(a) Were you in the active military or naval service (including Reserve or National Guard active duty or active duty for training) after September 7, 1939 and before 1968?	☐ Yes (If "Yes," answer (b) and (c))	☒ No (If "No," go to item 12)
	(b) Enter dates of service	FROM: (Month, Year)	TO: (Month, Year)
	(c) Have you ever been (or will you be) eligible for a monthly benefit from a military or civilian Federal agency? (Include Veteran's Administration benefits only if you waived military retirement pay.)	☐ Yes	☐ No
12.	Did you or your spouse (or prior spouse) work in the railroad industry for 5 years or more?	☐ Yes	☒ No
13.	(a) Do you have Social Security credits (for example, based on work or residence) under another country's Social Security System?	☐ Yes (If "Yes," answer (b))	☒ No (If "No," go to item 14)
	(b) List the country(ies):		
14.	(a) Are you entitled to, or do you expect to be entitled to, a pension or annuity (or a lump sum in place of a pension or annuity) based on your work after 1956 not covered by Social Security?	☐ Yes (If "Yes," answer (b) and (c))	☒ No (If "No," go to item 15)
	(b) ☐ I became entitled, or expect to become entitled, beginning	MONTH	YEAR
	(c) ☐ I became eligible, or expect to become eligible, beginning	MONTH	YEAR

I AGREE TO PROMPTLY NOTIFY the Social Security Administration if I become entitled to a pension or annuity based on my employment not covered by Social Security, or if such pension or annuity stops.

15.	(a) Have you ever been married?	☒ Yes (If "Yes," answer (b))	☐ No (If "No," go to item 16)

(b) Give the following information about your current marriage. If not currently married, write "None." (If "None," go on to item 15(c))

Spouse's name (including maiden name)	When (Month, day, year)	Where (Name of City and State)
Jane J. Doe	4/5/95	Los Angeles, CA

Marriage performed by:	Spouse's date of birth (or age)	Spouse's Social Security Number (If none or unknown, so indicate)
☒ Clergyman or public official		
☐ Other (Explain in Remarks)	9/5/72	111-22-3333

(c) Enter information about any other marriage if you:

- Had a marriage that lasted at least 10 years; or

- Had a marriage that ended due to the death of your spouse, regardless of duration; or

- Were divorced, remarried the same individual within the year immediately following the year of the divorce, and the combined period of marriage totaled 10 years or more. If none, write "None." None_____ Go on to item 15 (d) if you have a child(ren) who is under age 16 or disabled or handicapped (age 16 or over and disability began before age 22) and you are divorced from the child's other parent who is now deceased and the marriage lasted less than 10 years.

Spouse's name (including maiden name)	When (Month, day, year)	Where (Name of City and State)

How marriage ended	When (Month, day, year)	Where (Name of City and State)

Marriage performed by:	Spouse's date of birth (or age)	Date of spouse's death	Spouse's Social Security Number (If none or unknown, so indicate)
☐ Clergyman or public official			
☐ Other (Explain in Remarks)			

Form SSA-16, *Application for Disability Insurance Benefits* (Page 3)

Form **SSA-16** (06-2018) UF

15. (d) Enter information about any marriage if you:

- Have a child(ren) who is under age 16 or disabled or handicapped (age 16 or over and disability began before age 22); and
- Were married for less than 10 years to the child's mother or father, who is now deceased; and
- The marriage ended in divorce

  If none, write "None."   None

Spouse's name (including maiden name)	When (Month, day, year)	Where (Name of City and State)
Date of divorce (Month, day, year)	Where (Name of City and State)	

Marriage performed by: ☐ Clergyman or public official ☐ Other (Explain in Remarks)	Spouse's date of birth (or age)	Date of spouse's death	Spouse's Social Security Number (If none or unknown, so indicate)

Use the "REMARKS" space on page 5 for marriage continuation or explanation.

16. If your claim for disability benefits is approved, your children (including adopted children, and stepchildren) or dependent grandchildren (including stepgrandchildren) may be eligible for benefits based on your earnings record.

List below: FULL NAME OF ALL such children who are now or were in the past 12 months UNMARRIED and:

- UNDER AGE 18
- AGE 18 TO 19 AND ATTENDING ELEMENTARY OR SECONDARY SCHOOL FULL-TIME
- DISABLED OR HANDICAPPED (age 18 or over and disability began before age 22)

N/A

17. (a) Did you have wages or self-employment income covered under Social Security in all years from 1978 through last year?

☒ Yes   ☐ No

(If "Yes," go to item 18)   (If "No," answer (b))

(b) List the years from 1978 through last year in which you did not have wages or self-employment income covered under Social Security.

18. Enter below the names and addresses of all the persons, companies, or Government agencies for whom you have worked this year and last year. IF NONE, WRITE "NONE" BELOW AND GO TO ITEM 19.

NAME AND ADDRESS OF EMPLOYER (If you had more than one employer, please list them in order beginning with your last (most recent) employer)	Work Began		Work Ended (If still working show "Not Ended")	
	MONTH	YEAR	MONTH	YEAR
Bay Area Shipping Containers 12310 Front St., San Francisco, CA	August	1996	July	2006
Acme Security Services 1984 Ashley Ave., San Francisco, CA	Sept.	2006	Nov.	2011
Jewel's Food Services 400 W. 19th St., Los Angeles, CA	Feb.	2012	Sept.	2019

(If you need more space, use "Remarks".)

Form SSA-16, *Application for Disability Insurance Benefits* (Page 4)

Form **SSA-16** (06-2018) UF

19.	Complete item 19 even if you were an employee.	

(a) Were you self-employed this year or last year? ☐ Yes ☒ No
(If "Yes," answer (b))   (If "No," go to item 20)

(b) Check the year (or years) you were self-employed	In what type of trade/business were you self-employed? (For example, storekeeper, farmer, physician)	Were your net earnings from the trade or business $400 or more? (Check "Yes" or "No")
☐ This year		
☐ Last year		☐ Yes ☐ No

20.	(a) How much were your total earnings last year? Count both wage and self-employment income. (If none, write "None.") _____	Amount $ 32,500
	(b) How much have you earned so far this year? (If none, write "None.") _____	Amount $ 12,500
21.	(a) Are you still unable to work because of your illnesses, injuries, or conditions?	☒ Yes ☐ No (If "Yes," go to item 22) (If "No," answer (b))
	(b) Enter the date you became able to work.	MONTH, DAY, YEAR 9/1/2019
22.	Are your illnesses, injuries, or conditions related to your work in any way?	☒ Yes ☐ No
23.	Are you blind or do you have low vision even with glasses or contacts?	☐ Yes ☒ No
24.	(a) Have you filed, or do you intend to file, for any other public disability benefits (including workers' compensation, Black Lung benefits and SSI)?	☒ Yes ☐ No (If "Yes," answer (b)) (If "No," to item 25)
	(b) The other public disability benefit(s) you have filed (or intend to file) for is (Check as many as apply):	

☐ Veterans Administration Benefits   ☐ Welfare

☒ Supplemental Security Income   ☐ Other (If "Other," complete a Workers' Compensation/Public Disability Benefit Questionnaire)

25.	(a) Did you receive any money from an employer(s) on or after the date in item 9 when you became unable to work because of your illnesses, injuries, or conditions? If "Yes", give the amounts and explain in "Remarks".	☒ Yes ☐ No Amount $ 350.00
	(b) Do you expect to receive any additional money from an employer, such as sick pay, vacation pay, other special pay? If "Yes," please give amounts and explain in "Remarks".	☐ Yes ☒ No Amount $ _____
26.	Do you, or did you, have a child under age 3 (your own or your spouse's) living with you in one or more calendar years when you had no earnings?	☐ Yes ☒ No
27.	Do you have a dependent parent who was receiving at least one-half support from you when you became unable to work because of your disability? If "Yes," enter the parent's name and address and Social Security number, if known, in "Remarks".	☐ Yes ☒ No
28.	If you were unable to work before age 22 because of an illness, injury or condition, do you have a parent (including adoptive or stepparent) or grandparent who is receiving social security retirement or disability benefits or who is deceased? If yes, enter the name(s) and Social Security number, if known, in "Remarks" (if unknown, check "Unknown").	☐ Yes ☒ No ☐ Unknown

Form SSA-16, *Application for Disability Insurance Benefits* (Page 5)

Form **SSA-16** (06-2018) UF

REMARKS (You may use this space for any explanation. If you need more space, attach a separate sheet.)

I have developed high blood pressure, back pain, and arthritis in my hands and knees. The money my employer gave me when I left my last job was "sick pay" and there won't be any more.

I request my treating doctor be asked about how my medical problems interfere with my ability to perform activities before a decision is made on my disability claim.

Also, I request that a licensed medical doctor make any determination about the medical severity of my disorders in regard to whether I am disabled. I ask to be informed before SSA makes any denial determination, if a doctor has not reviewed my claim or if the SSA has not contacted my treating doctor for an opinion. I feel I have a right to have my medical record reviewed by a real doctor, not merely by a disability examiner, and that my treating doctor's opinion be considered.

I declare under penalty of perjury that I have examined all the information on this form, and on any accompanying statements or forms, and it is true and correct to the best of my knowledge. I understand that anyone who knowingly gives a false statement about a material fact in this information, or causes someone else to do so, commits a crime and may be subject to a fine or imprisonment.

SIGNATURE OF APPLICANT	Date (Month, Day, Year)
	9/05/2015
Signature (First name, middle initial, last name) (Write in ink)	Telephone Number(s) at which you may be contacted during the day. (Include the area code)
John D. Doe	310-555-1111

DIRECT DEPOSIT PAYMENT INFORMATION (FINANCIAL INSTITUTION)

Routing Transit Number	Account Number	☒ Checking ☐ Savings	☒ Enroll in Direct Express ☐ Direct Deposit Refused

Applicant's Mailing Address *(Number and street, Apt No., P.O. Box, or Rural Route) (Enter Residence Address in "Remarks," if different.)*

P.O. Box 24830

City and State	ZIP Code	County *(if any)* in which you now live
Los Angeles, CA	90025	Los Angeles

Witnesses are required ONLY if this application has been signed by mark (X) above. If signed by mark (X), two witnesses to the signing who know the applicant must sign below, giving their full addresses. Also, print the applicant's name in Signature block.

1. Signature of Witness	2. Signature of Witness
Address *(Number and street, City, State and ZIP Code)*	Address *(Number and street, City, State and ZIP Code)*

Form SSA-8000-BK, *Application for Supplemental Security Income (SSI)* (Page 1)

Form **SSA-8000-BK** (06-2019) UF
Discontinue Prior Editions
Social Security Administration

OMB No. 0960-0229

APPLICATION FOR SUPPLEMENTAL SECURITY INCOME (SSI)

Note: Social Security Administration staff or others who help people apply for SSI will fill out this form for you.	Do Not Write in This Space **DATE STAMP**
I am/We are applying for Supplemental Security Income and any federally administered state supplementation under Title XVI of the Social Security Act, for benefits under the other programs administered by the Social Security Administration, and where applicable, for medical assistance under Title XIX of the Social Security Act.	**Filing Date (MM/DD/YYYY)** ☐ Receipt ☐ Protective ☐ SNAP-SSA/APP ☐ SNAP-Referred **Preferred Language** Written: Spoken:

TYPE OF CLAIM ☑ Individual ☐ Individual with Ineligible Spouse ☐ Couple ☐ Child ☐ Child with Parents

PART 1 - BASIC ELIGIBILITY - Answer the questions below beginning with the first moment of the filing date month.

1.	(a) First Name, Middle Initial, Last Name Shirley L. Clark	Sex ☐ Male ☑ Female	Birthdate (MM/DD/YYYY) 07/15/1964	Social Security Number 234-56-7890

(b) Did you ever use any other names (including maiden name) or any other Social Security Numbers?	☐ YES Go to (c) ☑ NO Go to (d)

(c) Other Name(s)	Other Social Security Number(s) used

(d) If you are also filing for Social Security Benefits, go to #2; otherwise complete the following:

Parent 1's Name (s)	Parent 2's Name (s)
Parent 1's Other Name (s) (Including Name at Birth)	Parent 2's Other Name (s) (Including Name at Birth)

Go to #2

2. Applicant's Mailing Address (Number & Street, Apt. No., P.O. Box, Rural Route)

100 West 95th Street

City and State (U.S.)/State/Province/Region (Foreign) Los Angeles, CA	ZIP Code/Postal Code 90055	County/Country LA

3. Claimant's Residence Address (If different from applicant's mailing address)

City and State (U.S.)/State/Province/Region (Foreign)	ZIP Code/Postal Code	County/Country

4.	DIRECT DEPOSIT PAYMENT INFORMATION (FINANCIAL INSTITUTION)

Routing Transit Number	Account Number	☑ Checking	☑ Enroll in Direct Express
		☐ Savings	☐ Direct Deposit Refused

Form SSA-8000-BK, *Application for Supplemental Security Income (SSI)* (Page 2)

Form **SSA-8000-BK** (06-2019) UF

5.			
	(a) Are you married?	☑ YES Go to (b)	☐ NO Go to #6

(b) Date of marriage: (MM/DD/YYYY)

6/30/1995

(c) Spouse's Name (First, middle initial, last)	Birthdate (MM/DD/YYYY)	Social Security Number
Paul A. Clark	04/30/1961	234-56-6891

(d) Did your spouse ever use any other names (including maiden name) or Social Security Numbers?	☐ YES Go to (e)	☑ NO Go to (f)
(e) Other Name(s)	Other Social Security Number(s) Used	

(f) Are you and your spouse living together?	☑ YES Go to #6	☐ NO Go to (g)

(g) Date you began living apart :   (MM/DD/YYYY)

(h) Address of spouse or name of someone who knows where spouse is. (Complete only if spouse is age 65, blind or disabled.)

6.	(a) Have you had any other marriages?		**You**		**Your Spouse, if filing**	
	If never married, check this box ☐	☑ YES Go to (b)	☐ NO Go to 6(c)	☐ YES Go to (b)	☐ NO Go to 6(c)	

(b) Give the following information about your prior marriages. If there was more than one prior marriage, show the remaining information in Remarks. Go to #7.

	YOU	YOUR SPOUSE
FORMER SPOUSE'S NAME (including maiden name)	Mike Glenn	
BIRTHDATE (MM/DD/YYYY)	05/16/1960	
SOCIAL SECURITY NUMBER	Unknown	
DATE OF MARRIAGE (MM/DD/YYYY)	12/20/1987	
DATE MARRIAGE ENDED (MM/DD/YYYY)	03/18/1989	
HOW MARRIAGE ENDED	Divorce	

(c) Are you and another person living together in the same household and presenting to others or the community as a married couple?

☑ YES If YES, provide the date holding out began _____, then go to (d)*

☐ NO Go to #7

(d) Other person's Name (First, middle initial, last)	Other person's Social Security Number

*Use SSA-4178 to develop the holding out relationship.

Form SSA-8000-BK, *Application for Supplemental Security Income (SSI)* (Page 3)

Form **SSA-8000-BK** (06-2019) UF

		You		Your Spouse	
7.	If you are filing for yourself, go to (a); if you are filing for a child, go to (e).				

7. If you are filing for yourself, go to (a); if you are filing for a child, go to (e).

	You	Your Spouse
(a) Are you unable to work because of illnesses, injuries or conditions?	☑ YES ☐ NO Go to (b) Go to #8	☐ YES ☐ NO Go to (b) Go to #8
(b) Enter the date you became unable to work.	(MM/DD/YYYY) 06/01/2019	(MM/DD/YYYY)
(c) Are you blind or do you have low vision even with glasses or contacts?	☐ YES ☑ NO Go to (d) Go to (d)	☐ YES ☐ NO Go to (d) Go to (d)

(d) If you were unable to work because of illnesses, injuries, or conditions before you were age 22, do you have a parent who is age 62 or older, unable to work because of illnesses, injuries or conditions, or deceased?

☐ YES   Parent's Name: N/A

Social Security Number: _____

Address: _____

_____

_____

Parent's Name: _____

Social Security Number: _____

Address: _____

_____

_____

☐ NO
Go to #8

(e) When did the child become disabled?   (MM/DD/YYYY)
Go to (f)

(f) Is the child blind or do they have low vision even with glasses or contacts?	☐ YES Go to (g)	☐ NO Go to (g)

(g) Does the child have a parent(s) who is age 62 or older, unable to work because of illness, injuries, or conditions, or deceased?

☐ YES   Parent's Name: _____

Social Security Number: _____

Address: _____

_____

_____

Parent's Name: _____

Social Security Number: _____

Address: _____

_____

_____

☐ NO
Go to #8

8.	Birthplace	City	State	Country (if other than the U.S.)
	You	Chicago	Illinois	
	Your Spouse, if filing			Go to #9

Form SSA-8000-BK, *Application for Supplemental Security Income (SSI)* (Page 4)

Form **SSA-8000-BK** (06-2019) UF

9. Are you a United States citizen by birth?	You		Your Spouse, if filing	
	☑YES Go to #15	☐NO Go to #10	☐ YES Go to #15	☐ NO Go to #10
10. Are you a naturalized United States citizen?	☐ YES Go to #15	☐ NO Go to #11	☐ YES Go to #15	☐ NO Go to #11
11. (a) Are you an American Indian born outside the United States?	☐YES Go to (b)	☐NO Go to (c)	☐ YES Go to (b)	☐ NO Go to (c)

(b) Check the block that shows your American Indian status.

You	Your Spouse, if filing
☐American Indian born in Canada Go to #15	☐ American Indian born in Canada Go to #15
☐Member of a Federally recognized Indian Tribe; Name of Tribe Go to #15	☐ Member of a Federally recognized Indian Tribe; Name of Tribe Go to #15
☐Other American Indian Explain in Remarks, then Go to (c)	☐ Other American Indian Explain in Remarks, then Go to (c)

(c) Check the block below that shows your current immigration status

You	Your Spouse, if filing
☐Amerasian Immigrant Go to #12	☐ Amerasian Immigrant Go to #12
☐Asylee Date status granted: Go to #14	☐ Asylee Date status granted: Go to #14
☐Conditional Entrant Date status granted: Go to #14	☐ Conditional Entrant Date status granted: Go to #14
☐Cuban/Haitian Entrant Go to #14	☐ Cuban/Haitian Entrant Go to #14
☐Deportation/Removal Withheld Date: Go to #14	☐ Deportation/Removal Withheld Date: Go to #14
☐Lawful Permanent Resident Go to #12	☐ Lawful Permanent Resident Go to #12
☐Parolee for One Year Go to #14	☐ Parolee for One Year Go to #14
☐Refugee Date of entry: Go to #14	☐ Refugee Date of entry: Go to #14
☐Unknown/Other Explain in Remarks, then Go to (d)	☐ Unknown/Other Explain in Remarks, then Go to (d)

(d) If you have status or have applied for status as the spouse, child, or parent of a child of a US citizen or lawfully admitted permanent resident alien, Go to #13; otherwise Go to #15.

12. If you are lawfully admitted for permanent residence:

	You (MM/DD/YYYY)		Your Spouse (MM/DD/YYYY)	
(a) Date of Admission				
(b) Was your entry into the United States sponsored by any person or promoted by an institution or group?	☐YES Go to (c)	☐ NO Go to (d)	☐ YES Go to (c)	☐ NO Go to (d)

(c) Give the following information about the person, institution, or group, then Go to (d):

Name
Address
Telephone Number

Form SSA-8000-BK, *Application for Supplemental Security Income (SSI)* (Page 5)

Form **SSA-8000-BK** (06-2019) UF

		You		Your Spouse, if filing	
12.		Status:		Status:	
	(d) What was your immigration status, if any, before adjustment to lawful permanent resident?	(MM/DD/YYYY)		(MM/DD/YYYY)	
		From:		From:	
		To:		To:	Go to (e)
		You		Your Spouse, if filing	
	(e) If filing as an adult, did your parents ever work in the United States before you were age 18?	☐ YES Go to (f)	☐NO Go to #14	☐ YES Go to (f)	☐NO Go to #14
	(f) Name and Social Security Number of parent(s) who worked.				
	Name			Social Security Number	
	Name			Social Security Number	

		You		Your Spouse, if filing	
13.	(a) Have you, your child or your parent, been subjected to battery or extreme cruelty while in the United States?	☐YES Go to (b)	☐NO Go to #15	☐YES Go to (b)	☐NO Go to #15
	(b) Have you, your child, or your parent filed a petition with the Department of Homeland Security for a change in immigration status because of being subjected to battery or extreme cruelty?	☐YES Go to #14	☐NO Go to #15	☐YES Go to #14	☐NO Go to #15
14.	Are you, your spouse, or parent an active duty member or a veteran of the armed forces of the United States?	☐YES Explain in #60(b), then Go to #15	☐NO Go to #15	☐YES Explain in #60(b), then Go to #15	☐NO Go to #15
15.	(a) When did you first make your home in the United States?	(MM/DD/YYYY)		(MM/DD/YYYY)	
	(b) Have you lived outside of the United States since then?	☐ YES Go to (c)	☐ NO Go to #16	☐ YES Go to (c)	☐ NO Go to #16
	(c) Give the dates of residence outside the United States.	(MM/DD/YYYY) From: To:		(MM/DD/YYYY) From: To:	
16.	(a) Have you been outside the United States (the 50 states, District of Columbia and Northern Mariana Islands) 30 consecutive days prior to the filing date?	☐YES Go to (b)	☐NO Go to #17	☐YES Go to (b)	☐NO Go to #17
	(b) Give the date (MM/DD/YYYY) you left the United States and the date you returned to the United States.	Date Left: Date Returned:		Date Left: Date Returned:	

IF YOU ARE FILING ON BEHALF OF YOUR CHILD, GO TO #17.
IF YOU ARE MARRIED AND YOUR SPOUSE IS NOT FILING FOR SUPPLEMENTAL SECURITY INCOME AND YOU LIVED TOGETHER AT ANY TIME SINCE THE FIRST MOMENT OF THE FILING DATE MONTH, GO TO #17; OTHERWISE GO TO #18.

Form SSA-8000-BK, *Application for Supplemental Security Income (SSI)* (Page 6)

Form **SSA-8000-BK** (06-2019) UF

17.	(a) Is your spouse/parent the sponsor of an alien who is eligible for supplemental security income?	☐ YES Go to (b)	☑ No Go to #18
	(b) Eligible Alien's Name	Eligible Alien's Social Security Number	Go to #18

18.		**You**	**Your Spouse, if filing**
	(a) Do you have any unsatisfied felony warrants for your arrest?	☐ YES ☑ NO Go to (b) Go to #19	☐ YES ☐ NO Go to (b) Go to #19
	(b) In which State or Country was this warrant issued?	Name of State/Country Go to (c)	Name of State/Country Go to (c)
	(c) Was the warrant satisfied?	**You** ☐ YES ☐ NO Go to (d) Go to #19	**Your Spouse, if filing** ☐ YES ☐ NO Go to (d) Go to #19
	(d) Date warrant satisfied	(MM/DD/YYYY)	(MM/DD/YYYY)

PART 2 - LIVING ARRANGEMENTS - The questions in this section refer to the signature date.

19.	Check the block which best describes your present living situation:	Since (MM/DD/YYYY)	
	☑ Household	09/01/2005	Go to #24
	☐ Non-Institutional Care	Since (MM/DD/YYYY)	Go to #22
	☐ Institution	Since (MM/DD/YYYY)	Go to #20
	☐ Transient or homeless	Since (MM/DD/YYYY)	Go to #37

INSTITUTION

20.	Check the block that identifies the type of institution where you currently reside, then Go to #21:	
	☐ School	☐ Rehabilitation Center
	☐ Hospital	☐ Jail
	☐ Rest or Retirement Home	☐ Other (Specify)
	☐ Nursing Home	

21.	Give the following information about the INSTITUTION:	
	(a) Name of institution:	
	(b) Date of admission:	
	(c) Date you expect to be released from this institution:	Go to #37

NON-INSTITUTIONAL CARE

22.	Check the block that best describes your current residence, then Go to #23:
	☐ Foster Home ☐ Group Home ☐ Other (Specify)

Form SSA-8000-BK, *Application for Supplemental Security Income (SSI)* (Page 7)

Form **SSA-8000-BK** (06-2019) UF

23.	Give the following information about your Noninstitutional Care:

(a) Name of facility where you live:

(b) Name of placing agency

Address

Telephone Number

(c) Does this agency pay for your room and board?

☐ YES Go to #37

☐ NO If NO, who pays?

Go to #37

HOUSEHOLD ARRANGEMENTS

24. Check the block that describes your current residence, then Go to #25:

☐ House	☐ Mobile Home
☑ Apartment	☐ Houseboat
☐ Room (private home)	☐ Other (Specify)
☐ Room (commercial establishment)	

25. Do you live alone or only with your spouse?　☑ YES Go to #27　☐ NO Go to #26

26. (a) Give the following information about everyone who lives with you:

Name	Relationship	Public Assistance		Sex		Birthdate	Blind or Disabled		If Under 22				Social Security Number
									Married		Student		
		YES	NO	M	F	mm/dd/yy	YES	NO	YES	NO	YES	NO	
		☐	☐	☐	☐		☐	☐	☐	☐	☐	☐	
		☐	☐	☐	☐		☐	☐	☐	☐	☐	☐	
		☐	☐	☐	☐		☐	☐	☐	☐	☐	☐	
		☐	☐	☐	☐		☐	☐	☐	☐	☐	☐	
		☐	☐	☐	☐		☐	☐	☐	☐	☐	☐	
		☐	☐	☐	☐		☐	☐	☐	☐	☐	☐	

If anyone listed is under age 22 and not married, Go to (b); otherwise, Go to #27.

Form SSA-8000-BK, *Application for Supplemental Security Income (SSI)* (Page 8)

Form **SSA-8000-BK** (06-2019) UF

26.	(b) Does anyone listed in 26(a) who is under age 18, OR between ages 18-22 and a student, receive income?	☐ YES Go to (c)	☐ NO Go to #27
	(c) Child Receiving Income	Source and Type	Monthly Amount
			$
			$
			$
			$
			$
			$

27.	(a) Do you (or does anyone who lives with you) own or rent the place where you live?	☐ YES Go to #28	☑ No Go to (b)

(b) Name of person who owns or rents the place where you live

Donald Kemp

Address

114 Temple St, Los Angeles, CA

Telephone Number   **310-555-4444**

(c) If you live alone or only with your spouse, and do not own or rent, Go to #37; otherwise, Go to #31.

28.			
	(a) Are you (or your living with spouse) buying or do you own the place where you live?	☐ YES Go to (c)	☐ No If you are a child living with your parent(s) Go to (b); otherwise Go to #29
	(b) Are your parent(s) buying or do they own the place where you live?	☐ YES Go to (c)	☐ NO Go to #29

(c) What is the amount and frequency of the mortgage payment?

Amount: $
Frequency of Payment:

Go to (d)

(d) If you are a child living only with your parents, or only with your parents and their other children who are subject to deeming, or with others in a public assistance household, or living alone or with your spouse, Go to #37; otherwise Go to #31.

Form SSA-8000-BK, *Application for Supplemental Security Income (SSI)* (Page 9)

Form **SSA-8000-BK** (06-2019) UF

29.			
	(a) Do you (or your living with spouse) have rental liability for the place where you live?	☐ YES Go to (d)	☐ No If you are a child living with your parent(s) Go to (b); otherwise Go to (c)

(b) Does your parent(s) have rental liability?   ☐ YES   Go to (d)   ☐ NO   Go to (c)

(c) Does anyone who lives with you have rental liability for the place where you live?

   ☐ YES   Give name of person with rental liability: _____   Go to #30

   ☐   NO   Give name of person with home ownership:_____   Go to #31

(d) What is the amount and frequency of the rent payment?

   Amount: $

   Frequency of Payment: Go to #30

30.			
	(a) Are you (or anyone who lives with you) the parent or child of the landlord or the landlord's spouse?	☐ YES Go to (b)	☐ NO Go to (c)

(b) Name of person related to landlord or landlord's spouse

   Relationship

   Name and address of landlord (include telephone number and area code, if known):

(c) If you are a child living only with your parents, or only with your parents and their other children who are subject to deeming, or with others in a public assistance household, or living alone or with your spouse, Go to #37.

31.			
	(a) Does anyone living with you contribute to the household expenses? (NOTE: See list of household expenses in #36)	☐ YES Go to (b)	☐ NO Go to #32

(b) Amount others contribute: $ Go to #32

32.			
	(a) Do you eat all your meals out?	☐ YES Go to #33	☐ NO Go to (b)
	(b) Do you buy all your food separately from other household members:	☐ YES Go to #33	☐ NO Go to #33

33.	
Do you contribute to household expenses?	
☐ YES Average Monthly Amount: $_____ Go to #34	☐ NO Go to #34

34.			
	(a) Do you have a loan agreement with anyone to repay the value of your share of the household expenses?	☐ YES Go to (b)	☐ NO Go to #34(d)

(b) Give the name, address and telephone number of the person with whom you have a loan agreement :

(c) Will the amount of this loan cover your share of the household expenses?	☐ YES Go to #37	☐ NO Go to (d)

(d) **If you contribute** toward household expenses and you answered "NO" to both 32(a) & (b), Go To #35. If you answered "YES" to either 32(a) or 32(b), Go to #36.

If you do not contribute toward household expenses, go to #37.

Form SSA-8000-BK, *Application for Supplemental Security Income (SSI)* (Page 10)

Form **SSA-8000-BK** (06-2019) UF

35.	(a) Is part or all of the amount in #33 just for food?		
	☐ YES Give Amount: $ _____	Go to (b)	☐ NO Go to (b)
	(b) Is part or all of the amount in #33 just for shelter?		
	☐ YES Give Amount: $ _____	Go to #36	☐ NO Go to #36

36. What is the average monthly amount of the following household expenses:
(Show average over the past 12 months unless you have been residing at your present address less than 12 months. If so, show average for the months you have resided at your present address.)

CASH EXPENSES	AVERAGE MONTHLY AMOUNT
Food (complete only if #32(a) & (b) are answered NO)	$
Mortgage or Rent	$
Property Insurance (if required by mortgage lender)	$
Real Property Taxes	$
Electricity	$
Heating Fuel	$
Gas	$
Sewer	$
Garbage Removal	$
Water	$
TOTAL	$ 0.00 Go to #37

37. (a) Does anyone who does NOT LIVE with you pay for, or provide you or your household (if applicable), any of your food or shelter items?

☑ YES   Name of Provider (Person or Agency) John Ford

List of Items   Food

Monthly Value: $ 200.00

☐ NO

Go to (b)

(b) Does anyone who does NOT LIVE with you give you, or your household (if applicable), money to pay for any of your or your household's food or shelter items?

☑ YES   Name of Provider (Person or Agency) Betty Clark

List of Items   Electricity

Monthly Value: $ 100.00

☐ NO

Go to #38

38.			
(a) Has the information given in #19-37 been the same since the first moment of the filing date month?	☑ YES Go to (b)		☐ No Explain in Remarks, then Go to (b)
(b) Do you expect any of this information to change?	☐ YES Explain in Remarks, then Go to #39		☑ No Go to #39

Form SSA-8000-BK, *Application for Supplemental Security Income (SSI)* (Page 11)

Form **SSA-8000-BK** (06-2019) UF

PART 3 - RESOURCES - The questions in this section pertain to the first moment of the filing date month.

39.

(a) Do you own or does your name appear, either alone or with other people on any trust?

You		Your Spouse, if filing	
☐ YES	☑ NO	☐ YES	☐ NO
Go to (b)	Go to #40	Go to (b)	Go to #40

(b) If you answered "YES" to (a), give the following information:

Title of the Trust	Funding type, i.e., self-funded or third party funded alleged	Date established (MM/DD/YYYY)	Total alleged value	Specific assets contained within the trust, i.e., vehicles, homes, bank accounts, etc.

40.

(a) Do you own, or does your name appear (alone or with any other person's name) on the title of any vehicles (auto, truck, motorcycle, camper, boat, etc.)?

You		Your Spouse	
☐ YES	☐ NO	☑ YES	☐ NO
Go to (b)	Go to #41	Go to (b)	Go to #41

(b)

Owner's Name	Description (Year, Make & Model)	Used For	Current Market Value	Amount Owed
Paul Clark	1987 Ford	Personal	$200.00	$
			$	$
			$	$
			$200.00	$

41.

(a) Do you own, or does your name appear (alone or with any other person's name) on any land, houses, buildings, real property, property in foreign country, equipment, mineral rights, items in a safe deposit box, assets set aside for emergencies or heirs, or any other property of any kind that has not been shown anywhere else on the application

You		Your Spouse	
☐ YES	☐ NO	☐ YES	☐ NO
Go to (b)	Go to #42	Go to (b)	Go to #42

(b) Describe the property (including size, address, and how it is used. If the property is not used now, when was it last used? Do you plan to use the property in the future?

Item #1

Item #2

Owner's Name	Estimated Current Market Value	Owed on Item
	$	$
	$	$
	$	$
	$	$

Form SSA-8000-BK, *Application for Supplemental Security Income (SSI)* (Page 12)

Form **SSA-8000-BK** (06-2019) UF

42. (a) Do you own, or does your name appear on (either alone or with any other person's name) any of the following items?	You		Your Spouse	
	YES	NO	YES	NO
Cash at home, with you, or anywhere else	☐	☑	☐	☑
Financial Institution Accounts	☐	☑	☐	☑
Achieving a Better Life Experience (ABLE)	☐	☑	☐	☑
Checking	☐	☑	☐	☑
Savings	☐	☑	☐	☑
Credit Union	☐	☑	☐	☑
Christmas Club	☐	☑	☐	☑
Time Deposits/Certificates of Deposit	☐	☑	☐	☑
Individual Indian Money Account	☐	☑	☐	☑
Other (Including IRAs and Keough Accounts)	☐	☑	☐	☑

(b) If all the items in #42(a) are answered "NO", Go to #42(c). For any "YES" answer, give the following information:

Owner's Name	Name of Item	Value	Name & Address of Bank or Other Organization	Identifying Number
		$		
		$		
		$		
		$		

(c) Do you give us permission to obtain any financial records from any financial institution?	You		Your Spouse, if filing	
	☑ YES Go to #43	☐ NO Go to #43	☐ YES Go to #43	☐ NO Go to #43

43. (a) Do you own or does your name appear on any of the following items:	You		Your Spouse	
	YES	NO	YES	NO
Stocks or Mutual Funds	☐	☑	☐	☑
Bonds (Including U.S. Savings Bonds)	☐	☑	☐	☑
Promissory Notes	☐	☑	☐	☑
Other items that can be turned into cash	☐	☑	☐	☑

Form SSA-8000-BK, *Application for Supplemental Security Income (SSI)* (Page 13)

Form **SSA-8000-BK** (06-2019) UF

43. (b) If all the items in #43(a) are answered "NO", Go to #44. For any "YES" answer, give the following information:

Owner's Name	Name of Item	Value	Name & Address of Bank or Other Organization	Identifying Number
		$		
		$		
		$		
		$		

44. (a) Do you own or are you buying any life insurance policies?

You ☐ YES Go to (b) ☑ NO Go to #45

Your Spouse ☐ YES Go to (b) ☑ NO Go to #45

(b) Owner's Name	Name of Insured	Name & Address of Insurance Company	Policy Number
Policy (#1)			
Policy (#2)			
Policy (#3)			

	Face Value	Cash Surrender Value	Date of Purchase	Dividends		Accumu- lations	
				YES	NO	YES	NO
Policy (#1)				☐	☐	☐	☐
Policy (#2)				☐	☐	☐	☐
Policy (#3)				☐	☐	☐	☐

(c) Loans Against Policy?

☐ YES   Policy Number: _____

Amount: $ _____

☐ NO

Go to #45

45. (a) Have you or your spouse acquired any assets since the first moment of the filing date month?

☐ YES Go to (b)   ☑ NO Go to (c)

(b) Explain:

Form SSA-8000-BK, *Application for Supplemental Security Income (SSI)* (Page 14)

Form **SSA-8000-BK** (06-2019) UF

45. (c) Has there been any increase or decrease in the value of you or your spouse's resources since the first moment of the filing date month?	☐ YES Go to (d) ☑ NO Go to #46
(d) Explain:	

46. (a) Do you (either alone or jointly with any other person) own any:	You		Your Spouse	
	YES	NO	YES	NO
Life estates or ownership interest in an unprobated estate?	☐	☐	☐	☐
Items acquired or held for their value as an investment?	☐	☐	☐	☐

(b) Give the following information for any "Yes" answer in #46(a); otherwise, Go to #47.

Owner's Name	Name of Item	Value	Amount Owed	Name & Address of Bank or Other Organization
		$	$	
		$	$	
		$	$	
		$	$	

47. (a) Do you have any assets set aside for burial expenses such as burial contracts, trusts, agreements, or anything else you intend for your burial expenses? Include any items mentioned in #39, #41-45, and #49.	You		Your Spouse	
	☐ YES Go to (b)	☑ NO Go to #48	☐ YES Go to (b)	☑ NO Go to #48

(b) DESCRIPTION (Where appropriate, give name & address of organization and account/ policy number.)	Value	When Set Aside (MM/DD/YYYY)	Owner's Name
Item (#1)	$		
Item (#2)	$		

For Whose Burial	Is Item Irrevocable?		Will Interest Earned or Appreciation in Value Remain in the Burial Fund?	
Item (#1)	☐ YES	☐ NO	☐ YES Go to #48	☐ NO Explain in (c)
Item (#2)	☐ YES	☐ NO	☐ YES Go to #48	☐ NO Explain in (c)

(c) Explanation

Form SSA-8000-BK, *Application for Supplemental Security Income (SSI)* (Page 15)

Form **SSA-8000-BK** (06-2019) UF

48.	(a) Do you own any cemetery lots, crypts, caskets, vaults, urns, mausoleums, or other repositories for burial or any headstones or markers?		**You** ☐ YES Go to (b) · ☑ NO Go to #49		**Your Spouse** ☐ YES Go to (b) · ☐ NO Go to #49

(b) Owner's Name	Description	For Whose Burial	Relationship to You or Your Spouse	Current Market Value
				$
				$
				$ Go to #49

49.	(a) Have you or your spouse sold, transferred title, disposed of or given away, any money or other property, (including money or property in foreign countries), since the first moment of the filing date month or within the 36 months prior to the filing date month?	**You** ☐ YES · ☑ NO Go to (b)	**Your Spouse** ☐ YES · ☑ NO Go to (b)
	(b) If you co-owned any money or property with another person(s), did you or any co-owner sell, transfer, or give away any co-owned money or property within the 36 months prior to the filing date month?	☐ YES · ☑ NO	☐ YES · ☑ NO

IF YOU ANSWERED "YES" TO (a) OR (b), GO TO (c). IF "NO" TO BOTH, GO TO #50.

(c) Owner's/Co-Owner's Name	Description of Property	Date of Disposal
Item (#1)		
Item (#2)		
Item (#3)		

Name and Address of Purchaser or Recipient	Relationship to Owner	Value of Property and/or Amount of Cash Gift
Item (#1)		
Item (#2)		
Item (#3)		

Sales Price or Other Consideration	Are Other Consideration or Proceeds Expected? Explain.	Do You Still Own Part of the Property?
Item (#1)		
Item (#2)		
Item (#3)		

	Sold on Open Market?		Given Away?		Traded for Goods/ Services?	
Item (#1)	☐ YES	☐ NO	☐ YES	☐ NO	☐ YES	☐ NO
Item (#2)	☐ YES	☐ NO	☐ YES	☐ NO	☐ YES	☐ NO
Item (#3)	☐ YES	☐ NO	☐ YES	☐ NO	☐ YES	☐ NO

Form SSA-8000-BK, *Application for Supplemental Security Income (SSI)* (Page 16)

Form **SSA-8000-BK** (06-2019) UF

PART 4 - INCOME

50. (a) Since the first moment of the filing date month, have you (or your spouse) received or do you (or your spouse) expect to receive income in the next 14 months from any of the following sources?	You		Your Spouse	
	YES	NO	YES	NO
State or Local Assistance Based on Need	☐	☑	☐	☑
Refugee Cash Assistance	☐	☑	☐	☑
Temporary Assistance for Needy Families	☐	☑	☐	☑
General Assistance from the Bureau of Indian Affairs	☐	☑	☐	☑
Disaster Relief	☐	☑	☐	☑
Veteran Benefits Based on Need (Paid Directly or Indirectly as a Dependent)	☐	☑	☐	☑
Veteran Payments Not Based on Need (Paid Directly or Indirectly as a Dependent)	☐	☑	☐	☑
Other Income Based on Need	☐	☑	☐	☑
Social Security	☐	☑	☐	☑
Black Lung	☐	☑	☐	☑
Railroad Retirement Board Benefits	☐	☑	☐	☑
Office of Personnel Management (Civil Service)	☐	☑	☐	☑
Pension (Foreign Military, State, Local, Private, Union, Retirement or Disability)	☐	☑	☐	☑
Military Special Pay or Allowance	☐	☑	☐	☑
Unemployment Compensation	☐	☑	☐	☑
Workers' Compensation	☐	☑	☐	☑
State Disability	☐	☑	☐	☑
Insurance or Annuity Payments	☐	☑	☐	☑
Dividends/Royalties	☐	☑	☐	☑
Rental/Lease Income Not from a Trade or Business	☐	☑	☐	☑
Alimony	☐	☑	☐	☑
Child Support	☐	☑	☐	☑
Other Bureau of Indian Affairs Income	☐	☑	☐	☑
Gambling/Lottery Winnings	☐	☑	☐	☑
Other Income or Support	☐	☑	☐	☑

Form SSA-8000-BK, *Application for Supplemental Security Income (SSI)* (Page 17)

Form **SSA-8000-BK** (06-2019) UF

50. (b) Give the following information for any block checked YES in #50(a); otherwise, Go to #51

Person Receiving Income	Type of Income	Amount Received	Frequency of Payment	Date Expected or Received	Source (Name, Address of Person, Bank, Organization, or Company)	Identifying Number
		$				
		$				
		$				

IF YOU EVER RECEIVED SSI BEFORE, GO TO #51; OTHERWISE GO TO #52.

		You		Your Spouse	
51.	Are any overpayments being collected from benefits you receive from the Social Security Administration, Railroad Retirement Board, Office of Personnel Management, Veterans' Affairs, Military Pensions, Military Special Pay Allowances, Black Lung, Workers' Compensation, or State Disability or Unemployment Benefits?	☐ YES Explain in Remarks, then Go to #52	✔ NO Go to #52	☐ YES Explain in Remarks, then Go to #52	✔ NO Go to #52
52.	Since the first moment of the filing date month, have you received or do you expect to receive any meals or other gifts which are not cash?	☐ YES Explain in Remarks, then Go to #53	✔ NO Go to #53	☐ YES Explain in Remarks, then Go to #53	✔ NO Go to #53
53.	(a) Have you (or your spouse) received wages or sick pay since the first moment of the filing date month through the current month?	☐ YES Go to (b)	✔ NO Go to (e)	☐ YES Go to (b)	✔ NO Go to (e)

(b) Name and Address of Employer (include telephone number and area code, if known)

You

Go to (c)

Your Spouse

Go to (c)

(c)	Date last worked (MM/DD/YYYY)	Date last paid (MM/DD/YYYY)	Date next paid (MM/DD/YYYY)
You			
Your Spouse			

	Your Amount	Your Spouse's Amount
(d) Total monthly wages received (before any deductions)	$	$

	You		Your Spouse	
(e) Do you (or your spouse) expect to receive any wages in the next 14 months?	☐ YES Go to (f)	✔ NO Go to #54	☐ YES Go to (f)	✔ NO Go to #54

Form SSA-8000-BK, *Application for Supplemental Security Income (SSI)* (Page 18)

Form **SSA-8000-BK** (06-2019) UF

53. (f) Name and address of employer if different from #53(b) (include telephone number, if known)

You

Your Spouse

(g) Give the following information:

Rate of Pay	Amount Worked Per Pay Period	How Often Paid	Pay Day or Date Paid	Date Last Paid (MM/DD/YYYY)
You				
Your Spouse				

	You		Your Spouse	
(h) Do you expect any change in wage information provided in #53(g)	☐ YES Go to (i)	☐ NO Go to #54	☐ YES Go to (i)	☐ NO Go to #54

(i) Explain Change:

You

Your Spouse

54. (a) Have you been self-employed at any time since the beginning of the taxable year in which the filing date month occurs or do you expect to be self-employed in the current taxable year?

	You		Your Spouse	
	☐ YES Go to (b)	☐ NO Go to #55	☐ YES Go to (b)	☐ NO Go to #55

(b) Give the following information; then Go to #55

Date(s) Self-Employed	Type of Business	Last Year's: Gross Income	Last Year's: Net Profit	Last Year's: Net Loss
		$	$	$
Date(s) Self-Employed	Type of Business	This Year's: Gross Income	This Year's: Net Profit	This Year's: Net Loss
		$	$	$

55. If you or your spouse are blind or disabled, do you have any special expenses that you paid which are necessary for you to work?

	You		Your Spouse	
	☐ YES Explain in Remarks, then Go to #56	☑ NO Go to #56	☐ YES Explain in Remarks, then Go to #56	☑ NO Go to #56

Form SSA-8000-BK, *Application for Supplemental Security Income (SSI)* (Page 19)

Form **SSA-8000-BK** (06-2019) UF

56.	(a) Does your spouse/parent who lives with you have to pay court-ordered support?	☐ YES Go to (b)	✔ NO Go to NOTE

(b) Give amount and frequency of court-ordered support payment.

    Amount: $

    Frequency of Payment:

Go to (c)

(c) Give the following information about the person who receives these payments:

    Name:

    Address:

NOTE: IF YOU ARE FILING AS A CHILD AND YOU ARE EMPLOYED OR AGE 18 - 22 (WHETHER EMPLOYED OR NOT), GO TO #57; OTHERWISE, GO TO #58.

57.	(a) Have you attended school regularly since the filing date month?	☐ YES Go to (d)	☐ NO Go to (b)
	(b) Have you been out of school for more than 4 calendar months?	☐ YES Go to (c)	☐ NO Go to (c)
	(c) Do you plan to attend school regularly during the next 4 months?	☐ YES Explain absence in Remarks and Go to (d)	☐ NO Go to #58

(d) Name of School	Name of School Contact	Dates of Attendance		Course of Study
		From	To	
	Phone Number	Hours Attending or Planning to Attend		

PART 5 - POTENTIAL ELIGIBILITY FOR SUPPLEMENTAL NUTRITION ASSISTANCE PROGRAM (SNAP)/MEDICAL ASSISTANCE/OTHER BENEFITS

58.		You		Your Spouse, if filing	
	(a) Are you currently receiving SNAP benefits (formerly food stamps)?	☐ YES Go to (b)	✔ NO Go to (c)	☐ YES Go to (b)	☐ NO Go to (c)
	(b) Have you received a recertification notice within the past 30 days?	☐ YES Go to (e)	✔ NO Go to #59	☐ YES Go to (e)	☐ NO Go to #59
	(c) Have you filed for SNAP in the last 60 days?	☐ YES Go to (d)	✔ NO Go to (e)	☐ YES Go to (d)	☐ NO Go to (e)
	(d) Have you received an unfavorable decision?	☐ YES Go to (e)	✔ NO Go to #59	☐ YES Go to (e)	☐ NO Go to #59
	(e) If everyone in the household receives or is applying for SSI, Go to (f); otherwise Go to #59.				
	(f) May I take your SNAP application today?	✔ YES Go to #59	☐ NO Explain in (g)	✔ YES Go to #59	☐ NO Explain in (g)

(g) Explanation:

Form SSA-8000-BK, *Application for Supplemental Security Income (SSI)* (Page 20)

Form **SSA-8000-BK** (06-2019) UF

59. You may be eligible for Medicaid. However, you must help your State identify other sources that pay for medical care. Also, you must give information to help the State get medical support for any child(ren) who is your legal responsibility. This includes information to help the State determine who a child's parent is. If you want Medicaid, you must agree to allow your State to seek payments from sources, such as insurance companies, that are available to pay for your medical care. This includes payments for medical care for you or any person who receives Medicaid and is your legal responsibility. The State cannot provide you Medicaid if you do not agree to this Medicaid requirement. If you need further information, you may contact your Medicaid Agency.

IN STATES WITH AUTOMATIC ASSIGNMENT OF RIGHTS LAWS, Go to (b).

	You		Your Spouse, if filing	
(a) Do you agree to assign your rights (or the rights of anyone for whom you can legally assign rights) to payments for medical support and other medical care to the State Medicaid agency?	☑ YES **Go to (b)**	☐ NO Go to #60	☐ YES **Go to (b)**	☐ NO Go to #60
(b) Do you, your spouse, parent or stepparent have any private, group, or governmental health insurance that pays the cost of your medical care? (Do not include Medicare or Medicaid.)	☐ YES Go to (c)	☑ NO Go to (c)	☐ YES Go to (c)	☐ NO Go to (c)
(c) Do you have any unpaid medical expenses for the 3 months prior to the filing date month?	☑ YES Go to #60	☐ NO Go to #60	☐ YES Go to #60	☐ NO Go to #60

60. (a) Have you ever worked under the U.S. Social Security System? ☐ YES Go to (b)   ☑ NO Go to (b)

(b) Have you, your spouse, or a former spouse (or parent if you are filing as a child) ever:	You		Your Spouse/ Parent		Filed for Benefits	
	YES	NO	YES	NO	YES	NO
Worked for a railroad	☐	☑	☐	☑	☐	☑
Been in military service	☐	☑	☐	☑	☐	☑
Worked for the Federal Government	☐	☑	☐	☑	☐	☑
Worked for a State or Local Government	☐	☑	☐	☑	☐	☑
Worked for an employer with a pension plan	☐	☑	☐	☑	☐	☑
Belonged to union with a pension plan	☐	☑	☐	☑	☐	☑
Worked under a Social Security system or pension plan of a country other than the United States?	☐	☑	☐	☑	☐	☑

(c) Explain and include dates for any "Yes" answer given in #14 or #60(a); otherwise Go to #61.

You

Your Spouse, if filing/Your Parent, if filing as a child:

PART 6 - MISCELLANEOUS - (Answer #61 ONLY IF YOU ARE APPLYING ON BEHALF OF SOMEONE ELSE: OTHERWISE GO TO #62.

61. (a) Name of Person/Agency Requesting Benefits.	Relationship to Claimant	Your Social Security Number (or EIN)
(b) If SSA determines that the claimant needs help managing benefits, do you wish to be selected representative payee?	☐ YES	☐ NO (Explain in Remarks)
(c) Have you ever served as a representative payee for a Social Security beneficiary or SSI claimant?	☐ YES	☐ NO Go to #62

There is one exception to the requirement that you submit an original record to prove your age: You may give the SSA an uncertified photocopy of a birth registration notification where it is the practice of the local birth registrar to issue them in this way.

The SSA needs proof of your age, unless your eligibility for disability or your benefit amount does not depend on your age, as would be the case if you applied for SSI. The preferred evidence is a birth certificate or hospital birth record that was recorded before age five, or a religious record (such as a baptism record) that shows your date of birth and was recorded before age five. If you cannot obtain any of these, you will be asked for other convincing evidence of your date of birth or age at a certain time. Possible evidence includes the following (20 CFR § 404.701–716):

- original family Bible or family record
- school records
- census records
- statement signed by a physician or midwife present at your birth
- insurance policies
- marriage record
- passport
- employment record
- delayed birth certificate, or
- immigration or naturalization record.

b. Medical Records

The SSA will need several kinds of medical records, including the following:

- information from your doctors, therapists, hospitals, clinics, and caseworkers
- laboratory and test results
- names, addresses, phone numbers, and fax numbers of your doctors, clinics, and hospitals, and
- names of all medications you take.

You might not have your medical records when you first apply for benefits. If so, your medical providers will receive a request for that information from the DDS, the agency that processes the medical portion of your application on behalf of the SSA. (See Section E, below.) Waiting for medical records is one of the biggest causes of delays in the disability process. The more medical records you can turn over to the SSA with your application, the faster a decision on your claim is likely to be made. Also, if you claim that your disability began many years back, the SSA has to obtain those old medical records, and this can further delay your claim.

The SSA will never send your disability forms to your treating doctors. In fact, the SSA specifically requests that you not send your paperwork to your doctor. This is good advice, because your form might get lost or be delayed for months in a doctor's office. Your doctor is not responsible for completing your forms—you are, and your doctor probably would not appreciate receiving your paperwork to complete. Instead, the SSA will request specific medical information it wants directly from your doctors without your needing to do anything other than identify the doctors. If you want to get involved, call your doctor's office and make sure your doctor responds to the SSA's request for information and sends in a complete and accurate report.

> ! CAUTION
>
> **Ask your doctors to send you a copy of the reports they send the SSA.** This is extremely important. Review each one carefully. If a doctor states that you are capable of doing things that you cannot do, you will need to get that physician to send a corrected report.

c. Employment Information

You will need to indicate the names of your employers and your job duties for the last 15 years. If you can't remember, write "unknown" in the space where the information is required, but do not leave it blank. You will also be asked if your medical disorder affected your attendance at work or the hours you could work, and whether your employer had to give you special help in order for you to do your job. Adding this information helps you, as it might result in a finding that your disability started further back in time. In some instances, it might even be critical in determining whether you are disabled.

Specific information about your work history can be extremely important. You'll need to give your job title, type of business,

dates worked, days per week, and rate of pay. Again, if you can't remember, state that in the appropriate spaces. Do not leave parts of the form blank. Where you can remember, you'll be asked to describe your basic job duties, such as:

- the machines, tools, and equipment you used and the operations performed
- the technical knowledge or skills involved in your work
- the type of writing you did and the nature of any reports, and
- the number of people you supervised and the extent of your supervision.

You will be asked to describe the kind and amount of physical activity you did at work, including walking, standing, sitting, and bending. In addition, the SSA wants to know about the lifting and carrying you did on the job.

You don't have to answer all questions about your work at the time you apply for disability benefits, but the information will have to be given to the SSA at some time before a disability determination is made. If you omit any information, you'll hear from the SSA or the agency processing the medical portion of your application (DDS). If you don't understand a question, contact an SSA representative at the Field Office or the disability examiner who has been assigned your claim once it leaves the Field Office.

d. Activities of Daily Living

The claims representative or interviewer may give you forms asking detailed questions about your activities of daily living, called ADLs. The ADL form, *Function Report— Adult*, is Form SSA-3373-BK. This form asks specific questions about what you do during a typical day to give the SSA an idea of how your impairment affects your daily life. ADLs are important in all kinds of disabilities, especially mental disorders. Questions typically deal with your ability to do household chores, cook, shop, visit friends, attend social activities, and attend to finances.

If you don't answer the questions about your ADLs when you apply, the Disability Determination Services (DDS)—the state agency that receives your file from the Field Office to process your claim—will send you forms requesting the information. (The DDS is discussed in Section B6, below.) Some people just put "none" in answer to all questions about what they do during a typical day. These answers are considered uncooperative and will not help your claim, because everyone does something. Even sitting in a chair all day watching TV is an activity. Try to explain how your mental or physical impairments are related to what you can or cannot do during the day.

Don't rely on your doctor to answer these questions. Few doctors actually know what their patients do during the day. If you want your doctor to have this information, discuss your daily activities with your doctor. This will help with your credibility when officials contact your doctor, who can then verify the limitations you have reported.

e. School Records

If you are applying for disability for a child, you will need to provide school records regarding your child's disability. (This is explained in more detail in Chapter 3.)

f. Income and Asset Information

To receive SSI, your income and assets cannot exceed a certain limit. You will need records, such as bank statements, rent receipts, and car registration to show what you earn and your financial worth.

In addition, the SSA will want a copy of your most recent W-2 form, if you are employed, or your tax return, if you're self-employed. All of this information is to help determine your income and assets.

3. Field Office Observations

If you don't apply over the phone, the Field Office representative will observe you while you complete your application form. He will note how you perform reading, writing, answering, hearing, sitting, understanding, using your hands, breathing, seeing, walking, and anything else that might relate to your claim. You won't be given any medical tests at the Field Office, and the person who takes your application is not a doctor. But the representative will write down these observations.

The SSA reviewers will pay attention to these observations, which don't determine the outcome of your claim but are weighed with the other data. If the Field Office representative stated you had no difficulty walking while the medical information says you do, then the observation would be disregarded. But usually, Field Officers bring things to the attention of the evaluator that otherwise might be missed. For example, a Field Office representative can note if you need special assistance in completing your application because of apparent mental illness or limited English skills. A person who cannot speak English has fewer work opportunities, which can be important in the final decision on whether or not to award benefits.

4. Onset of Your Disability

On your disability application, you will have to state the date you became disabled. This is called the "alleged onset date" (AOD). (See Chapter 10 for more on the onset date.)

If you are applying for SSDI, you set the date of your AOD. But the SSA won't allow you to receive benefits for any time when you were engaged in substantial gainful activity and earning too much money to qualify for SSDI. So the SSA gives you an "established onset date" (EOD), which, can be different from the AOD that you stated; it is influenced by both nonmedical eligibility factors (see the next section) and the date the SSA considered you unable to do substantial gainful work.

If you're applying for SSI only, your alleged onset date does not matter. That is because SSI benefits are never awarded for earlier than the first day of the month after you file for disability.

5. Nonmedical Eligibility Requirements

Having a medical disorder that prevents you from working is only one factor in determining your eligibility to receive disability benefits. First, it must be established that you are covered under SSDI or you are qualified to apply for SSI benefits because of low income and resources. You must satisfy the nonmedical eligibility requirements before your medical disorder is even considered by the SSA. Determining whether or not you satisfy nonmedical requirements is the job of the Field Office. Nonmedical criteria include your age, employment, marital status, Social Security coverage information, and other factors.

Age, education, and work experience can be important later in your claim. (These are called "vocational factors" and are discussed in Chapter 9.)

6. Processing Your Application (or Claim)

The Disability Determination Service, or DDS, is the state agency that determines whether your medical disorder is severe enough to qualify you for benefits. Your file is sent there once the SSA Field Office determines that you meet the nonmedical eligibility requirements based on information in your application and your interview with the SSA representative. Several states with large populations have more than one DDS office, but most states have only one. (Your local SSA Field Office can give you the contact information for the DDS that will handle your claim.)

Although Field Offices deal with all kinds of Social Security issues, the DDS is concerned only with determining your medical eligibility for disability benefits. The DDS employees and consultants are hired by your state, not by the SSA.

CAUTION
It is not the job of the SSA Field Office to make a medical determination about you. This is the responsibility of the DDS. If you meet the nonmedical eligibility requirements, the SSA Field Office must forward your application to the DDS. SSA representatives at Field Offices and contact stations are not doctors and should not give you an opinion regarding whether or not you are medically disabled.

Once the DDS receives your file, representatives there collect more information, especially medical information, and decide whether you are eligible for disability benefits. The DDS sends requests to your treating doctors and hospitals for your medical records, based on the information you provide. The DDS might also obtain nonmedical information, such as detailed data about your work activities or skills.

If the DDS needs more information, the examiner will contact you by telephone or in writing. It is vital that the DDS be able to communicate with you to obtain full and accurate information and, in some cases, to request that you undergo medical examinations or laboratory tests at the SSA's expense. (Types of evidence the DDS might need are discussed in Chapter 5.) (The DDS is discussed more fully in Chapter 6.)

C. The Role of Health Care Professionals

Health care professionals play a vital role in the disability determination process and participate in the process in a variety of ways. These professionals include:
- "treating sources," who provide medical evidence and opinions on behalf of their patients
- "consultative examination" (CE) sources, who perform necessary examinations or tests
- "medical consultants," who review claims, and
- "medical experts" (MEs), who testify at administrative hearings.

1. Treating Sources

A treating source is the physician, psychologist, or other acceptable medical source who has treated or evaluated you and has or had an ongoing treatment relationship with you. Your treating source is usually the best source of medical evidence about the nature and severity of your condition. If the DDS or SSA needs additional examinations or tests to process your claim, your treating source is usually the preferred person to perform the examination or test.

The treating source is neither asked nor expected to decide if you are disabled. But the treating source will usually be asked to provide a statement about your ability to do work-related physical or mental activities, despite your condition. (Acceptable medical sources are discussed in Chapter 5.)

2. Consultative Examination (CE) Sources

If your treating sources don't provide sufficient medical evidence for the DDS to make a disability determination, the DDS may request "consultative examinations" (CEs) or tests. These examinations or tests are performed by physicians, osteopaths, psychologists, or in certain circumstances, other health professionals. Other health professionals include people such as audiologists to test hearing, and speech therapists (also known as speech language pathologists) to evaluate speech. All consultative examiners must be currently licensed in your state and have the training and experience to perform the type of examination or test requested.

If you must undergo exams or tests by a consulting examination source, you will not have to pay a fee.

If you are denied benefits and then appeal, the SSA can ask the DDS to administer the tests or examinations if it needs more information.

Medical professionals who serve as consultative examiners must have a good understanding of the SSA's disability programs and the type of evidence required to make a disability determination. The DDS is responsible for oversight of its consultative examination program.

The DDS advises these medical professionals of their responsibilities and obligations regarding confidentiality, as well as the administrative requirements for scheduling examinations and tests and issuing a report. (Consultative examinations are discussed more fully in Chapter 5.)

3. Medical Consultants

The medical consultants who review claims for disability benefits on behalf of the DDS or SSA include licensed medical doctors of virtually all specialties, osteopaths, and psychologists with a Ph.D. The work is performed in a DDS office, an SSA regional office, or the SSA's central office. It is strictly a paper review; the consultant usually has no contact with you. (Medical consultants are discussed in more detail in Chapter 6.)

Life-Threatening Situations

If you have had a consultative examination (known as a CE, and discussed in Section 2, above), and the examining doctor detects something that might be life threatening, the DDS must send a copy of the CE medical report to your treating doctor if it appears your treating doctor might be unaware of the problem. A DDS doctor may also have an examiner call or write to you stating that there is a potentially serious problem you should have evaluated. In all cases, the DDS will include in your file any action it took regarding life-threatening situations.

In general, any doctor who examines you should inform you of any serious impairments. But this might not happen if the doctor assumes the DDS will tell you, or if you are no longer around when the doctor gets the results of some test. For example, the DDS has you undergo a chest X-ray. By the time the report is done, but before the doctor can tell you about a suspicious and possibly cancerous tumor, you have left the hospital. A DDS medical consultant who sees the X-ray report should ask the examiner to send a copy of the report to your treating doctor, provided you consent to the release. A DDS medical consultant must exercise medical judgment regarding the urgency of the situation and method of informing you, assuming that the examiner shows the information to a medical consultant.

4. Medical Experts

If you are denied benefits and you appeal, an administrative law judge (ALJ) in the Office of Hearings Operations (OHO) will hear your case. To help them in their work, ALJs sometimes request expert testimony on complex medical issues from "medical experts" (MEs). Unlike medical consultants, medical experts have no official authority regarding whether you should be allowed benefits; they only testify in hearings.

Each hearing office maintains a list of medical experts who are called to testify as expert witnesses at hearings. The SSA pays the medical experts a fee for their services. Medical experts don't work in state or federal agencies. They never examine disability claimants in person, though they may review your medical records. (Appeals and medical experts are covered in Chapter 12.)

D. How Other Disability Payments May Affect Social Security Benefits

Workers' compensation benefits or benefits you receive from another public disability program affect the amount of Social Security disability benefits you receive.

1. Workers' Compensation and Public Disability

Workers' compensation payments are made to a worker because of a job-related injury or illness or to the workers' dependents if the worker is killed. Workers' comp, as it is known, might be paid by a government workers' compensation agency, an employer, or an insurance company on behalf of employers. In most states, employers are required to participate in workers' compensation insurance programs.

No state's workers' comp program covers all jobs; however, many of the states cover most jobs. Some states cover only work considered dangerous; others cover only employers with a minimum number of employees. Coverage varies for agricultural workers and domestic workers, meaning people who work in private homes doing work such as cleaning, babysitting, and cooking. All laws include some or all diseases attributable to the worker's occupation. Most states exclude coverage for injuries due to the employee's intoxication, willful misconduct, or gross negligence.

Other public disability payments that may affect your Social Security benefits are those paid under a federal, state, or local government plan that covers conditions that are not job related. Examples are civil service disability benefits, military disability benefits, state temporary disability benefits, and state or local government retirement benefits based on disability.

SEE AN EXPERT

Workers' compensation and public disability benefit cases can be legally complex

and vary among states, especially when combined with Social Security disability benefits. If you might be eligible for both, consider using the services of an attorney experienced in the interaction of Social Security disability and other programs to make sure you obtain all the benefits you are entitled to.

a. How Much Your Disability Benefits May Be Reduced

Your Social Security disability benefit will be reduced so that the combined amount of your Social Security benefit plus your workers' compensation and public disability payment does not exceed 80% of your average current earnings. But the SSA should deduct legal, medical (including future medical expenses paid by workers' compensation), and rehabilitation expenses from a workers' compensation award before reducing your Social Security disability benefit.

To calculate your SSDI disability benefit, first the SSA will calculate your "average current earnings." (All earnings covered by Social Security, including amounts above the maximum taxable by Social Security, can be used when figuring average current earnings.)

Average current earnings are the highest of the following:

- the average monthly earnings the SSA used to figure your Social Security disability benefit

- your average monthly earnings from any work you did covered by Social Security during the five highest years in a row after 1950, or
- your average monthly earnings from work during the year you became disabled or in the highest year of earnings you had during the five-year period just before you became disabled.

The SSA uses your average earnings and a complex formula to calculate your disability benefit. Then your monthly disability benefit, including any benefits payable to your family members, is added to your workers' compensation or other public disability payment. If this sum exceeds 80% of your average current earnings, the excess amount is deducted from your Social Security benefit. But the amount of the combined benefits will never be less than the total Social Security benefits before they were reduced. The reduction will last until the month you reach age 65 or the month your workers' compensation and/or other public disability payment stops, whichever comes first.

Some states offset (reduce) their workers' compensation benefits to account for SSDI, rather than the other way around. Social Security will not reduce an SSDI payment when the state is already offsetting its workers' compensation payment.

b. Reporting Other Benefits to the SSA

You must notify the SSA if any of the following occurs:

- The amount of your workers' compensation or public disability payment changes. This may affect the amount of your Social Security benefits.
- Your workers' compensation or public disability payment ends. If your workers' compensation or public disability payment stops, your Social Security benefit may increase.
- You receive a lump sum disability payment. If you get a lump sum workers' compensation or other disability payment to settle your claim, your Social Security benefits may be reduced.

2. Railroad Retirement Act and Social Security Disability

The Railroad Retirement Act (RRA) sets up a system of benefits for railroad employees and their dependents and survivors. The RRA works with the Social Security Act to provide disability (as well as retirement, survivors, and dependents) benefits payable on the basis of a person's work in the railroad industry and in work covered by the Social Security Act.

An important distinction is made between railroad workers who have worked less than ten years and those who have worked ten years or more. The RRA transfers to the Social Security system the compensation records of people who, at the onset of disability, have less than ten years of work in the railroad industry. This compensation is considered wages under the Social Security Act.

The wages of those with ten or more years of work generally remain under the RRA. The distinction has primary importance when you seek survivors benefits based on the death of the insured railroad worker, and so the details are not covered here. But if it might apply to you, be aware of the distinction and ask your local SSA office for more information.

3. Black Lung Benefits and Social Security Disability

Black lung benefits are payments to coal miners—and their survivors—who become disabled from a lung disease known as pneumoconiosis as a result of breathing fine dust-like particles of coal while working in the mines. The Federal Coal Mine Health and Safety Act of 1969 assigned initial responsibility for processing black lung benefit claims to the SSA. The Labor Department (DOL) assumed eventual responsibility.

For many years, the SSA handled some aspects of the black lung program for the DOL, such as taking initial applications and deciding black lung benefit appeals. However, as of March 30, 2012 the SSA no longer has any responsibility or involvement in the black lung program. If you want to apply for black lung benefits, appeal denial of benefits, or have any questions about that program, you will need to contact the DOL.

4. What Payments Do Not Affect Your Social Security Disability Benefits?

The SSA does not count certain types of payments in considering whether to reduce your disability check. These include:

- Veterans Administration (VA) benefits
- federal benefits, if the work you did to earn them was covered by Social Security
- state and local government benefits, if the work you did to earn them was covered by Social Security
- private pensions or insurance benefits, and
- Supplemental Security Income (SSI) payments.

E. Availability and Disclosure of Confidential Records

Several laws and regulations govern access to and disclosure of confidential information and official records entrusted to the SSA, the DDS, and other nonfederal entities or individuals.

1. Your Medical Records

Under the Privacy Act, you or your authorized representative have the right to examine federal government records pertaining to you.

(Public Law 93-579; 5 U.S.C. § 552a; 20 CFR §§ 401.30–401.200.) Your "authorized representative" is someone you appoint in writing to pursue your rights under the Social Security Act. You can name any responsible person, including a family member, as your authorized representative.

This right means that you can request to see the medical and other evidence used to evaluate your application for SSDI or SSI benefits. Make this request in writing to the SSA Field Office handling your claim (see below for more details on the SSA procedure for releasing records). Medical records include:

- records kept by physicians or other health professionals
- records derived from reports by physicians or other health professionals
- medical evaluations and determinations on Social Security forms, including rationales and diagnoses, and
- records created by laypeople relevant to your claim (such as statements by witnesses who saw epileptic seizures or signs of mental impairment).

This law concerns your own requests to see your medical records. You cannot directly access your child's medical records. Instead, you must name a physician or another health professional (excluding family members) to receive the records as a designated representative.

The SSA will release your records to you as long as the SSA doesn't think they will have an "adverse effect" on you. According to the SSA, such an adverse effect is an effect likely to occur if direct access by an individual to his or her medical records is expected to:

- disrupt a doctor-patient relationship
- interfere with the patient's medical management, or
- negatively affect the patient in some other way.

Here are some of the SSA's own examples of adverse effect.

EXAMPLE 1: You have been diagnosed as diabetic. The medical record indicates a good prognosis with treatment involving medication, diet, weight control, and exercise. An adverse effect is not likely, and the SSA is likely to release the records.

EXAMPLE 2: You have a severe heart impairment. The doctor has noted in the medical record that your knowing the severity of your condition could cause complications. An adverse effect is likely, and the SSA is not likely to release the records.

EXAMPLE 3: A doctor has included very candid remarks in the report that might incite you to threaten the doctor. An adverse effect is likely, and the SSA is not likely to release the records.

There is one exception: Direct disclosure of medical information may be made to you, upon request, in any case in which you have requested a hearing or a review by the Appeals Council.

The person at the SSA deciding whether or not you should see your medical records doesn't have to be a doctor. Nondoctors in SSA Field Offices can make that determination, or they can refer your file to doctors working for the SSA. If the SSA thinks that releasing your medical records will have an adverse effect on you, you won't be told. The SSA policy instruction specifically states: "Do not tell an individual that direct access of a medical record is likely to have an adverse effect on him/her."

Instead, you will be told that Privacy Act regulations require that you designate a representative to receive your records. Ironic, isn't it? Under the law that is meant to protect your privacy, the SSA has concluded that someone other than you must get your records. You are not alone in thinking this sounds paternalistic. Few people know about this policy because few people ask to see their medical records.

Until very recently, if you were forced to have a designated representative, that person could withhold any of your own records from you indefinitely. However, based on a federal court case against the SSA, your representative must ultimately provide all of your records to you. The SSA has not said, however, how

long the representative has in which to turn over the records to the claimant.

Sample Letter When SSA Wants a Designated Representative

Dear [*claimant*]:

You asked for copies of medical records we used in your [*type of*] claim. We reviewed the records. We decided that we must give them to someone you choose who will review and discuss the information with you. Because this is medical information, we prefer you choose a doctor or a health worker.

Please give us the name and address of the person you want to receive your medical records. You may use the office address shown above to send us this information.

If you have any questions, you may call, write, or visit any Social Security office. If you call or visit our office, please have this letter with you and ask for [*name of SSA representative*]. The telephone number is [*xxx-xxx-xxxx*].

If you receive a letter like the one above, the SSA clearly thinks that your seeing your records will have an adverse effect on you. If you do not follow through by naming a designated representative, the SSA will send you a form letter like the one below.

Sample Letter If You Don't Give a Designated Representative

Dear [*claimant*]:

We are writing to you about your request for copies of medical records we used in your [*type of*] claim.

As we told you earlier, we require that you choose someone to receive your records. This person will review the information and discuss it with you. Because this is medical information, you may wish to choose a doctor or a health worker to review your records.

Since you have not yet chosen someone, we want to give you some suggestions about groups that might be able to help. We have found that the following groups are often willing to help people by reviewing their records:

- local social services
- local public health services
- legal aid societies, and
- other public agencies.

When you give us the name and address of the person you want to review your medical records, we will make sure they get the records. You may use the office address shown above to send us this information.

If you have any questions, you may call, write, or visit any Social Security office. If you call or visit our office, please have this letter with you and ask for [*name of SSA representative*]. The telephone number is [*xxx-xxx-xxxx*].

If you still don't name a representative, the SSA will mail your file to the SSA's central Office of Disability (OD) in Baltimore. If this happens, you will have to wait months for a response to any further requests for your file.

2. Consultative Examination (CE) Records

The SSA may require that you be examined by a doctor or have laboratory tests done in order to evaluate your claim for disability. You must give permission for the SSA to obtain your medical records from your treating doctor and also for those records to be released to a doctor whom the SSA has chosen to do a CE exam.

The SSA cannot release the results of your CE exam to your treating doctor without your consent. It is generally to your benefit to have CE exams sent to your treating doctor. These CE exams often involve information your treating doctor doesn't have. Therefore, it is to your advantage to let your treating doctor see it.

But the SSA doesn't have to share the findings of your CE exam with you, except in life-threatening situations. (See "Life-Threatening Situations," in Section C, above.) Most claimants don't ask CE doctors for personal copies of their examinations or tests. If they do, the CE doctor must contact the DDS for permission to release the information.

3. Disclosure With Consent

Most disclosures by the SSA require your consent. Consent must be in writing, be signed by you or your authorized representative, be dated, and specify what information is to be disclosed. Specifically, the SSA or DDS must obtain your consent in order to:

- contact your treating sources for information necessary to review your claim
- release your records, particularly your medical records, to the SSA, and
- disclose information about you to any third party, such as physicians and medical institutions, with the exception of parties permitted disclosure without your consent. (See Section E4, below.)

In most situations, any consent statement you sign will include a revocation clause, allowing you to take back your consent, or else it will be valid for only a specified time.

4. Disclosure Without Consent

Under the U.S. Privacy Act, the SSA can disclose your records without your consent for certain purposes. The SSA must keep a record of all such disclosures. Permissible reasons for disclosure without consent include the following:

- sharing information within an SSA agency on a need-to-know basis
- complying with the Freedom of Information Act (FOIA)
- for a routine use (a purpose compatible with the reason the information was collected, such as disability determination)
- assisting the Census Bureau in planning or carrying out a census, survey, or related activity
- for research and statistical purposes
- transferring records to the National Archives of the United States when its historical or other value warrants its continued preservation
- cooperating with another government agency's civil or criminal law enforcement activity
- helping someone whose health and safety is affected by compelling circumstances (after notice of disclosure is sent to you)
- informing the House of Representatives or the Senate, to the extent necessary, on a matter within its jurisdiction
- cooperating with the Comptroller General while performing duties of the General Accounting Office, or
- a court order.

More specific examples of disclosures that are covered under the above list include the following:

- information to your representative payee (the person designated to receive your payments) or authorized representative to pursue a Social Security claim or to receive and account for payments

- medical information to your designated representative
- payment information to the IRS to conduct an audit, collect Social Security taxes, or investigate a tax crime
- information to the Department of Justice (DOJ) or U.S. Postal Service for law enforcement purposes, or
- nontax-return information (and usually nonmedical information) to the president, individual members of Congress, and their staffs if necessary to answer inquiries from you or your authorized representative.

Finally, if the SSA sends your records to someone without your consent, the SSA does not have to inform you of that action.

5. Penalties for Violating Disclosure Laws

Your privacy rights are protected by a variety of federal statutes.

Social Security Act. Under the Social Security Act, the following violations are punishable as misdemeanors by a fine of up to $1,000 and/or a year in prison:

- disclosure by an SSA employee of tax return information, files, records, reports, or other SSA papers or documents, except as permitted by regulation or federal law, or
- misrepresentation by an individual who purports to be an employee or agent

of the United States, with the intent to elicit information regarding another person's date of birth, employment, wages, or benefits.

Freedom of Information Act (FOIA). The FOIA provides that agency officials found to have arbitrarily and capriciously withheld disclosable records may be subject to disciplinary action recommended by the Special Counsel to the Merit Systems Protection Board.

Privacy Act (PA). You can sue the SSA in a U.S. District Court for various reasons, including:

- refusing to amend your Social Security record
- refusing to let you (or another person chosen by you) view your record and obtain a copy of it
- failing to disclose that you dispute information in your record, or
- failing to accurately maintain your record.

If the court determines that the SSA acted intentionally or willfully, it may assess against the United States the attorneys' fees, other litigation costs, and actual damages you sustain. The court can award you at least $1,000 in damages in such cases.

The SSA might be found guilty of a misdemeanor, mostly due to the willful disclosure of information in violation of the PA. You cannot normally bring criminal actions against an SSA employee unless you convince the Justice Department that the employee "willfully and knowingly" disclosed information. If convinced, the DOJ may prosecute.

Finally, an SSA employee may be subject to disciplinary action for knowing and willful violations of the PA.

Internal Revenue Code (IRC). Under the IRC, a federal employee who discloses information found on a federal tax return may be found guilty of a felony and fined $5,000 and/or sentenced to five years in prison. Furthermore, you can sue the IRS and any person who knowingly or negligently discloses federal tax returns or return information.

Alcohol and Drug Abuse Patient Records. Any person who violates the Drug Abuse and Treatment Act or the Comprehensive Alcohol Abuse and Alcoholism Prevention, Treatment, and Rehabilitation Act by disclosing such information may be fined as much as $500 for a first offense and as much as $5,000 for each subsequent offense.

6. Reporting Possible Violations

If you suspect an SSA employee has violated one of the above laws, report the incident to the employee's supervisor or call the SSA's Office of Inspector General (OIG) Hotline at 800-269-0271; TTY 866-501-2101. You can also write to the SSA on the Internet at www.socialsecurity.gov/oig. Click "Reporting Fraud."

F. Fraud and Other Crimes

Both SSA personnel and DDS officers are looking for fraud—for example, allegations of disability that are not consistent with other information and indications that an individual may have been coached.

The SSA says fraud has occurred when someone, with the intent to wrongfully obtain a benefit, right, or credit, knowingly makes a false statement, causes a false statement to be made, willfully attempts to conceal a material fact, or fails to disclose a material fact. (§§ 208 and 1632 of the Social Security Act.)

Claimants have been known to allege impairments they do not have. Sometimes this is innocent. Sometimes it is not, such as when a person alleges a serious illness where medical records show no such diagnosis. Some treating doctors lie about a person's having a serious illness. Some doctors' medical records show they know the diagnoses given to the SSA are not valid.

The SSA rarely goes after treating doctors or claimants for fraud. This may be because the SSA needs the goodwill of the public and medical profession, or because it is difficult to prove intentional lies. But the SSA doesn't ignore fraud. It ignores statements it knows are false when making the disability determination.

The SSA may identify fraud anywhere in the claims process. If the SSA identifies fraud after determining that a person is eligible for benefits, the SSA can reopen the file and redo the determination, ignoring the false information.

It is a crime to do any of the following:

- furnish false information in connection with your Social Security records or to obtain someone else's records
- use an SSN obtained through false information
- use someone else's SSN
- disclose or force the disclosure of or use an SSN in violation of U.S. law
- forge or falsify SSA documents
- conspire over a false claim
- knowingly buy, sell, or alter an SSN card, or
- process an SSN card or counterfeit an SSN card.

Civil penalties can also be imposed for fraud. In 2006, Public Law 108-203 was amended to impose civil penalties (up to $5,000 per occurrence) for not notifying the SSA of changed circumstances that affect eligibility or benefit amounts. These penalties apply when a person or organization knew or should have known that a withheld fact could affect benefits and that the failure to come forward was misleading. For example, penalties would apply if an individual who has a joint bank account with a beneficiary continues to receive the beneficiary's Social Security checks after the beneficiary's death, or if an individual receives benefits under one SSN while working under another SSN.

Civil penalties may also apply for engaging in the following activities:

- selling services to the public that are available for no cost from SSA, unless clearly disclosing that fact
- converting a beneficiary's benefit to a third party
- claiming that your services are endorsed by the SSA, including the misleading use of SSA symbols or emblems, and
- marketing products or services using certain prohibited words (such as "Death Benefits Update," "Federal Benefit Information," "Funeral Expenses," or "Final Supplemental Program").

You should be aware of these changes because they are meant to protect the public, including Social Security disability beneficiaries.

Disability Benefits for Children

About 1,000,000 children receive disability benefits from the Social Security Administration (SSA). This chapter is for the parents and caregivers of children—generally considered to be people under the age of 18—with disabilities, and for the parents and caregivers of adults who have been disabled since childhood.

Although some of this information appears in other chapters, we bring it together here to provide one place for important information needed by caregivers of children.

The person who handles the benefits on behalf of a child is called, in Social Security lingo, the "representative payee," and must be a responsible person. The representative payee is usually a child's parents.

CAUTION

The representative payee is not the same as the authorized representative. An authorized representative is any person, including an attorney, named in writing by the claimant/recipient, to act in place of the claimant/recipient in pursuing his or her rights under the Social Security Act.

You can use the information in this chapter to understand the kinds of Social Security Disability Insurance (SSDI) and Supplemental Security Income (SSI) available to an eligible child and to learn how the SSA evaluates disability claims for children.

A. Three Benefit Programs for Children

There are three ways a child might be eligible for SSDI or SSI benefits.

1. SSDI Auxiliary Benefits for Children Under 18

Although this is a book about disability benefits, children eligible for dependents' or survivors' benefits need not be disabled. A child is eligible for Social Security benefits simply because he or she is the dependent of someone receiving disability benefits or the surviving child of someone who died while receiving benefits.

Social Security dependents' benefits are available to unmarried children younger than 18 based *on the record* of a parent who collects Social Security or disability benefits. Social Security survivors' benefits are available also to children younger than 18 based *on the record* of a deceased parent who was entitled to Social Security disability benefits. "On the record" means benefits are paid based on the earnings record of someone else—the insured worker who paid enough Social Security taxes to qualify for SSDI benefits. "Parent" means biological parent, adoptive parent, or stepparent.

Child dependents' and survivors' benefits are known as "auxiliary benefits," because they are based on the disability and earning record of a parent, not a child's disability. The theory behind the benefits is that a disabled parent needs more money to take care of dependent children, and that a surviving spouse of a deceased disabled worker needs more money to take care of children.

A child found to be eligible for these benefits can receive them until attaining the age of 18—or 19 if enrolled as a full-time student in elementary or high school. For full-time students, twice a year—at the beginning and end of the school year—the SSA sends the students a form asking whether they are still in school. The SSA may terminate benefits if the student (or living parent) doesn't send back a completed form.

If the child turns 19 during a school term, the SSA can continue the benefits for up to two months to allow the student to complete the term. Before turning 19, a student may receive benefits during a vacation period of four months or less if the student plans to go back to school full time at the end of the vacation.

If the student leaves school, changes from full time to part time, or changes schools, the student or parent must notify the SSA immediately. Also let the SSA know if the student is paid by an employer for attending school. A student over 18 who stops attending school generally can receive benefits again upon returning to school full time before age 19. The student must contact the SSA to reapply for benefits.

If your stepchild receives benefits on your earnings record, and you and the child's parent divorce, the stepchild's benefit will end the month following the month the divorce becomes final. (This is not the case with biological or legally adopted children.) You must notify the SSA as soon as the divorce becomes final.

2. SSDI Benefits for Adults Disabled Since Childhood

Social Security dependents or survivors benefits normally end when a child reaches age 18, or age 19 if the child is a full-time student. If the young adult is disabled, however, the benefits can continue as long as the recipient is disabled.

The rules require both of the following:

- The disability began prior to age 22.
- The recipient is the child of someone receiving Social Security retirement or disability benefits or of someone who was insured for Social Security retirement or disability benefits but is now deceased.

Someone who qualifies is said by the SSA to be an "adult child," or "adult disabled since childhood." Although most recipients of these benefits are in their 20s and 30s, the benefit is considered a "child's benefit" because of the eligibility rules.

Sometimes, a person doesn't become eligible for a disabled child's benefit until well into adulthood.

EXAMPLE: John retires and starts collecting Social Security retirement benefits at age 62. He has a 38-year-old son, Ben, who has had cerebral palsy since birth. Ben could not collect Social Security benefits before John retired because John was still working and not collecting benefits. When John retired, however, Ben started collecting a disabled child's benefit based on John's Social Security record. (If, instead, Ben had become disabled when he was 23 or older, he would have to rely on his own earnings record to collect SSDI, or try to qualify for SSI.)

3. SSI Benefits for Children

SSI is a program that pays monthly benefits to elderly and disabled people with low incomes and limited assets. Children under the age of 18 can qualify for SSI if they meet the SSA's definition of disability (see Section C, below) and if their income and assets—or more likely, the income and assets of their parents—fall within the eligibility requirements.

The income and asset limits vary from state to state, and were discussed in Chapter 1. Check with your local Social Security office to find out the SSI eligibility levels in your state. (You can call 800-772-1213 from 7 a.m. to 7 p.m. Monday through Friday to find the location of an SSA office near you, or access the Internet at www.ssa.gov/regions/regional.html.)

The SSA considers a child who has turned 18 to be an adult, and eligibility for SSI is no longer determined under the rules for children. For example, a child's parent's income and assets are not relevant in deciding if he is eligible to receive SSI. Instead, his own income and resources are used to determine eligibility. This means that a child who was not eligible for SSI before his 18th birthday because his parents' income and assets were too high might become eligible as an adult when he reaches age 18. Of course, this assumes his own income and resources are low enough and he satisfies all other eligibility requirements for disability "in-kind income" (and that he qualifies under the adult medical disability criteria).

Note that if the young adult at age 18 still receives food and shelter paid for by his parents, the government considers these as in-kind income, which may result in a lower disability benefit payment, even if he qualifies as a medically disabled adult.

B. Applying for SSDI or SSI Benefits

You can apply for SSDI or SSI benefits for your child by calling or visiting your local SSA office. Bring the child's Social Security card—or at least the number—and birth certificate with you. If you are applying for SSI for your child, you also will need to provide records that show your income and your assets, as well as those of the child.

You will be sent or given SSA-3820-BK, *Disability Report—Child*, to fill out. We provide a sample form here. Look at the form to see what information you will need to gather to fill it out.

Form SSA-3820-BK, *Disability Report—Child* (Page 1)

SOCIAL SECURITY ADMINISTRATION

Form Approved
OMB No. 0960-0577

Form SSA-3820-BK (03-2017) UF

Page 1 of 12

DISABILITY REPORT - CHILD

SECTION 1 - INFORMATION ABOUT THE CHILD

A. CHILD'S NAME (First, Middle Initial, Last)	B. CHILD'S SOCIAL SECURITY NUMBER
Penny A. Reeves	335-67-8901

C. YOUR NAME (If agency, provide name of agency and contact person)

Marilyn Reeves

YOUR MAILING ADDRESS (Number and Street, Apt. No. (if any), P.O. Box, or Rural Route)

4301 West Markham Street

CITY	STATE	ZIP CODE
Oklahoma City	OK	73999

YOUR EMAIL ADDRESS (Optional)   PAReeves@yahoo.com

D. YOUR DAYTIME PHONE NUMBER   (If you do not have a phone number where we can reach you, give us a daytime number where we can leave a message for you.)

405   555-1111

Area Code   Number   ☑ Your Number   ☐ Message Number   ☐ None

E. What is your relationship to the child?   parent/mother

F. Can you speak and understand English?   ☑ YES   ☐ NO

If "NO", what is your preferred language?

NOTE: If you cannot speak and understand English, we will provide you an interpreter, free of charge. If you cannot speak and understand English, is there someone we may contact who speaks and understands English and will give you messages?

☐ YES (Enter name, address, phone number, relationship)   ☐ NO

NAME _____   RELATIONSHIP TO CHILD _____

ADDRESS _____

(Number, Street, Apt. No. (if any), P.O. Box, or Rural Route)

DAYTIME PHONE _____

City   State   ZIP   Area Code   Number

Can you read and understand English?   ☑ YES   ☐ NO

G. Does the child live with you?   ☑ YES   ☐ NO   If "NO", with whom does the child live?

NAME _____   RELATIONSHIP TO CHILD _____

ADDRESS _____

(Number, Street, Apt. No. (if any), P.O. Box, or Rural Route)

DAYTIME PHONE _____

City   State   ZIP   Area Code   Number

Can this person speak and understand English?   ☐ YES   ☐ NO

If "NO", what is this person's preferred language? _____

Can this person read and understand English?   ☐ YES   ☐ NO

Disability Report - Child - Form SSA-3820-BK

Form SSA-3820-BK, *Disability Report—Child* (Page 2)

SECTION 1 - INFORMATION ABOUT THE CHILD

H. Can the child speak and understand English?   ☑ YES   ☐ NO

    If "NO," what languages can the child speak? _____

    If the child understands any other languages, list them here: _____

I. What is the child's height (without shoes)?   56 in.

    What is the child's weight (without shoes)?   80 lbs.

J. Does the child have a medical assistance card? (for example Medicaid, Medi-Cal) ☐ YES   ☑ NO

    If "YES", show the number here: _____

SECTION 2 - CONTACT INFORMATION

A. Does the child have a legal guardian or custodian other than you?

    ☐ YES (Enter name, address, phone number, relationship)   ☑ NO

    NAME _____

    ADDRESS _____
                   (Number, Street, Apt. No. (if any), P.O. Box, or Rural Route)

    City   State   ZIP

    DAYTIME PHONE NUMBER _____ _____
                       Area Code   Number

    RELATIONSHIP TO CHILD _____

    Can this person speak and understand English?   ☐ YES ☐ NO

       If "NO", what is this person's preferred language? _____

    Can this person read and understand English?   ☐ YES ☐ NO

B. Is there another adult who helps care for the child and can help us get information about the child if necessary?

    ☑ YES (Enter name, address, phone number, relationship)   ☐ NO

    NAME OF CONTACT   Betty Slocum

    ADDRESS   300 West Pine Street
                  (Number, Street, Apt. No. (if any), P.O. Box, or Rural Route)

    Oklahoma City   OK   73998

    City   State   ZIP

    DAYTIME PHONE NUMBER   405   555-1789
                      Area Code   Number

    RELATIONSHIP TO CHILD   Aunt

    Can this person speak and understand English?   ☑ YES ☐ NO

       If "NO", what is this person's preferred language? _____

    Can this person read and understand English?   ☑ YES ☐ NO

Form SSA-3820-BK, *Disability Report—Child* (Page 3)

SECTION 3 - THE CHILD'S ILLNESSES, INJURIES OR CONDITIONS AND HOW THEY AFFECT HIM/HER

A. What are the child's disabling illnesses, injuries, or conditions?

Intellectual disability

Heart disease from birth

B. When did the child become disabled?

April	14	2009
Month	Day	Year

C. Do the child's illnesses, injuries or conditions cause pain or other symptoms? ☑ YES ☐ NO

SECTION 4 - INFORMATION ABOUT THE CHILD'S MEDICAL RECORDS

A. Has the child been seen by a doctor/hospital/clinic or anyone else for the illnesses, injuries or conditions?

☑ YES ☐ NO

B. Has the child been seen by a doctor/hospital/clinic or anyone else for emotional or mental problems?

☑ YES ☐ NO

Form SSA-3820-BK, *Disability Report—Child* **(Page 4)**

SECTION 4 - INFORMATION ABOUT THE CHILD'S MEDICAL RECORDS

Tell us who may have medical records or other
information about the child's illnesses, injuries or conditions.

C. List each DOCTOR/HMO/THERAPIST/OTHER. Include the child's next appointment.

1. NAME Dr. Jessica Cook, psychologist (Ph.D.)			DATES
STREET ADDRESS 1001 Polk Street			FIRST VISIT November 2009
CITY Oklahoma City	STATE OK	ZIP 73888	LAST VISIT January 2016
PHONE 405 555-1234 Area Code Number	Patient ID # (If known)		NEXT APPOINTMENT January 2017

REASONS FOR VISITS

Penny's intellectual disability

WHAT TREATMENT WAS RECEIVED?

Mental tests (IQ and others); advice about Penny's behavior and limitations

2. NAME Dr. John Barrow			DATES
STREET ADDRESS 95 Capitol Avenue			FIRST VISIT May 18, 2009
CITY Oklahoma City	STATE OK	ZIP 73887	LAST VISIT July 2016
PHONE 405 555-3333 Area Code Number	Patient ID # (If known)		NEXT APPOINTMENT July 2017

REASONS FOR VISITS

Evaluation of Penny's heart problem

WHAT TREATMENT WAS RECEIVED?

Heart surgery to repair defects present at birth

Form SSA-3820-BK, *Disability Report—Child* (Page 5)

Form SSA-3820-BK (03-2017) UF

SECTION 4 - INFORMATION ABOUT THE CHILD'S MEDICAL RECORDS

DOCTOR/HMO/THERAPIST/OTHER

3. NAME			DATES
Peggy Hall, M.D.			
STREET ADDRESS			FIRST VISIT
975 Fairview Drive			June 2009
CITY	STATE	ZIP	LAST VISIT
Oklahoma City	OK	73888	October 2015
PHONE 405 555-4444 Area Code Number	Patient ID # (If known)		NEXT APPOINTMENT October 2016

REASONS FOR VISITS

Regular medical check-ups. Dr. Hall is Penny's pediatrician

WHAT TREATMENT WAS RECEIVED?
Immunizations, treatment of colds and other problems children have. Also prescribes drugs for Penny's heart condition, consulting with Dr. Barrow.

If you need more space, use Section 10.

D. List each HOSPITAL/CLINIC. Include the child's next appointment.

1. HOSPITAL/CLINIC	TYPE OF VISIT	DATES	
NAME	☑ INPATIENT STAYS (Stayed at least overnight)	DATE IN	DATE OUT
Children's Hospital		April 2009	June 2009
STREET ADDRESS	☑ OUTPATIENT VISITS (Sent home same day)		
183 Popular Avenue			
CITY Oklahoma City	☐ EMERGENCY ROOM VISITS	DATE FIRST VISIT	DATE LAST VISIT
STATE OK ZIP		Sept. 2009	Sept. 2009
PHONE Area Code Number		DATES OF VISITS Once 2009 as above	

Next appointment   None

The child's hospital/clinic number   unknown

Reasons for visits
Penny's heart had an irregular rhythm, and she was short of breath.

What treatment did the child receive?
Oxygen and drugs to make her heart rhythm regular.

What doctors does the child see at this hospital/clinic on a regular basis?
Mostly Dr. Hall, but sometimes other doctors have substituted.

Form SSA-3820-BK, *Disability Report—Child* (Page 6)

SECTION 4 - INFORMATION ABOUT THE CHILD'S MEDICAL RECORDS

HOSPITAL/CLINIC

2. HOSPITAL/CLINIC	TYPE OF VISIT	DATES	
NAME	☐ **INPATIENT STAYS** *(Stayed at least overnight)*	DATE IN	DATE OUT
STREET ADDRESS	☐ **OUTPATIENT VISITS** *(Sent home same day)*		
CITY	☐ **EMERGENCY ROOM VISITS**	DATE FIRST VISIT	DATE LAST VISIT
STATE **ZIP**		DATES OF VISITS	
PHONE *Area Code Number*			

Next **appointment**   The child's hospital/clinic **number**

Reasons for visits

What **treatment** did the child receive?

What **doctors** does the child see at this hospital/clinic on a regular basis?

If you need more space, use Section 10.

E. Does **anyone else have medical records or information** about the child's illnesses, injuries or conditions (foster parents, social workers, counselors, tutors, school nurses, detention centers, attorneys, insurance companies, and/or Worker's Compensation), or is the child scheduled to see anyone else?

☐ YES *(If "YES," complete information below.)*   ☑ NO

NAME	DATES
ADDRESS	**FIRST** VISIT
CITY **STATE** **ZIP**	**LAST** SEEN
PHONE *Area Code Number*	**NEXT APPOINTMENT**
CLAIM NUMBER *(If any)*	
REASONS FOR VISITS	

If you need more space, use Section 10.

Form SSA-3820-BK, *Disability Report—Child* (Page 7)

Form SSA-3820-BK (03-2017) UF   Page 7 of 12

SECTION 5 - MEDICATIONS

Does the child currently take any medications for illnesses, injuries or conditions?   ☑ YES   ☐ NO

If "YES", tell us the following: (Look at the child's medicine containers, if necessary.)

NAME OF MEDICINE	IF PRESCRIBED, GIVE NAME OF DOCTOR	REASON FOR MEDICINE	SIDE EFFECTS THE CHILD HAS
propranolol	Dr. Hall	irregular heart	feels tired, sleepy

If you need more space, use Section 10.

SECTION 6 - TESTS

Has the child had, or will he/she have, any medical tests for illnesses, injuries or conditions?

☑ YES   ☐ NO   If "YES", tell us the following (give approximate dates, if necessary).

KIND OF TEST	WHEN WAS/WILL TESTS BE DONE? (Month, day, year)	WHERE DONE (Name of Facility)	WHO SENT THE CHILD FOR THIS TEST
EKG (HEART TEST)	2009, 2011 and other dates	Hospital and office	Dr. Hall
TREADMILL (EXERCISE TEST)	None		
CARDIAC CATHETERIZATION	2009	Children's Hospital	Dr. Barrow
BIOPSY - Name of body part	None		
SPEECH/LANGUAGE	Currently	Fair Park School	School
HEARING TEST	Yes, forgot date	Dr. Hall's office	Dr. Hall
VISION TEST	Yes, forgot date	Dr. Hall's office	Dr. Hall
IQ TESTING	2013	Dr. Cook's office	Dr. Cook
EEG (BRAIN WAVE TEST)	2009	Children's Hospital	Dr. Hall
HIV TEST	None		
BLOOD TEST (NOT HIV)	CBC, liver, others	Children's Hospital	Dr. Hall
BREATHING TEST	No		
X-RAY - Name of body part	No		
MRI/CAT SCAN - Name of body part __Heart__	MRI 2009, 2012	Children's Hospital	Dr. Barrow

If the child has had other tests, list them in Section 10.

Form SSA-3820-BK, *Disability Report—Child* (Page 8)

SECTION 7 - ADDITIONAL INFORMATION

A. Has the child been tested or examined by any of the following?

Headstart (Title V) ☐ YES ☑ NO

Public or Community Health Department ☐ YES ☑ NO

Child Welfare or Social Service Agency or WIC ☐ YES ☑ NO

Early Intervention Services ☐ YES ☑ NO

Program for Children with Special Health Care Needs ☐ YES ☑ NO

Mental Health/Mental Retardation Center ☑ YES ☐ NO

B. Has the child received Vocational Rehabilitation or other employment support services to help him or her go to work?

☐ YES ☑ NO

If you answered "YES" to any of the above in A. or B., please complete C. below:

C. 1. NAME OF AGENCY   Community Mental Health Center

ADDRESS   1001 Polk Street

(Number, Street, Apt. No. (if any), P.O. Box, or Rural Route)

Oklahoma City	OK	93888
City	State	ZIP

PHONE NUMBER   405   555-6666

Area Code   Number

TYPE OF TEST Achievement test	WHEN DONE Don't remember
TYPE OF TEST IQ test	WHEN DONE 2013

FILE OR RECORD NUMBER   don't know

2. NAME OF AGENCY

ADDRESS

(Number, Street, Apt. No. (if any), P.O. Box, or Rural Route)

City	State	ZIP

PHONE NUMBER

Area Code   Number

TYPE OF TEST	WHEN DONE
TYPE OF TEST	WHEN DONE

FILE OR RECORD NUMBER

If there are any other agencies, show them in Section 10.

Form SSA-3820-BK, *Disability Report—Child* (Page 9)

SECTION 8 - EDUCATION

A. Is the child currently enrolled in any school? ☑ YES, grade: 1st ☐ NO, too young

☐ NO, other reason (complete B)

B. Other reason the child is not enrolled in school:

_____

_____

_____

_____

_____

_____

_____

_____

_____

C. List the name of the school the child is currently attending and give dates attended. If the child is no longer in school, list the name of the last school attended and give dates attended.

NAME OF SCHOOL Peabody Elementary

ADDRESS 2500 Pine Street

(Number, Street, Apt. No. (if any), P.O. Box, or Rural Route)

Oklahoma City	Polk	OK	93777
City	County	State	ZIP

PHONE NUMBER 405 555-7777

Area Code Number

DATES ATTENDED 8/2014 - Current

TEACHER'S NAME Ms. Harrison

Has the child been tested for behavioral or learning problems? ☑ YES ☐ NO
If "YES", complete the following:

TYPE OF TEST IQ WHEN DONE 2015

TYPE OF TEST _____ WHEN DONE _____

Is the child in special education? ☑ YES ☐ NO

If "YES", and different from above, give:
NAME OF SPECIAL EDUCATION TEACHER Ms. Ramirez

Is the child in speech/language therapy? ☑ YES ☐ NO

If "YES", and different from above, give:
NAME OF SPEECH/LANGUAGE THERAPIST Mr. Johnson

Form SSA-3820-BK, *Disability Report—Child* (Page 10)

SECTION 8 - EDUCATION

D. List the names of all other schools attended in the last 12 months and give dates attended.

NAME OF SCHOOL ___ see above ___

ADDRESS _____
(Number, Street, Apt. No. (if any), P.O. Box, or Rural Route)

City   County   State   ZIP

PHONE NUMBER _____
Area Code   Number

DATES ATTENDED _____

TEACHER'S NAME _____

Was the child tested for behavioral or learning problems? ☐ YES ☐ NO
If "YES", complete the following:

TYPE OF TEST _____ WHEN DONE _____

TYPE OF TEST _____ WHEN DONE _____

Was the child in special education? ☐ YES ☐ NO
If "YES", and different from above, give:

NAME OF SPECIAL EDUCATION TEACHER _____

Was the child in speech/language therapy? ☐ YES ☐ NO

If "YES", and different from above, give:

NAME OF SPEECH/LANGUAGE THERAPIST _____

If there are other schools, show them in Section 10.

E. Is the child attending Daycare/Preschool? ☐ YES ☑ NO

If "YES", complete the following:

NAME OF DAYCARE/
PRESCHOOL/CAREGIVER _____

ADDRESS _____
(Number, Street, Apt. No. (if any), P.O. Box, or Rural Route)

City   County   State   ZIP

PHONE NUMBER _____
Area Code   Number

DATES ATTENDED _____

TEACHER'S/CAREGIVER'S NAME

Form SSA-3820-BK, *Disability Report—Child* (Page 11)

Form SSA-3820-BK (03-2017) UF

SECTION 9 - WORK HISTORY

A. Has the child ever worked (including sheltered work)? ☐ YES ☑ NO
   If "YES", complete the following:

   DATES WORKED _____

   NAME OF EMPLOYER _____

   ADDRESS _____

   (Number, Street, Apt. No. (if any), P.O. Box, or Rural Route)

   City   County   State   ZIP

   PHONE NUMBER _____
            Area Code   Number

   NAME OF SUPERVISOR _____

B. List job title, and briefly describe the work and any problems the child may have had doing the job.

_____

_____

_____

_____

_____

_____

_____

_____

SECTION 10 - DATE AND REMARKS

Please give the date you filled out this disability report.

1/11/2016

Date (MM/DD/YYYY)

Use this section for any additional information about your child.

Penny tires easily and is frustrated by not being able to learn as fast as other children. Her teachers say she is falling further and further behind in her school work. Dr. Hall says Penny's heart is becoming more irregular and increasing in size. She says Penny needs more tests in the hospital and might even need surgery again, but we can't afford the costs. Penny's doctors and teachers say they will provide any information requested. Please contact me, Penny's mother, if there is any problem obtaining Penny's medical or school records. Also, I request Penny's medical information be evaluated by a real doctor to determine her disability and also that Penny's treating doctors' opinions be considered.

Form SSA-3820-BK, *Disability Report—Child* (Page 12)

Form SSA-3820-BK (03-2017) UF

SECTION 10 - REMARKS

CAUTION
You must use forms provided by the SSA. You can obtain them at your local SSA Field Office or by calling the SSA hotline at 800-772-1213, Monday through Friday (except holidays), from 7 a.m. to 7 p.m. If you are deaf or hard of hearing, TTY service representatives are available at the same times at 800-325-0778. You can also download many necessary forms from the SSA website at www.ssa.gov.

If the child meets the initial nonmedical eligibility requirements, the child's file is forwarded to a state agency called the Disability Determination Service (DDS). There, a disability evaluation team, made up of a nondoctor examiner and a medical consultant, reviews the child's case to decide if the SSA's definition of disability has been met. (See Chapter 6 for more on DDS agencies, examiners, and medical consultants.)

The doctors at the DDS need thorough and detailed medical records to help them decide if your child is disabled. You can speed up the process by providing your child's medical records to the SSA, or more likely, helping the SSA get them. When you fill out the application for your child, you will be asked to provide names, addresses, and telephone numbers of all doctors, hospitals, clinics, and other specialists your child has visited. Be as thorough as you can. If you have them, provide the dates of visits to doctors and hospitals, insurance policy numbers, and any other information that

will help the SSA get your child's medical records as soon as possible.

In addition, if your child is under age 18 and applying for SSI, you will be asked to describe how your child's disability affects the ability to function in the same way as another child of similar age. To help the DDS in its evaluation, be ready to provide the names of teachers, day care providers, and family members who can give information about how your child functions in his or her day-to-day activities. If you can get any school records, bring them along.

In many communities, the SSA has made special arrangements with medical providers, social service agencies, and schools to help it get the information it needs to process your child's claim. Most DDSs have Professional Relations Officers who work directly with these organizations. But don't rely solely on these officers to get the information. It's your child; you need to be an active participant in your child's quest for benefits.

C. Disability Evaluation

SKIP AHEAD
The first section below applies only to children applying for SSI. Under SSDI, children can receive benefits at any age (paid to the parents) if the parent is a disabled, retired, or deceased worker who has paid sufficient Social Security taxes. Such children cannot receive SSDI benefits based on their own medical problems,

no matter how severe. A child of an eligible worker can receive benefits based on her own medical problems, however, once she passes her 18th birthday, as long as she becomes medically disabled before age 22.

Under SSI, children can qualify for disability based on their own medical problems. (As explained previously, the SSA considers anyone under age 18 a child.) All claimants, both children and adults, must pass through a specific set of disability evaluation steps called sequential evaluation.

1. Disability in Children for SSI

A child's disability obviously cannot be evaluated using work-related adult criteria. Instead, a child will be considered disabled if the child satisfies all nonmedical eligibility rules and has an impairment that is medically both *marked* and *severe*. Rather than proving your child can't work, you'll need to prove that your child has severe functional limitations in day-to-day activities.

To prove a child is disabled, you must submit all of the child's medical records to the SSA, or the SSA will obtain them from the child's doctor. Then they are forwarded to the DDS. If the available records are not thorough enough for the DDS team to decide if your child qualifies as disabled, you may be asked to have your child undergo a special examination called a "consultative examination" (CE), which is paid for by the government.

a. Marked and Severe

"Marked and severe" is a legal standard in the Social Security Act. It applies to the disabling conditions that either satisfy a specific medical requirement listing in the SSA's Listing of Impairments or result in equivalent functional limitations. (The Listings are discussed further in Section C2, below, and are explained in detail in the Medical Listings on Nolo's website.) The phrase is meant to emphasize the intent of Congress to grant disability benefits only to children with the worst medical conditions. When used by the SSA, marked and severe indicates that a child's impairments are disabling enough to qualify under a specific listing in the Listing of Impairments.

Some listings mention only the level of medical severity required rather than functional severity because they presume that extreme functional limitations result from the disorder. For example, if a child has been diagnosed with acute leukemia, the child will meet the listing and be granted benefits without considering the child's functional limitations.

MEDICAL LISTINGS

Remember: The Medical Listings are on Nolo's website (see Appendix D for the link). Parts 1 through 14 contain the Medical Listings, which is the medical information the SSA uses to determine whether an impairment meets the requirements to obtain disability benefits.

Defining Marked and Severe

Marked means more than moderate and less than extreme. The listings authorize the granting of benefits when a child's condition causes marked limitations in two areas of functioning or extreme limitations in one area of functioning. The exact areas of functioning depend on the type of impairment. For example, the ability to walk and use the hands is often compromised in arthritis and nervous system disorders. In mental disorders, memory, ability to relate to other people, and ability to think clearly are often in question. Limitations in function are considered in light of what is age appropriate. The SSA requires that its doctors use medical judgment in making these decisions.

Severe means a *condition* that is more than mild or slight. A condition that is only mild or slight is called "not severe" or "nonsevere" by the SSA. Keep in mind that the common meaning of severe implies a medical condition worse than moderate, but the SSA requires only worse than mild or slight. (See Chapter 7 for a more detailed explanation of a severe condition.)

---

b. Child Listing of Impairments

A DDS medical consultant initially checks to see whether the child's medical condition is on the Listing of Impairments found in the Social Security regulations, or whether the child has an impairment of equivalent severity. These listings say what sort of symptoms, signs, or laboratory findings show that a physical or mental condition is severe enough to disable a child. For example, the listings specify exactly what symptoms are necessary for your child to qualify under autistic disorders. If your child's condition is on the list or equivalent to something on the list, your child is considered disabled for SSI purposes.

In comparing your child's condition against the Listing of Impairments, the medical consultant reviews evidence from treating doctors and other health professionals, as well as your child's teachers, counselors, therapists, and social workers. All of these people have knowledge of how your child functions day-to-day and how your child has functioned over time. (Parts 1 through 14 of the Medical Listings can be found on Nolo's website. See Appendix D for the link.)

c. Special Rules for Children With Severe Disabilities

The disability evaluation process generally takes several months. But the SSI eligibility law includes special provisions for people, including children, whose condition is so severe that they are presumed to be disabled. In these cases, SSI benefits begin immediately and are paid for up to six months while the formal disability decision is being made. (The child must, of course, meet the other nonmedical eligibility requirements.) These payments are called "presumptive disability payments." (See Chapter 4 for more details.)

If the SSA makes these payments and later decides that the child's disability is not severe enough to qualify for SSI benefits, the money does not have to be paid back.

Is Your Child in Special Education?

Your child will not be automatically found disabled for SSI purposes because of enrollment in special education classes. At the same time, just because your child is mainstreamed does not automatically mean that he or she won't be found disabled for SSI purposes. The DDS evaluation is based on different criteria.

---

d. Special Rules for Children With HIV Infection

Children with HIV infection may differ from adults in the way the infection is acquired and in the course of the disease. DDS disability examiners and doctors use extensive guidelines when evaluating claims for children with HIV infection.

Some children may not have the conditions specified in the SSA's current guidelines for evaluating HIV infection, but might have other signs and symptoms that indicate an impairment that affects

their ability to engage in activities expected of children of the same age. This kind of evidence might help show that your child is disabled for SSI purposes. (See Part 14 of the Medical Listings for more detailed discussion of children with HIV and AIDS.)

2. Disability in Adult Children for SSDI

A child older than 18 who is applying for SSDI disability for the first time or who is being converted from a child's benefit will be evaluated using the adult disability criteria. It is important to remember that these claimants are adults, not children, and that their nonmedical eligibility depends on having a parent worker who is insured for SSDI benefits by having paid enough Social Security taxes.

Briefly, to qualify for disability as an adult, a person must have a physical or mental impairment that is expected to rule out doing any substantial work for at least a year or is expected to result in death. Generally, if the claimant holds a job that pays $1,260 or more per month (in 2020), the work is considered substantial, and will disqualify the claimant from getting disability benefits. (See Chapter 1, Section B, for more on defining disability.)

The claimant's condition is compared to a list of impairments that are considered to be severe enough to prevent working for a year or more. These are called the "Listing of Impairments." A claimant who is not working and has an impairment that is on the list (or equivalent to a condition on the adult listing) is considered disabled for Social Security purposes.

If the DDS cannot match the claimant's impairment with one on the list, the DDS assesses the claimants current ability to perform the type of work done in the past—if any. A young adult usually won't have a past work history, so the DDS considers his or her ability to do any kind of suitable work—based on the claimant's age, education, and experience. A claimant found to be unable to do any substantial work then qualifies for SSDI benefits. (For more information on this issue, see Chapter 7.)

D. Continuing Disability Reviews for SSI Children

Once a child is found disabled by the SSA, the law requires that the SSA periodically do a "continuing disability review" (CDR) to determine whether or not a child younger than age 18 is still disabled. The CDR must be done on the following schedule:

- at least every three years for recipients under 18 whose conditions are likely to improve
- not later than 12 months after birth for babies whose disability is based on low birth weight, and
- sometime during the 18th year, if the person received benefits for at least one

month before turning age 18 (after turning 18, the eligibility will be based on the adult criteria).

Continuing disability reviews for SSI recipients younger than 18 whose conditions are not likely to improve are done at the SSA's discretion. Despite legal requirements, the SSA frequently stops doing CDRs when the agency is short of money. This means that actual intervals for CDRs may be longer than described above.

One thing you must show during a CDR is that the child is and has been receiving treatment that is considered medically necessary for the disabling condition. The only time the SSA does not require this evidence is when the agency determines that it would be inappropriate or unnecessary. If the SSA requests this evidence and you refuse to provide it, the SSA will suspend payment of benefits to you and select another representative payee if that would be in the best interest of the child. If the child is old enough, the SSA may pay the child directly.

Generally, if the child is younger than 18, the SSA will make payments only to a representative payee. Under certain circumstances, however, the SSA will make direct payments to a beneficiary under age 18 who shows the ability to manage such benefits. Examples of these circumstances are:

- The child beneficiary is also a parent who files for herself and/or her child and has experience in handling her own finances.

- The child is capable of using the benefits to provide for her needs, and no qualified payee is available. (The SSA determines whether the child is "capable.")
- The child is within seven months of reaching age 18 and is filing an initial claim for benefits.

(CDRs are discussed further in Chapter 14).

E. Other Health Care Concerns

Federal law recognizes that disabled children need more than simply monthly cash benefits for their health care. Some types of health care assistance available to disabled children are summarized below and are especially directed toward helping children who receive SSI.

1. Medicaid

Medicaid is a health care program for people with low incomes and limited assets. In most states, children who receive SSI also qualify for Medicaid. In many states, Medicaid comes automatically with SSI eligibility. In other states, you must sign up for it. And some children can qualify for Medicaid coverage even if they don't qualify for SSI. Check with your local Social Security office or your state or county social services office for more information.

2. Children With Special Health Care Needs

If the SSA determines that a child is disabled and eligible for SSI, the SSA refers the child for health care services under the Children with Special Health Care Needs (CSHCN) provision of the Social Security Act. CSHCN services are generally administered through state-run health agencies, and most provide specialized services through arrangements with clinics, private offices, hospital-based outpatient, and inpatient treatment centers, or community agencies.

Depending on your state, the CSHCN program might be called the Children's Special Health Services, Children's Medical Services, the Handicapped Children's Program, or something else. Even if your child is not eligible for SSI, you might be able to obtain some kind of health service for your child through a CSHCN program. Contact a local health department office, social services office, or hospital to find out how to contact your CSHCN program.

3. Children in Certain Medical Care Facilities

Living in a public institution may affect an SSI claimant's or recipient's eligibility and payment amount. That's because residents of public institutions generally are not eligible for SSI. For SSI purposes, a "public institution" is one operated by or controlled by a federal, state, or local government agency, and housing 17 or more residents.

There are exceptions to this rule. If a child lives for an entire month in a public institution or private medical care facility where more than 50% of the costs are covered by private insurance, Medicaid, or a combination of the two, the child may be eligible for a $30 monthly SSI payment. (20 CFR § 416.211 (b)(1)(i)(ii).) This exception also applies if a child spends part of a month in a public institution and part in a private medical facility where more than 50% of the costs are covered by private insurance, Medicaid, or a combination of the two. (Examples of medical facilities are hospitals, skilled nursing facilities, and intermediate care facilities. However, any medical facility can qualify.) There is no limitation on the SSI payment if the child is in a private facility and does not receive or expect to receive more than 50% of the cost of the child's care from private insurance or Medicaid. (Program Operations Manual System (POMS) SI 00520.001.)

> EXAMPLE: Matthew, a disabled child, was born at Tall Oaks Multi-Care Center on October 4. He remained in the hospital until January 5, when he was released to live with his parents at home. Private health insurance paid for more than 50% of the cost of Matthew's care for the months of October and November. For December and January, more than 50% of the cost of his care was paid for by a combination of private insurance and Medicaid. Matthew is eligible for the $30 per month benefit.

Because of the complexity of laws involving SSI for children living in institutions, call your local Social Security Field Office if your disabled child who receives SSI is going to be in a facility. In fact, the SSA requires that you report if your child is admitted or discharged from a medical facility or another institution. (See Chapter 13 for details.)

4. Medicare

Medicare is a federal health insurance program for people 65 or older and those who have received SSDI benefits for at least two years. Because children do not qualify for SSDI benefits on their own until they turn 18 (if they qualify at a younger age, they are receiving auxiliary dependents or survivors benefits through their parents), no child can get Medicare coverage while reaching 20 years of age. The only exception is for children with chronic renal disease who need a kidney transplant or maintenance dialysis. Those children will be eligible for Medicare only if a parent receives SSDI or has worked enough to be insured by Social Security.

Getting Benefits During the Application Process (SSI)

Presumptive disability (PD) payments are made to a person who is *initially applying* for SSI benefits and whose medical condition is such that there's a strong likelihood the person will be found eligible for disability payments. The person must meet all nonmedical factors of eligibility—such as having low income and few assets. If you are an SSDI claimant—a worker who has paid Social Security taxes—you are not entitled to presumptive disability. If you apply simultaneously for SSI and SSDI, any presumptive disability you might qualify for will be based on the SSI claim only.

SKIP AHEAD

If you are only applying for SSDI benefits, you do not need to read this chapter. You may proceed to Chapter 5.

If the SSA agrees that you are presumptively disabled, you may receive payments for up to six months while your application for disability benefits is pending. Payments begin in the month in which the SSA made the presumptive disability finding. If, after six months of presumptive disability payments, the SSA has not made a formal determination on your disability application, the presumptive disability payments end until this formal determination is made.

People applying for SSI based on a disability are commonly awarded presumptive disability cash payments. It never hurts to request them. If you are granted presumptive disability, you can also receive free health care under Medicaid earlier than would otherwise be possible. But being granted presumptive disability does not necessarily mean that the SSA will make a favorable final determination on your disability application. And if the SSA denies your request for benefits before you have received a full six months of presumptive disability benefits, you will not receive the balance.

You will not have to pay back any of the presumptive disability payments you were given before your claim was denied, except in some unusual situations (20 CFR § 416.537(b)1):

- The SSA later determines that you did not qualify under the nonmedical eligibility requirements—this exception primarily targets those people who commit fraud to obtain benefits.
- The SSA made an error in computing your monthly presumptive disability payment—in this situation, you need only repay the amount of money that went over the amount you were supposed to receive. Even in this situation, the SSA can waive the requirement that you repay the money if both of the following are true:
  - You were not at fault.
  - Repayment would defeat the purpose of the SSI law, would be unfair, or

would interfere with administration of SSI law due to the small amount of money involved.

NOTE: The sponsor of an immigrant who is denied disability may be responsible for repaying the immigrant's presumptive disability payments. (20 CFR § 416.550.)

Emergency Payments

In cases of extreme hardship, the law permits a one-time emergency cash advance payment to people who appear to qualify for presumptive disability through SSI. (42 U.S.C.A. § 1383(a)(4)(A); 20 CFR 416.520.) Extreme hardship means that without the payment, you risk an immediate threat to your health or safety, such as the lack of food, clothing, shelter, or medical care.

This advance payment is not extra benefit money. The SSA eventually gets the money back by deducting it from your presumptive disability checks, usually spread out over a period of six months.

If you think you need an emergency advance payment, tell the Social Security Field Office when you are applying for SSI benefits. If you are eligible, you will receive an emergency payment, which will take seven to ten days to process. The amount of the payment for one person cannot exceed $783 (the federal benefit rate in 2020), plus any applicable state supplementary amount.

Emergency Versus Immediate Payments

Do not confuse "emergency payments" with "immediate payments." The SSA will issue "immediate payments" through a Field Office in critical cases within 24 hours. (You must already be receiving SSI or SSDI payments to collect an immediate payment, so immediate payments do not apply to presumptive disability.)

Immediate payments can be made to both SSI and SSDI claimants who qualify. To qualify, you must have a financial emergency or present a potential public relations problem for the SSA. Critical cases are those involving delayed or interrupted benefit payments. Examples might include the loss of a benefit check in the mail or a natural disaster like a hurricane or tornado wiping out parts of a town and interfering with normal benefit check delivery to a number of people.

For immediate payments, the maximum amount payable for either SSI or SSDI is $999. The exact amounts vary and must be calculated by the SSA Field Office.

A. Applying for Presumptive Disability

You apply for presumptive disability at your local SSA Field Office when you apply for SSI. The SSA Field Office can grant presumptive disability at that time if you have any of a limited number of impairments (see Section B, below). Most applications, however, are forwarded to the state Disability Determination Services (DDS) without an award of presumptive disability. But the DDS also has wide discretion to grant presumptive disability. So even if your condition isn't listed below, once your file is forwarded to the DDS, be sure to ask the examiner handling your claim about presumptive disability (see Section C, below).

B. Impairments Qualifying for Presumptive Disability by Field Office

An SSA Field Office representative has the power to grant six months of presumptive disability payments when you apply for benefits, if there is a reasonable basis for believing that you have a disabling impairment. Of course, Field Office representatives are not doctors, but they can award presumptive disability to claimants who are obviously disabled. This is one way the SSA is trying to speed up providing low-income disabled people with financial assistance.

The Field Office may grant presumptive disability in three ways: based on the representative's observations, based on the claimant's statements, or after requesting confirmation from another source. The sections below cover each method.

1. Observation

Under federal regulations, the Field Office representative can award presumptive disability upon seeing that a claimant has one of the following disabling conditions:

- amputation of two limbs, or
- amputation of a leg at the hip.

2. Statement by the Claimant or Guardian

The Field Office representative can award presumptive disability payments based on the word of the claimant (or the claimant's parent or guardian, in the case of a child) that he or she has certain disabling impairments. The disabling impairments must be very severe, because the Field Office personnel are not doctors and are screening only for obvious cases. Note that the actual medical severity needed to ultimately qualify for disability benefits based on one of these disorders may be less than what is required to receive presumptive disability payments. The disabling impairments are as follows:

- total blindness
- total deafness
- bed confinement or immobility without a wheelchair, walker, or crutches due to a long-standing condition—such as a chronic condition that is not likely to improve with further treatment and has been present for a year or more
- a stroke more than three months in the past with continued marked difficulty in walking or using a hand or an arm— marked means more than moderate, but less than extreme but does not require an inability to walk or total paralysis in an arm

- cerebral palsy, muscular dystrophy, or muscle atrophy along with marked difficulty in walking without using braces, in speaking, or in coordination of the hands or arms
- Down syndrome characterized by intellectual disability, abnormal development of the skull, short arms and legs, and hands and feet that tend to be broad and flat, and
- severe intellectual disability in someone who is at least seven years of age—severe means the person depends on others for meeting personal care needs and in doing other routine daily activities.

Saying you, or the claimant, in case of a child, are disabled isn't enough. A statement by you or a child claimant's parent or guardian that the claimant is disabled won't establish presumptive disability if the SSA Field Office representative believes the allegation may be false, based on personal observation. For example, if a claimant alleges total blindness but the Field Office representative sees her reading a book, the SSA will not grant presumptive disability at the time of the application.

3. Disorders Requiring Confirmation From Another Source

With certain impairments, the Field Office may need to confirm the claimant's allegation before granting presumptive disability. This situation arises when the alleged impairment is not observable by the Field Office representative or when the representative's observations are inconsistent with the claimant's statements. These are some of the conditions that can qualify for PD but require confirmation:

- symptomatic human immunodeficiency virus (HIV) infection
- terminal illness (a physician must confirm by telephone or in a signed statement that an individual has a terminal illness with a life expectancy of six months or less, or a physician or hospice official, such as a hospice coordinator, staff nurse, social worker, or medical records custodian, must confirm that an individual is receiving hospice services because of a terminal illness)
- a child six months or younger with a birth weight below 1,200 grams (2 pounds, 10 ounces)
- a child 12 months or younger whose birth weight was as listed in the following chart:

Gestational Age (in weeks)	Weight at Birth
37–40	under 2,000 grams (4 pounds, 6 ounces)
36	1,875 grams or less (4 pounds, 2 ounces)
35	1,700 grams or less (3 pounds, 12 ounces)
34	1,500 grams or less (3 pounds, 5 ounces)
33	1,325 grams or less (2 pounds, 15 ounces)

- a spinal cord injury producing an inability to move without the use of a walker or bilateral hand-held assistive device for more than two weeks (with confirmation of such status from an appropriate medical professional)
- end stage renal disease (ESRD) requiring chronic dialysis (Form CMS-2728-U3, *End Stage Renal Disease Medical Evidence Report - Medicare Entitlement and/or Patient Registration*, must be filled out), and
- amyotrophic lateral sclerosis (ALS), also known as Lou Gehrig's disease.

To confirm allegations for presumptive disability (except for HIV infection—see "Special Confirmation Needed With HIV Infection," below), the Field Office representative must do all of the following:

- Record the information given by the claimant on a Report of Contact (RC) form, which is placed in the claimant's file.
- Explain the presumptive disability procedures to the claimant, and the need to contact a source to verify the allegation (claimant's statement) in order to make a presumptive disability finding.
- Ask the claimant or guardian for the name and telephone number of a reliable source who can verify the allegation. An appropriate source might include school personnel, a social service agency worker, a doctor, a member of the clergy, or another member of the community who knows of the condition based on frequent contacts or a long-term association with the claimant.
- Contact an appropriate source to determine if the claimant meets the presumptive disability criterion.
- Record the information obtained from the source on the RC form in the claimant's file.
- Inform that claimant.

Special Confirmation Needed With HIV Infection

If a claimant alleges HIV infection, including AIDS, the Field Office must send the claimant's treating doctor a form requesting information about the severity of the infection. The medical severity required for presumptive disability is like that described in the Listing of Impairments that deals with HIV infection. (See Part 14 of the Medical Listings.)

C. Qualifying for Presumptive Disability Through the DDS

Once the SSA determines you are legally entitled to presumptive disability benefits, it leaves the initial determination of medical eligibility for SSI benefits to a state agency called the Disability Determination Service, or DDS.

If you fail to win presumptive benefits during the initial application process at the SSA Field Office, you can try again when your case is forwarded to the DDS for the SSI disability determination. (A DDS representative has much wider discretion in granting presumptive disability than a Field Office representative.) The presumptive disability determinations that DDS can make fall into three general categories.

1. High Potential for Presumptive Disability

The DDS is most likely to grant presumptive disability for the following disabilities:

- severe intellectual disability
- cancer
- central nervous system diseases resulting in paralysis or difficulty in walking or using hands and arms
- irreversible kidney disease, and
- symptomatic HIV infection.

2. Caution in Granting Presumptive Disability

The DDS uses caution in granting PD in the following disabilities because of the difficulty in predicting severity or duration of the impairment:

- diabetes
- epilepsy
- high blood pressure
- heart disease caused by high blood pressure
- peptic ulcer
- cirrhosis of the liver, and
- bone fractures.

3. Low Potential for Presumptive Disability

The DDS rarely authorizes presumptive disability payments for the following disorders:

- mental impairments (with the exceptions of severe intellectual disability or where there is convincing evidence of prolonged severe psychosis or chronic brain syndrome)
- breathing disorders, because medical tests of breathing ability are crucial to a determination of disability for most respiratory impairments, and
- back conditions, except in cases involving traumatic injury to the spinal cord (in which case, an award of PD benefits is more likely).

Proving You Are Disabled

All claimants who file a disability claim for SSDI or SSI are responsible for providing medical evidence to the Social Security Administration (SSA) showing that they are impaired, or "medically eligible" for disability benefits. You do not have to physically provide medical reports to the SSA (although you can, to help expedite a decision). If you give your permission, the SSA will request your reports from medical sources (doctors) that have treated or evaluated you.

Once you have established the existence of an impairment, the SSA considers both medical and nonmedical evidence to assess the severity of your impairment. For this, the SSA requests copies of medical evidence from hospitals, clinics, or other health facilities where you have been treated—if the SSA doesn't already have those records.

A. Acceptable Medical Sources

When considering both the existence and severity of your impairment, the SSA evaluates reports from all medical providers who have treated you, called your treating sources. These include doctors, chiropractors, naturopaths, and other alternative providers. But to trust a medical opinion and obtain medical information necessary for accurate disability determination, the SSA must have medical information from what it calls "acceptable medical sources." Reports from these sources enhance the credibility of your disability claim.

EXAMPLE: You apply for disability benefits, but your only treating source for your back pain is your chiropractor. Any information provided to the SSA by that chiropractor, no matter how detailed, is not sufficient for the SSA to make a disability determination. You will be sent to an acceptable medical source for an examination of your back complaints.

Only the following are considered acceptable medical sources:

- **Licensed physicians.** Licensed physicians hold an M.D. degree with a valid license to practice medicine in the states in which they practice. Chiropractic, homeopathic, naturopathic, and other alternative providers do not qualify.
- **Licensed osteopaths.** Licensed osteopaths hold a D.O. degree with a valid license in the states in which they practice.
- **Licensed or certified psychologists.** A licensed or certified psychologist holds a doctorate degree (Ph.D.) in psychology. For the purpose of establishing severe intellectual disability or learning disabilities, a licensed or certified psychologist includes a school psychologist or another licensed or certified individual with a different title who performs the function of a school psychologist in a school setting. Psychologists must be licensed in the state in which they practice.
- **Licensed optometrists.** An optometrist holds an O.D. degree. The SSA

will recognize medical evidence from optometrists as acceptable and sufficient for diagnostic purposes (establishing the presence of visual disorders only), as well as measuring visual acuity and visual fields. An exception: Optometrists in the U.S. Virgin Islands can only measure visual acuity and visual fields, not provide a diagnosis. Optometrists must be validly licensed in the states in which they practice. Medical doctors (M.D.s) or osteopaths (D.O.s) who specialize in the treatment of disease of the eye are called ophthalmologists, and should not be confused with optometrists.

- **Licensed podiatrists.** Licensed podiatrists hold a D.P.M. degree and are validly licensed in the states in which they practice. Podiatrists are an acceptable medical source only to establish impairments of the foot—or foot and ankle, depending on the laws of the state in which they practice.
- **Speech-language pathologists.** Qualified speech-language pathologists are fully certified by the state education agency in the state in which they practice, are licensed by the state professional licensing board, or hold a Certificate of Clinical Competence from the American Speech-Language-Hearing Association. A speech-language pathologist is an acceptable medical source only to establish speech or language impairments.

- **Licensed audiologists** for impairments of hearing loss, auditory processing disorders, and balance disorders, within the licensed scope of their practice (which can vary state by state). Effective March 27, 2017.
- **Licensed advanced practice registered nurses (APRNs),** advanced registered nurse practitioners (ARNPs), or other advanced practice nurses with a different title, within their licensed scope of practice (which can vary by state). Effective March 27, 2017.
- **Licensed Physician Assistants (PAs),** within their licensed scope of practice (which can vary by state). Effective March 27, 2017.

B. Medical Evidence From Treating Sources

Many disability claims are decided on the basis of medical evidence from treating sources (your doctors), if they are acceptable medical sources. For example, the doctor who treats you for high blood pressure is often the best medical source of information for how serious your condition is. SSA regulations, in some situations, place special emphasis on evidence from your treating doctors—especially if they are acceptable medical sources—because they are likely to provide the most detailed and long-term picture of your impairment. They may also bring a perspective to the medical evidence that cannot be obtained from the medical findings alone or from reports of examinations or brief hospitalizations.

1. All Relevant Medical Records

The SSA revised and clarified its regulations in 2015 (§§ 404.1512, 416.912) to require you or your lawyer to submit *all* records that relate to your disability claim. By "relate," the SSA means anything that has a logical or causal connection to your medical condition, whether it is favorable or unfavorable to your claim.

Since the SSA is required by law to consider the totality of your impairments—even those that you didn't include on your application, the agency wants all of the available medical records. For example, if you had back surgery and also a worker's compensation claim, the SSA wants any medical evidence from both. As another example, if you have a mental impairment and physical impairment, both are relevant and should be mentioned on the application, and you, your doctor, or your lawyer should submit all of the relevant physical and mental medical records.

If you have a mental impairment that interferes with your ability to obtain accurate records, or you're homeless, the disability examiner can help. Relevant nonmedical records must also be submitted, such as information about your education, vocational skills, and employment.

When lawyers or other representatives are representing applicants, they are not free to choose what information to submit— for example, withholding medical or nonmedical evidence that they think might be unfavorable to a claim. For instance, you or your representative cannot submit evidence from a medical event or hospitalization but hold back certain pieces that might appear unfavorable. Say you were hospitalized for a possible heart attack, but your cardiac scan was normal—that information must be included with the other evidence from that hospitalization.

Communication between you and your representative, however, is privileged information and does not have to be given to the SSA. Furthermore, any investigation your representative makes into the merits of your claim is protected information, including discussions between your representative and your doctor regarding the severity of your disorders or your lawyer's personal opinion about your disability. Also note that neither you nor your representative is required to request an opinion from any doctor about the medical severity of your condition. However, if you or your representative does ask your doctor for a "treating source opinion" on the severity of your condition, then you must submit the response to the SSA.

2. Timely, Accurate, and Sufficient Medical Records

Timely, accurate, and sufficient records from your treating doctors can greatly reduce or eliminate the need for the SSA to obtain additional medical evidence, which means you can get a faster determination on your disability claim. Timely, accurate, and sufficient mean the following:

- **Timely** records are recent enough to be relevant to your current medical condition. How recent is a matter of medical judgment, depending on the disorder. A condition that is rapidly changing requires more up-to-date information than one that is slowly progressive or has been unchanged for years. Generally, the SSA likes to have records no older than six months. (That doesn't mean older records aren't important. Records dating back for many years may help provide the medical big picture and establish when your disability began.)

- **Accurate** records correctly describe your condition according to the standards of acceptable medical sources. To use a common example, a chiropractor may describe subluxation (slippage) of your spine on X-rays, but this will not be considered accurate if an acceptable medical source (see Section A, above) reports normal X-rays. Also, acceptable medical sources must report their information accurately. For instance, a treating medical doctor's records that say you can't walk one block because of chest pain will be rejected if specific exercise testing shows that you can do much more exercise.

- **Sufficient** medical records contain enough accurate information from acceptable medical sources to allow the SSA to make an independent medical judgment regarding the nature and severity of your medical condition. For example, an allegation (claim) and diagnosis of cancer is not sufficient. The SSA will want to know: Did a biopsy prove the cancer's presence? What kind? Where in the body? When did symptoms appear? What did a physical examination show? What did X-rays and other imaging tests show? What did blood tests show? Did you have surgery? Did it remove all of the cancer? Did you have chemotherapy? What side effects did you suffer, if any? Did you have radiation therapy? What were the results?

It is not enough for your doctor to start keeping detailed records only when you apply for disability.

> **EXAMPLE:** You were sick for six months before you applied for disability and were unable to work during that time. You might be eligible for a retroactive award of benefits for the six months you couldn't work and before you applied for disability. But if your doctor does not have detailed medical records for the entire period he has been seeing you, you might not be able to prove you were unable to work during those six months.

There is no way for your doctor to believably recreate detailed medical records from memory. If your doctor does remember something not in the written records, the SSA will evaluate such statements on a case-by-case basis. For example, if your doctor remembers that you have always had pain in the joints of your hands, that is more believable than remembering that you had ten degrees of motion in the second joint of your left little finger three years ago. In all instances, however, the SSA knows that memory is not as reliable as written records.

3. Thorough Medical Records

The medical records of a treating doctor are of critical importance to a disability claim, and they should be as comprehensive as possible. Luckily, doctors usually write things down about their patients and their treatment—and patients expect their doctors to remember them and their conditions. But not all doctors record complaints, diagnoses, and treatments with the same detail. A doctor can see as many as 30 or 40 patients a day. Even if your doctor sees only 20 people in a day, your doctor may have seen, evaluated, and treated as many as 400 patients from the time of your first visit to your next one a month later. You might not even see the same doctor on each visit, depending on your health care provider. Unless your doctors keep good medical records in writing, you cannot reasonably expect them to have an adequate knowledge of your condition.

Medical consultants working for the SSA and in a DDS see the records kept by thousands of doctors on their patients. The quality of these records varies greatly. Some are typed, mention all of the patient's complaints, show the results of examination,

note what treatment was given, state the response to treatment, and mention future plans. Many records are unreadable, however, or don't contain enough information to determine disability.

EXAMPLE: Many people apply for disability benefits based on arthritis. When a disability examiner reviews the records provided by a treating doctor, often the file contains a few scribbles that the patient has joint pains and arthritis, and further notes that some form of treatment has been given. Often, medical records contain no description of diseased joints, no range-of-motion test results, and no X-rays. The SSA spends extensive time and money each year obtaining data from joint examinations, X-rays, and other lab tests.

The SSA cannot evaluate medical records that are scribbled and unreadable, nor can they evaluate medical records that lack significant information about your condition. But if your files are incomplete, understand that it is not necessarily because of malice or incompetence on the part of your doctor. Doctors don't routinely document their files for disability purposes. Their records are to help them treat their patients. On the other hand, the SSA often does see treating doctor records that are of quite poor quality, either for treatment or disability determination purposes.

EXAMPLE: To qualify for disability based on epilepsy, you must have had a certain number of seizures during a specified time period. But physicians—even neurologists who specialize in treating epileptics—often do not record the number of seizures patients have had between visits, even though they should, in the event that adjustments of medication might be needed. Nor do physicians usually describe seizures in detail in their records, though they will note the type of seizures involved and drugs given. The SSA requires this information and a number of other things to evaluate the severity of epilepsy, such as whether or not you cooperate in taking medication and the blood levels of drugs used to treat the epilepsy. This information is often missing from a treating doctor's file.

You need to make sure the records your doctor keeps on your health are thorough enough to prove your case to the SSA. If they are not, you should augment the information they contain. It will speed up the disability determination process if you can deliver your records to the SSA—either when you make your application or later, to the claims examiner at the DDS.

4. The Weight of Your Treating Doctor's Opinion

For disability applications filed before March 27, 2017, federal regulations required the SSA to accept your treating doctor's assessment unless the SSA's own decision maker (such as a DDS medical consultant or administrative law judge on appeal cases) could give a reasonable explanation for rejecting it. This was informally known as "The Treating Source Rule." Specific information about your condition from your treating doctor was supposed to be given greater weight than the opinion of other doctors who may have seen you only once—be they doctors who examine you for the DDS or even specialists.

Effective March 27, 2017, this policy favoring the opinion of your treating doctor is no longer in effect. Instead, the new rule about medical evidence says that the most persuasive medical opinion will be given the most weight, and that the key factors that will be considered in evaluating the persuasiveness of an opinion are "supportability" and "consistency."

The first factor, supportability, means that a medical opinion should be backed up by medical tests, such as X-rays or blood tests, other signs, and a doctor's clinical notes. The second factor, consistency, refers to whether the medical opinion is consistent with the rest of the evidence in the file (for instance, the applicant's statements and other doctors' opinions).

Only if there are opinions from two or more doctors (for instance, the treating doctor and a consultative examiner) that are equally well-supported by the evidence and consistent with the applicant's file will Social Security consider the length of the patient's relationship with the doctor and whether the doctor is a specialist. However, the doctors' familiarity with Social Security rules and with the applicant's disability file will also be considered, and this factor tends to be in favor of Social Security's consultative doctors.

This change in the rule is likely to have little practical effect for several reasons. At the initial application level, medical consultants have never blindly followed treating doctor opinions anyway; regulations said that medical consultants and claims examiners didn't have to give weight to a treating doctor's opinion if it was inconsistent with other evidence in the file or if it wasn't supported by medically acceptable diagnostic techniques. Medical consultants have always weighed all of the evidence in a file, including different opinions from different treating doctors, to make a well-informed decision. The SSA has found by its own studies that the most important thing in cases is objective analysis of the totality of evidence, not reliance on any one person's opinion. It is the actual evidence that is most important.

For example, if your doctor says you can't lift more than ten pounds because of arthritis in your hands, the opinion has little weight without evidence of activity-limiting arthritis. If she says you can't lift more than ten pounds because of arthritis, describes your physical abnormalities, and provides X-ray reports showing the arthritis, her opinion will be noted and considered. However, the SSA will make its own determination of your physical abilities, using all of the evidence in file, based on federal regulations.

Note that a change in regulations in 2015 (under Section 223(d)(5)(C)(i) of the Social Security Act) made it possible for the SSA to refuse to consider medical evidence from treating sources, including acceptable medical sources, in some circumstances. This can happen if your treating source has ever been convicted of a felony, excluded from a federal health care program, or has been found to have submitted false evidence.

Some exceptions to these rules are allowed, however: If the evidence is a laboratory test that seems reliable, or if the treatment evidence was obtained before the treating source was convicted of a felony or excluded from a federal health care program, the SSA may be required to consider the evidence.

5. Treating Source Statements and Medical Assessments About Your Ability to Function

If your treating doctor gives a medical opinion about your ability to function, the SSA must consider that opinion. These opinions are called *treating source statements*. It's useful for you to have such statements from your treating doctor(s), provided they are backed up by objective evidence. The SSA will weigh such opinions in the context of all the medical evidence, but your doctors' opinions will have no effect unless the SSA thinks they are reasonable. As discussed above, the SSA will no longer give special weight to your treating doctors' opinions, but it's still worthwhile to have a supportive doctor's opinion. For one, if you have doctors who are very familiar with your case, they can point out medical problems and limitations that might otherwise be overlooked.

6. Obtaining and Reviewing Records From Your Treating Doctor

Many doctors consider medical records their property, even though the records state your health history; in rare instances, doctors might be reluctant to give you copies of your medical records. Laws vary across the country on a doctor's obligation to hand over your medical records. The best approach is to ask politely for them. For most people, a call to the doctor's office explaining that you are applying for disability is sufficient.

If your treating doctor is hesitant to let you have copies of your records, don't just say, "Thanks a lot," and hang up. Explain again that you need to see your records for your disability claim, and ask why you can't have a copy. If you are dealing with resistant office personnel who simply say it is an office policy, ask to speak with the doctor. If you get a runaround on talking to the doctor, write a letter explaining why you want your records. Write "personal and confidential" on the envelope to make sure the doctor gets the letter.

If your doctor still refuses to let you have a copy of your file, won't answer your questions regarding your medical conditions, gives you rude answers, treats you like an idiot, has a cold demeanor, or has little time for you, then you should consider finding a new treating doctor. An uncooperative doctor probably won't cooperate with the SSA on your behalf anyway. The SSA cannot force a doctor or hospital to turn over medical records, and it is not unusual for the SSA to wait months to receive medical records from treating doctors. If you are really determined to get records from an uncooperative doctor, you may need the services of an attorney who may be able to force the doctor to turn over your records. However, that would be an expensive option. Fortunately, most doctors will give you a copy of your records simply for the asking.

Be sure to review the records when you get them and make sure that all information contained in them is correct.

7. Obtaining and Reviewing Records From Hospitals and Medical Centers

Like most treating doctors, most hospitals and medical centers will let you have copies of your records without any problem. Just call the hospital and say you want a copy of your medical records; you don't have to ask your doctor's permission.

Note that some hospitals charge high per-page copy fees to former patients—as high as a dollar a page! It is not reasonable to have to pay such a high fee when copying costs only a few cents per page. If a hospital can provide copies of records to the SSA for a small fee, there is no reason they should charge a private citizen a large fee. So express mild outrage at the fee and tell the hospital you know they make records available to the SSA for a small fee.

Releasing Records for Mental Disorders

Psychiatrists and psychologists are more likely to release medical records to the SSA than to patients. Some won't even release records to the SSA. These records may contain comments about a claimant's mental disorder that could harm the doctor-patient relationship or the claimant's relationship with other people.

One simple way to avoid this problem is to talk with your treating professional about writing a summary of his or her findings on your mental condition only as it relates to your disability claim.

This summary should contain detailed comments about the kind of information the SSA wants in evaluating a mental disorder (see Part 12 of the Medical Listings on Nolo's website), while omitting personal information irrelevant to the disability determination. In fact, this might be the preferable solution if your psychologist or psychiatrist has voluminous records on you.

Before writing a summary, your treating professional should review the listing requirements of your disability in the SSA listings of impairments to see what the SSA is looking for. A summary or letter that does not address the requirements of a medical listing will do little or no good to your claim.

If the hospital still refuses, you can call the facility's social services department and ask for help. You can also look for free legal aid clinics in your area that may be able to negotiate on your behalf. Of course, you can also wait until the hospital sends the records to the SSA and then review them when they are in your file. But hospitals are often slow in sending files to the SSA.

It is very important for you to review hospital records being used to determine your eligibility for disability. Some of the information may be incorrect. It is common for doctors of hospitalized patients to focus on the immediate cause of admittance to the hospital and ignore other problems. For example, a doctor examining a patient for a heart problem may report that all other areas of the body are normal, even if they have not done a complete physical examination.

Such a practice is not uncommon, even with patients the doctor has never seen before. This can lead to serious errors and conflicts in your medical records. Doctors often do this to cut corners while satisfying hospital rules that require complete exams of hospitalized patients.

You should ask yourself: Did the doctor really examine all parts of your body they reported as normal? Did the surgeon who did your abdominal surgery really look in your eyes, ears, nose, and throat? Did they really check your reflexes and your skin sensation? Examine your joints for arthritis? If you were hospitalized for a heart attack, did the cardiologist look at anything but your heart and lungs before dictating an "otherwise normal" physical examination into hospital records?

Doctors tend to concentrate on their areas of specialty, but when they report "normal" for the other areas they didn't examine, it can be a real problem for you in establishing disability. If you find that this has happened in your case, make sure that you call or write to the SSA and tell them that various parts of your body were not actually examined and are not normal. In these instances, the SSA should arrange for an independent consultative examination.

8. Evidence the SSA Needs From Treating Sources

In general, here is the basic evidence the SSA needs:

- your medical history
- clinical findings, including the results of physical or mental status examinations
- laboratory findings, such as the results of blood pressure tests or X-rays
- your doctor's diagnosis of your condition
- your doctor's prescribed treatment, as well as your response to that treatment and your doctor's prognosis—that is, the prospect for your recovery from a medical condition, and
- your doctor's opinion about what you can do despite your impairments, based on the medical findings. This statement should describe your ability to perform work-related activities, such as sitting, standing, walking, lifting, carrying, handling objects, hearing, speaking, and traveling. In

cases involving mental impairments, the statement should describe your ability to understand, carry out, and remember instructions, and to respond appropriately to supervision, coworkers, and work pressures. For a child, the statement should describe the child's ability to function effectively in an age-appropriate manner. (If you are legally blind (vision worse than 20/200 best corrected in both eyes or visual fields of 20 degrees or less), you'll be granted benefits, and your doctor need not describe your ability to perform the above activities.)

Keep in mind that your claim could be denied no matter how much information your doctor provides if you don't fit the criteria for disability or if you are found ineligible based on nonmedical reasons. If you are denied benefits, the SSA will tell you the reasons for denial. (See Chapter 12 for more on appealing a denial.)

9. If Your Records Provide Insufficient or Unhelpful Evidence

Once you see your medical records, you may be concerned that they are insufficient for Social Security purposes. Don't necessarily blame your doctor. The files of many treating doctors are incomplete from the point of view of the SSA, but contain a perfectly reasonable amount of information to treat their patients. Furthermore, your medical file might omit certain symptoms or conditions, simply because you forgot to tell your doctor about them.

Doctors are often bogged down with paperwork: Insurance companies, workers' compensation programs, employers, government agencies, lawyers, patients, and other physicians all request written information from doctors. Few doctors enjoy tasks that take them away from seeing patients.

In addition, your doctor may never have thought about the kind of evidence the SSA needs. Let your doctor know that to support your claim of disability, the SSA will require specific medical evidence about your impairments and how your impairment affects your day-to-day functioning—not merely a letter stating that you are disabled. If your doctor sends the SSA a brief letter and no other medical information, you will be required to undergo an examination paid for by the SSA.

If your doctor wants to send a letter to the SSA, emphasize that it must contain extensive detail about your impairment and how it affects your ability to function—including your ability to walk, breathe, or use your hands and arms. It might be helpful if your doctor fills out an "RFC" form to detail your abilities and limitations (see Chapter 8 for more information). Don't assume that your doctor knows all of your impairments and how they limit your daily activities. Make sure you tell your doctor the details of your limitations.

Some doctors are willing to simply write that you are "permanently and totally disabled," even if you don't have that much wrong with you. They want to please their patients. But federal law requires that your SSA file contain actual objective evidence showing how your impairments limit your ability to function.

Your doctor doesn't have to become an expert in job performance. Your doctor may be inclined to write the SSA saying that you cannot work at all. Although this may be well intended, your doctor is not a vocational counselor. The SSA has vocational specialists who determine what jobs can be done with various impairments. Many people are capable of some kind of work, even though their doctors think the medical evidence shows them to be disabled. Many people who qualify for disability benefits do so because of both nonmedical (age, education, and work experience) and medical factors. The SSA, not your doctor, ultimately determines whether or not you are disabled—that is, whether or not you can work given your particular impairments.

Most people applying for disability would be granted benefits if it were up to their treating doctors. Doctors want to help and maintain a good relationship with their patients. But their opinions about their patients and their patients' claims are far from unbiased. Even if those doctors can give neutral opinions, they can't make the final disability determination and shouldn't. Doctors would become the targets of irate disability advocate organizations and the subject of lawsuits and political scrutiny. Making final decisions about disability is the role of the government, not the medical profession.

Nevertheless, your doctor can have much influence on the ultimate outcome of your claim for disability by providing ample medical information about your impairments. It will help your case enormously if your doctor provides detailed evidence of your physical or mental medical disorders and how they limit your functioning.

MEDICAL LISTINGS

The Medical Listings on Nolo's website (see Appendix D for the link) provide details on what constitutes a disability for purposes of SSDI and SSI. If your doctor needs help determining what kind of evidence the SSA will need, the information included in the Medical Listings can help. In addition, Section D, below, includes information related to symptoms.

C. The Role of Consultative Examinations in Disability Determination

If the evidence provided by your treating doctor and other medical sources is inadequate to determine whether you are disabled, the SSA may seek additional medical information by paying for you to visit a doctor for a "consultative examination" (CE).

1. When Are Consultative Examinations Used?

A significant percentage of disability claims involve the use of CEs. The SSA spends many millions of dollars on CEs every year.

The SSA must order a large number of CEs for several reasons:

- Many claimants don't have treating doctors.
- Medical records from treating doctors may be too old.
- Claimants have complaints they have never mentioned to their treating doctors.
- Some treating doctors refuse to provide records.
- Some treating doctors' records aren't useful for disability determination.

2. Who Performs Consultative Examinations?

If your treating doctor has the necessary skills, the SSA prefers that physician to administer the CE. But some doctors are not willing to administer CEs to their own patients on behalf of the SSA. That's because it could strain relations between the doctor and patient if the SSA denies a disability claim based on the CE. In that situation, an independent doctor, called a consultative examiner, will perform the exam.

3. When an Independent Doctor Performs the Consultative Examination

If your treating doctor refuses to administer the CE, the SSA will arrange it with an independent doctor.

Even if your doctor is willing to administer your CE, the SSA can send you to a different CE doctor if any of the following is true:

- Your doctor does not have the equipment to provide the specific data needed.
- Conflicts or inconsistencies in your medical file will not be resolved by using your doctor.
- You prefer that someone other than your doctor administer the CE and you have a good reason for wanting it—for example, you don't want to compromise your relationship with your doctor.
- The SSA has prior experience with your doctor and does not believe that this individual will conduct a proper CE. This might happen, for example, if the DDS knows from past experience that your treating doctor does a poor job in conducting CEs. In other instances, treating doctors do adequate CE examinations, but are so slow sending the results to the DDS that a case can be held up for many unnecessary months.

4. Who Serves as Independent Consultative Examiners?

All consultative examiners used by the SSA are acceptable medical sources (see Section A, above) in private practice. For example, the SSA may have your hearing tested by an audiologist. (An audiologist's report may be all that's needed in some cases. However, the SSA will always want to know what disorder is causing a hearing loss, and that may require examination by a ENT medical doctor, if such exam is not already in the claimant's file.) On the other

hand, the SSA will never send you to a chiropractor, naturopath, herbalist, or other alternative healer for an examination.

Consultative Examiners Versus Medical Consultants

Doctors who do CEs for the SSA are not the same as DDS medical consultants. This can be confusing, because CE doctors may also work as medical consultants for the DDS. When they are performing work for the DDS, they are called "DDS medical consultants."

Here is the difference: A CE doctor examines a claimant and sends a report to the SSA with an opinion on what a claimant can do, given the claimant's medical condition. CEs do not necessarily have the training or authority to make a medical disability determination.

On the other hand, DDS medical consultants do not actually examine claimants but do have the authority to make disability determinations based on the special training by the SSA/DDS that they must undergo before being allowed to make decisions, as well as ongoing training they receive.

---

5. Who Pays for the Consultative Examination?

The SSA pays for all CE examinations and reports—even if your own treating doctor administers the CE.

6. Contents of a CE Report

A complete CE is one in which the doctor administers all the elements of a standard examination required for the applicable medical condition. If you undergo a complete CE, the doctor's report should include the following information:

- your chief complaints
- a detailed history of the chief complaints
- details of important findings, based on your history, examination, and laboratory tests (such as blood tests and X-rays), as related to your main complaints. This should include abnormalities that you do have (positive findings such as swollen joints in physical disorders or presence of delusions in mental disorders), as well as abnormalities that could have but didn't show up during your exam (negative findings). (Abnormalities found during a physical exam or with laboratory testing should also be reported, even if you didn't know of them or complain of them.)
- the results of laboratory and other tests (such as X-rays or blood tests) performed according to the Listing of Impairments. (See Chapter 7 and Parts 1 through 14 of the Medical Listings on Nolo's website.)
- the diagnosis and prognosis for your impairments, and
- a statement about what you can do despite your impairments; this is the same kind of information that the SSA requests from your treating doctor,

except that your treating doctor's opinion generally carries more weight than an independent doctor's.

Consultative examination doctors cannot decide whether or not you qualify for disability. Their assessments can be useful but usually do not carry the weight of your treating doctor's medical assessments supported by evidence.

Many CEs are not complete physical or mental examinations but are specific tests, such as breathing tests or X-rays. For example, many claimants who complain of shortness of breath caused by lung damage from cigarette smoking are sent for breathing tests only; their treating doctor or a prior CE already provided the necessary physical examination data. Many claimants are sent for blood tests required by the Listing of Impairments, or that are otherwise necessary to determine a disability. X-rays are another kind of CE frequently performed without a full examination.

A CE doctor who administers only a specific test is not expected to provide an opinion regarding what you can do given your impairments.

7. Your Protections in a Consultative Examination

It is the SSA's responsibility to make sure that consultative examiners provide professional and reasonable care. Examining rooms should be clean and adequately equipped, and you should be treated with courtesy. The DDS is supposed to ask you questions about your CE—how long you had to wait, whether you were treated with courtesy, how long the examination took, and whether it seemed complete. If you have a complaint about your CE experience and have not been asked about it by the DDS, call the public relations department at the DDS to voice your concern.

The SSA tries to screen out doctors who violate adequate standards for a CE or who provide incomplete or repeatedly inaccurate reports. Doctors may take shortcuts with a CE because the SSA doesn't pay much for them and doctors are often in a hurry. A nurse can record a part of your history, as long as the doctor reads what the nurse wrote and reviews the important parts with you. But no one other than a doctor (or another acceptable medical source, like a nurse practitioner or advanced practice nurse) should examine you.

The SSA provides CE doctors with detailed instructions regarding the requirements for an adequate and complete examination. These standards are generally accepted by the medical profession as needed for the competent examination of any patient in the specialty concerned.

> **EXAMPLE:** You are sent to an arthritis specialist (rheumatologist) because you complained of joint and back pains. The doctor has a nurse take your history and spends ten minutes with you, looking briefly at some of your joints. The doctor does not test how well the joints move or how well you can walk. This inadequate exam will be unacceptable to the SSA.

8. If the Consultative Examination Is Inadequate

If you did not receive an adequate consultative examination—particularly if the doctor did not examine you about your complaint—contact the DDS examiner who arranged it. Call, but also send your complaint in writing to be added to your SSA file.

If you have appealed your denial of disability and are at the administrative hearing level, complain to the administrative law judge. Tell the DDS examiner or judge about the inadequate examination and ask to be sent to someone who will examine you properly. If your complaint is not taken seriously, write to the DDS public relations department and the DDS director. If that doesn't work, call the SSA's hotline number (800-772-1213) and ask for assistance.

D. Evidence of Symptoms

The SSA will investigate many areas of your life and the effect of symptoms—such as pain, shortness of breath, or fatigue—on your ability to function.

1. Evidence Related to Symptoms

Evidence of your symptoms will include the following kinds of information provided by your treating doctor and other sources:

- your daily activities—what you do during a typical day. Especially important is how these "activities of daily living" (called ADLs in SSA lingo) are affected by your pain and other symptoms.

- the location, duration, frequency, and intensity of the pain or other symptoms—where you have pain or other symptoms, how long the symptoms last, how often the symptoms occur, and the severity of the symptoms
- precipitating and aggravating factors—what activities or other factors are known to cause or exacerbate your symptoms
- the type, dosage, effectiveness, and side effects of any medication—whether prescribed or purchased over the counter, the dosage used, whether or not the medication helps pain or other symptoms, and the type and severity of any side effects. Medications include herbal or other alternative medicine remedies. Be sure to let your treating doctor know if you are taking anything he or she hasn't prescribed.
- treatments, other than medications, for the relief of pain or other symptoms —including things like hydrotherapy, music therapy, relaxation therapy, biofeedback, hypnosis, massage, physical therapy, transcutaneous electrical nerve stimulators, and meditation
- any measures you use or have used to relieve pain or other symptoms— information that may offer the SSA insight into the nature and severity of your condition

- other factors concerning your functional limitations due to pain or other symptoms.

> **CAUTION**
>
> **If you reveal to the SSA that you use marijuana, even if it is clearly for medical reasons, the SSA might be compelled by federal law to consider it a drug abuse or alcoholism (DAA) problem that could affect the outcome of your disability determination.** (DAA problems are discussed in Chapter 11, Section F.)

2. The SSA Evaluation of Symptoms

The SSA makes its determinations based on your individual symptoms, not a general perception. For instance, rarely would the SSA give any weight to your allegation of headaches, because in most people, headaches are not frequent enough or severe enough to prevent work. But some people have severe, frequent migraine headaches that last hours or even days at a time, and which do not respond to treatment by doctors. It is rare to see headaches this severe, but if you have them, the SSA can use them to allow disability benefits in your individual case. In the case of a disorder like headaches, where a physical examination shows very little abnormality, it is particularly critical that your treating doctor has good records about the severity, duration, and frequency of the headaches. These records will provide credibility to your allegation that the headaches are disabling.

Just because you say you have certain symptoms, you will not automatically be granted disability. Although the SSA must give consideration to your individual symptoms, the SSA is not obligated to believe that you have the symptoms you say you have or to believe that they are as severe as you say they are. Remember—an acceptable medical source must provide objective evidence that reasonably supports the severity of the symptoms you allege.

What you do regarding your symptoms is much more important than what you say. If you have back pain and have frequently seen doctors in an attempt to improve the pain, this indicates that you might really have severe back pain. But your statement about severe pain becomes less believable when you haven't seen a doctor. And if you have seen an acceptable medical source, then that doctor's evaluation and treatment are very important.

EXAMPLE 1: You have back pain. You have had multiple back surgeries to address what your doctor believes to be the abnormalities that cause the problem. But the pain has continued. Your doctor has given you injections of steroids in an attempt to block pain and you have used a TENS electrical stimulator unit for pain. You take pills for pain. When you say that you are highly restricted in what you can do because of pain, the SSA should give considerable weight to your statements.

EXAMPLE 2: You have back pain. But you've never had surgery, have no abnormalities on physical examination, and have normal X-rays of your back. When you say you can't do anything because of back pain, the SSA is not likely to believe you.

Almost all people who apply for disability have pain or other symptom complaints, such as dizziness, weakness, fatigue, nervousness, or shortness of breath. Any DDS or SSA medical consultant or administrative law judge who does not ask about your symptoms or who does not take them into account is in violation of federal regulations.

3. The SSA Evaluation of Pain

Pain and other symptoms often go to the heart of the restrictions on your activities of daily living. As explained in Chapter 2, you must complete forms describing what you do during an average day and what you cannot do.

In back pain cases, it is important to measure how long you can sit and stand in one continuous period. Inability to sit or stand very long can be very critical to the outcome of your claim, if the SSA believes your symptoms. If your doctor writes the SSA about your back pain, make sure the report remarks on your ability to lift, bend, and stoop. Your doctor should also state an opinion as to how long you can stand and sit in one continuous period, as well as the total time you can sit and stand during a typical workday.

4. If Physical Evidence Does Not Support Your Claim of Pain

If you allege that you have severe restrictions from pain, but no doctor (your own or a CE doctor) can find any reasonable physical basis for it, the SSA is likely to consider the possibility that you have a mental disorder of some kind.

> EXAMPLE: You apply for disability, and the evidence indicates there is very little wrong with you physically. But you say you must use crutches to walk, or even use a wheelchair, and have been living that way for some time. This suggests a mental disorder, and the SSA is likely to ask you to go to a mental examination by a clinical psychologist or psychiatrist.

In obvious cases of malingering (pretending an illness), the SSA would not request a mental examination. In fact, now and then a claimant will rent a wheelchair or crutches just for a CE, and is then seen by the doctor walking normally to a car after the exam. Most CE doctors can tell when there is no medical reason for a wheelchair, crutches, or walker. In other words, attempted fraud when no condition exists is not likely to be successful. But claimants who have significant impairments may sometimes successfully exaggerate the severity of their conditions. Such dishonesty is difficult to detect, but is sometimes exposed when the SSA obtains treating doctor records showing less severity.

E. Other Evidence

Information from sources other than your treating physician and any consultative examiner might help show the extent to which your impairments affect your ability to function. Other sources include public and private social welfare agencies, teachers, day care providers, social workers, family members, other relatives, clergy, friends, employers, and other practitioners, such as physical therapists, audiologists, chiropractors, and naturopaths.

If you want evidence from these types of individuals and practitioners, ask them to write a letter to be put in your file for the DDS to review. You may also mail in the records of any practitioner yourself or give them to the SSA Field Office representative when you file your claim.

However, if the evidence contradicts the evidence of acceptable medical sources described in Section A above or does not consist of evidence generally acceptable to the medical community, the evidence will be given little weight in evaluating your claim.

F. Expedited Determinations

In response to complaints about how slowly disability claims are processed, the SSA now has two programs for serious or advanced illness, called "Compassionate Allowances" and "Terminal Illness" programs.

1. Compassionate Allowances Cases

The Social Security Administration (SSA) provides expedited processing for medical conditions that are listed in the Compassionate Allowances List (CAL). Compassionate allowance cases don't involve any special criteria for qualifying for disability benefits. Rather, CAL cases are those involving such severe impairments that they would always satisfy one of the SSA's disability listings.

CAL cases are selected for fast processing through a DDS based solely on the allegations of a claimant or parent of a child claimant. If the allegations fit the SSA's predictive model that the claim will result in an approval with minimal objective information necessary (such as a positive biopsy for esophageal cancer), the claim will qualify for CAL treatment.

The evidence the DDS needs is truly minimal—just enough information to establish the correct diagnosis. The type of information you need to provide for a CAL case depends on the nature of your condition. For example, most CAL cases involve cancer. If you have leukemia or another form of cancer, the most important thing is the biopsy report. Along with a hospital discharge summary or letter from your doctor, that would be sufficient evidence.

However, hospitals or treating doctors may require weeks or months to respond to a DDS request for basic medical records. Therefore, you can speed up processing of your claim by submitting basic medical information along with your application, or sending it to the disability examiner at DDS yourself.

Because minimal objective information is required—proof of the medical condition is sufficient to assume disability—these cases can be allowed in much less time. That is the "compassion" component: SSA gives them priority, so that a CAL case is decided in a matter of days rather than months. In that sense, these cases are similar to Quick Disability Determination (QDD) cases (see Chapter 6). However, unlike a QDD claim, a medical consultant is needed to medically assess and sign a CAL case before approval or denial.

Here is a complete list of CAL impairments:
- Acute Leukemia
- Adrenal Cancer—with distant metastases or inoperable, unresectable, or recurrent
- Adult Non-Hodgkin Lymphoma
- Adult Onset Huntington Disease
- Aicardi-Goutieres Syndrome
- Alexander Disease (ALX)—Neonatal and Infantile
- Allan-Herndon-Dudley Syndrome
- Alobar Holoprosencephaly
- Alpers Disease
- Alpha Mannosidosis—Type II and III
- ALS/Parkinsonism Dementia Complex
- Alstrom Syndrome
- Alveolar Soft Part Sarcoma
- Amegakaryocytic Thrombocytopenia
- Amyotrophic Lateral Sclerosis (ALS)
- Anaplastic Adrenal Cancer—with distant metastases or inoperable, unresectable, or recurrent

- Angelman Syndrome
- Angiosarcoma
- Aortic Atresia
- Aplastic Anemia
- Astrocytoma—Grades III and IV
- Ataxia Telangiectasia
- Atypical Teratoid/Rhabdoid Tumor
- Batten Disease
- Beta Thalassemia Major
- Bilateral Optic Atrophy—Infantile
- Bilateral Retinoblastoma
- Bladder Cancer—with distant metastases or inoperable or unresectable
- Breast Cancer—with distant metastases or inoperable or unresectable
- CACH—Vanishing White Matter Disease, Infantile and Childhood Onset Forms
- Canavan Disease (CD)
- Carcinoma of Unknown Primary Site
- Caudal Regression Syndrome—Types III and IV
- CDKL5 Deficiency Disorder
- Cerebro Oculo Facio Skeletal (COFS) Syndrome
- Cerebrotendinous Xanthomatosis
- Child Neuroblastoma—with distant metastases or recurrent
- Child Non-Hodgkin Lymphoma—recurrent
- Child T-Cell Lymphoblastic Lymphoma
- Chondrosarcoma—with multimodal therapy
- Chronic Idiopathic Intestinal Pseudo Obstruction
- Chronic Myelogenous Leukemia (CML)—Blast Phase

- Coffin-Lowry Syndrome
- Congenital Lymphedema
- Congenital Myotonic Dystrophy
- Cornelia de Lange Syndrome
- Corticobasal Degeneration
- Creutzfeldt-Jakob Disease (CJD)—Adult
- Cri du Chat Syndrome
- Degos Disease—Systemic
- DeSanctis Cacchione Syndrome
- Dravet Syndrome
- Early-Onset Alzheimer's Disease
- Edwards Syndrome (Trisomy 18)
- Eisenmenger Syndrome
- Endometrial Stromal Sarcoma
- Endomyocardial Fibrosis
- Ependymoblastoma (Child Brain Tumor)
- Erdheim Chester Disease
- Esophageal Cancer
- Esthesioneuroblastoma
- Ewing Sarcoma
- Farber's Disease (FD)—Infantile
- Fatal Familial Insomnia
- Fibrolamellar Cancer
- Fibrodysplasia Ossificans Progressiva
- Follicular Dendritic Cell Sarcoma—metastatic or recurrent
- Friedreichs Ataxia (FRDA)
- Frontotemporal Dementia (FTD), Picks Disease—Type A—Adult
- Fryns Syndrome
- Fucosidosis—Type 1
- Fukuyama Congenital Muscular Dystrophy
- Fulminant Giant Cell Myocarditis
- Galactosialidosis—Early and Late Infantile Types
- Gallbladder Cancer

- Gaucher Disease (GD)—Type 2
- Giant Axonal Neuropathy
- Glioblastoma Multiforme (Adult Brain Tumor)
- Glioma Grades III and IV
- Glutaric Acidemia (neonatal)
- Head and Neck Cancers—with distant metastasis or inoperable or unresectable
- Heart Transplant Graft Failure
- Heart Transplant Wait List—1A/1B
- Hemophagocytic Lymphohistiocytosis (HLH)—Familial Type
- Hepatoblastoma
- Hepatopulmonary Syndrome
- Hepatorenal Syndrome
- Histiocytosis Syndrome
- Hoyeaal-Hreidarsson Syndrome
- Hutchinson-Gilford Progeria Syndrome
- Hydranencephaly
- Hypocomplementemic Urticarial Vasculitis Syndrome
- Hypophosphatasia Perinatal (Lethal) and Infantile Onset Types
- Hypoplastic Left Heart Syndrome
- I Cell Disease
- Idiopathic Pulmonary Fibrosis
- Intracranial Hemangiopericytoma
- Infantile Free Sialic Acid Storage Disease
- Infantile Neuroaxonal Dystrophy (INAD)
- Infantile Neuronal Ceroid Lipofuscinoses
- Inflammatory Breast Cancer (IBC)
- Intracranial Hemangiopericytoma
- Jervell and Lange-Nielsen Syndrome
- Joubert Syndrome
- Junctional Epidermolysis Bullosa—Lethal Type
- Juvenile Onset Huntington Disease

- Kidney Cancer—inoperable or unresectable
- Kleefstra Syndrome
- Krabbe Disease (KD)—Infantile
- Kufs Disease—Type A and B
- Large Intestine Cancer—with distant metastasis or inoperable, unresectable, or recurrent
- Late Infantile Neuronal Ceroid Lipofuscinoses
- Left Ventricular Assist Device (LVAD) Recipient
- Leigh's Disease
- Leiomyosarcoma
- Leptomeningeal Carcinomatosis
- Lesch-Nyhan Syndrome (LNS)
- Lewy Body Dementia
- Liposarcoma—metastatic or recurrent
- Lissencephaly
- Liver Cancer
- Lowe Syndrome
- Lymphomatoid Granulomatosis—Grade III
- Malignant Brain Stem Gliomas—Childhood
- Malignant Ectomesenchymoma
- Malignant Gastrointestinal Stromal Tumor
- Malignant Germ Cell Tumor
- Malignant Melanoma—with metastases
- Megacystis Microcolon Intestinal Hypoperistalsis Syndrome
- Megalencephaly Capillary Malformation Syndrome
- Malignant Multiple Sclerosis
- Malignant Renal Rhabdoid Tumor
- Mantle Cell Lymphoma (MCL)

- Maple Syrup Urine Disease
- Marshall-Smith Syndrome
- Mastocytosis—Type IV
- MECP2 Duplication Syndrome
- Medulloblastoma—with metastases
- Menkes Disease—Classic or Infantile Onset Form
- Merkel Cell Carcinoma—with metastases
- Merosin Deficient Congenital Muscular Dystrophy
- Metachromatic Leukodystrophy (MLD)—Late Infantile
- Mitral Valve Atresia
- Mixed Dementias
- MPS I, formerly known as Hurler Syndrome
- MPS II, formerly known as Hunter Syndrome
- MPS III, formerly known as Sanfilippo Syndrome
- Mucosal Malignant Melanoma
- Multicentric Castleman Disease
- Multiple System Atrophy
- Myoclonic Epilepsy with Ragged Red Fibers Syndrome
- Neonatal Adrenoleukodystrophy
- Nephrogenic Systemic Fibrosis
- Neurodegeneration with Brain Iron Accumulation—Types 1 and 2
- NFU-1 Mitochondrial Disease
- Niemann-Pick Disease (NPD)—Type A
- Niemann-Pick Disease—Type C
- Nonketotic Hyperglycinemia
- Non-Small-Cell Lung Cancer—with metastases to or beyond the hilar nodes or inoperable, unresectable, or recurrent
- Obliterative Bronchiolitis
- Ohtahara Syndrome
- Oligodendroglioma Brain Tumor— Grade III
- Ornithine Transcarbamylase (OTC) Deficiency
- Orthochromatic Leukodystrophy with Pigmented Glia
- Osteogenesis Imperfecta (OI)—Type II
- Osteosarcoma, formerly known as Bone Cancer—with distant metastases or inoperable or unresectable
- Ovarian Cancer—with distant metastases or inoperable or unresectable
- Pallister-Killian Syndrome
- Pancreatic Cancer
- Paraneoplastic Pemphigus
- Patau Syndrome (Trisomy 13)
- Pearson Syndrome
- Pelizaeus-Merzbacher Disease— Classic Form
- Pelizaeus-Merzbacher Disease— Connatal Form
- Peripheral Nerve Cancer—metastatic or recurrent
- Peritoneal Mesothelioma
- Peritoneal Mucinous Carcinomatosis
- Perry Syndrome
- Phelan-McDermid Syndrome
- Pitt-Hopkins Syndrome
- Pleural Mesothelioma
- Pompe Disease—Infantile
- Primary Cardiac Amyloidosis
- Primary Central Nervous System Lymphoma
- Primary Effusion Lymphoma
- Primary Peritoneal Cancer

- Primary Progressive Aphasia
- Progressive Bulbar Palsy
- Progressive Multifocal Leukoencepha-lopathy
- Progressive Supranuclear Palsy
- Prostate Cancer—Hormone Refractory Disease—or with visceral metastases
- Pulmonary Atresia
- Pulmonary Kaposi Sarcoma
- Retinopathy of Prematurity—Stage V
- Rett (RTT) Syndrome
- Revesz Syndrome
- Rhabdomyosarcoma
- Rhizomelic Chondrodysplasia Punctata
- Richter Syndrome
- Roberts Syndrome
- Salivary Tumors
- Sandhoff Disease
- Schindler Disease—Type 1
- Seckel Syndrome
- Severe Combined Immunodeficiency —Childhood
- Single Ventricle
- Sinonasal Cancer
- Sjogren-Larsson Syndrome
- Small Cell Cancer (of the Large Intestine, Ovary, Prostate, Thymus, or Uterus)
- Small Cell Lung Cancer
- Small Intestine Cancer—with distant metastases or inoperable, unresectable, or recurrent
- Smith Lemli Opitz Syndrome
- Soft Tissue Sarcoma—with distant metastases or recurrent
- Spinal Muscular Atrophy (SMA)— Types 0 and 1
- Spinal Nerve Root Cancer—metastatic or recurrent
- Spinocerebellar Ataxia
- Stiff Person Syndrome
- Stomach Cancer—with distant metastases or inoperable, unresectable, or recurrent
- Subacute Sclerosing Panencephalitis
- Superficial Siderosis of the Central Nervous System
- Tabes Dorsalis
- Tay Sachs Disease—Infantile Type
- Tetrasomy 18p
- Thanatophoric Dysplasia—Type 1
- Thyroid Cancer (anaplastic)
- Transplant Coronary Artery Vasculopathy
- Tricuspid Atresia
- Ullrich Congenital Muscular Dystrophy
- Ureter Cancer—with distant metastases or inoperable, unresectable, or recurrent
- Usher Syndrome—Type I
- Walker Warburg Syndrome
- Wolf-Hirschhorn Syndrome
- Wolman Disease
- X-Linked Lymphoproliferative Disease
- X-Linked Myotubular Myopathy
- Xeroderma Pigmentosum
- Zellweger Syndrome

Compassionate allowances apply to both SSDI and SSI claims. The five-month waiting period for SSDI claims is not waived by having a compassionate allowance. The waiting period is established by federal law and cannot be reversed by SSA's compassionate allowance initiative.

2. Terminal Illness Cases

The Social Security Administration (SSA) expedites disability decisions for applicants with terminal illnesses through its "terminal illness" (TERI) program. Terminal illness cases are those that are expected to result in death; the DDS is expected to handle these cases quickly and with sensitivity to the claimant's condition.

SSA and the DDS are alerted to possible TERI cases by any of the following situations:

- An allegation (e.g., from the claimant, a friend, family member, doctor, or other medical source) is made that the illness is terminal.
- An allegation or diagnosis is made of amyotrophic lateral sclerosis (ALS), known as Lou Gehrig's Disease.
- An allegation or diagnosis is made of acquired immune deficiency syndrome or acquired immunodeficiency syndrome (AIDS).
- The claimant is receiving inpatient hospice care or is receiving home hospice care; e.g., in-home counseling or nursing care.

Some examples of TERI cases include, but are not limited to, the following:

- chronic dependence on a cardio-pulmonary life-sustaining device
- awaiting a heart, heart/lung, lung, liver, or bone marrow transplant (excludes kidney and corneal transplants)
- chronic pulmonary or heart failure requiring continuous home oxygen and an inability to care for personal needs

- any malignant neoplasm (cancer) that is:
  - metastatic (has spread)
  - defined as Stage IV
  - persistent or recurrent following initial therapy, or
  - inoperable or unresectable
- an allegation or diagnosis of:
  - cancer of the esophagus
  - cancer of the liver
  - cancer of the pancreas
  - cancer of the gallbladder
  - mesothelioma
  - small-cell or oat-cell lung cancer
  - cancer of the brain, or
  - acute myelogenous leukemia (AML) or acute lymphocytic leukemia (ALL)
- comatose for 30 days or more, or
- newborn with a lethal genetic or congenital defect.

If your claim fits the CAL list or you think it may be a TERI case, you should tell SSA that when you first apply for benefits. That way, it will be expedited from the very start.

Note that QDD (see Chapter 6) and CAL cases (see above) do not necessarily imply terminal illness, although they could involve such a prognosis. Like a CAL case, a medical consultant is required to make a TERI determination, and some CAL cases are also TERI cases.

Note that if an SSA Field Office classifies a claim as a TERI claim, the DDS has the authority to remove that classification if the DDS finds that the medical evidence does not justify it. Unfortunately, the SSA's operating guidelines do not require the

DDS to use a medical consultant to remove TERI status. Of course, if the issue is merely something like a typographic error such as entering "ALS" (amyotrophic lateral sclerosis) instead of an intended "ACL" (anterior cruciate ligament) tear, it makes sense that a doctor isn't required to remove a TERI classification because the error doesn't require medical knowledge. However, the SSA says, in an example, that an examiner could remove the TERI classification when "the claimant's neoplastic disease is responding to multimodal therapy." One would think that only a medical doctor would be qualified to determine whether there is meaningful improvement in cancer, but the SSA does not require a doctor to make this decision.

3. Wounded Warriors

The SSA processes "military casualty/ wounded warrior" (MC/WW) cases under expedited procedures similar to TERI (but does not classify them as TERI cases without the indication of terminal illness). If you are a wounded veteran or active duty servicemember who became disabled while on active duty, it is helpful to let the SSA know you have that MC/WW status because wounded warrior cases are evaluated more quickly than might otherwise be the case. The SSA's processing of claims involving military or former military personnel can be complex; for example, military wages alone may not determine whether a servicemember is doing substantial gainful activity, because servicemembers usually continue to receive full military pay even if they are too sick or injured to work.

If you are a MC/WW person applying for Social Security disability, you should take copies of all Department of Defense (DOD) Forms DD 214 (DD Form 214) to the Field Office where you apply for disability. The DDS needs all the information possible to determine the onset date of your disability and possible closed periods of disability.

If you apply for disability online, you should still make sure these forms reach your disability examiner once you are informed of who it is and how to contact that person. However, you should not delay applying for disability to obtain these documents from DoD. The Field Office can forward them to your disability examiner later if you do not do so directly yourself. Since these forms contain dates of active duty and other useful information in disability adjudication, it is in your best interest to make sure they are submitted. The SSA has more information for wounded warriors on its website, including a brochure called "Disability Benefits for Wounded Warriors."

Who Decides Your Claim?

After the Social Security Administration Field Office finds that you meet the nonmedical eligibility requirements for disability benefits, your file is sent to the state agency responsible for making a decision on your application. This agency is known as the Disability Determination Services, or DDS. Your file will contain your application, the few administrative documents you completed at the SSA Field Office, and copies of any medical records or other relevant papers you provided to the SSA when you applied.

A. DDS Basics

DDS offices are run by each state, but they are federally funded and must follow the federal laws and regulations. Each DDS has a computer system connected to the SSA federal computers in Baltimore and to the local SSA Field Offices. These computers allow the DDS and the SSA to quickly communicate.

1. Types of Claims Handled by DDS

The DDS handles several types of disability claims, including:

- a new application, called an "initial claim"
- a "reconsideration claim," if you are turned down
- a "second initial claim"—in fact, you can file as many initial claims as you want, and

- "continuing disability reviews" (CDRs), in which the DDS periodically reviews the files of disability recipients to see if their health has improved.

2. Contacting Your DDS

Your DDS will have a toll-free telephone number you can use from anywhere in your state. If you don't have this number, check the government section of your phone book, call the SSA Field Office where you made your application, call the general number for the SSA, 800-772-1213, or check the SSA website at www.ssa.gov.

3. When the Outcome of a Claim Is Uncertain

If you apply for disability when you are acutely sick or hurt and the outcome of your treatment is not clear, the DDS may "diary" your claim. This means that the DDS holds your file to see how your illness or injury progresses to see if you will have an ongoing or permanent disability. Diaries usually last up to three months but can sometimes last as many as six. Heart-impairment claims often require diaries because claimants apply for disability soon after they've had a heart attack or heart surgery, and the outcome of their treatment is unknown.

Other claimants who might need a diary include people who apply soon after incurring multiple serious fractures in an automobile wreck or soon after incurring a brain injury.

How Claims Examiners Work

Claims examiners sometimes are taught about basic medical principles by the DDS medical consultants. This is to help them better understand the medical issues involved in claims but does not qualify them to make determinations about the medical severity of your impairments. Unfortunately, this doesn't stop some examiners from trying. Under current regulations, however, examiners cannot legally make medical determinations.

As might be expected, claims examiners vary greatly in their intelligence and motivation. Some meticulously consider and document every detail. Others care only about processing claims as fast as they can with the least amount of work.

DDS offices have internal quality-assurance reviews that are supposed to catch poor work. Examiners have supervisors who are supposed to monitor their work. But supervisors also vary in how conscientious they are and in their willingness to make sure their examiners are doing good work. In addition, a DDS office may not conduct the number of internal quality-assurance reviews called for. This raises the likelihood of claims being done incorrectly and escaping the agency undetected.

If a DDS office is understaffed and underfunded, the number of cases an examiner has to handle increases. If your examiner has a caseload in the hundreds, the probability of errors increases greatly.

The more you know about the disability determination process, the more likely you will be able to spot an examiner who improperly handles your claim or an issue in your file that was decided wrongly.

Here are some hints. Watch out if:

- You know a decision was made without sufficient medical information. For example, the DDS denies your claim for a vision problem without requesting and reviewing your treating doctor's records or sending you for a consultative examination of your eyes. It is illegal for a DDS office to ignore all of your medical allegations.

- The examiner or a supervisor appears evasive or unable to answer your questions on the telephone.

- An examiner or a supervisor promises to call you back to answer a question and fails to do so.

- The examiner or a supervisor says there is no need to take your claim to a DDS medical consultant for an evaluation of your medical records, or won't tell you whether a doctor will be asked to look at your records. It is a violation of federal regulations for an examiner to make a medical determination of disability or to determine your residual functional capacity (see Chapter 8). But it happens.

B. DDS Claims Examiners

When the DDS receives your file, it assigns a disability claims examiner to your case. The claims examiner's job is to obtain the medical records listed on your application, maintain contact with you, and do other administrative work as necessary (discussed below). Claims examiners are your point of contact with the DDS.

There are various types of claims examiners: those who handle initial claims, those who do reconsideration claims, those in the quality-assurance department who review the work of other examiners, and those who evaluate people already receiving benefits to see if they still qualify.

It's important that you understand the job of the claims examiner and the kinds of work pressure the claims examiners are under. Examiners are responsible for evaluating the nonmedical aspects of all claims—other than nonmedical eligibility issues that were already handled by the SSA Field Office. The number of nonmedical issues potentially involved in a claim is so large that it is impossible to list them here. But they do include:

- deciding the date you actually stopped work for disability purposes
- determining your vocational factors, including age, education, and work experience
- arranging for consultative examinations and coordinating your attendance

- contacting your treating sources for your medical records, and
- asking DDS medical consultants for advice on the nature and severity of medical impairments, as well as on what kind of additional medical evidence is needed to decide your claim.

Examiners have difficulty keeping up with the endless, changing rules. They refer to a huge, multivolume publication called the "Program Operations Manual System" (POMS). If the POMS does not have the answer to a question, the examiners ask their immediate supervisors, who can ask higher supervisors. If the DDS personnel don't know the answer, they send the question to the SSA Regional Office. You can access the POMS yourself online at www.SSA.gov, but you should be careful, as some sections are not up to date, it is loaded with bureaucratic terms, and it can be very complex.

C. DDS Organization

DDS offices have administrative personnel besides claims examiners. The other administrative personnel you might encounter include secretaries and vocational analysts. "Vocational analysts" are specially trained examiners who assess your ability to work based on the severity of your medical impairments, your work experience, and your education. Vocational analysts are often assistant supervisors of a group of examiners.

"Claims examiners" are usually arranged into units, each with a supervisor and perhaps an assistant supervisor. The supervisors in turn answer to their supervisor—usually an operations manager, quality-assurance manager, or assistant director. The position titles may vary, but the general idea is that there is a bureaucracy with many levels of authority.

You would ordinarily meet only your claims examiner and, in many cases, even that contact would be limited to the telephone. A vocational analyst (see below) could also call you to discuss specific issues about the work you did or your education. You can also demand to speak to an examiner's immediate supervisor. You would not routinely come into contact with higher-level personnel, but it is possible. Claimants who are angry about their treatment and not satisfied by the supervisor could be referred to an assistant director. Other claimants don't wait for referral up through the chain of command—they call the DDS director on their own initiative.

The DDS director may be appointed by a state governor, which could mean frequent turnover. The agency director sets the tone of the agency. How a particular agency runs, therefore, depends on the director's integrity, intelligence, dedication, managerial ability, motivation, and desire to provide good public service. Agency directors do not have the legal authority to make the medical part of disability determinations—only an SSA medical consultant or disability hearing officer (or administrative law judge) can do that.

D. Medical Consultants

"Medical consultants" are the people who ultimately review the medical aspect of your claim for disability benefits. A medical consultant (MC) must be a licensed medical doctor, osteopath, or psychologist with a Ph.D. If you apply for disability based on physical impairments, a medical doctor or osteopath will evaluate your file.

If you apply for disability based on a mental impairment, a consulting psychiatrist (either a medical doctor or osteopath) or a qualified psychologist will evaluate your file.

If you apply for disability based on both a physical and a mental impairment, a consulting psychologist can evaluate only the mental impairment. A consulting medical doctor or osteopath must evaluate the nonmental impairment. The overall medical part of the determination of disability must be made by a consulting medical doctor or osteopath, unless the mental impairment alone would justify a finding of disability.

Federal law requires the SSA to have a qualified medical or psychological consultant review all initial claim applications (Public Law 114–74, 129 Stat. 584, 613, which is also known as the Bipartisan Budget Act of 2015). This law reversed the SSA's previous policy of letting disability examiners decide some claims without consulting a doctor. Note that although the law was enacted in 2015, the SSA didn't stop its policy until December 28, 2018. And it is important to understand that the 2015 law only applied to "initial" applications, not other types of evaluations, such as continuing disability claims to decide if those already receiving benefits will continue to do so. (Fortunately, the SSA has not adopted a policy of letting examiners decide such claims without professional medical input about the decision.) Also, federal law used the word "initial" without clarifying, so it is not clear if the SSA is prohibited from letting claims examiners alone decide reconsideration appeals at the DDSs. If you feel it was possible that your claim was denied because of a lack of professional medical evaluation, you could probably get it re-reviewed without filing a formal appeal (which can take a long time) by contacting the DDS director or even your governor and your federal politicians. They can ask that the DDS look at your claim again. (The author reviewed many such claims as a DDS chief medical consultant, no small number of which were reversed into allowances.)

Questions about specific cases should be directed to the local SSA Field Office or the state's disability determination agency.

1. The Medical Consultant's Job

A medical consultant's work is performed mostly at a desk, in an office. It is strictly a paper review; the consulting physician or psychologist usually has no contact with you. The work of determining whether or not you qualify for disability includes the following:

- evaluating medical evidence to determine if your impairment meets the requirements of the Listing of Impairments (see Chapter 5, Section D1)

- assessing the severity of your impairments and describing your remaining physical or mental abilities (called your "residual functional capacity," or RFC) and your limitations in abilities that are caused by the impairments (see Chapter 8)

- discussing with the DDS other ways to get medical evidence, including suggesting ways to improve communication between the DDS and treating sources. For example, the medical records department of a hospital might tell a claims examiner that it doesn't have a biopsy report showing that a claimant has cancer. The medical consultant can suggest that the examiner call the pathology department of the hospital. Or a claims examiner might not be able to get a treating doctor on the telephone to ask questions about impairments that were not covered in your doctor's medical records. A medical consultant, as a doctor, has a better chance of getting a treating doctor on the telephone. Because of time constraints, however, medical consultants do not usually talk to the treating doctors.

- evaluating medical questions asked by a claims examiner. For example, a claims examiner may need to know whether it is reasonable to award a particular SSI claimant presumptive disability. Or a claims examiner may need to know the probability of a medical condition improving in order to schedule a re-review of the file. Or a claims examiner may need to know exactly what medical records are needed. The medical consultant would answer these questions.

- reviewing requests for consultative examinations (CEs) to make sure they are necessary and will address the issue in question
- suggesting alternatives when a claimant cannot or will not attend a CE, or cannot or will not cooperate with the disability determination in other ways. For example, some claimants refuse to attend a CE, feeling that their treating doctor has the information. If the treating doctor has not provided the DDS with the information, the medical consultant can suggest that the claimant visit his or her doctor and personally obtain the records. On the other hand, for example, if the claimant won't attend a CE because she has agoraphobia—a fear of leaving her house—the medical consultant can intervene to have a consulting psychologist or psychiatrist sent to the claimant's home.
- reviewing consultative exam reports that don't give enough medical information for a disability determination and

recommending to the CE doctor ways to avoid deficient reports
- participating in the vocational rehabilitation screening and referral process, by advising whether you are medically capable of undergoing training for new job skills
- reviewing disability determinations to assure that the decision is based on medical evidence, and
- signing disability determination forms.

If a Medical Consultant Gives Medical Evidence

Medical consultants who furnish any of the medical evidence for a particular disability case (that is, act as treating doctors) should disqualify themselves from determining disability—that is, from working as a medical consultant on that case. This is not as unusual a situation as it might sound. A doctor who works as a DDS medical consultant might, for example, also see patients privately, and one of his patients might apply for disability. In that case, the doctor can provide medical information as the treating doctor but cannot act as the medical consultant for the DDS in the disability determination for that claimant. This policy protects the doctor-patient relationship and attempts to assure that the disability decision is made without any personal bias for or against the claimant.

2. Reviewing the Medical Consultant's Decision

Depending on the state, medical consultants may be employees of the DDS or consultants who charge an hourly fee. Some medical consultants work only part time, which can be a problem. The complexities of Social Security medical evaluations can rarely be fully grasped by someone who does the work only part time.

If you are unhappy with the medical consultant's decision (that is, your claim is denied for a medical reason), what you can do about it depends on how strongly you feel about the matter. If you are concerned that your application received an inappropriate medical review, ask the director of the DDS the following:

- the name and medical specialty of the doctor who reviewed your claim
- how long that doctor has worked for the DDS, and
- the average amount of time the doctor spends at the DDS per day or week.

The director should be able to answer these questions. In addition, the doctors' contracts are probably available as public records in your state's finance and administration department, because the doctors are paid for through state coffers.

If you are really concerned about the doctor who reviewed your claim, ask the DDS director to have your records reviewed by a different medical consultant—specifically, one with more experience or knowledge of your medical condition. If the SSA has already denied your claim, ask the DDS director to recall your claim and reopen it. You can make this request for any reason up to a year after you have been denied benefits. (Reopenings and revisions are discussed in Chapter 12.)

E. If Your Claim Is Granted

The DDS medical consultant approves the medical part of the determination, and the examiner approves the nonmedical portions. Both the consultant and the examiner sign the appropriate final disability determination form. The DDS then returns your file to the SSA Field Office. The SSA will complete any outstanding nonmedical paperwork, compute the benefit amount, and begin paying benefits.

The SSA is responsible for notifying you of the approval. A notice should be mailed to you between seven and ten days after the DDS decision. However, the time it actually takes for the necessary paperwork to be completed depends on workloads. Also, your claim could be slowed by months if, after the DDS decision, it is chosen for a quality review by an SSA Disability Quality Branch (DQB) located at an SSA Regional Office. You will not be told if your case has been selected for review, but you can find out by asking your DDS examiner. Still, there is nothing you can do to speed up the process if your case has been chosen for review.

The SSA Field Office sometimes makes errors in benefit computation. Chapter 13 contains information about benefit computation, but this is a complex area. If you have any question about receiving the right amount of money, don't hesitate to call your local Field Office and discuss it with them.

Remember that being found entitled to benefits doesn't necessarily mean you will get money at the same time. SSDI claimants can't get money until after a five-month waiting period, and SSI claimants can't get money until the month after they apply (see Chapter 10).

F. If Your Claim Is Denied

If the DDS denies your claim, you might want to find out the details behind that decision. This information may be important to you if you plan to appeal. The SSA keeps disability information in an "electronic folder" (EF), and much of that information is available to you. (Electronic folders are discussed in more detail in Chapter 12.)

If you get your folder, look for Form SSA-831, *Disability Determination and Transmittal*—it's usually at the front of the folder. The DDS claims examiner and the medical consultant must complete this form in every initial and reconsideration application. If you have applied more than once, your folder (also called your disability file) will contain multiple forms.

Even if the form was signed by a medical consultant, it may not have been reviewed by a doctor. To see if the medical consultant who signed the form reviewed your disability file, look for medical notes or a residual functional capacity (RFC) rating form completed by the medical consultant. If you can't find notes or an RFC form, it's quite possible that your claim was not reviewed by the medical consultant. (Children do not receive RFCs, so no such form would be expected in their disability file, but you would still expect to find the medical consultant's notes.)

If it appears that your file was not reviewed by a medical consultant, write and call the DDS director. State that your file contains no evidence that your claim was reviewed by a doctor, except for a signature on the Disability Determination and Transmittal Form. Demand that your claim be recalled and reviewed by a medical consultant. If the director won't help you, contact your senator or congressional representative, as well as your governor and local state legislator. You have a right to have your medical records reviewed by a medical consultant.

Of course, your claim may be denied whether or not it is reviewed by a DDS medical consultant. (Chapter 11 contains a discussion of the different ways claims can be denied. Chapter 12 discusses the various types of appeal available to you.)

G. DDS Corruption and Incompetence

Corruption and incompetence involving the DDS are probably the last thing on earth you want—or the SSA wants you—to think about. Still, it's possible that your claim is or will be denied for reasons unrelated to the criteria established under Social Security disability rules and regulations. This section helps you understand why corruption and incompetence might have an impact on your claim—and what you can do about it.

There are two basic reasons you should be interested in corruption and incompetence in the DDS:

- As a claimant, you may be cheated out of a fair decision on your claim.
- As a taxpayer, your money may be spent in ways other than intended.

Unfortunately, anyone engaged in corrupt activity isn't going to make it easy for you to detect—but hopefully this section will help you know what to watch out for.

1. How Corruption and Incompetence Can Influence Your Claim

Honest error and missing information can play a role in denials of deserving claimants. Unfortunately, denials may also result from corruption or incompetence. The SSA may not be aware of the corruption or incompetence in a particular DDS—or may overlook what it does know.

Here are some real-life examples of the kinds of activities that can go on.

a. Corrupt Directors

DDS directors are appointed by state governors. Some directors may be appointed by a governor with more interest in political goals than in delivering quality service. A corrupt director isn't necessarily as concerned with the overall allowance or denial of benefits as with which claims are allowed or denied. For example, a corrupt director might try to allow large numbers of claims that are politically sensitive— such as children—while keeping a medical consultant in the agency who unfairly denies large numbers of adult claimants. Typically, a director or senior level manager pressures others into doing something wrong. This hides the director's activities. A few specific instances of the practical application of corruption are given below.

Developing Illegal Policies. It is illegal for a director to manipulate the DDS's allowance rate by pressuring medical consultants and other staff to allow a specific quota of favored types of claims. It is also against the law to speed up claim processing by giving examiners authority they do not have under law—such as making medical determinations on whether impairments are not severe (slight) or qualify under the Listing of Impairments, or completing residual functional capacity (RFC) forms.

This means that medically unqualified people may have influenced your determination, such as the DDS director (see below).

Blocking Finished Claims. A corrupt DDS director can order DDS employees to hold a finished claim and not forward the decision to the SSA unless the decision is one the director wants. For example, one DDS director physically held many hundreds, if not thousands, of finished claims that were denials. Only allowances were put into the DDS computer that was connected to the SSA. The result was an artificially high allowance rate, which allowed the agency to escape criticism by certain political action groups. Unfortunately, the denials sat for months and had many claimants wondering where their claims had gone. This prevented the denied claimants from going on to a timely appeal.

Controlling the Chief Medical Consultant. The chief medical consultant (CMC), as you might guess, is the head of the medical staff at a DDS. A corrupt director can anonymously control all medical determinations by controlling the CMC. If the CMC is weak or dishonest, the director can insist that he or she approve medical policies the director favors. Again, this means a medically unqualified person (the director) may be influencing your medical determination.

For example, a CMC might agree to pressure medical consultants to sign RFC forms that were actually completed by claims examiners. In this phony assessment, medical consultants are allowed to read the files in order to give the impression that they control the medical assessment but are required to sign the RFC forms whether or not they agree with the claims examiner's opinion. Medical consultants are not allowed to change the RFCs to conform to their own medical opinions, even though they have to sign the forms as if they did so.

To make the process appear legitimate and give some cover to medical consultants, the medical consultants are told they will only be required to sign such claims if the claims examiner assures them that the examiner's medical assessment cannot affect the decision (allowance or denial) outcome of the claim. Thus, if caught, a medical consultant could make the weak argument that, "It didn't make any difference to the outcome," and people not familiar with how disability determinations are made might accept that excuse. However, federal regulations specifically require medical consultants to make the RFC determinations, and there is no legal excuse for not doing so using their own judgment. Indeed, state medical boards do not look favorably on doctors letting others use their signatures.

To make matters worse, claims examiners cannot accurately assure a medical consultant that other medical assessments than what they propose won't make any difference. Why? Because a particular

RFC can result in allowance or denial of a claim based on the vocational factors of age, education, and work experience (see Chapter 8). These vocational decisions can be subjective, and administrative law judges frequently disagree with what a claims examiner decides in regard to analyzing vocational factors. There can be erroneous denials and allowances, as well as uncertainty about the validity of medical consultant signatures, at all levels of appeal.

This kind of corruption is difficult to detect, even at higher review levels by the SSA or attorneys representing claimants, because there is nothing in the file saying that medical consultants signed an RFC they didn't agree with. If a paper RFC form was completed and the handwriting is that of the claims examiner, that is a strong hint. However, when such forms are completed on computer in a DDS, that clue is missing.

If your claim was denied based on medical ineligibility and no doctor was consulted, you should strongly insist that your claim be re-reviewed by a real doctor. Also, if you appeal such a denial, lack of professional medical review of your file is a strong argument that you were denied a fair hearing.

b. Incompetent Directors

Good administration of a DDS requires education, knowledge, skill, and experience. However, a governor might appoint an unqualified person. For example, the director might have no experience with Social Security disability or fail to have the necessary education. You should be able to find out about the director's qualifications by calling or writing the director himself, or the governor's office. It is in your best interest to know the director's qualifications and to make sure the governor knows what you think.

c. Problematic Medical Consultants

Sometimes, a file is incorrectly handled at a DDS because of medical consultants who are either not able or not willing to make medical decisions according to the SSA's rules and regulations. Some can be pressured by a DDS director to make the medical determinations that the director wants.

Lacking Ability or Judgment. Some medical consultants have serious emotional problems that can affect their ability to use the clear, rational thinking that is needed to make accurate disability determinations. Others may be affected by drug or alcohol abuse. A medical consultant with a limited knowledge of English can make mistakes in interpreting and discussing medical data.

Some consultants have specific limitations that can affect your claim. As an example, a blind medical consultant cannot evaluate the meaning and validity of medical data, such as heart tracings (EKGs), visual field charts, or breathing tests. In other words, they are unable to provide an independent evaluation of test results, as required by federal regulations for disability determination. An independent evaluation requires a medical consultant to personally examine the various graphs and tracings to make sure the test was performed correctly and that the laboratory's reported results are accurate. This requires good vision. Such data is a large part of many files—especially the files of claimants with heart or lung disease. It does no good for a blind consultant in these instances to have an aide to read to them, because the aide would not be qualified to interpret such raw medical data. A blind consultant should not make determinations in these types of claims.

Acting With Malice. Some medical consultants routinely deny claimants because of personal bias against people receiving disability. At one DDS, a medical consultant commonly denied claimants with terminal cancer, terminal heart disease, severe arthritis, and terminal lung disease. He denied about 800 claimants a year who were legally entitled to benefits. Conscientious examiners would not take serious impairments to him, for fear he would deny the claimants. Other examiners, however, were quick to give him cases in order to get a fast decision. No DDS director would terminate the medical consultant's contract because he—and those who were happy to work with him—moved along enormous numbers of cases. This DDS looked good in federal statistics—it had one of the fastest processing times in the country. This consultant's unfair reign of terror ended only when he died.

Stealing Time. Some DDS medical consultants work at other medical jobs while supposedly working at the DDS. Imagine a doctor who does telephone consulting work or takes calls from private patients while supposedly reviewing disability files. Obviously, there are many problems with this. First, the doctor is double-dipping, getting paid by the government while not working for the government. Second, the doctor has less time to review claims while lining his pockets with extra money. One of those delayed claims could be yours.

Signers. It is unfortunate, but some medical consultants are known as "signers," meaning they will sign medical assessments an administrator asks them to sign although they would otherwise have reached a different conclusion. This is fraud, but it is difficult to prove: if questioned, the administrator would deny any influence and the consultant would say the rating was their own medical opinion. An example will show how this kind of corruption works. A state governor wants to get allowance of disability benefits for someone. The governor calls the DDS director and asks that a particular person's claim be "looked at" again. This part is actually legal, but if the governor states that the person is disabled or indicates it in some other way, then the line is crossed into corruption because the agency director is under pressure to please the governor. In cases like this, the agency director would make it clear to a medical consultant that the governor thinks the person is disabled. A "signer" consultant will oblige, and this is very convenient for politicians who want to hand out favors. "Signers" are an insidious form of corruption, and no DDS will admit they exist—but they do. The SSA has no procedures for preventing this type of corruption.

d. Problematic Claims Examiners

Some claims examiners are lazy. They cut corners everywhere they can and do the minimum amount of work necessary. One DDS director lowered state performance standards so the worst examiners could keep their jobs. Other examiners might try to manipulate medical determinations by removing written medical opinions they don't like from files and then taking the claim to a different medical consultant, hoping for a different decision. Their supervisors may do the same thing. Additionally, examiners—like medical consultants—can have emotional, alcohol, drug abuse, or other problems.

e. Disregarding Federal Laws and Regulations

Federal regulations require the SSA to take the disability determination procedures away from a DDS that doesn't follow the law. It's rare, however, for the SSA to take such action. Various DDS offices around the country have been found guilty of violations such as not reviewing medical information from treating doctors and not considering a claimant's age, education, and work experience—but these violations were decided by federal courts, not by the SSA. And the punishment was minimal: Making the DDS re-review the claims. Such gross and intentional negligence can be disastrous to your claim.

f. Political Pressure and "Crazy Checks"

An SSA problem known as "crazy checks" illustrates how badly things can go wrong with the SSA's administration of its disability program.

In 1990, the U.S. Supreme Court ordered the SSA to change the way child disability claims were evaluated. Following the court's order, the SSA created new child disability regulations. Special interest groups pressured some DDS directors into seeing the new regulations as an opportunity to allow most child claims. At many DDS offices, more than 90% of child claims were granted. Directors felt secure (claimants don't complain about getting approved for benefits). Medical consultants, however— particularly those with expertise in the diagnosis and treatment of child disorders— felt otherwise. Some resigned their jobs. Others, especially those who tried to expose the problem, were terminated.

The DDS offices that continued objective evaluations of child claims had only a modest increase in the percentage of child claims allowed. Certain special interest groups labeled their states "aberrant." The SSA was pressured into sending the aberrant state list to all DDS offices; many offices were terrified at seeing their state on the list. Being on the list subjected every DDS office in that state to having more claims reviewed by the SSA's Regional Offices and to receiving negative news media coverage. To avoid being on the aberrant state list, a DDS had to grant an extremely high percentage of child claims.

Word got around to parents receiving SSI that it was easy to get a "crazy check" for their child, and SSI child applications increased. DDS offices granted these applications more and more for minor disorders.

Allowance awards (disability approvals) were so out of hand that the U.S. General Accounting Office, state legislatures, and many newspapers investigated why nondisabled children were receiving benefits. At first, the SSA denied that there was a problem. That didn't work, so the SSA tried to quiet criticism by doing its own studies that supported the SSA position. That didn't work either. Finally, the SSA claimed that the excessive allowances were caused by misunderstandings in the DDS offices.

Congress wasn't impressed and amended the law, changing the definition of child disability. Large numbers of nondisabled children were removed from the benefit rolls, as the SSA was forced to undo its mistakes.

Special interest groups and newspaper articles again attacked the SSA for removing children from the disability rolls. To escape

being called nasty and mean, the SSA again claimed it was all a misunderstanding by the DDS offices. The SSA held national retraining classes for DDS medical consultants and examiners. After these sessions, thousands of cases were sent back to the DDS offices for re-review as often as was necessary until benefits were granted.

2. What You Can Do About Corruption and Incompetence

Your goal is to get a fair decision on your disability claim, not to get into a personal conflict with DDS personnel or to accuse them of malfeasance. But you have the right to have an intelligent, capable, and unbiased person review your claim. So here is how to minimize the effect of these problems on your claim.

Take Preventive Action

You can try to prevent any problems by notifying the DDS in writing that you expect only actions on your claim that are authorized by federal law, and only qualified, competent individuals to work on your claim. Send the letter (see the sample below) to the DDS as soon as you file your application, with copies to your state and federal representatives. This alerts DDS personnel that you will pay careful attention to exactly what they do. This alone will maximize your chance of a good quality review. The DDS is required to make all correspondence from you a part of your

Sample Letter to DDS

Date: 12/12/20

Bob Smythe
Disability Determination Services
1234 Bobson Lane
Bobtown, VA

Dear Mr. Smythe:

I have applied for disability because of the following impairments:

1. Depression
2. Heart Disease
3. Lung Cancer

I hereby request assurance in writing that my claim will be reviewed by a licensed medical doctor or osteopath (for physical impairments) or by a licensed psychiatrist or properly qualified psychologist (for mental impairments). I object to and want to be informed of nondoctors participating in the medical part of my disability determination. If my claim is not reviewed by a medical consultant, I hereby request that you tell me in writing the personal qualifications that allow the reviewing individual to make medical evaluations on my claim, including all licenses to practice medicine or psychology in this state.

If an examiner or consultant receives instructions from a supervisor who is not licensed to practice medicine, osteopathy, or psychology regarding the medical severity of my impairments, I hereby object to the use of such instructions and request that I be notified of these instructions before a final determination on my claim is made.

Furthermore, I do not want my claim reviewed by any medical consultant the DDS knows has problems that may interfere with his or her ability to review my file and make competent medical determinations. Specifically, I do not want my claim reviewed by a medical consultant with an uncontrolled serious mental disorder such as schizophrenia or manic-depressive illness; a medical consultant who has had serious strokes or other type of brain disease or brain damage sufficient to affect his or her ability to think clearly; a medical consultant who is known to have an active drug or alcohol abuse problem; or a medical consultant who is unable to read my medical records or to see what documents to sign, unless that medical consultant has an aide who is qualified to interpret medical records.

I also do not want my claim reviewed by any medical consultant whom the DDS knows or has reason to know is "denial oriented"—that is, who denies a significantly higher percentage of claims than do other medical consultants working in the same agency on the same types of claims. I demand a fair consideration.

I also request that my claim not be handled by a claims examiner who has any of the types of problems described above.

If this DDS office is involved in any type of special pilot project for the SSA that means my claim will be handled in ways different from the way claims are handled in other states, please inform me of the nature of such project so that I may protect my rights.

Finally, I request that this letter remain in my file for use in my appeal, if necessary. Under no circumstances do I authorize removal of this letter from my file.

Sincerely yours,

Bill Smith

Bill Smith
1234 William Drive
Williamsburg, VA

cc: Rep. Bob Williams (D-Va.)
     Sen. Will "Bob" Williams
     Rep. Woody "Will" Williamson

file. If you have an attorney, that person's signature to a letter like this will make the DDS pay even more attention.

3. Remain Actively Involved in Your Claim

If you become aware of a specific problem involving the handling of your claim, you are not helpless. Here are some suggestions on how to proceed:

- Call your claims examiner and that examiner's supervisor, if necessary, to discuss the problem. If, for example, the claims examiner did not show your claim to a medical consultant, the examiner might do so when reminded of your right to such review—let the examiner know you will complain to the agency director if you don't get what you're entitled to. Be sure to follow up with a letter outlining your complaint. This ensures that your file contains your complaint and your understanding of what the claims examiner or supervisor said to you.

- Call the DDS director and state that if the problem is not resolved to your satisfaction, you will write the governor's office and your state and federal representatives. Calling a director is effective because it puts the director on the spot—with you on the other end of the telephone, this person is more likely to agree to take

some action on your complaint than would be taken in response to a letter, which can be filed away and forgotten. But always follow up this call with a letter outlining your complaint and the director's response.

- Write your legislators and send a copy to the DDS director. Your complaint will become a part of your file, and the DDS director will know that you are serious—not just somebody who made a telephone call and gave up.

- Write the SSA's Office of Inspector General (OIG), which is charged with investigating SSA (including DDS) wrongdoing—fraud, waste, abuse, and mismanagement. (Send copies to the DDS director and your state and federal representatives.) There is no guarantee that the OIG will think your complaint has merit, but you have nothing to lose by trying. Do not be afraid the DDS will take some kind of revenge because you complained to the OIG; the opposite is more likely. If the DDS director knows you have gone so far as to complain to the OIG, the office will handle your claim with kid gloves.

The OIG can be reached in various ways:
SSA Fraud Hotline
P.O. Box 17768
Baltimore MD 21235
800-269-0271 (voice)
410-597-0118 (fax)
http://oig.ssa.gov

Also consider talking to your local newspaper. The DDS offices and the SSA don't want bad publicity, and a mistreated claimant can often get a story in the newspaper. Too much bad publicity may embarrass the governor, and you can be sure the DDS director will be asked about it.

 SEE AN EXPERT

You may find that attorneys are reluctant to spend too much time on the DDS process. A disability lawyer may tell you that it is useless to deal with and complain to the DDS, since it denies most claims. But DDS officials typically allow about 30%–40% of initial claims and 10%–15% of reconsideration claims—about half of all requests. It is not useless to deal with the DDS. A good attorney will do everything possible to get the DDS the information it needs about a claimant. Appeals beyond the DDS can take a year or longer—even several years—so you want to avoid that, if possible.

H. Quick Disability Determination Unit (QDD)

In the DDS, a special unit known as the "Quick Disability Determination Unit" (QDD) might review your claim. If all of the important issues in your claim (such as your onset date—the date your disability began—and the degree of severity of your impairments) can be resolved within 20 days, then you could receive benefits quickly.

You cannot refer your own claim to the QDD; the DDS will make this decision internally. But because the disability claims examiner handling your file has input into whether your claim will go to the QDD, there is no reason you cannot ask the examiner whether your claim will go to the QDD and the reason for that decision.

You'll have the best chance of obtaining a favorable QDD review if you ensure all of the following:

- All of your important medical and nonmedical records have been provided to the DDS.
- You are not alleging a disability onset date that is far back in time (see Chapter 10 to learn more about onset dates).
- There are no complex vocational factors (age, education, or work experience) complicating a decision in your particular case (see Chapter 9 for more about these factors).

If the QDD doesn't approve your claim, or doesn't agree with your alleged onset date, the claim will be referred back to regular DDS functions so that any outstanding issues can be resolved.

How Claims Are Decided

Any time your claim for disability is evaluated—whether at the DDS, on appeal to an administrative law judge (ALJ), or in federal court—SSA procedures require that specific issues be addressed in a specific order. This is done to make sure that everyone gets the same consideration. If at any point in this sequential evaluation process, the DDS, SSA, ALJ, or federal court judge determines that your impairments justify disability, the evaluation ends. This chapter explains the sequence of events that is used at every level in the disability determination process. (See Chapter 12 for more on the different levels of disability appeals.)

Step 1. Are You Engaged in Substantial Gainful Activity?

If you are working and making a certain amount of money, you may be engaged in what is called "substantial gainful activity" (SGA). If so, you are not eligible for disability. (SGA is discussed in Chapter 1.) If the Field Office and the DDS claims examiner find that you are not performing SGA, the analysis proceeds to Step 2.

Step 2. How Severe Are Your Impairments?

The second step involves a determination of the severity of your impairments. If they do not (or should not) significantly limit the work you could do, your impairment will be considered "not severe" (or "nonsevere," "mild," or "slight"). Your claim will be denied if your impairments individually or combined are not severe.

The presence of one or more impairments doesn't necessarily mean you are disabled. Their effect on your ability to function mentally or physically is what matters. For example, you have severe hypertension (high blood pressure) that limits the amount of physical work you can safely do. But if your hypertension is controlled with drugs so that your blood pressure is normal, your impairment would be considered not severe.

Similarly, a nearsighted person for whom everything is a blur without glasses but clear with glasses does not have a severe impairment. On the other hand, if you have retinal disease that blurs your vision and cannot be corrected with glasses, your impairment would be more than not severe. So would painful arthritis in your spine that cannot be improved surgically. Many medical conditions cover the range of severity from not severe to incapacitating.

If your impairments are determined to be "significant"—that is, they are more than "not severe"—the analysis proceeds to Step 3.

Step 3. Do You Meet the Listing of Impairments?

At the first stage of review, the DDS will compare your disability to a list—called the "Listing of Impairments"—to see if your impairments are severe enough to "meet or equal" the SSA requirements. The listings are federal regulations, found at 20 CFR Part 404. If you are denied at the DDS level, each level of appeal will also use the Listing of Impairments to consider whether the DDS should be overruled.

TIP

Remember: The Medical Listings are on Nolo's website (see Appendix D for the link). The listings contain the medical information the SSA uses to determine whether your particular impairment, such as coronary artery disease, meets the requirements to obtain disability benefits.

Each impairment in the listings specifies a degree of medical severity which, if met by an applicant, presumes the inability to function well enough to perform any type of substantial work. The listings differ for adults and for children.

The listings cover most frequently found impairments. If any of your impairments exactly match the criteria of a listing, you will be found disabled and granted benefits regardless of your age, education, or work experience. For example, say you have an aortic aneurysm. If an imaging test shows that the aneurysm is dissecting (the arterial lining is pulling away from the artery wall), and it isn't controlled by treatment, you will be approved for disability benefits.

If none of your impairments meet the requirements of a listing, then the reviewer must determine if your impairments are equivalent to the severity required for a similar impairment. (This is called

an "equal.") Allowing benefits based on the equal standard recognizes that it is impossible for the SSA to put all impairments in the listings. If the SSA says your impairments are as severe as those in the listings, you will be granted benefits.

For your impairments to be considered equal to a listing, the reviewer must find one of the following to be true:

- Your impairment is not listed, but it is of the same medical severity as a listed impairment.
- You don't meet the criteria of a listing, but your medical findings have the same meaning as the listing criteria. For example, you might have a laboratory test not mentioned by the listing that shows the same thing as the type of test in the listing.
- You have a combination of impairments. None alone is severe enough to meet a listing, but together they are equivalent to listing-level disability. For example, you have heart disease and lung disease, which together cause you much greater severity than either would alone.
- For a child applying for SSI, the impairment is considered a "functional equal" of those that satisfy the listings. The functional equal standard allows benefits to children who don't quite have the medical severity needed to meet one of the above three points but whose impairments cause the same amount of functional loss. Relatively

Reading the Listings

SSA staff, DDS examiners and medical consultants, hearing officers, administrative law judges, appeal council judges, and federal judges all refer to listing letters and numbers to identify specific listings. These numbers come directly from the federal regulations governing Social Security, namely, 20 CFR Part 404. It is important that you understand this system so you can communicate clearly with the SSA and DDS. A typical listing may be expressed using familiar letters and numbers:

#.##		
A.		
	1.	
		a.
		b.
		c.
	2.	
		a.
		b.
B.		
	1.	
	2.	
		a.
		b.

The #.## represents the listing number. Adult heart disease, for example, is listing 4.04. Each capital letter introduces a new condition that might qualify for a listing. The numbers further subdivide a condition; usually, you will qualify if you meet one of the numbers. What this means, for example, is that you might meet a listing if you meet B1. The lowercase letters add another level of complexity. In some cases, you must meet all those conditions; in other cases, only one. For example, you might meet a listing if you match A1a, A1b, and A1c. Or, you might meet a listing if you have only B2b. What qualifies varies from listing to listing.

few children have impairments that qualify as functional equals.

If your impairments or combination of impairments do not meet or equal any listing or combination of listings, the analysis proceeds to Step 4.

Step 4. Can You Do Your Prior Job?

If your impairments do not meet or equal any listing, the reviewer will consider whether your limitations are severe enough to prevent you from doing your prior work (if any). If your limitations are not that severe, your claim will be denied with the rationale that you can return to your prior work. To determine how severe your limitations are, the DDS claims examiner will create a "residual functional capacity" (RFC) rating for you. (RFCs are discussed in detail in Chapter 8.)

If you cannot perform your prior work, the analysis proceeds to Step 5.

Step 5. Can You Do Any Other Job?

If your limitations prevent you from doing your prior work, the reviewer will consider whether or not there are other jobs in the national economy that you can do. If so, your claim will be denied with the rationale that there are jobs that you can perform. If you can transfer your skills to other work, your claim will be denied.

Be clear about this: The SSA does not have to find you a particular job, or a job of equal pay, or a job of equal skill, or jobs near where you live in order to deny your claim.

In order to determine whether there are other jobs you can be expected to do, given your age, education, and skill set, the SSA will perform a "medical-vocational assessment." (This analysis is discussed in Chapter 9.)

Whether You Can Do Some Work: Your RFC

If your medical impairments are more than slight or mild, but not severe enough to meet or equal a listing, then the SSA will consider what it calls your residual functional capacity, or RFC. (Listings are discussed in Chapter 7.) RFC assessments are done only on adult claims.

An RFC analysis is an assessment of what the SSA thinks you are physically or mentally capable of doing despite the limitations from your impairments and related symptoms. In other words, an RFC outlines what remaining (residual) capacities you have to do things (function) in a medical sense; an RFC might also specify some things that you cannot do. For example, an RFC might say that you can lift 50 pounds occasionally, but that you cannot work in places where there is an excessive amount of dust and fumes.

The RFC assessment is a medical decision, not a determination as to whether or not you are disabled. (An RFC does not state whether you can do specific types of jobs, but it can state that you are limited to doing a certain level of work, such as sedentary work.) SSA examiners and vocational analysts use it to determine the types of work you might be able to do.

Before we get into how the RFC analysis is done, let's look further at how it's used in the disability determination. If your remaining capabilities make it possible for you to continue with your prior job, the SSA can deny your claim because you can return to that type of work. The SSA doesn't have to actually find you a job or call your previous employers and ask them if they will take you back.

If your RFC restricts you so much that you cannot return to any of your past jobs (say your RFC is for light work but your past jobs all required heavy work), the SSA will consider your age, education, and work experience (called your "vocational factors") to determine whether you can do any other work. If the SSA concludes that you cannot, then you will be allowed disability payments. (Vocational factors are discussed in Chapter 9.) If the SSA awards you benefits based on your impairments and your RFC assessment, you receive a "medical-vocational allowance"; if your claim is denied after this kind of analysis, you receive a "medical-vocational denial."

If the RFC limits you to jobs that pay significantly less than your current or previous work, the SSA will not pay you the difference; there are no partial disability payments under Social Security—it is an all-or-nothing decision.

TIP

Learn who did your RFC. A doctor must determine your RFC during your initial claim, reconsideration claim, or continuing disability review at the DDS. On appeal, an administrative law judge or federal judge can do the RFC assessment. If your RFC was done at the DDS and the handwriting on the assessment doesn't match the doctor's signature, a doctor may not have done your RFC. This would be a violation of current federal regulations, and you should contact the SSA's Office of Inspector General at 800-269-0271 or on the Internet at www.socialsecurity.gov/oig.

Your RFC is developed based upon all relevant evidence, including your description of how your symptoms affect your ability to function. In addition, the SSA might consider observations of your treating doctors or psychologists, relatives, neighbors, friends, coworkers, the SSA intake person, and others. The SSA uses your statement, the observations of others, and your medical records to decide the extent to which your impairments keep you from performing particular work activities. The SSA must have reasonably thorough medical evidence.

The SSA has two different RFC assessments: one for physical impairments and one for mental impairments. The medical consultant will not do a physical assessment if you have only a mental impairment. Nor will the consultant do a mental rating if you have only a physical impairment. Many cases, however, require both.

RFCs are not assessed in numbers, percentages, or other scores. Instead, work abilities are put into categories. The lower your RFC category, the less the SSA believes you are capable of doing. For example, a physical RFC for light work is lower than a physical RFC for medium work. A mental RFC for unskilled work is lower than a mental RFC for semiskilled or skilled work. Your RFC might be additionally lowered if you cannot perform certain work-related activities very often, such as pushing and pulling.

The lower your RFC category, the less likely the SSA will say there is some work you can do. That is because the SSA cannot say that you can do work that falls into a higher RFC category than the RFC you received. For example, if you receive a physical RFC for sedentary work, you cannot be expected to do a job requiring light, medium, or heavy work. Similarly, if your mental RFC is for unskilled work, you cannot be expected to do semiskilled or skilled work.

A. RFC Analysis for Physical Impairments and Abilities

This section focuses on how the SSA assesses a physical RFC in general. The Medical Listings on Nolo's website (see Appendix D for the link) provide commentary on what an RFC should look like for each of the SSA listings for specific physical disorders. How the SSA combines a physical RFC with the vocational factors of age, education, and work experience to do a medical-vocational analysis is discussed in Chapter 9.

When the SSA assesses your physical RFC abilities, it first makes a medical judgment about the nature and extent of your physical limitations. If you have limited ability to perform certain physical activities associated with working, such as sitting, standing, walking, lifting, carrying, pushing, pulling, reaching, handling, stooping, or crouching, the SSA might conclude that you cannot do your past work or any other work.

A physical RFC itself will not take your age into consideration, except in certain continuing disability review claims (see Chapter 14). In other words, your RFC will not be lower because you are 60 years old and not as energetic as you were at age 30. But the SSA does not ignore age; it is considered when the SSA is determining whether you can do any work during the "medical-vocational analysis," discussed in Chapter 9. For example, if you are given a sedentary RFC, but your past jobs required heavy work and you are over 50, have no high school diploma, and have only unskilled work experience, you should be considered disabled.

Not only doesn't your age matter for your RFC itself, but your sex and physical strength are also irrelevant unless they are related to your impairments. Here's how this plays out. Never in your life have you been able to lift 50 pounds, much less 100 pounds. But if there is nothing significantly wrong with you, the SSA may give you an RFC saying you can lift 100 pounds. At first glance, this seems illogical and unfair. But restricting RFCs for nonmedical reasons would result in granting benefits to some people who have no significant impairments, and that would defeat the meaning of the disability system.

The areas assessed in a physical RFC are described in the rest of this section.

1. Exertion

In the "exertion" category, the SSA evaluates lifting, carrying, standing, walking, sitting, and pushing and pulling. Many claimants have exertional restrictions on their RFC because of impairments that affect physical strength and stamina. Other claimants, especially those suffering from arthritis of the joints or spine, have reduced exertional ability on their RFC because of pain. Disorders of the nervous system, lung diseases, and heart and blood vessel diseases also account for large numbers of exertional restrictions because of decreased strength and stamina, and because of symptoms such as fatigue, pain, and short-ness of breath. (If your impairments don't affect your ability to lift, carry, push, pull, and so on, you could still be given an RFC for nonexertional limitations if you have difficulty seeing or hearing or if you cannot work in certain environments. More on this below.)

If your RFC restricts your exertion, it must explain why your impairments justify the limitations.

Lifting or carrying exertional abilities are measured by the descriptive words "frequent-ly" and "occasionally." Frequently means you can lift or carry for at least one-third but less than two-thirds (cumulative, not continuous) of an eight-hour workday. Occasionally means you can lift or carry for less than one-third of an eight-hour workday.

Pushing and pulling exertional abilities are measured in terms of "unlimited," "frequently," and "occasionally." Frequently means you can push or pull for at least one-third but less than two-thirds of an eight-hour workday. Occasionally means you can push or pull for less than one-third of an eight-hour workday. A lot of jobs, especially those involving heavy equipment, require pushing or pulling. Any impairment that affects use of the hands, arms, or legs could result in a restricted RFC with pushing and pulling restrictions. Arthritis is probably the most frequent cause of limitations. Strokes, with the weakness they can cause, usually involve one arm and one leg on the same side of the body, and are another common reason for limitations in ability to push and pull.

Exertional abilities are divided into five categories, as follows.

Heavy work. "Heavy work" is the ability to lift or carry 100 pounds occasionally and 50 pounds frequently and to stand or walk six to eight hours a day. The SSA rarely gives an RFC for heavy work. In general, the SSA believes that a person who can do heavy work has no exertional restriction and is rated not severe—that is, not disabled.

Medium work. "Medium work" is the ability to lift or carry 50 pounds occasionally and 25 pounds frequently and to stand or walk six to eight hours daily. Medium work is an RFC given to claimants whose exertional ability is moderately limited. What is moderate? That's a matter of medical judgment.

Light work. "Light work" is the ability to lift or carry 20 pounds occasionally and ten pounds frequently, and to stand or walk six to eight hours daily. Light work is an RFC given to claimants who can't do medium work, but are not restricted to sedentary work. Again, this is a matter of medical judgment. A claimant with a missing hand or arm is usually restricted to no more than light work. If you can't stand or walk at least six hours daily, you will not be able to do light work. That means that your RFC can't be for more than sedentary work. This is to your advantage as an applicant for disability benefits because it markedly limits the jobs you can do.

Sedentary work. "Sedentary work" requires lifting no more than ten pounds at a time and occasionally lifting or carrying articles like small files or small tools. Although the work is done primarily while seated, up to two hours per day of walking and standing may be necessary.

If the SSA says you can stand four hours daily, then your RFC is between sedentary and light work. Although this is possible, the SSA tries to avoid such blurry distinctions. Such an RFC would require a vocational analyst to carefully evaluate how it affects your ability to return to your prior or other work. (See Chapter 9 about medical-vocational evaluation.)

Although sedentary work does not require much lifting or standing, even unskilled sedentary jobs often require good use of the hands and fingers for repetitive hand-finger actions. A sedentary RFC is often given to those claimants whose impairments are not quite severe enough to qualify under a listing.

Less than sedentary. "Less than sedentary" is not an official RFC category, but it is an RFC rating sometimes given. It will almost always result in allowance of the disability claim, because the examiner or vocational analyst will not be able to find any jobs the claimant can do. However, there are rare exceptions of some highly trained claimants who had less than sedentary jobs when they applied for disability; the SSA might return these people to their prior work.

Sedentary work requires good use of the hands. If you can't stand or walk at least two hours daily, and you don't have excellent use of both of your hands, then you cannot do even sedentary work. Similarly, if you start out with a sedentary RFC but need to use one hand for an assistive device to help you walk, such as a cane or crutch, then you actually have a less than sedentary RFC although your hands and arms may be normal.

In addition, if you must periodically alternate between sitting and standing to relieve pain or discomfort, this medical restriction eliminates most sedentary jobs and will result in a less than sedentary RFC. Most claimants who must alternate sitting and standing have very severe back pain. Because this restriction applies so infrequently, the SSA requires a special explanation as part of the RFC assessment.

In many instances, claimants with a less than sedentary RFC should have equaled a listing or combination of listings without their claims ever having to go on to the RFC step of the sequential evaluation process.

2. Posture

"Postural exertional abilities" include bending, stooping, climbing, balancing, kneeling, crouching, and crawling. In technical language, posture is the attitude, or directional orientation, of the body.

Postural exertional abilities are described on an RFC as "never," "frequently," or "occasionally." Frequently means you can do the activity at least one-third but less than two-thirds of an eight-hour workday. Occasionally means you can do the activity less than one-third of an eight-hour workday. If the RFC gives any restrictions of posture, it must explain why the impairments justify the limitations.

Bending. An ability to bend the back (or stoop) is often needed for jobs that require lifting and carrying. This fact, coupled with the fact that many claimants allege back pain as a basis for disability, makes bending extremely important in disability determination. Degenerative arthritis and degenerative disc disease of the spine cause most back pain in claimants. How well you can bend your back is often the most important aspect of your physical evaluation.

Claimants with significant back pain almost always have difficulty bending and are usually limited to only occasional bending. This limitation can be very important because most medium or heavy work requires frequent bending. If you receive a medium restriction regarding lifting and carrying and an occasional restriction for bending, you are likely to be referred for only light work (that is, given a light RFC) to be used in the medical-vocational analysis. Depending on your age, education, and work experience, this change can make the difference between allowance and denial of your claim.

Some claimants cannot bend their spine to any significant degree. This usually happens in people who have surgical fixation of the spine because of spinal fractures, advanced osteoarthritis of the spine, or an inflammatory disease known as ankylosing spondylitis. But even these people will not automatically qualify for disability—depending on the vocational factors, some will not be granted disability.

Balancing and climbing. Difficulties in balancing are most frequently caused by significant impairments of the nervous system or inner ear. In such a situation, an RFC should include a statement that the claimant should not be required to do work requiring good balance. Climbing, except for steps with handrails, would also be prohibited when balancing is restricted.

Limiting climbing when balance is not restricted might occur in cases of weakness in an arm or leg or in cases of arthritis in a hip or knee joint. The RFC may need to specify the kind of climbing that is limited—such as ramps, stairs, ladders, ropes, or scaffolds. An RFC will not simply limit all balancing or climbing. If it did, the claimant would not be able to walk and would qualify under a listing.

Kneeling, crouching, and crawling. Limitations in kneeling, crouching, and crawling are most frequently caused by arthritis in the knees. The ability to crouch may also be decreased by back pain. Limitations in these areas can be decisive in allowance or denial of a claim.

3. Manipulation

"Manipulation" means the ability to use the hands for various tasks. Manipulative abilities include reaching in all directions, including overhead; handling (gross manipulations); fingering (fine manipulations); and feeling (skin receptors). Manipulative abilities on an RFC assessment are described as "limited" or "unlimited." An RFC with any restrictions of manipulation must explain why the impairments justify the limitations. Manipulative abilities are especially relevant when a claimant is limited to using his or her hands less than one-third of a workday.

Reaching and handling. Reaching is most often limited by arthritis in a shoulder or elbow joint, or weakness in an arm, such as from a stroke.

Strokes are a frequent cause of decreased handling ability, due to weakness and numbness in the hands. Arthritis in the hands can also affect handling ability. Fractures of bones involving the wrist can result in markedly decreased use of a hand, even after optimum healing. These limitations can be caused by damaged soft tissues, such as ligaments, tendons, and nerves, as well as by the lack of bone healing or the development of arthritis due to a fracture in a joint space.

Fine manipulations and feeling. "Fine manipulations" require coordinated, precise movements of the fingers.

Impairments that result in little limitation in handling abilities can still affect fine manipulation. Disorders of the nervous system, such as strokes or tremors, can affect the ability to perform fine manipulations but might not be severe enough to affect handling. Arthritis or other disorders that are associated with swelling of the fingers can affect fine manipulations. Missing fingers might not affect handling but would prevent fine manipulations. Diabetes can damage the nerves from skin receptors involved in feeling, resulting in numbness that can affect fine manipulative ability, even though the ability to do handling remains.

Fractures of wrist bones can decrease ability to perform fine manipulations, even after optimum healing. Carpal tunnel syndrome is a frequent problem of workers performing repetitive activities with their hands and wrists that can cause pain, numbness, and weakness in the hands that affect manipulative ability.

Difficulty with fine manipulations has little effect on the SSA's ability to refer a claimant to jobs requiring light, medium, or heavy work. Many such jobs don't require fine manipulations. Fine manipulations, however, are very important in the ability to do sedentary work. This means that if you have an RFC for sedentary work but you cannot perform fine manipulations, your RFC drops to less than sedentary work, and your claim will probably be allowed.

4. Vision

RFCs describe "visual abilities" as "limited" or "unlimited." If an RFC gives any restrictions of vision, it must explain why the impairments justify the limitations. Visual tests and visual impairments are discussed in Part 2 of the Medical Listings on Nolo's website.

The RFC rating for visual limitations takes into account the following six factors.

Near acuity. "Near acuity" is important for seeing close up, such as reading a book or typewritten papers. Good near acuity is not required for many jobs for light work or higher. Also, some sedentary jobs don't require good near acuity. Therefore, being allowed disability on the basis of limited near acuity is unlikely—especially in young claimants who have flexibility in transferring to different kinds of jobs. Cataracts and retinal diseases are the most likely causes of decreased near acuity that cannot be corrected with glasses or contacts.

Distance acuity. "Distance acuity" is important for seeing objects more than a few feet away. Most decreases in distance acuity can be corrected with glasses or contact lenses and are not considered limiting; some cases, such as those involving cataracts, can be cured with surgery. If distance acuity is limited and uncorrectable but does not meet or equal a listing, you still may be unable to perform your prior work. For example, some types of manual labor might not require good distance acuity, but a modest decrease in acuity can disqualify a person from having a driver's license—including the ability to drive commercial vehicles such as trucks.

Whether the SSA would say you can do other work besides your prior job would depend on the types of other medical problems you have and your vocational factors of age, education, and work experience (see Chapter 9).

Depth perception. "Depth perception" is the ability to perceive how far something is from you. Depth perception is affected when a claimant is blind in one eye. Jobs such as being a pilot require good depth perception, but many other jobs don't. An examiner or vocational analyst can usually refer a claimant with limited depth perception to a job not requiring depth perception, even if the claimant can't return to prior work.

Accommodation. "Accommodation" means the ability of the lens of the eye

to change thickness in order to focus on near objects. The most common cause of inability to do this is a stiff lens resulting from normal aging; this is easily correctable with glasses. Limited accommodation is rarely a basis for disability.

Color vision. "Color vision" means the ability to distinguish different colors. Limitations in color vision are usually genetic and are most often limited to green and red colors. Many people with color vision deficit can still see some color. Even if you suffer complete loss of color vision, the SSA can identify general jobs that don't require color vision.

Field of vision (peripheral vision). Field of vision" refers to the ability to see objects away from the center of vision. Limited fields of vision are most often the result of glaucoma, strokes, and diabetic retinal disease. Claimants who have significant restriction in their fields of vision but not enough to meet or equal a listing, might still need to be restricted from work where lack of good peripheral vision can endanger their lives or the lives of others. Specifically, the RFC analysis should restrict the claimant from driving, working at unprotected heights, or working around hazardous machinery.

5. Communication

The most important work-related communication abilities are hearing and speaking. On an RFC, communication abilities are described as "limited" or "unlimited." If an RFC gives restrictions on hearing or speaking, it must explain why the impairments justify the limitations. Hearing and speaking impairments, as well as tests for those impairments, are discussed in Part 2 of the Medical Listings on Nolo's website.

Hearing. Claimants frequently allege hearing impairments, and both awareness that someone is speaking and understanding the spoken word are important in many jobs. Hearing problems, however, can often be improved with hearing aids. Most claimants who have hearing impairments do not qualify under a listing but have a significant hearing loss that requires an RFC. Still, the SSA can identify general jobs that most claimants can perform, despite some difficulty hearing.

Speaking. The ability to speak involves clarity of speech, as well as adequate volume and production of enough words fast enough to meaningfully communicate with other people. A significant speaking impairment that doesn't qualify under a listing requires an RFC. Still, the SSA can identify general jobs that most claimants can perform, despite some difficulty speaking. Many jobs require minimal speaking.

6. Environment

"Environmental factors" that might place limitations on a claimant's RFC include sensitivity to extreme cold, extreme heat, wetness, humidity, noise, vibration, fumes (odors, dusts, gases, poor ventilation), and avoidance of certain dangers, such as working around hazardous machinery or at unprotected heights. Limitation of exposure to a particular environmental factor can be expressed on the RFC as unlimited, avoid concentrated exposure, avoid even moderate exposure, and avoid all exposure. If the RFC gives any environmental restrictions, it must explain why the impairments justify the limitations.

A patient evaluated in an office or a hospital is in a special environment, one that may be very different from the environment found at many jobs. Therefore, when an examiner or vocational specialist needs to determine whether you can return to your past work or do some other type of work, the DDS medical consultant must note any relevant environmental restrictions on the RFC. The examiner or vocational analyst may need to discuss with you the kinds of environmental exposures you have had in your job.

Two impairments almost always give rise to environmental restrictions on an RFC:

- **Epilepsy.** Claimants with epilepsy who have had a seizure in the past year are restricted from working around or driving hazardous machinery and from working at unprotected heights where they might injure themselves or others if they suffer a seizure.

- **Lung disease.** Claimants with significant lung disease are usually restricted from exposure to moderate dust and fumes. Restriction from all exposure is not feasible, because there are dust and fumes everywhere, even in people's homes.

Two other conditions may give rise to environmental restrictions on an RFC:

- **Heart or blood vessel disease.** Claimants with severe heart disease or vascular disease of the arteries might be restricted from concentrated exposure to extreme heat or cold because temperature extremes can put dangerous stress on the heart and blood vessel system. In some instances, restriction from even moderate exposure might be required.
- **Skin disorder.** Claimants whose skin disorders are affected by constant contact with wetness should be restricted from performing work that could worsen the condition. For instance, if you have an inflammatory condition of the skin of the hands (dermatitis) that worsens with constant dipping of your hands in water, your RFC should restrict you from concentrated exposure. In some instances, restriction from even moderate exposure might be required.

Vibration is an environmental factor that does not usually make a difference in the outcome of a claim but it can in some cases. For example, claimants have been granted disability because the only work they could perform involved riding on equipment, such as a tractor, that caused too much pain from the vibration.

Noise is not an important environmental factor in most cases, but it can be in some. This is most often the case with people with hearing impairments whose jobs required them to communicate in noisy environments; their ability to understand words is likely to be affected in the noisy environment.

7. Symptoms

The medical consultant completing an RFC should consider any symptoms—such as pain, nausea, and dizziness. (Symptoms important to disability determination are discussed in Chapter 5.)

The RFC must address the following three concerns regarding symptoms:

- whether symptoms are caused by a medically determinable impairment— that is, whether or not they are real
- whether the alleged severity or duration of the symptoms is medically reasonable based on the impairments, and
- whether the severity of the symptoms is consistent with your alleged ability to function, taking into account the medical and nonmedical evidence— your statements, statements of others, observations regarding your activities of daily living, and changes in your usual behavior or habits.

The important point is that the SSA should recognize that symptoms can limit your ability to work. Joint and back pain are common symptoms, usually related to arthritis. Restrictions for arthritis are most often for pain—especially for back pain. People vary considerably in the amount of pain they feel, and the SSA must evaluate each case on an individual basis. Although individual claimants can reasonably vary in the amount of pain they feel or other symptoms they exhibit, the SSA is not likely to accept a very low RFC due to pain or other symptoms when the claimant has very minor physical abnormalities.

Pain is not the only symptom that can influence an RFC. For example, some claimants have severe nausea and dizziness from inner ear disease. These people require the same kinds of restrictions as epileptics—no work around hazardous machinery or at unprotected heights.

Other claimants have nausea, weakness, numb hands and feet, or potential side effects from medication taken to treat their impairments. The SSA should factor this into the RFC.

8. Statements of the Treating Physician

The RFC must specify whether your treating doctor's statements about your physical capacities are in the file. If so, the medical consultant and/or administrative law judge will specify whether their conclusions about what you can and cannot do significantly differ from your treating doctor's. If they differ, the medical consultant or ALJ will explain in detail why the treating or examining doctor is wrong (see Chapters 6 and 12). The SSA no longer needs to accept your treating doctor's opinion regarding your functional abilities, especially if that opinion is not persuasive.

(See Chapter 5 for more information about treating and examining source opinions.)

B. Mental Impairments and Abilities

This section focuses on how the SSA assesses a mental RFC (an assessment of residual functional capacity), including how RFC factors relate to the ability to work. (See Part 12 of the Medical Listings on Nolo's website for the SSA listings and RFCs for specific mental disorders.)

At the initial, reconsideration, or continuing disability review (CDR) level, a psychologist or psychiatrist does a mental RFC assessment. On appeal, an ALJ or a federal court judge can rule on mental RFCs.

The SSA is looking for the degree of limitation of function a claimant has in each assessed area. All areas to be assessed are rated as "not significantly limited," "moderately limited," "markedly limited," "no evidence of limitation in this category," or "not ratable on available evidence." If an area is not ratable on available evidence, the SSA is obligated to obtain more information. The difference between no evidence of limitation in this category and not significantly limited is the difference between no limitation at all and a mild limitation.

The objective of a mental RFC is to produce an assessment by which a claims examiner or vocational analyst can determine if a claimant with a mental impairment can do skilled, semiskilled, or unskilled work—or whether the claimant is incapable of doing even unskilled work. (See Chapter 9 for more on the definition of these types of work.) The examiner or analyst uses the information to determine if the claimant can return to his or her prior work or perform some other kind of work.

The most important determination in a mental RFC analysis is whether you are mentally capable of doing unskilled work. The reason for this is that even if you are no longer capable of returning to your prior job that required semiskilled or skilled work, the SSA can still identify unskilled jobs. For example, a lawyer, whose work is skilled, is in an automobile accident and suffers brain injury, resulting in significant permanent mental impairment. Because of the brain damage, he is no longer capable of skilled or even semiskilled work. This lawyer, however, is capable of unskilled work. Under these conditions, the SSA could deny the lawyer's claim for disability benefits by identifying unskilled jobs that he could perform. This is a reminder of the important principle in disability determination: Claimants must be incapable of performing any work to be considered disabled—not just their prior jobs.

Consider, on the other hand, a mental RFC that shows a claimant with chronic schizophrenia or severe depression who cannot do even unskilled work. The SSA would allow the claim, regardless of the claimant's age, education, or work experience.

Because of the large number of unskilled jobs in the economy, a claimant with a mental impairment alone who has a mental RFC for unskilled work is almost never going to be allowed benefits. (For the rare exceptions, see Chapter 9, Section C3.) This does not mean that mental RFC assessments that indicate a capacity for unskilled work—or even for more than unskilled work—are meaningless. Such RFCs become important when the claimant also has a physical RFC. (See Section C, below.)

A mental RFC contains four areas of function to be assessed, covered in Sections 1 through 4, below. These include the basic abilities needed for any job. The limitation assigned to each area is a matter of medical judgment, derived from the evidence. If any one area is assessed as markedly (severely) limited, the claimant will be considered unable to do even unskilled work.

If the RFC contains various combinations of moderately limited and not significantly limited ratings, the DDS examiner or vocational analyst, ALJ, or federal court judge (depending on who has the claim) will have to determine whether the claimant can return to prior or other work. This is not the job of a doctor, such as a DDS medical consultant, because most doctors are not experts in vocational (job-related) issues. (The vocational application of RFCs is discussed in Chapter 9.)

1. Understanding and Memory

The SSA evaluates the following areas of understanding and memory function:

- remembering locations and work-like procedures—if markedly limited, you cannot perform unskilled work
- understanding and remembering very short and simple instructions—if markedly limited, you cannot perform unskilled work, and
- understanding and remembering detailed instructions—if markedly limited, you cannot perform semiskilled or skilled work.

2. Sustained Concentration and Persistence

The SSA evaluates your ability to do the following related to concentration and persistence:

- carry out very short and simple instructions—if markedly limited, you cannot perform unskilled work
- carry out detailed instructions—if markedly limited, you cannot perform semiskilled or skilled work
- maintain attention and concentration—if markedly limited, you cannot perform unskilled work
- perform activities within a schedule, maintain regular attendance, and be punctual within customary tolerances—if markedly limited, you cannot perform unskilled work

- sustain an ordinary routine without special supervision—if markedly limited, you cannot perform unskilled work
- work in coordination with or proximity to others without being unduly distracted by them—if markedly limited, you cannot perform unskilled work
- make simple work-related decisions—if markedly limited, you cannot perform unskilled work, and
- complete a normal workday and work-week without interruptions caused by mental symptoms and perform at a consistent pace without an unreasonable number and length of rest periods—if markedly limited, you cannot perform unskilled work.

3. Social Interaction

The SSA evaluates your ability to sustain the following social interactions:

- interact appropriately with the general public—no general rule can be given for limiting this area because jobs vary so greatly
- ask simple questions or request assistance—if markedly limited, you cannot perform unskilled work
- accept instructions and respond appropriately to criticism from supervisors—if markedly limited, you cannot perform unskilled work
- get along with coworkers or peers without distracting them or exhibiting

behavioral extremes—if markedly limited, you cannot perform unskilled work, and

- maintain socially appropriate behavior and adhere to basic standards of neatness and cleanliness—no general rule can be given for limiting this area because jobs vary so greatly.

4. Adaptation

Finally, the SSA evaluates your ability to do the following regarding adaptation:

- respond appropriately to changes in the work setting—if markedly limited, you cannot perform unskilled work
- be aware of normal hazards and take appropriate precautions—if markedly limited, you cannot perform unskilled work
- travel in unfamiliar places or use public transportation—no general rule can be given for limiting this area because jobs vary so greatly, and
- set realistic goals or make plans independently of others—if markedly limited, you cannot perform semiskilled or skilled work.

5. Statements of Your Treating Physician

The SSA no longer needs to accept your treating doctor's opinion regarding your functional abilities, especially if that opinion is not persuasive. If the SSA does not accept that opinion, the RFC will contain an explanation of the conclusions that differ from the treating source's conclusions or your allegations.

In addition to the RFC rating areas described in this section, the DDS mental consultant must complete what is called a Psychiatric Review Technique Form (PRTF). This document is based on diagnostic categories of mental disorders and is supposed to serve as sort of a checklist to help the person assessing the mental RFC (such as a DDS psychologist or psychiatrist or an ALJ) be sure all relevant medical evidence has been considered. Possible improper completion of the mental RFC or PRTF is something you or your authorized representative should look for if you are reviewing your file and planning an appeal (see Chapters 6 and 12). Especially look for opinions expressed on these documents that are not backed up by evidence in the file.

C. Claims With Both Physical and Mental RFCs

Because of the large numbers of unskilled jobs in the economy, it is very rare for a claimant with a purely mental impairment who is capable of unskilled work to be granted benefits. In fact, the medical-vocational rules in Appendix C always require claimants to have significant physical impairments (those that require a physical RFC) for allowance of a claim. Of course, if you have a mental RFC for less than unskilled work, your claim will be allowed regardless of any physical impairments you have or the medical-vocational rules.

Many claimants have both mental and physical impairments requiring RFCs. In these cases, depending on the claimant's vocational factors, an approval of benefits may be possible, even if the claimant is capable of unskilled work.

The problem for claimants with both mental and physical disorders is that nobody at the DDS is likely to evaluate, or even be qualified to evaluate, their combined severity. Assessing whether mental and physical impairments "combine" to create a more disabling condition than on their own requires expertise about both physical and mental impairments. At the DDS, mental consultants generally evaluate only the mental part of a claim, and physical consultants evaluate only the physical part of a claim. Mental consultants who are psychiatrists (M.D.s) could evaluate the physical impairment and the mental impairment in a claim, but most psychiatrists today would not want to evaluate physical impairments due to claim complexity and medical data complexity.

Typically, what happens is that disability examiners, if they consult with doctors at all, ask for separate medical assessments for the physical and mental disorders in the same case. The physical and mental conditions are then evaluated separately as to whether they should be approved as disabilities. Examiners are not qualified to evaluate the combined effect of physical and mental disorders, which is more difficult than assessing the severity of either alone. So what happens is that no combined evaluation is done in most cases at DDS, and some claims are unfairly denied because of this.

If you are restricted to sedentary work physically but unskilled work mentally, you should bring it to the attention of the DDS so that a medical consultant qualified in both physical and mental impairments can consider the combined effects of your physical and mental conditions. If you've been denied, be sure to bring it up in your appeal. In this case, the medical consultant and examiner, or the administrative law judge, might be able to find that your combined impairments are equal in severity to listings by combination, naming both a mental listing and a physical listing.

How Age, Education, and Work Experience Matter

As discussed in Chapter 8, if you have a significant impairment, but one not severe enough to meet or equal an entry on the Listing of Impairments, the SSA will determine what abilities you do have (known as residual functional capacity, or RFC) to see if you can return to your *past* work. If you cannot, the SSA may then consider your age, education, and work experience—called the vocational factors—to determine if you can do *any* work. If you cannot, you will be considered disabled. This chapter is about the medical-vocational analysis that takes place to see if you can be expected to learn to do, and do, any other work.

The SSA has published tables that consider RFC ratings along with age, education, and work experience. The tables direct the SSA to find someone "disabled" or "not disabled," depending where the person falls. The tables are known as the "medical-vocational rules" or, more informally, the "medical-vocational guidelines" or "grid." They appear in Appendix C, along with instructions on how to use them. If you fall into a disabled grid in the medical-vocational guidelines, the SSA will consider you to be a "medical-vocational allowance," which means you will be awarded disability.

Table 1 considers sedentary work RFCs along with vocational factors; Table 2 deals with light work RFCs, and Table 3 with medium work RFCs. Heavy work RFCs are not included in the medical-vocational rules because they essentially are considered the same as a not severe (slight) impairment that does not produce any significant limitation in physical ability; thus the SSA would find a claimant capable of doing heavy work not disabled.

Turn to Appendix C and look at Table 1. You can see that nine medical-vocational rules result in allowance when vocational factors are combined with sedentary RFCs. These are: 201.01, 201.02, 201.04, 201.06, 201.09, 201.10, 201.12, 201.14, and 201.17. Now turn to Table 2. Five medical-vocational rules result in allowance for claimants with light RFCs. These are: 202.01, 202.02, 202.04, 202.06, and 202.09. Finally, look at Table 3. Now you see that only three medical-vocational rules result in allowance for claimants with medium RFCs. These are: 203.01, 203.02, and 203.10. This makes sense, given that being able to tolerate medium work means there's a greater chance that there's some job you could do.

How age, education, and work experience are evaluated under the medical-vocational rules is considered below. This material will be clearer to you if you refer to the tables in Appendix C.

A. Age

Your disability application will be evaluated under one of the following categories:
- Younger than 50 years (younger individuals)
- age 50–54 years (closely approaching advanced age)

- age 55–59 years (advanced age)
- age 60–64 (advanced age and also closely approaching retirement age).

Age is an important vocational factor affecting your ability to adapt to new work situations and to compete with other people. The lower your RFC at a particular age, the greater chance you will be found disabled under a medical-vocational rule. Similarly, the older you are, the greater the chance you will be found disabled with a particular RFC. In other words, a 55-year-old claimant with a sedentary RFC has a better chance of being allowed than a claimant of the same age with an RFC for light, medium, or heavy work. Similarly, a 55-year-old claimant with a sedentary RFC has a better chance of being allowed under the rules than a 25-year-old with the same RFC.

1. Sedentary Work and Age

Claimants 55 years of age and older are especially likely to be found disabled under a medical-vocational rule for disability when they have RFCs for sedentary work. As Table 1 shows, the only "not disabled" claimants of this age group are those with past skilled or semiskilled work experience whose skills can be transferred to new jobs or whose recent education permits them to do skilled work. Also, to be found "not disabled" in this age group, Table 1 requires claimants to be able to do a new job with little or no adjustment in their tools, work processes, work settings, or industry. In other words, to be 55 or older

and denied benefits with a sedentary RFC, claimants would have to fit into a job with little difficulty and perform the work as if they had been doing it for years. The same rules apply for claimants 50–54 years old with a sedentary RFC.

What about claimants younger than 50 with a sedentary RFC? As Table 1 shows, these claimants will have a much harder time being granted a medical-vocational allowance.

If you are 45–49, you can be found disabled with a sedentary RFC under Medical Vocational Rule 201.17 only if all of the following are true:

- You are unskilled and have no skills that can be transferred to a new job.
- You have no past work that is relevant to your current ability to work or you can no longer perform your past work.
- You are either illiterate or unable to communicate in English.

If you are between 18 and 44, under the SSA's rules, you will not be granted disability with a sedentary RFC (but if you also have nonexertional limitations or a mental RFC, this can change).

2. Less-Than-Sedentary Work and Age

RFCs for less-than-sedentary work are not part of the medical-vocational rules, but such an RFC will almost always result in allowance of benefits at any age, regardless of education and past work experience. Less-than-sedentary RFCs are discussed in Chapter 8, Section A1.

3. Other Work Levels and Age

If you are in the 60–64 age range, you will be found disabled under the medical-vocational rules of Table 1 for sedentary work and Table 2 for light work, unless you have highly marketable, transferable skills or recent training for skilled work. Note also on Table 2 that many claimants ages 55–59 with RFCs for light work or less are allowed benefits.

In general, few claimants are found disabled with an RFC for medium work, however; claimants 55 or older with a medium RFC may be found disabled if they have a limited education and a history of no past work or of unskilled work. See Table 3, Medical-Vocational Rules 203.01, 203.02, and 203.10.

If you are under 50, the only way you can get disability benefits under these rules is to have an RFC for sedentary work and be illiterate.

4. Age Examples

Age 55 is frequently the threshold that separates allowance and denial of disability benefits. Two examples demonstrate this fact and show how allowance or denial can turn on fine points.

EXAMPLE 1: Rita is 54 years old, has moderate arthritis in her spine so that she can't do more than light lifting, and receives an RFC for light work. But she has a college degree and has done desk work most of her life. If she has skills that could be transferred to another job, she'll be denied benefits under Medical-Vocational Rule 202.15. Even if she doesn't have any transferable skills, she'll still be denied benefits under Medical-Vocational Rule 202.14. The SSA will deny her claim.

EXAMPLE 2: Lou is just a year older, 55, and has moderate arthritis in his spine so that he can't do more than light lifting. If he has skills that can be transferred to another job, he will be denied benefits under Medical-Vocational Rule 202.07. If he doesn't have transferable skills, he might be denied benefits under Medical-Vocational Rule 202.08—but only if he can do other skilled work specified by the SSA, without further training. If he doesn't have transferable skills and can't do other skilled work without training, then he will be granted benefits under Medical-Vocational Rule 202.06.

B. Education

"Education" means formal schooling or other training that contributes to your ability to meet vocational requirements—for example, reasoning ability, communication skills, and arithmetic skills. Lack of formal schooling does not necessarily mean that you are uneducated or don't have these abilities. You may have acquired meaningful work skills through job experience, on-the-job training, or other means that did not involve formal school learning. Past work experience and work responsibilities may show that you have intellectual abilities, although you may have little formal education. In addition, your daily activities, hobbies, or test results may show that you have significant intellectual ability that can be used for work.

1. How the SSA Evaluates Education

How much weight the SSA places on education may depend upon how much time has passed between the completion of your education and the onset of your impairments and on what you have done with your education in work and other settings. The SSA knows that formal education completed many years ago may no longer be meaningful in terms of your ability to work. This is especially true regarding skills and knowledge that were a part of your formal education but which you haven't used in a very long time. Therefore, the numerical grade level you completed may not represent your actual educational level, which could be higher or lower. But if the SSA has no evidence to show that your actual education differs from your grade level, the SSA will use your numerical grade level to determine your educational abilities.

When you file your application for disability benefits, you will be asked about your education. The SSA will accept your word about your educational level, unless you've given them some reason to doubt it—such as being a certified public accountant and saying you never completed the fifth grade. If you have any additional or written documentation about your education that you want in your file, give it to your SSA Field Office, and someone there will send it to the DDS; or you could send it to the claims examiner at the DDS handling your claim.

The effect of your education on your ability to work is evaluated in the following categories.

Illiteracy. "Illiteracy" means the inability to read or write. The SSA considers someone illiterate if the person cannot read or write a simple message such as instructions or inventory lists, even though the person can sign his or her name.

Marginal education. "Marginal education" means sufficient ability in reasoning, arithmetic, and language skills to do simple, unskilled types of jobs. The SSA generally considers formal schooling to the sixth grade or lower to be a marginal education.

Limited education. "Limited education" means some ability in reasoning, arithmetic, and language skills, but not enough to allow a person to do most of the complex job duties needed in semiskilled or skilled jobs. The SSA generally considers a formal education that ended somewhere between seventh and eleventh grade to be a limited education.

High school education and above. "High school education and above" means abilities in reasoning, arithmetic, and language skills acquired through formal schooling that included completing high school and may have included more education. The SSA generally considers someone with these educational abilities able to do semiskilled through skilled work.

Note that the SSA also generally considers a claimant's ability to communicate in English. Because the ability to speak, read, and understand English is generally learned or increased at school, the SSA often considers this as part of the educational factors. Because English is the dominant language of this country, someone who doesn't speak and understand English may have difficulty doing a job, regardless of the education achieved in another language.

2. Education and Medical-Vocational Rule Tables

Your education is an important vocational factor because it relates to the types of mental skills that you may be able to bring to a job. Turn again to Appendix C to see how various educational levels at sedentary, light, and medium work RFCs affect the allowance or denial of a claim. Under each table, lower educational levels make allowance of benefits more likely. This is particularly true as age increases and work experience and skills decrease.

A high school education or above is a critical threshold and greatly decreases your chance of being allowed benefits, although it does not eliminate them entirely. If you have a high school education or more, your education doesn't provide you with any skills you can easily use in a job, you have a history of unskilled or no work, you are at least 55 years old, and you have a sedentary RFC, you would be disabled under Medical-Vocational Rule 201.04 (Table 1). With the same findings and an RFC for light work, you would be disabled under Rule 202.04 (Table 2). With the same findings and a medium RFC, however, you would be denied under Rule 203.14 (Table 3). In fact, a high school education and a medium RFC could get you denied even as old as age 64 (Rule 203.06).

With a limited education, your chance of being found disabled greatly increases. As you can see on Table 1, if you have a sedentary RFC, your education is limited or less, and you are at least 50 years old with a history of no work or only unskilled work, you will be allowed disability benefits under Medical-Vocational Rule 201.09. If you have skilled work abilities that can't be transferred to a new job, you would be allowed under Rule 201.10.

If you are at least age 55 with limited education, have an RFC for light work, and have no or unskilled work experience, you could be allowed under Rule 202.01. With the same age and education, even if you have experience with semiskilled or skilled work, you could still be allowed under Rule 202.02, provided your skills can't be transferred to a new job. If you have a light RFC and are at least 50 years old, you can be allowed under Rule 202.09, if you are illiterate and have no work history or only did unskilled work.

3. Education Examples

Two examples help illustrate the rules discussed above.

> **EXAMPLE 1:** Dom has only a third-grade education, has done no work his entire life, is 55 years old, and has an RFC for medium work because of intermittent back pains and age-related degenerative changes in his spine. Medium work means Dom can lift up to 50 pounds and stand six to eight hours a day. That's more physical ability than many healthy people have. Yet Dom is going to be allowed SSI benefits under Medical-Vocational Rule 203.10 because his chance of learning a new job that he can perform is small. (See Table 3 in Appendix C.)

> **EXAMPLE 2:** Chuck is also age 55, has a high school education, has worked in semiskilled jobs, and has paid Social Security taxes throughout his life. He also has occasional back pains and age-related degenerative changes in his spine, and his RFC rating says the most he can do is medium work. His claim for SSDI may be denied under Medical-Vocational Rules 203.15, 203.16, or 203.17 because his education will supposedly enable him to perform some type of work. Even if he has never worked, he could be denied under Medical-Vocational Rule 203.14 because of his education.

C. Work Experience

"Work experience" means the skills you have acquired through work you have done and indicates the type of work you may be expected to do. Your work experience should be relevant to your ability to perform some type of currently existing job.

The SSA has three considerations in deciding whether your past work experience is relevant:

- The SSA recognizes that the skills required for most jobs change after 15 years. Therefore, the general SSA rule is that any work you did 15 or more years before applying for disability is not relevant to your current job skills. If you are applying for SSDI and your "date last insured" (DLI) is earlier than the application date, the SSA applies the 15-year rule described above to the DLI. (The DLI is the date at which your eligibility for SSDI benefits ran out, usually because you stopped working some years earlier. After your DLI, you can still sometimes receive benefits if you became disabled before your DLI.)
- Your work experience must have lasted long enough for you to acquire actual experience.
- Your work must have been substantial gainful activity. (See Chapter 1, Section B1.)

1. Information About Your Work

If your impairment is significant but does not meet or equal a listing, the SSA will ask you about the work you have done in the past. If you cannot give the SSA all the information it needs, the SSA will try, with your permission, to get it from your employer or another person who knows about your work, such as a relative or a coworker. When the SSA needs to decide whether you can do work that is different from what you have done in the past, you will be asked to tell the SSA about all of the jobs you have had during the past 15 years.

You must tell the SSA the dates you worked, your duties, and the tools, machinery, and equipment you used. You also need to tell the SSA about the amount of walking, standing, sitting, lifting, and carrying you did during the workday, as well as any other physical or mental duties of your job.

2. Work in the National Economy

If the SSA denies your claim, saying you can perform a particular type of work, it means that the SSA believes there are significant numbers of jobs open for doing similar work in the "national economy." "Significant numbers" is not an exact number; it is only meant to ensure that there is a reasonable chance that such work would be available. In other words, the SSA will not deny you benefits by referring to jobs that are isolated and exist in very limited numbers in relatively few locations. The SSA does not have to refer to a particular location in the country where you might find a job, however.

a. How the SSA Finds Job Information

The SSA must refer to reliable job information before saying there are jobs in the national economy that you can do. The SSA looks at statistics from state employment agencies, the Bureau of Labor Statistics, and the Census Bureau but relies most heavily on the Department of Labor's *Dictionary of Occupational Titles* (DOT).

You can refer to the DOT yourself. It's a big book—nearly 1,500 pages—and can be purchased from the U.S. Government Printing Office (www.gpo.gov). It's available in most large public libraries, law libraries, university libraries, and on the Internet at https://occupationalinfo.org. The DOT was officially replaced by the O*NET, at www.doleta.gov/programs/onet, but the SSA continues to use the DOT as its main reference for vocational analysis. The DDS should have a copy to let you look at—just ask your claims examiner.

The DOT lists various jobs, along with the physical and mental abilities required and the amount of education needed. An important consideration is the "specific vocational preparation" (SVP). The SVP is expressed as a number (the lower the number the less skill needed) and is the amount of time required to learn the techniques, acquire information, and develop the quickness needed for average performance in a specific job. The examiner or vocational analyst working on your claim will refer to the DOT to determine your SVP. With the SVP, the examiner or vocational analyst can find out the skill level required in your past work experience, which is important when looking at the medical-vocational rules.

b. Factors Not Considered in SSA's Work Decision

When the SSA decides there is work you can perform, the following factors do not matter:

- your inability to get work
- the lack of work in your local area
- the hiring practices of employers
- technological changes in the industry in which you have worked
- changing economic conditions
- that there are no job openings for you
- that an employer might not hire you, even if you are capable of doing the work, and
- that you do not wish to do a particular type of work.

3. Skill Requirements for Work

Certain mental abilities (skills) are necessary to perform various kinds of work. Abilities needed for the most basic, unskilled kinds of work are simply a part of normal human ability and do not require any advanced education or even work experience. More advanced skills can be obtained by work experience and education. The three levels of skills considered by the SSA are unskilled, semiskilled, and skilled.

a. Unskilled Work

"Unskilled work" is work that needs little or no judgment. It involves simple tasks that can be learned on the job in a short period of time. The job may or may not require considerable strength. The SSA considers a job unskilled if the primary work duties are handling materials, placing or removing materials into or out of automatic machines or machines operated by others, or machine tending; whether the job can be learned in 30 days or less; and whether little specific job skill preparation and judgment are needed. A person does not gain work skills by doing unskilled jobs.

If you have a mental impairment, your abilities are rated on a mental RFC (see Chapter 8, Section B2). Jobs listed in the DOT with an SVP of 1 or 2 are considered to be unskilled work.

Some examples of unskilled jobs are farmhand, garbage collector, maid, and delivery person. Determining whether work experience is unskilled is not always simple, because some unskilled jobs might require abilities in common with semiskilled work. For example, a delivery person might be required to provide summaries and reports of the daily delivery route.

The basic mental abilities needed to perform unskilled work are those required to perform even the simplest job. If you have no significant mental impairment, the SSA will assume that there is no significant limitation in your ability to perform unskilled work.

There are several important special concepts and considerations about unskilled work that can influence your claim—"less-than-unskilled work," "unskilled work and mental disorders," and "work that has been arduous and unskilled." Each of these is discussed below.

Less-than-unskilled work. If you can't meet the basic mental demands for unskilled work, you can be found disabled regardless of your age, education, or work experience.

The SSA looks for whether you've had a "substantial loss" of abilities. The SSA does not exactly define substantial loss, but it is similar to being "markedly limited" in an ability on a mental RFC, discussed in Chapter 8. Moderate limitations in multiple unskilled abilities on a mental RFC might be enough for an allowance of disability benefits, but the vocational analyst would have to apply subjective judgment to determine if there was work you could do.

Just as there are no medical-vocational rules for a less-than-sedentary physical RFC, there are no medical-vocational rules for a less-than-unskilled-work mental RFC. Because these are below the lowest medical-vocational rule classification, they strongly suggest that the claimant should have met or equaled a listing and that an RFC was never needed in the first place.

Why is this a category then? The answer is that not everyone in the SSA who reviews disability claims does things exactly right in regard to the "coding" of a claim—that is, how the allowance is classified as qualifying under a listing or as an RFC resulting in a medical-vocational allowance. For example, a psychiatrist or psychologist (the medical consultant) reviewing a mental impairment claim at a DDS might determine that one or more of the abilities needed to do unskilled work is markedly limited on a mental RFC they are completing. As discussed in Chapter 8, this will always lead to a medical-vocational allowance. At this point, the medical consultants should say to themselves, "I should go back and code this case to meet or equal a listing." Instead, they might just go ahead and leave the mental RFC in such a way that the examiner or vocational analyst will be forced to allow the claim on a medical-vocational basis. It is not that the medical consultant is doing the vocational determination in deciding the claim has to be allowed with certain medical restrictions—it's just that the consultant knows what the outcome will have to be in these instances. Unfortunately, some medical consultants try to get around the requirements of a listing by manipulating a mental RFC in a way they know will force the examiner or vocational analyst to allow it on a medical-vocational basis. In these cases, they're guessing and doing sloppy work rather than getting the detailed medical information necessary. But the use of "less-than-unskilled mental RFCs" is a common enough practice by some DDSs (and administrative law judges) that you should know about it.

Unskilled work and mental disorders. What if a claimant has a significant mental disorder and a mental RFC, but no significant physical disorder? How does the SSA rate these claims, given that the medical-vocational rules require a physical RFC (sedentary, light, or medium work restrictions)? Any claimant with a mental impairment who can do unskilled work will almost always be denied benefits. There are many unskilled jobs with no physical exertional restrictions to which the SSA can refer a claimant.

In a few rare instances, a claimant might be considered disabled with a mental impairment and the ability to do unskilled work. An example of such a case is one in which the claimant is close to retirement age, has no more than a limited education, and has essentially spent her lifetime in an unskilled job that she cannot now do because of her mental impairment. Of course, these are claimants who do not meet or equal a listing but receive a mental RFC for unskilled work.

Work that has been arduous and unskilled. It is important for the SSA to recognize claimants who have performed only arduous, unskilled work for many years. These people are often granted benefits because the SSA cannot name jobs that they could perform, once they can no longer do their past work. "Arduous unskilled work" has three elements:

- It is primarily physical work requiring a high level of strength or endurance.
- It usually involves physical demands that are classified as heavy.

- If it does not have heavy demands, then it requires a great deal of stamina or activity such as bending and lifting at a very fast pace.

If all of your work in the past 15 years has been arduous and unskilled, and you have very little education, the SSA will ask you about all of your jobs from when you first began working. This information could help you to get disability benefits because the SSA might decide that you cannot do lighter work. Specifically, SSA regulations provide that you will be found disabled if the following are true:

- You have only a marginal education.
- You have 35 years or more work experience during which you did arduous unskilled physical labor.
- You are not currently working.
- You are no longer capable of arduous work because of your impairment (an RFC for medium work or less).

Disability attorneys often refer to this special medical-vocational profile as the "worn-out worker" rule.

EXAMPLE: Mr. B is a 60-year-old miner with a fourth grade education who has a lifelong history of arduous physical labor. Mr. B has arthritis of the spine, hips, and knees, and other impairments. Medical evidence establishes that these impairments prevent Mr. B from performing his usual work or any other type of arduous physical labor. Although his disability is not severe enough for him to meet or equal a listing, his job history shows he does not have the skills or capabilities needed to do lighter work. Under these circumstances, the SSA will find Mr. B disabled on a medical-vocational basis.

b. Semiskilled Work

"Semiskilled work" requires some skills but does not include complex work duties. Semiskilled jobs may require alertness and close attention to watching machine processes; inspecting, testing, or looking for irregularities; tending to or guarding equipment, property, materials, or persons against loss, damage, or injury; or other types of activities. A job may be classified as semiskilled where coordination and dexterity are necessary, such as when hands or feet must be moved quickly to do repetitive tasks.

Semiskilled jobs include quality control inspector, typist, receptionist, security guard, truck driver, and secretary. Some semiskilled jobs have elements of skilled work in them, which means that determining if work experience is semiskilled or skilled is not always simple.

Jobs listed in the DOT with an SVP of 3 or 4 are considered to be semiskilled work.

c. Skilled Work

"Skilled work" requires judgment to determine the equipment to use and operations to be performed to obtain the proper form, quality, or quantity of material to be produced. Skilled work may require laying out work, estimating quality, determining the suitability and needed quantities of materials; making precise measurements; reading blueprints or other specifications; or making necessary computations or mechanical adjustments to control or regulate the work. Other skilled jobs may require dealing with people, facts, figures, or abstract ideas at a high level of complexity.

Examples of skilled jobs include engineer, doctor, pilot, accountant, attorney, and architect. Skilled work, however, is not confined to people who have college and advanced degrees. Machinists perform skilled work, and some assembly-line work is considered skilled. Computer programmers, mechanics working on today's highly specialized automobiles, many types of electronic technicians, and numerous other skilled jobs don't necessarily require a college degree.

Jobs listed in the DOT with an SVP of 5 or higher are considered to be skilled work.

d. Transferable Skills

The SSA will not award you disability just because you can't do your former jobs. If you can't do jobs you previously held because your RFC is for work lower than you used to do, then the SSA will look into whether you have "transferable skills" from your past work that you could use for other work. This issue is an important part of the medical-vocational analysis. If your skills can be usefully transferred, then you will be denied benefits. If they can't, you may get benefits as a medical-vocational allowance, depending on your RFC and other vocational factors. Note that whether one has transferable skills concerns only those who have done semiskilled and skilled work—because unskilled work does not produce work skills, there are no skills to transfer.

The SSA considers the transferability of skills most meaningful between jobs in which all of the following are true:

- The same or a lesser degree of skill is required.
- The same or similar tools and machines are used.
- The same or similar raw materials, products, processes, or services are involved.

The degree of transferability of skills ranges from very close similarities to remote and incidental similarities. A complete similarity of the three above factors is not necessary for the SSA to consider you to have transferable skills, however. When skills are so specialized or have been acquired in such an isolated work setting (like many jobs in mining, agriculture, and fishing) and are not readily usable in other jobs, however, the SSA considers that they are not transferable.

D. Use of Vocational Analysts

The medical-vocational rules in Appendix C can help you figure out if you are likely to be considered disabled or not disabled on a medical-vocational basis. Remember from Chapter 8, however, that these rules will be applied exactly as written only if your RFC rating has no special restrictions or nonexertional limitations. With special restrictions, the SSA must decide based on your individual circumstances, within the framework of the rules.

"Vocational analysts" are people with expert training in how claimants' vocational factors influence their ability to perform various kinds of jobs. In the DDS, vocational analysts handle complex issues when RFCs or vocational factors do not exactly fit into the medical-vocational rules. At the hearing level, the administrative law judge, in reaching a decision, often uses the opinion of vocational analysts (called "vocational experts"). At this level, the vocational analysts do not work for the DDS but are private consultants under contract with the Office of Hearings Operations.

> **EXAMPLE:** Mary Ellen has lung disease and arthritis, neither of which is severe enough to meet or equal a listing. Regarding her lung disease, Mary Ellen's RFC specifies that she do no more than light work and avoid exposure to excessive dust and fumes. Because of her arthritis, Mary Ellen cannot use her hands to perform certain kinds of functions such as fine manipulations or pinching. Such a complex RFC would require a vocational analyst before fairly judging this claim.

To see the RFC in your file and make sure it has all the necessary information, see Chapter 2, Section E. However, it is possible to make sure the important medical details are considered in your RFC without all the hassle of seeing your file.

Call your claims examiner and ask whether your RFC considers all of your medical limitations. Review every impairment you have. Be specific in your questions—using the above example, Mary Ellen should ask if the RFC limits her use of her thumb. If you have lung disease, make sure your RFC restricts you from excessive exposure to dust and fumes; if you have epilepsy, your RFC should restrict you from working at unprotected heights or around hazardous machinery; if your back pain is so severe you can't bend over, your RFC should restrict your bending.

If the claims examiner says that an important work-related limitation was not addressed on your RFC, ask the examiner to return the RFC to the medical consultant who prepared it to correct the oversight. If the examiner states that your treating doctor's medical records don't show a problem or otherwise don't address your concern, insist that you do have a problem and you want it evaluated before your claim is decided. Ask to speak to the examiner's supervisor and, if necessary, call the DDS director. Federal laws and regulations require that every one of your complaints be fully addressed by the SSA.

If the problem is your treating doctor, ask the examiner to hold your file until you can contact your doctor and find out why your medical records are incomplete. You will probably get full cooperation from your doctor. If you don't, you must insist to the examiner that you have a problem and want

it evaluated. This will almost invariably result in the DDS ordering another doctor to evaluate you. If your claim is at the hearing level and your file doesn't contain information on all of your problems, tell the administrative law judge that you have a problem that was not addressed by the DDS when it denied your claim.

Make Sure Your File Has Vocational Details

The devil is in the details. Not all SSA examiners are conscientious about getting vocational details from claimants about their prior work experience and skills, and a vocational analyst can work only with the information provided. If you needed any special consideration to perform your past work, make sure everyone at the SSA handling your claim is aware of that fact. Also, some medical consultants do not include important details on the RFC form for the vocational analyst. For example, you might have done a particular sewing job for many years and can do only jobs requiring similar skills. But you have arthritis in your thumb joint because of the repetitive movement required by the job. The medical consultant fails to note that you can't do work requiring frequent and repetitive thumb movement, although he restricts you to light work. The vocational analyst gets your claim and because your prior work was less than light, sends you right back to the very type of thing you can't do.

E. Vocational Rehabilitation

"Vocational rehabilitation" (VR) is the process of restoring a disabled person to the fullest physical, mental, vocational, and economic usefulness of which that person is capable. The SSA refers some SSDI and SSI claimants to vocational rehabilitation.

Vocational rehabilitation is a public program administered by a VR agency in each state to help people with physical or mental disabilities to become gainfully employed. A rehabilitation counselor evaluates your vocational disability, based on medical and vocational findings, to determine your eligibility for services. If you are eligible for services, the counselor will work with you to plan a program of rehabilitation.

The SSA will not refer certain claimants to a state VR agency. This includes claimants who have the following:

- an illness in terminal state—irreversible or irremediable
- a physical or mental impairment so severe that work adjustment, training, or employment would be precluded
- chronic brain syndrome with marked loss of memory and understanding
- a long-standing neurological or psychiatric impairment not responding to treatment, substantiated by poor employment or poor social history
- advanced age, with impairment of such severity that potential to adjust to or sustain work is doubtful
- advanced age (usually older than 55) with a significant impairment and either a sparse work record or a record of performing arduous unskilled labor for at least 35 years, having a marginal education with no transferable skills, or
- younger than 15, unless the claimant's circumstances indicate a readiness to begin VR services.

When Benefits Begin

The Social Security system uses the term "onset date" to refer to the date you became disabled. This date is important because the SSA may pay you SSDI benefits retroactively to the date you were disabled, even if you don't apply for disability until later. (The SSA does not pay SSI benefits until the first day of the month following the date of your application.) Not surprisingly, however, the date of onset isn't always clear and can be influenced by medical and nonmedical factors.

Actually, there are three different onset dates.

Alleged onset date (AOD). The "alleged onset date" is the date you state on your disability application that you became unable to work due to your impairment. If the SSA states that your impairment was not disabling at the AOD, the SSA must have contrary evidence to disregard your AOD and select another date.

Medical onset date (MOD). The "medical onset date" is the date your impairment is medically severe enough to find you disabled. In some cases, this is the same date as your AOD. But the MOD is not necessarily the same date you become eligible for disability benefits, because you must also meet nonmedical eligibility factors to qualify for the benefits.

Established onset date (EOD). The "established onset date" is the date that the SSA finds you became eligible to receive disability benefits. On this date, all of the following must be true:

- Your impairment must be sufficiently severe to qualify you for disability.
- You must have satisfied the nonmedical eligibility factors (see Chapter 1, Section A).
- You cannot be engaged in substantial gainful activity (see Chapter 1, Section B).
- Your impairment must be expected to last at least 12 months or result in your death.

The EOD is the onset date used by the SSA and may or may not be the same as the AOD or MOD. Three primary factors affect what your established onset date (EOD) will end up being—medical evidence about your condition, your work experience, and whether you are applying for SSDI or SSI.

A. Medical Evidence

Medical evidence serves as the primary element in the SSA's determination of your onset date. The SSA should review reports from all of your medical sources that bear upon the onset date to determine when your impairment became disabling. The EOD must be consistent with the medical evidence in your record. If the SSA is unable to obtain sufficiently detailed medical reports from your treating doctors or hospitals, you may not get an onset date that's as early as you deserve. (See Chapter 5 for information on how to get good medical evidence into your file.)

B. Work Experience

The date you stopped substantial gainful activity (SGA) is an important one for establishing your EOD if you are applying for SSDI. Even if the medical evidence shows that you were disabled before you stopped working, the SSA is likely to set your EOD at the date your SGA ended. Determining when your SGA stopped is not necessarily clear-cut.

In deciding whether your work is substantial gainful activity, the SSA can consider the nature of your duties, your hours worked, your productivity, your pay, and any other factors related to the value of the services your work provided. But usually, the best gauge of whether your work is considered SGA is the amount of pay you received. Under current Social Security regulations, any work that averages more than $1,260 a month is considered SGA (in 2020). If you are blind, the amount is $2,110. These amounts are adjusted annually.

If your employer had to provide special help for you to work, the value of the special assistance may be considered a subsidy and subtracted from your earnings in the SGA calculation. Additionally, impairment-related work expenses you must pay can be deducted from your earnings.

If you were working but not doing SGA, the SSA may find your EOD to be a date while you were still employed.

Failed Work Attempts

If you tried to go back to work again but failed due to your medical condition, this can allow your onset date to be earlier than your last day of work at this failed work attempt. In other words, the date you originally quit work due to disability (or were fired) can be your onset date if your later attempt at work counts as an "unsuccessful work attempt" (UWA). Your attempt at work must have lasted less than six months, and you must have left (or reduced your work below the SGA level) because of your medical impairment, either because you couldn't do the work or special conditions that you needed to do the work were removed. Special conditions include:

- assistance from other employees in doing your job
- special equipment to help do your job
- special arrangements, such as help getting you ready for work or getting to and from work
- permission to work irregular hours
- permission to take frequent rest breaks
- permission to work at a lower level of productivity than other employees
- work assignments specially suited to your medical condition, or
- being allowed to work despite your impairment because of a family or past work relationship with your employer or other philanthropic reasons.

You don't apply for a UWA determination; it is something the SSA does internally.

EXAMPLE 1: When Caesar injured his back, he could no longer carry the heavy loads that his construction job required. His employer allowed his coworkers to do the heavy lifting and carrying for him. Six months after his injury, he applied for SSDI benefits. When he was working, he earned $1,300 per month, but the SSA deducted $350 per month because his boss provided special considerations that he had to have in order to perform the job. Therefore, Caesar really earned only $950 per month, well below the SGA level. The SSA found his EOD to be the date he injured his back.

EXAMPLE 2: Suyan, a blind medical consultant, was hit by a truck and paralyzed. A month later, she applied for SSDI disability benefits. Before her paralysis, Suyan could do her job only with special considerations. Other medical consultants did part of the medical work for her, such as reading medical graphs, charts, and tracings. In addition, others read files to her, escorted her to business meetings, and recorded documents on audio tape for her to listen to. She could not take notes in meetings or see films or slides. She could not work with computers, complete medical forms, or read what she signed. Her employer estimated that the value of her special considerations was at least $5,000 per month, or $56,000 yearly. But Suyan's annual salary was $100,000, way over the SGA level, even with the $56,000 deduction. Therefore, Suyan's EOD could not be earlier than the date of her paralysis.

C. SSDI or SSI Claimant

The SSA distinguishes between the onset dates in SSDI claims and SSI claims. If you apply for both SSDI and SSI at the same time based on the same impairment, these concurrent claims may have different onset dates.

1. Waiting Period for SSDI Claimants

If you are an SSDI claimant, you may be entitled to retroactive (past) benefits if the SSA finds that your EOD fell on a date earlier than your application date. Even if the SSA makes such a finding, however, the SSA will not automatically pay you benefits from your EOD to the present. The SSA requires that at least five full calendar months, known as the "waiting period," pass beyond your EOD before you are owed any benefits.

Once the SSA establishes your EOD, it waits until the first day of the following month (unless your EOD is on the first of the month), and then counts an additional five months to determine the date you are eligible for benefits. For example, if your EOD is March 2, the SSA doesn't count March as a part of your waiting period. Instead, your waiting period is made up of April, May, June, July, and August. The SSA will pay disability benefits retroactively to September 1—assuming you qualify for benefits and you applied after September 1.

If you otherwise qualify, the SSA may establish an EOD as far back as 17 months before you apply for benefits, and then count the five-month waiting period. What this means, essentially, is that even if you apply for SSDI well after becoming disabled, the SSA will not pay you retroactive benefits for more than 12 months. This is a requirement of federal law, so even if a doctor at the SSA states that you satisfied the medical severity requirements many years in the past, you still cannot have an earlier EOD.

To get maximum retroactive benefits of a full 12 months, you need to have an EOD that causes the 17th month before your application to be counted as a waiting period month. To accomplish this, the EOD must be no later than the first day of the 17th month before your application. Any medical onset date of 18 or more months before the application date would have the same effect, because the SSA would then set the EOD the earliest it can legally be, which would be the first day of the following month—the 17th month.

> **EXAMPLE:** Jerry, a 57-year-old bricklayer and long-time cigarette smoker, stopped working July 2, 2018—two years before applying for SSDI on July 1, 2020. He states that he had to stop work because of shortness of breath and had been financially supported by his children until recently. His medical records confirm lung disease and markedly decreased breathing capacity associated with emphysema.
>
> Based on the evidence, Jerry's medical condition is severe enough to qualify for benefits when he stopped working two years previously, and the DDS medical consultant reviewing Jerry's claim states he could have a medical onset date all the way back to July 2, 2018.
>
> However, knowing that an onset 17 full months before the application date is the most the claimant can have under law, the examiner handling Jerry's claim then establishes the onset for disability purposes as March 1, 2019. This effectively gives him the full 12 months of benefits before his application date that is permissible under law. (Note that Jerry loses the benefits he could have had between July 2, 2018 and March 1, 2019 because he didn't apply soon enough. The fact that his children were helping him with living expenses would not have disqualified him for SSDI benefits.)

There are two exceptions to the waiting period rule. First, if you were approved for SSDI benefits, went back to work, and stopped receiving benefits, and then become disabled again, you will not have to wait five months to receive benefits, as long as no more than five years has passed between the first EOD and the second. (See Chapter 13.)

Second, if you are applying for benefits as the child of a disabled worker, your application is not subject to any waiting period. (See Chapter 3.)

2. No Waiting Period for SSI Claimants

As stated previously, the established onset date for an SSI claimant cannot be earlier than the first day of the month following the date of application. This is true regardless of how long you have been disabled. In other words, you are not entitled to any retroactive payments at the time you apply. If, however, you don't get approved right away (for example, you had to appeal the denial of your SSI claim), you can start building up past-due benefits between the first day of the month following your initial application date and the date your claim is allowed, if it is.

EXAMPLE: John has heart disease and arthritis. He applies for disability July 5, 2020. On his application, he alleges an onset date of sometime in February 2018. Review of his medical records shows that from a medical severity standpoint, he could have a medical onset date as far back as February 2018. John is not eligible for SSDI, however—only SSI. Therefore, the SSA determines his EOD as established August 1, 2020—the first day of the month following his application date. But John's claim isn't approved until February 2021. He is owed back payments from August 1, 2020.

Appeal of Onset Date

If you are granted SSDI benefits, the SSA may establish an EOD later than you think is correct. In that situation, you can appeal the onset date by asking the DDS to do a reconsideration of the onset. Of course, there is little point in arguing about onset date if the date the SSA established covers the full 17 months before your application. Also, when you ask for an onset appeal, the entire decision may be reviewed, including the decision to grant you disability benefits. (For more information on appealing an onset date, see Chapter 12.)

Reasons You May Be Denied Benefits

When applying for Social Security disability, most people naturally think about the reasons why they should be granted benefits. You may find it useful, however, to turn the perspective around and understand the reasons why you might be denied benefits. In some cases, the reasons are beyond your control. In other instances, though, you may be able to avoid doing something that results in denial.

A. You Earn Too Much Income or Have Too Many Assets

The most basic reason to be denied benefits is that you work above the substantial gainful activity (SGA) limit when you apply. This means you earn too much money. If you are an SSDI or SSI applicant who is not blind, you are considered above the SGA limit if you make over $1,260 per month. If you are a blind SSDI applicant, you are considered above the SGA limit if you make over $2,110 per month. (These numbers are current as of January 2020. The limits adjust each year.) Income from investments does not count toward the SGA—only work income counts.

TIP

Once disability benefits begin, earning money does not always result in a termination of benefits. For example, SSDI recipients can usually keep their benefits during a "trial work period." Also, SSI recipients can receive cash, under certain conditions, in excess

of the SGA levels, provided they do not exceed acceptable SSI income levels. (See Chapter 13.)

For SSDI, there is no such thing as partial disability based on how much money you earn. In other words, if you make $1,260 per month or less as a nonblind person, you will receive the total amount of your SSDI disability check. If you make more than the $1,260 SGA limit, you will receive no benefits (although there are temporary exceptions for those already receiving benefits when they attempt to return to work, as described in Chapter 13).

This maximum assumes that you have no impairment-related work expenses (IRWEs) such as a prosthesis or bus fare to work. If you do, you may actually be allowed to earn more than this maximum.

For SSI recipients, SGA can be confusing, because the SSI income limit is different. Your SSI check will be reduced by part of your earnings. If you have no income other than job earnings and your SSI payment, as an individual, you could technically earn up to $1,650 per month (in 2020) before your SSI will stop because you are over the income limit (financially ineligible for SSI).

The income limit also depends on the state where you live. In some states, the SSA pays a supplement (an additional payment) on top of the federal SSI benefit, so that you can earn even more before your SSI cash payments stop. But you are still subject to the $1,260 SGA limit (unless you are blind) when you apply for benefits. If you make over that amount, you will be medically ineligible for SSI.

The best way to find out about your state's SSI benefits and how much you can safely earn is to contact your local Field Office. (Also, for additional information about SSI income and resource limits, see Chapter 1, Section D, and Chapter 13.)

B. Your Disability Won't Last Long Enough

Another reason to be denied benefits is that your disability is considered temporary. To qualify for SSI or SSDI benefits, the SSA must believe that your impairment is severe enough to last at least 12 months or result in your death. The only exception to this duration requirement is with blind SSI applicants.

Many claims—often based on bone fractures resulting from acute trauma, such as automobile or motorcycle accidents—are denied because they are not likely to cause disability for 12 months. Almost all bone fractures heal in less than a year. If you have severe bone fractures unhealed after six months, however, the SSA is likely to think your impairment will last a year. But each case is evaluated on an individual basis.

> EXAMPLE: Reg has an acute bone fracture from an automobile accident two months ago and he cannot walk. He clearly is severely impaired and unable to work. But his application for SSDI is denied because the DDS assumes that his fracture will heal in less than 12 months.

TIP

You may be eligible for temporary disability benefits. A few states offer temporary disability benefits (TDI or SDI) for those who are unable to work for less than a year. If you live in California, Hawaii, New York, New Jersey, or Rhode Island, contact your state labor or employment department to apply.

C. The SSA Cannot Find You

The SSA (and the DDS) must be able to communicate with you regarding your application. If the SSA cannot schedule examinations or communicate with you about critical matters, your benefits may be denied. If you name a representative, such as an attorney, to handle your paperwork, you may not need to get in touch with the SSA, but be sure to stay in touch with your representative. If you move while your application is being considered, make sure the SSA knows how to contact you. Claimants get denied every day because the SSA cannot find them.

D. You Refuse to Cooperate

Your medical records may be vital to granting your disability. If you refuse to release those records to the SSA, your claim could be denied.

Similarly, the SSA may need additional information about your impairments, either because your treating doctor's medical records are incomplete or because you have no regular treating doctor. In these instances, the SSA will request that you be examined in something called a consultative examination (CE) with an SSA doctor, at government expense. In some cases, the SSA will require you to attend more than one CE.

If you refuse to attend a CE, or request that the SSA make a determination based on the medical records already in your file, you may be denied disability because of inadequate medical information or failure to attend the CE.

If you can't make it to a scheduled CE because of the time or location, talk to your claim examiner so the DDS can schedule a CE at a time or place that is convenient for you. If you repeatedly fail to show up for a CE, however, your claim will most likely be denied. (See Chapter 5, Section C, for more on CE examinations.)

E. You Fail to Follow Prescribed Therapy

If you are being treated by a doctor but fail to follow the doctor's prescribed treatment recommendations when you have the ability to do so, you can be denied disability benefits. For the SSA to deny your claim for this reason, the therapy that you fail to follow must be one that is clearly expected to restore your ability to do economically meaningful work (substantial gainful activity). (For a child applying for SSI, the issue is whether the prescribed therapy will restore the child's ability to function in an age-appropriate manner.) For example, if you refuse to take medications that make it possible for you to work (even though you can afford them and you don't have a mental issue that prevents you from taking them), you could be denied benefits.

If your treating doctor tells the SSA that the prescribed treatment or medication is not likely to result in your ability to work, the SSA won't fault you if you don't follow such therapy. If your treating doctor's statement is clearly contrary to the general medical opinion, however, the SSA is not bound by it. Such opinions by your treating doctor are evaluated like other medical source opinions. (See Chapter 5, Section B.)

The SSA recognizes certain legitimate excuses for failing to follow prescribed therapy.

1. Acceptable Medical Excuses

Failure to follow prescribed therapy can be excused for reasons beyond your control. They include, but may not be limited to, the following:

- You have a mental illness so severe that you cannot comply with prescribed therapy. Severe mental disorders include mania, major depression, dementia, or psychosis, such as schizophrenia.
- You have cataracts from diabetes so severe that your vision is too poor to accurately measure your insulin dose.

- You have below normal intelligence. For example, if your IQ is 70, you would not be expected to self-administer home dialysis for kidney failure. But you would be expected to swallow a pill three times a day.
- You physically cannot follow prescribed therapy without assistance—for example, because of paralysis of the arms.
- You have a fear of surgery so intense that surgery would not be appropriate. Your treating doctor must confirm the severity of your fear to the DDS consulting doctor. If your treating doctor cannot, the SSA may ask you to undergo a psychiatric examination. The SSA will not accept a refusal to have prescribed surgery because its success is not guaranteed or because you know someone for whom the treatment was not successful.
- The prescribed treatment is for major surgery and you've already undergone unsuccessful major surgery for this impairment.
- The prescribed treatment is cataract surgery for one eye, and your other eye has a severe visual impairment that cannot be improved through treatment.
- The prescribed treatment is very risky because of its magnitude (such as open heart surgery), unusual nature (such as an organ transplant), or another reason.

- The prescribed treatment involves amputation of an extremity or a major part of an extremity.
- A doctor who has treated you advises against the treatment prescribed by another doctor.

CAUTION
Parents or caregivers must follow the prescribed therapy for their children. Young children cannot be expected to reliably administer treatments to themselves or to take pills on a regular schedule. Parents or other caregivers are responsible for children following prescribed therapy, however, or they face the risk of benefits being denied to the child.

2. Acceptable Nonmedical Excuses

It is possible that you cannot follow a prescribed therapy for a reason that has nothing to do with your medical condition. Acceptable nonmedical excuses for failing to follow prescribed therapy are described in this section.

a. Lack of Money to Pay for Treatment

The SSA should not deny you benefits for failing to follow treatment prescribed by your doctor if you don't have enough money to pay for the treatment. This frequently happens with SSI applicants who have epilepsy.

If you don't have enough money to pay for drugs or other treatments for any of your impairments, make sure the SSA knows this. Informing the SSA about your lack of money for medication is extremely important; do not assume that a claims examiner will know or even care about your financial plight. However, if the SSA can find a source of free treatment for you, then you cannot use lack of money as an excuse for not following the prescribed therapy given by your doctor.

> EXAMPLE: Anna has frequent epileptic seizures because she can't afford the drugs necessary to control her seizures. Her medical records show that her epilepsy is well controlled when she takes medication. The SSA finds a free clinic in a university medical center that is willing to give her free drugs and help her obtain transportation to the clinic for treatment. In this instance, Anna cannot use lack of money as an excuse for failing to follow her doctor's prescribed treatment.

Also, if you have money and spend it on some luxury items rather than on medications, the SSA may reasonably conclude that you could afford to buy your drugs. The most common examples involve claimants who say they have no money for medications but have money to buy cigarettes or alcohol.

CAUTION

Alcohol interferes with the action of antiepileptic drugs. Avoid alcohol if you are being treated for epilepsy. If you drink alcohol, the SSA will assume that your epilepsy would improve if you stopped drinking, or that you are failing to follow prescribed treatment recommended by your doctor. If your medical records show that you drink alcohol despite advice to the contrary from your doctor, you are likely to be denied benefits. (See Section F, below, for more information.)

b. Religious Reasons

Some people's religious convictions prohibit them from receiving medical therapy. The SSA will not deny you disability for not following a prescribed therapy that is contrary to the established teaching and tenets of your religion. The SSA makes this determination by:

- identifying the church affiliation
- confirming your membership in the church, and
- documenting the church's position concerning the medical treatment by requesting relevant church literature or obtaining statements from church officials about the teachings and tenets of the church.

If you are a Christian Scientist, the SSA needs only to verify your membership in the church, because church teachings forbidding medical treatment are well established.

> EXAMPLE: Dwight, a middle-aged truck driver, applied for disability benefits. He submitted a color photograph showing a huge, gaping hole several inches in diameter that looked like he had been shot through the chin and neck with a bullet. The wound

was gruesome, and Dwight stated that the reason he could no longer work was that he did not want to be seen in public.

He had seen a local doctor when there was only a very small skin cancer on his chin that could have easily been treated without even leaving much of a scar. However, he refused treatment because his preacher told him to pray and place his faith in Jesus to cure him. He accepted this advice, despite the progressive worsening nature of the abnormality over a period of several years.

The DDS examiner evaluating the nonmedical evidence in his claim verified his church affiliation, confirmed his membership, and documented through church literature and talking to the preacher that the church taught salvation through Jesus without medical care. The DDS medical consultant wanted more medical information because Dwight's old medical records didn't establish disability, and the only evidence of a severe impairment was the alleged photograph taken by his wife.

With difficulty, Dwight was persuaded to go to a consultative examination paid for by the DDS, and the CE doctor on physical examination confirmed the huge, gruesome hole as a probable advanced cancer. By this time, Dwight was confined to a wheelchair and still putting his faith in Jesus. His claim was allowed.

c. Your Doctor Prescribes Incorrect Treatment

Sometimes, people receive treatment from a doctor that is not effective for their impairments. The SSA cannot interfere with the therapy given by treating doctors. If you follow your doctor's prescribed therapy, even if it is silly, you should not be faulted—that is, you should not be denied benefits.

EXAMPLE 1: Sal, a young man in his 20s, applied for disability benefits on the basis of arthritis. Review of his medical records showed that he had extremely severe and rapidly progressive rheumatoid arthritis affecting most of the joints in his body. Not only did he suffer from painful inflammation around most joints, but he also had irreversible destruction of many joints.

When Sal first went to a medical doctor, competent treatment could have saved his joints. But his incompetent doctor treated him only with injections of vitamin B12. Over a period of several months, Sal's faith in his doctor resulted in permanent, crippling arthritis. The SSA could not tell him that his doctor was incompetent—the SSA cannot even report such doctors to state medical authorities. Sal's disability was no fault of his own, and the SSA granted him benefits.

EXAMPLE 2: Susan has poorly controlled epilepsy of such severity that she qualifies for disability. She takes her medications as she is supposed to, but the DDS medical consultant reviewing her file can easily see that her treating doctor gives her only older types of drugs used to treat epilepsy. Newer drugs might be very effective, but apparently the treating doctor doesn't even know they exist. Susan is granted benefits.

At the same time, if you refuse to follow your treating doctor's prescribed therapy and the SSA feels the treatment would not result in a significant improvement in your impairments, the SSA should not deny your claim for failing to follow prescribed treatment.

> **EXAMPLE:** Biff developed epileptic seizures following a head injury while playing football in high school. Following the advice of friends, he went to a medical doctor who said that treatment should consist of cleansing enemas, herbal teas, and large doses of vitamins. The doctor said that these "natural" treatments would be effective and even sold the treatments in his office. The treatments were ineffective, uncomfortable, and expensive, however, so Biff stopped doing what the doctor said. He continued to have seizures, had no money to see another doctor, and so applied for disability. He was granted the benefits—and not surprisingly, he read shortly thereafter in a newspaper that the state medical board had revoked the doctor's medical license.

Keep in mind that the SSA will consider treatment prescriptions only from a medical doctor or osteopathic doctor for a physical or mental disorder. If you have a mental impairment, your treating doctor could be a licensed psychologist with a Ph.D. degree. (This doesn't matter as far as not following prescribed medication, however, because a psychologist cannot prescribe drugs.)

If an alternative practitioner is treating you, you will not be denied benefits for failing to follow a prescribed therapy if that treatment is not a reasonable therapy generally recognized by the medical community.

> **EXAMPLE:** Wilma has severe joint pains and suspects she has arthritis. She visits a doctor of naturopathy, who performs a test on her called iridology that involves analyzing the iris of her eyes. The iris is the pigmented (colored) muscle that controls the size of the pupil. The naturopath suggests to Wilma that she visit her local health food store and buy certain herbs to cleanse the toxins from her body. A friend of Wilma's had been prescribed a similar treatment, which did nothing. So Wilma doesn't comply with the recommendation. In this case, Wilma will not be denied benefits for failing to follow prescribed therapy.

d. You Don't Have a Treating Doctor

The SSA should never deny your claim for not following therapy for your condition if you do not have a treating doctor and, therefore, have no prescribed therapy, even if you have the money to see a doctor.

The SSA does not define what it means to have a treating doctor. You will be considered to have a treating doctor for a particular condition if a doctor treats you in some way meant to improve your impairment and you have an ongoing treatment relationship with that doctor. You do not have to see the doctor a particular number of times, but visits should be frequent enough to reasonably believe that doctor has knowledge of your current condition. For example, you saw a doctor several times, your medical condition stabilized with treatment, and you were given a return appointment for six months later. That doctor would certainly be your treating doctor. But if you haven't seen a doctor for over six months, the SSA may conclude that you no longer have a meaningful treatment relationship with that doctor.

Doctors who perform SSA consultative examinations on you are not considered treating doctors. You are not obligated to follow their treatment recommendations.

> **EXAMPLE:** Hiro has cataracts and is blind. He applies for disability benefits. If he has the cataracts removed, he will probably be able to see fairly well. Hiro, however, doesn't have the money for such treatment. Because he cannot afford to pay an eye specialist to submit a report to the DDS, he is sent to a consultative eye examination at the expense of the SSA. The examining doctor submits a report to the DDS, stating that although Hiro is essentially blind, he would be able to see quite well with cataract surgery and placement of artificial lenses in his eyes. The doctor gave this recommendation to Hiro. The SSA should not deny Hiro's claim, however, because the prescribed treatment was recommended by the SSA doctor, not a treating doctor.

F. Drug Addiction or Alcoholism Contributes to Your Disability

The SSA will deny benefits to someone whose "drug addiction or alcoholism" (DAA) is a contributing factor to the disability.

The decision whether DAA contributes materially to a disability is left to the SSA or DDS. In general, the medical consultant who makes the disability determination is responsible for making the determination about whether your DAA contributes to your disability. Opinions from medical sources (including treating, nontreating, and nonexamining sources), however, will be considered when making the determination. But the medical consultant will attach no special significance to the source of the opinion.

1. Is the DAA Relevant to Your Impairment?

The SSA must decide if your drug addiction or alcoholism is relevant to your disability. This determination is separate from your disability determination, and is made only if all of the following are true:

- You are found to have medical impairments severe enough to be disabling.
- Medical evidence supplied by an acceptable medical source—such as a medical doctor, osteopath, or licensed psychologist—indicates that you have a DAA.

- The medical evidence is sufficient to establish the existence of a DAA—that is, it satisfies the diagnostic requirements for drug addiction or alcoholism in the *Diagnostic and Statistical Manual of Mental Disorders*. This is a book published by the American Psychiatric Association and is found in most large libraries and bookstores. It is usually just referred to as the DSM-III, DSM-IV, or DSM-V, depending on the edition. The DSM describes the diagnostic criteria needed for various mental disorders and is an attempt to standardize the way such disorders are diagnosed. (The SSA's medical criteria for disabling mental impairments is based on the DSM.)

CAUTION
Independent corroborative evidence of your drug or alcohol abuse is required. The most convincing and likely information that the SSA can use is from medical records of hospitalization for drug or alcohol abuse. A statement such as, "I am an alcoholic," or "I take drugs"—even recorded in your medical records by a physician or a psychologist—is insufficient evidence of drug addiction or alcoholism. Moreover, alcoholism and drug addiction imply a pattern of compulsive use. (Note that the labels do not apply to children who have physical or mental impairments resulting from their mothers' use of alcohol or drugs during pregnancy.)

2. Making a DAA Determination

If you are found to have a drug or alcohol addiction and it is considered relevant, the DDS will decide if it should prevent you from getting disability benefits. The key factor a DDS medical consultant must consider when making a DAA determination is whether or not the SSA would still find you disabled if you stopped using drugs or alcohol. The medical consultant must answer two questions:

- Which of your current physical and mental limitations would remain if you stopped using drugs or alcohol?
- Would any of these remaining limitations be disabling?

EXAMPLE: Dot drinks alcohol heavily, resulting in alcoholic inflammation of her liver (alcoholic hepatitis). Although she will eventually kill herself if she keeps drinking, the medical evidence suggests that if she stopped drinking, her condition would probably improve significantly. Despite the fact she is too drunk most of the time to work, the SSA will not find her disabled. Under the circumstances, it is reasonable for the SSA to assume she would improve if she stopped drinking.

The law does not say that permanent damage done to your body by drugs or alcohol cannot be the basis of disability. If you have some type of permanent impairment that would still be present if you stopped abusing alcohol or drugs, that impairment could be the basis of disability.

EXAMPLE 1: Billy drinks alcohol heavily and has done so for many years. His blood clots abnormally slowly, and he is physically weak. Billy's liver is so damaged from alcoholic scarring (cirrhosis) that it is shrunken and obviously incapable of self-repair, even if he stopped drinking. In this instance, Billy's prognosis is grim, and he would be allowed benefits—although payments would be made to a representative payee who is supposed to keep Billy from spending the money on alcohol.

EXAMPLE 2: Gretchen uses large amounts of alcohol, cocaine, and other drugs. She has been hospitalized for detoxification numerous times but as soon as she hits the street, she goes back to her old habits. Because she is unkempt and paranoid from drug abuse, her job prospects are grim, and she is obviously unemployable. Besides, work is the furthest thing from her mind. She is exceptionally weak and barely gets around. She has used up all the goodwill of family members and friends for money. She applies for SSI and is sent for medical evaluations.

A doctor discovers that Gretchen has a heart infection known as endocarditis that resulted from her intravenous injection of drugs with dirty needles. Her heart is so damaged that it is unlikely she will survive more than a few months, even with treatment. Normally, Gretchen's drug abuse would prevent her from getting benefits. Her heart damage would remain if she stopped using drugs, however, and would itself be disabling. In this instance, Gretchen will be allowed benefits—again, through a representative payee.

G. You Have Been Convicted of a Crime

Certain conditions related to conviction of a crime or imprisonment will prevent you from receiving Social Security benefits. They are as follows:

- **Incarceration for a felony conviction.** If you are in a prison after being convicted of a felony, you can't get disability benefits. The one exception is if you are in a court-approved rehabilitation program that is likely to result in your getting a job when you get released from prison, and your release is within a reasonable amount of time. For example, if you won't be leaving prison for another five years, the SSA won't grant you benefits.

- **Injured during a felony.** If you were injured while committing a felony and were convicted of the crime, you can't get disability benefits based on that injury. The impairment that you suffered—or the worsening of an existing impairment—during the commission of a felony of which you have been convicted cannot be used as a basis for benefits.

- **Injured in prison.** If you were injured while in prison for a felony, the impairment that you suffered—or the worsening of an existing impairment—while you are in prison cannot be used to obtain disability benefits. However, in these instances, you can receive benefits after being released from prison.

H. You Commit Fraud

If you obtain disability benefits by dishonest means, the SSA can terminate your benefits and prosecute you for fraud. If you obtained benefits through fraud on the part of someone working for the SSA, your benefits can also be terminated.

Appealing If Your Claim Is Denied

I f the SSA decides that you are not eligible for benefits, that your current benefits will end, or that the amount of your payments should change, you'll be sent a letter explaining the decision. If you don't agree with the decision, you can ask the SSA to reconsider. This is called a "request for reconsideration," also known as the "first level of appeal." When you ask for an appeal, the SSA will look at the entire decision, even those parts that were in your favor.

If you disagree with the result of the appeal, you have further recourse. You can appeal first to an administrative law judge (see Section E3, below), then to the SSA Appeals Council (see Section E4, below), and finally, to a federal district court judge (see Section E5, below). Before filing an appeal, however, you should consider your chances of winning.

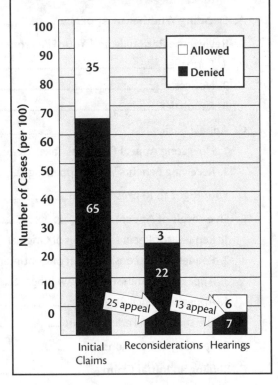

Progression of Cases Through the Disability Process

NOTE: Data based on total appeals in fiscal year 2018, not a longitudinal tracking of individual cases.

A. Deciding Whether to Appeal

A higher percentage of claimants are granted disability on appeal than at the initial application stage. See the chart below for the SSA's reporting of statistics on cases granted after an appeal (from the SSA website).

TIP
There are no costs for filing an appeal with the SSA. This is true regardless of whether you are filing a request for reconsideration or appealing to an administrative law judge or the Appeals Council. You can fill out the forms yourself and appear to defend your case. If you choose to hire an attorney or an authorized representative, however, you will have to pay for their services. And if you file an appeal in federal court, you will need to pay court fees and other costs.

Here are some issues to consider when deciding whether to appeal:

- **How medically severe are your impairments?** If you have an impairment that qualifies under an SSA listing—such as cancer—and the severity of your impairment is close to the requirements of the listing, then your claim should not have been denied, and you have a very good chance of prevailing during an appeal. The closer your disability fits into a listing (see the Medical Listings on Nolo's website), the greater chance you have of winning an appeal.

- **Is your impairment going to last at least a year?** Often, claimants apply for disability benefits based on bone fractures or other injuries associated with accidents. Most often these kinds of disabilities will not last a year, which is a requirement to obtain disability, and so these claims are denied. If lack of duration was noted as a reason for your denial, and your accident-related injuries have lasted a year or almost a year by the time you are ready to appeal, you have a good chance of winning.

- **How old are you?** The probability of getting benefits increases with age. (See Chapters 7 and 8 for more on this issue.) If you are 55 or older, your chances are generally much better than if you are younger. However, the more severe your disability, the less your age matters. (In other words, if your medical condition is severely disabling, it doesn't matter if you are only 25.)

- **What is your education?** The chance of being allowed benefits decreases with the greater amount of education you have. (See Chapters 7 and 8 for more on this issue.) If you have a high school education or more, your chances of obtaining benefits radically decrease, unless your medical condition is so severe that you meet an impairment listing or your disability leaves you with a residual functional capacity (see Chapter 8) for less than sedentary or less than unskilled work. But if you have not worked for many years in a field for which you are educated, this may not be a factor.

- **What is your work experience?** The more work experience you have—especially more skilled experience—the greater the chances that the SSA will decide you can do some kind of work.

- **Can you undertake an appeal on your own or pay someone to do it for you?** Are you able to physically and mentally do the paperwork involved? Do you want to get involved in reviewing your file and commit enough of your time to the appeal process? Or are you willing to pay part of your benefits to a disability lawyer or an authorized nonlawyer representative who will help you?

- **Why was your claim denied?** After reviewing your SSA file, can you see incorrect statements or opinions that you can challenge? What does the file say about your impairment severity, your age, your education, your work experience? Are any of these statements in your file incorrect? Can you show that they are wrong? If you can, your chances of winning an appeal are increased.

- **Is it in your best interests to appeal?** The SSA may grant you benefits after an appeal, even though you are capable of doing some sort of work. Some people can work even if they qualify and can make more money working part time than collecting benefits. For example, there are many legally blind or totally deaf people who have rewarding jobs making many times the amount of money they could receive on disability, although they would easily qualify for benefits.

Your decision to appeal should not be based on any one of the above factors, but on a consideration of all of them together. If you are younger than age 55, speak English, and don't qualify under an impairment listing, then you are facing a likely denial in the DDS reconsideration. On the other hand, if you don't mind a long process of appeal to an administrative law judge, then there is a good possibility that you could be approved even if your medical condition is not particularly severe. A few examples of cases and probable outcomes are given below.

EXAMPLE 1: Rick is 56 years old and has a third-grade education. He has done only arduous, unskilled, heavy work his whole life. He fell from a roof doing construction work and fractured his spine. After a lengthy hospitalization, it is obvious that he cannot return to his job, and he applies for Social Security disability. He has back pain if he sits or stands too long or lifts over 20 pounds. Additionally, he has difficulty bending his back. A poorly trained DDS medical consultant reviewing his initial claim ignores his symptoms, ignores his treating doctor's statement that he can't lift over 20 pounds, and ignores reports that he has difficulty bending. He is given an RFC for full medium work, which involves standing and walking six to eight hours daily, and lifting up to 50 pounds, and has no restrictions on bending. Rick has a virtual certainty of being approved for benefits on a DDS reconsideration appeal of his claim to a different medical consultant and examiner, both because his RFC was too high and because the examiner should have allowed his claim even with a medium RFC, based on his age, education, and work experience.

EXAMPLE 2: Jay is 25 years old and suffered multiple bone fractures, cuts, abrasions, and bruises in a motorcycle accident. He lost so much blood that right after the accident, his life was in danger. Because of his injuries, he cannot return to his carpentry job for about six months. He applies for Social Security disability right away and is surprised to find that the DDS denies his initial and reconsideration claims based on the fact that his fractures will be healed in less than a year. Jay's situation is like that of many claimants with serious injuries who apply for benefits but are expected to recover. Unless enough time has passed so that Jay can successfully argue that his fractures are not going to heal in 12 months, his chances of being allowed benefits even on appeal are small.

Appeal Myths Versus Reality

Beware of myths about the way the SSA and DDS agencies operate. One prevalent myth is that the SSA denies every initial application as a matter of policy. Not true. It would require a conspiracy of every DDS medical consultant, DDS director, and DDS examiner to disregard federal laws and regulations. The truth is that about 35% of initial claims are granted, as are about 10% of reconsideration claims.

Lawyers tell some claimants that the initial decision doesn't matter—that going before an administrative law judge (ALJ) after a denial is what's important. But if the DDS denies you benefits and you have to appeal, your case could be delayed a year or more. So from your point of view, what happens at the DDS level does matter.

However, it's true that your chances of prevailing are better at a hearing before an ALJ. Typical ALJs allow about half of claims they hear.

EXAMPLE 3: Jay's brother Jim, age 27, was also injured in the motorcycle accident, but he was not wearing a helmet and suffered a serious head injury. He had a fractured skull with bone fragments pushed into his brain. He was in the hospital for a month after brain surgery before he was finally allowed to go home to the care of his wife, Lorraine. He has severe difficulty with memory and thinking, characteristic of traumatic brain injury. With intense rehabilitation, he has

been slowly improving. Before he left the hospital, Lorraine filed for disability benefits on his behalf, but Jim's claim was denied. The denial notice indicated that, although Jim's brain injury was disabling at the present time, it was expected that he would recover in less than 12 months.

As Jim's guardian, Lorraine decided to review Jim's file and found that the DDS medical consultant had predicted that, based on Jim's slow improvement with rehabilitation, he would be capable of at least unskilled work within 12 months after his injury. Lorraine discovered two serious problems with Jim's denial.

First, the DDS medical consultant was a neurologist rather than a psychiatrist, and should not have been evaluating Jim's mental condition. She knew that the consultant was a neurologist because of the specialty code entered on the Form SSA-831-C3/U3: *Disability Determination and Transmittal* (see "DDS Medical Consultant Codes" in Section E1c, below, for the codes).

Second, based on the discussion of traumatic brain injury in Medical Listings Part 11, she knew that SSA policy doesn't allow cases of severe traumatic brain injury to be denied on the presumption they will improve to a denial level of severity in 12 months. The SSA may delay a decision until three to six months after the accident.

Lorraine arranged for Jim to appeal for reconsideration at the DDS, pointing out both in writing and telephone calls to the agency director that Part B of the listing for traumatic brain injury, Listing 11.18, allows for disability if the claimant has marked limitations in both mental and physical functioning. Lorraine informed the director that she knows that evaluation of mental disorders must be done by a psychiatrist or psychologist in regard to Part B, and also that the consultant should not have guessed that Jim's condition would improve. The DDS director was embarrassed and assured Lorraine that on reconsideration Jim's claim would be assigned to a medical consultant who would properly evaluate it. Within a week, Jim's claim for benefits was allowed, after being reviewed by a DDS psychiatrist who properly applied the law.

EXAMPLE 4: Maude has been on disability for three years because of severe chest pain and weakness related to blockages of her coronary arteries. Last year, Maude had coronary artery bypass surgery. Her heart-related chest pain has disappeared, and her heart tests show that she is now capable of considerably more physical activity than simply sitting. Maude's treating doctor's statements in her medical records indicate that Maude has improved significantly. Maude's physical condition appears compatible with work Maude used to do. Maude has no real reason to appeal the SSA's decision to terminate her benefits.

B. Review the Rationale and Your File From the SSA

The SSA uses hundreds of specialized forms and notices to communicate with claimants and recipients. Here is an explanation of some of the paperwork you may receive from the SSA when your claim is denied.

1. Forms

Forms are the way the SSA obtains basic information, such as claimant names and addresses and dates and types of claims. The SSA also uses forms to communicate its activities, such as disability determinations, or to transmit important information between the DDS and the SSA. Many forms are designed to be completed by claimants. At the same time, you will never see some forms unless you review your file during an appeal.

2. Notices

Notices are SSA form letters used to communicate with claimants. The SSA must send a written notice to you notifying you of any determination or decision about your entitlement to benefits or planned action that will adversely affect your current or future entitlement to benefits.

For example, a notice may tell you whether your claim is denied or allowed, or whether your claim is going to undergo a continuing disability review. Most notice forms have some type of identifier that begins with the letter L, such as SSA-L1675-U2, *Notice of Reconsideration*.

In addition to regular notices, the SSA sometimes sends out advance predetermination notices to SSDI claimants. These advance notices:

- inform you of action the SSA plans to take—such as a termination of benefits because you are performing substantial gainful activity

- summarize the evidence in your file that supports the proposed determination
- advise you how to present evidence that may change the planned action, and
- tell you how long you have to respond to the notice.

3. Rationales

"Rationales" are explanations of SSA determinations and are sent on Form SSA-4268. The form contains your name, Social Security number, and type of claim, and then a rationale—either a personalized explanation or a technical explanation.

The purposes of the disability determination/hearing decision rationales are to:

- identify the medical and nonmedical factors that have been considered
- explain the process the SSA used to arrive at the determination, and
- provide a permanent record of evidence of the reasons underlying the conclusion.

Rationales are extremely important when your claim is denied. Mistakes contained in SSA rationales can help you understand what went wrong and provide the basis for an appeal.

a. Personalized Explanation Rationales

If you receive an unfavorable decision notice —such as one denying your application or ending your benefits—it will include a personalized explanation "rationale." You may also receive an attachment with the notice, detailing additional reasons for your denial.

Personalized explanations are written to be understood by someone with at least a sixth-grade education. They are supposed to avoid abbreviations, jargon, technical terms, complex medical phrases, or personal statements about you that have nothing to do with your actual disability determination. Although the SSA uses some stock sentences in personalized explanations, your specific personal disability determination must be explained.

The personalized explanation rationales must contain the following elements.

All medical and nonmedical sources used in evaluating your claim. All medical sources used in evaluating your claim, such as doctors and hospitals, should be listed by name. Nonmedical sources (such as school guidance counselors, welfare departments, vocational rehabilitation agencies, day treatment facilities, sheltered workshops, social workers, and family members) should be listed as evidence sources but not identified by name.

An explanation for the denial. The explanation depends on the type of claim you have. In the denial of an initial claim, the SSA might say: "We have determined that your condition is not severe enough to keep you from working. We considered the medical and other information, your age, education, training, and work experience in determining how your condition affects your ability to work."

A list of the impairments evaluated. If you have a mental impairment or are unaware of the exact nature of your condition, the rationale may be worded in such a way as to not offend or upset you. For example, if you are unaware of a mental impairment, the SSA will say something general such as, "The evidence does not show any other conditions that significantly limit your ability to work."

A brief description of your medical condition. The rationale will include a description of your impairments as the SSA understands them. Read this carefully to see whether you agree with the description and to make sure nothing has been left out.

If the denial is because the SSA believes your condition won't last 12 months or result in your death, the personal explanation rationale must address this issue.

If the denial is because the SSA believes you can do your prior work, the letter will include the job the SSA thinks you can return to. The SSA does not have to include information about your residual functional capacity (see Chapter 8) if the job the SSA thinks you can return to is consistent with your description of your past work. (See Example 1, below.) If the physical or mental work you did and described to the SSA differed from what is generally required for the job, the SSA will advise you that you can return to the job as it is generally performed.

The following three examples are personalized explanation rationales of the type that might be included with an initial claim denial notice.

Note that the examples have had doctor and hospital names and dates removed that must be listed in actual notice rationales. If the DDS fails to list some of your important medical sources, you can assume that they were not used in your disability determination. This can be the basis for an appeal.

Form SSA-4268, Example 1

We have determined that your condition is not severe enough to keep you from working. We considered the medical and other information, your age, education, training, and work experience in determining how your condition affects your ability to work. You said that you are unable to work because of a back condition. The medical evidence shows that you were operated on for a slipped disc. There are no signs of severe muscle weakness or nerve damage. While you cannot do heavy work, you are now able to do light work not requiring frequent bending. Based on your description of the job of rug inspector that you performed for the past 15 years, we have concluded that you can return to this job. If your condition gets worse and keeps you from working, write, call, or visit any Social Security office about filing another application.

If the denial is because the SSA believes you can do work other than your prior work, a statement will be included saying you have the ability to do work that is less demanding than your prior work. The SSA will generally refer to your physical and mental abilities and skill level and will state that you can do a job that requires less physical effort than your previous work. The SSA will say this in general terms, rather than refer to specific jobs. For example, it might say: "You can do lighter work." (See Examples 2 and 3, below.)

Form SSA-4268, Example 2

We have determined that your condition is not severe enough to keep you from working. We considered the medical and other information, your age, education, training, and work experience in determining how your condition affects your ability to work. You said that you were unable to work because of "nerves." The medical evidence shows that you have anxieties that make it difficult to return to your prior work as a traveling saleswoman. You also complained that you have arthritis in your hands and back.

We realize that your conditions prevent your return to any type of work requiring frequent interaction with the public or heavy lifting. However, your condition does not prevent you from performing other types of jobs requiring less mental stress or performing light lifting. Based on your age (45), education (high school graduate), and past work experience, you can do other work. If your condition gets worse and keeps you from working, write, call, or visit any Social Security office about filing another application.

Form SSA-4268, Example 3

We have determined that your condition is not severe enough to keep you from working. We considered the medical and other information, your age, education, training, and work experience in determining how your condition affects your ability to work. You said that you are unable to work because of pain and stiffness in your knees and lower back.

The medical evidence shows that you have arthritis in your knees and back that causes you discomfort. We realize that your condition prevents you from doing any of your past jobs, but it does not prevent you from doing other jobs that require less physical effort. Based on your age (52), education (9th grade), and past work experience, you can do other work. If your condition gets worse and keeps you from working, write, call, or visit any Social Security office about filing another application.

If the SSA does not include the above elements in its personalized explanation rationale, it has been deficient in its explanation and possibly in the determination of your claim, and you should consider appealing.

b. Technical Rationales

"Technical rationales" are more detailed than personalized explanations, are medically complex, and may refer to specialized references, such as the *Dictionary of Occupational Titles* and specific medical-vocational rules. The SSA does not send you the technical rationale, but it is a part of every file and can give deep insight into why a claim was denied.

We have included a number of actual technical rationales in Appendix B. It is useful to review them when considering whether to file an appeal of a denial of benefits.

Personalized explanation rationales for denial notices you received in the mail won't be in your DDS file, but the technical rationales and official determination forms will be. Your DDS only retains your file for about six months. After that, it is sent to a storage facility. You should ask your local SSA Field Office for help locating the file and getting you a copy.

Continuing Disability Review Rationales

In personalized explanations for continuing disability review (CDR) claims, the rationale will also include the dates and reasons you were granted disability in the prior decision and why you are no longer considered disabled—for example, you have had medical improvement, you have started working, or there was an error in the prior determination. (CDR claims are covered in Chapter 14.)

C. Appeal Basics

Enclosed with the notice from the SSA denying or terminating your benefits will be information on how to appeal the decision.

You must appeal in writing within 60 days of the date that you receive the notice. The SSA assumes that you received the letter five days after the date on the letter, unless you can show you received it later. (In other words, the deadline is generally 65 days from the date the notice was sent.)

If you fail to appeal within 60 days, you probably lose your right to appeal—the SSA rarely makes exceptions. Of course, if you have a problem like an unexpected hospitalization, the SSA might be willing to overlook a late appeal request.

TIP

If you miss the appeal deadline. You can always start over again with a new initial claim, have it denied, and then appeal. Given the time involved, however, try to avoid starting over.

Starting the appeal process is not difficult. You simply call your local Social Security Field Office and state that you want to appeal a decision to deny you or terminate your benefits. The SSA will send you the proper forms and tell you where to mail them when they are completed. The different levels of appeal are each discussed in detail in Section E, below.

You can also file an appeal online at www.socialsecurity.gov/disability/appeal. The process is too lengthy to reproduce here, but the SSA guides you through the form step by step with instructions and examples. You can even complete part of the form and return at a later time to finish it.

If you are nearing the 60-day deadline for filing the appeal forms, write a letter stating that you will be appealing and asking for the forms.

If you live near an SSA Field Office, the easiest way to speed things along might be to go in person to complete the forms and ask any questions you might have of the Social Security representative. Remember, however, that even if you are completing the forms in your home, you can still call the Field Office for help completing them. Here are details on different types of appeals:

- To appeal from a denial of initial benefits, you must file Forms SSA-561-U2, SSA-3441-BK, and SSA-827. This starts your first level of appeal for reconsideration. (These forms are discussed in more detail in Section E1a, below, and are filed at your local Social Security Field Office.)

- To appeal from an initial termination of benefits, you must file Forms SSA-789-U4 and SSA-3441-BK. This starts your first level of appeal for reconsideration. (These forms are discussed in more detail in Section E2a, below, and are filed at your local Social Security Field Office.)

- To appeal from a denial by the SSA of a reconsideration claim, you must file Forms HA-501-U5, SSA-3441-BK, and SSA-827. This starts your appeal to an administrative law judge (ALJ). (These forms are discussed in more detail in Section E3a, below, and are filed at your local Social Security Field Office.)

- To appeal from denial of a claim before an ALJ, you must file Form HA-520-U5.

This starts your appeal to the Appeals Council. (This form is discussed in more detail in Section E4a, below, and is mailed directly to the Appeals Council.)

- To appeal from denial by the Appeals Council, you can sue the SSA in federal district court, as discussed in more detail in Section E5, below.

It is possible to have your claim reopened and evaluated again without actually appealing. Reopenings are explained in Section F, below. Also, if you lose all of your appeals, you can file another initial claim and start all over again, as discussed in Section G, below.

1. How Long Appeal Decisions Take

The first level of appeal in most states—reconsideration of an initial denial by the DDS—is the quickest, because your file is likely still at the DDS.

In a reconsideration, your file is simply reviewed by a different medical consultant and examiner from the pair that made the original decision. If the DDS does not have to wait for additional medical records and the agency's caseload is not too high, you might get a decision in a few weeks to a month. However, the reconsideration review could take four months or longer in a DDS with a heavy caseload.

Similarly, if you are appealing a termination of benefits (where a disability hearing officer (DHO) reviews the decision to terminate), it might be completed in less than a month if the DHO doesn't have a large backlog of claims for hearings and all of the records you want reviewed are already in your file. But it is more likely you will have to wait several months.

Once you get to the next level of appeal (an administrative law judge hearing), decisions really slow down—you could easily wait for a year or longer for a hearing. On further appeal to the Appeals Council, you'd probably be lucky to get any kind of answer within a year.

Appeals to a federal court typically take about a year for a decision—but several years is also quite possible. Federal court judges are not special judges who decide only disability claims; they have many kinds of cases on their schedule that have nothing to do with Social Security disability, so your claim will have to wait its turn.

2. Receiving Benefits While Appealing

If you are receiving benefits and the SSA decides to terminate your benefits after a continuing disability review (see Chapter 14), you may continue receiving your benefits while you appeal, up until the ALJ's decision (42 U.S.C. § 1383(a)(7)), if the SSA decided any of the following:

- You are no longer eligible for SSDI because your condition has improved.
- You are no longer eligible for SSI.
- Your SSI will be reduced.

If you want your benefits to continue, you must tell the SSA within ten days of when you receive the denial notice, by signing and returning Form SSA-795. The local SSA Field Office should send you this form along with the termination notice. But beware: if you continue benefits through your appeals and lose, you may have to repay the SSA. (See Chapter 12 for more information.)

TIP

More information on appeals. If you have questions about your right to appeal, call the SSA at 800-772-1213 or call your local SSA Field Office. All calls to the SSA are confidential. You can also find a considerable amount of information about appeals, including many forms and informational booklets, on the SSA's website at www.ssa.gov or at www.disabilitysecrets.com.

D. Your Right to Representation

Some people handle their own Social Security appeal. But you can appoint a lawyer, a friend, or someone else, called your "authorized representative," to help you. The SSA will work with your lawyer or representative just as it would work with you. At the first level of appeal—reconsideration by the DDS—many claimants do not have representation. But this changes as the appeals move further along; 80% of claimants use a lawyer or another representative when they appeal to an administrative law judge.

Your representative can act for you in most Social Security matters and will receive a copy of all SSA correspondence. Your representative cannot charge or collect a fee from your disability benefits without first getting the SSA's written approval.

(For more information on using and paying a lawyer or representative, see Chapter 15.)

E. Five Levels of Appeal

In most states, there are four levels of appeal of an SSA decision. The appeal levels are:

1. reconsideration of claim by DDS
2. administrative law judge (ALJ) hearing
3. Appeals Council review, and
4. federal court review.

Each step is discussed below. The request for reconsideration is discussed twice—once for original claims and once for terminations or reductions following a continuing disability review.

1. Request for Reconsideration of Original Claim

If your application for benefits is denied, you will receive a notice to that effect. The exact language of the notice depends on whether your claim is for SSDI, SSI, a combination of both, or subcategories such as auxiliary benefits (see Chapter 1). The denial notice example below is for an initial SSDI claim, but shows the kind of language you can expect in any denial of an initial claim.

In addition to telling you that you are not entitled to benefits, the denial notice may explain other basic information about Social Security disability claims (not included here), as well as your right to appeal. A personalized explanation paragraph about your medical condition either will be merged into the text of the denial notice or be on a separate attachment.

Reconsideration Returns to All States

Over the past 20 years, Social Security ran an experiment that eliminated the reconsideration step of the appeal process in some states. As of early 2020, reconsideration is back as the second step of the appeals process in every state. Reconsideration returned to Alabama, California, Colorado, Louisiana, Michigan, New Hampshire, New York, and Pennsylvania in 2019 and Alaska and Missouri in early 2020.

Contact your local Field Office for help initiating your reconsideration appeal. Do not contact the DDS directly, as they do not accept appeal applications. (The Field Office will send the DDS your prior file for reconsideration and the DDS will then contact you, as was done on your initial claim. Once a DDS reconsideration examiner has your file, you will communicate with the DDS officer.) Of course, you can still call the Field Office and ask any general questions about appeals that you want, but issues regarding the disability determination decision rests with the DDS.

The denial notice on the following pages is the kind you might expect to see if your initial DDS claim was denied.

Notice From Social Security Administration Denying Initial DDS Claims (Page 1)

Social Security Notice

From: Social Security Administration

Date:

Claim Number:

☐ Disability Insurance Benefit

☐ Disabled Widow/Widower Benefits

☐ Childhood Disability Benefit

We have determined that you are not entitled to disability benefits based on the claim that you filed. The attached page explains why we decided that you are not disabled. However, you may appeal this determination if you still think you are disabled.

The determination on your claim was made by an agency of the state. It was not made by your own doctor or by other people or agencies writing reports about you. However, any evidence they gave us was used in making this determination. Doctors and other people in the state agency who are trained in disability evaluation reviewed the evidence and made the determination based on Social Security law and regulations. The law is explained on the back of this page.

In addition, you are not entitled to any other benefits based on this application. If you applied for other benefits, you will receive a separate notice when a decision is made on that claim(s).

YOUR RIGHT TO APPEAL

If you think we are wrong, you can ask that the determination be looked at by a different person. This is called a reconsideration. IF YOU WANT A RECONSIDERATION, YOU MUST ASK FOR IT WITHIN 60 DAYS FROM THE DATE YOU RECEIVE THIS NOTICE. IF YOU WAIT MORE THAN 60 DAYS, YOU MUST GIVE US A GOOD REASON FOR THE DELAY. Your request must be made in writing through any Social Security office. Be sure to tell us your name, Social Security number, and why you think we are wrong. If you cannot write to us, call a Social Security office or come in and someone will help you. You can give us more facts to add to your file. However, if you do

Notice From Social Security Administration Denying Initial DDS Claims (Page 2)

not have the evidence yet, you should not wait for it before asking for a reconsideration. You may send the evidence in later. We will then decide your case again. You will not meet with the person who will decide your case. Please read the enclosed leaflet for a full explanation of your right to appeal.

NEW APPLICATION

You have the right to file a new application at any time, but filing a new application is not the same as appealing this decision. You might lose benefits if you file a new application instead of filing an appeal. Therefore, if you think this decision is wrong, you should ask for an appeal within 60 days.

Enclosures:

SSA Publication No. 05-10058

Form SSA-L443-U2 (2-90)

a. Complete the Forms

The forms you need to request a reconsideration are:

- Form SSA-561-U2, *Request for Reconsideration*
- Form SSA-3441-BK, *Disability Report —Appeal*, and
- Form SSA-827, *Authorization for Source to Release Information to the SSA*.

> ⚠ CAUTION
>
> **You must use forms provided by the SSA.** You can obtain them at your local SSA Field Office or by calling the SSA hotline at 800-772-1213, Monday through Friday (except holidays), from 7 a.m. to 7 p.m. If you are deaf or hard of hearing, TTY service representatives are available at the same times at 800-325-0778. You can also download many necessary forms from the Social Security Administration website at www.ssa.gov. These forms are not available from the DDS. Each form comes with its own instructions. Also, if you ask, the SSA will assist you in completing them.

i. Form SSA-561-U2, *Request for Reconsideration*

If you are uncertain whether this is the appropriate request to file, look at the letter you received from the SSA. Use this form if the letter says you have a right to file a request for reconsideration. If you have further questions, call 800-772-1213 or contact your local SSA office.

Here are instructions on how to fill out the form. A completed sample follows.

❶ **Name of Claimant:** Enter your name or the name of the person on whose behalf this reconsideration is being filed.

❷ **Claimant SSN:** Enter your Social Security number (or that of the person on whose behalf this reconsideration is being filed).

❸ **Claim Number:** Enter the claim number if different from the Social Security number.

❹ **Issue being appealed:** Simply put in the broad issue, such as "disability."

❺ **"I Do Not Agree. ... My Reasons Are:"** Briefly state the decision with which you disagree and why you disagree with the decision—use the back of the form or a continuation sheet if you need more room. For example, "I don't agree that I can lift 50 pounds and stand 6–8 hours daily. I intend to submit more medical information, as well as my treating doctor's opinion about my limitations."

❻ This section explains the different ways to handle an SSI appeal. Read it and mark your preference here.

❼ On the left side, sign the form (this is optional) and enter your address. If a legal representative is handling your appeal (see Chapter 15), that person must sign on the right side and enter an address, and must complete and return Form SSA-1696, *Appointment of Representation*. The SSA cannot discuss your case with your legal representative until it receives Form SSA-1696.

❽ Provide your daytime phone number.

Form SSA-561-U2, *Request for Reconsideration* (Page 1)

Form **SSA-561-U2** (06-2019) UF (06-2019)
Destroy Prior Editions
Social Security Administration

OMB No. 0960-0622

REQUEST FOR RECONSIDERATION

NAME OF CLAIMANT:	CLAIMANT SSN:	CLAIM NUMBER: *(If different than SSN)*
❶ Myrtle Johnson	987-65-4321 ❷	❸

ISSUE BEING APPEALED: *(Specify if retirement, disability, hospital or medical, SSI, SVB, overpayment, etc.)*
❹ Disability

I do not agree with the Social Security Administration's (SSA) determination and request reconsideration.
My reasons are:
❺ Arthritis and my illness is chronic. Also, I reviewed my denial, and no real doctor in SSA saw the evidence. I want a real doctor to look at my medical evidence, not just a bureaucrat.

SUPPLEMENTAL SECURITY INCOME (SSI) OR SPECIAL VETERANS BENEFITS (SVB) RECONSIDERATION ONLY
THREE WAYS TO APPEAL

I want to appeal your determination about my claim for **SSI** or **SVB**. I have read about the three ways to appeal.
I have checked the box below:

❻ ☒ **CASE REVIEW - You can pick this kind of appeal in all cases.** You can give us more facts to add to your file. Then we will decide your case again. You do not meet with the person who decides your case.

☐ **INFORMAL CONFERENCE - You can pick this kind of appeal in all SSI cases except for medical issues. In SVB cases, you can pick this kind of appeal only if we are stopping or lowering your SVB payment.** You will meet with a person who will decide your case. You can tell that person why you think you are right. You can give us more facts to help prove you are right. You can bring other people to help explain your case.

☐ **FORMAL CONFERENCE - You can pick this kind of appeal only if we are stopping or lowering your SSI or SVB payment.** This meeting is like an informal conference, but we can also get people to come in and help prove you are right. We can do this even if they do not want to help you. You can question these people at your meeting.

CONTACT INFORMATION

CLAIMANT SIGNATURE - *OPTIONAL:*	NAME OF CLAIMANT'S REPRESENTATIVE: *(If any)*
MAILING ADDRESS: ❼ 2300 Illard Way	MAILING ADDRESS:

CITY:	STATE:	ZIP CODE:	CITY:	STATE:	ZIP CODE:
Baltimore	MD	43202			

TELEPHONE NUMBER: *(Include area code)*	DATE:	TELEPHONE NUMBER: *(Include area code)*	DATE:
❽ (555) 555 - 5555	1/27/2020		

TO BE COMPLETED BY SOCIAL SECURITY ADMINISTRATION

1. HAS INITIAL DETERMINATION BEEN MADE? ☐ Yes ☐ No	FIELD OFFICE DEVELOPMENT (GN 03102.300)
	☐ NO FURTHER DEVELOPMENT REQUIRED
2. IS THIS REQUEST FILED TIMELY? ☐ Yes ☐ No	☐ REQUIRED DEVELOPMENT ATTACHED
(If "NO", attach claimant's explanation for delay. Refer to GN 03101.020)	☐ REQUIRED DEVELOPMENT PENDING, WILL FORWARD OR ADVISE STATUS WITHIN 30 DAYS
SOCIAL SECURITY OFFICE ADDRESS AND DATE APPEAL RECEIVED:	SSI CASES ONLY - GOLDBERG KELLY (GK) (SI 02301.310) RECIPIENT APPEALED AN ADVERSE ACTION:
	☐ WITHIN 10 DAYS AFTER RECEIVING THE ADVANCE NOTICE;
	☐ AFTER THE 10-DAY PERIOD AND GOOD CAUSE EXISTS FOR EXTENDING THE TIME LIMIT
	☐ PAYMENT CONTINUATION APPLIES AND INPUT MADE TO SYSTEM

NOTE: Take or mail the **completed original** to your local Social Security office, the Veterans Affairs Regional Office in Manila, or any U.S. Foreign Service post and keep a copy for your records.

Claims Folder

ii. Form SSA-3441-BK, *Disability Report—Appeal*

Use this form to update your disability information when appealing. Here are instructions on how to fill it out. A completed sample (that was completed by a spouse) follows.

❶ **Section 1:** Complete this section to give the SSA your name, daytime telephone number, and other basic information.

❷ **Section 2:** Put the contact information here for someone like a spouse or friend. If there's no one you can put down, enter n/a.

❸ **Section 3:** Here you record changes in your medical condition since you last completed a disability report form. Answer the questions as thoroughly as possible. Mention all changes in your impairments, symptoms, limitations, daily needs, and daily activities. In the example given, the person's mental disorder has worsened and she has a new heart problem.

❹ **Section 4:** Here you provide any new information about your medical treatment and include information such as tests, hospitals, clinics, doctors, or other facilities involved in your treatment.

❺ **Section 5:** Here you are asked what other people might have information about your condition. It could be almost anyone, such as attorneys, welfare agencies, vocational rehab services, insurance companies, and even correctional facilities. You are not limited by the examples the form provides.

❻ **Section 6:** Here you provide information about any medications you are currently taking.

❼ **Section 7:** Here you describe any changes in your activities since the last disability decision. Specify here how your condition has worsened. If needed, you can include more detail in Section 10, Remarks.

❽ **Section 8:** Here you describe any work or type of special job training or trade or vocational school you have had since you last completed a disability report form.

❾ **Section 9:** Here you indicate whether you have had any vocational rehabilitation, employment, or other support services since you last completed a disability report form.

❿ **Section 10:** Use this space to continue your answer to any questions (make sure you note the question number to which you are referring). You can also use this section to show any other information you feel the SSA should consider in the appeal process. For example, if the DDS didn't consider a certain impairment or relied on incorrect information provided by your treating physician, state that.

If you run out of room, attach a blank sheet of paper as a continuation sheet—at the top write your name, Social Security number, and SSA-3441-BK, Continued.

Form SSA-3441-BK, *Disability Report—Appeal* (Page 1)

Form **SSA-3441-BK** (04-2018) UF
Discontinue Prior Editions
SOCIAL SECURITY ADMINISTRATION

OMB No. 0960-0144

DISABILITY REPORT – APPEAL

For SSA use only. Please do not write in this box.

Related SSN _____   Number Holder _____

If you are filling out this report for someone else, please provide information about him or her. When a question refers to "you" or "your," it refers to the person who is applying for disability benefits.

❶ **SECTION 1 – INFORMATION ABOUT THE DISABLED PERSON**

1. A. Name (First, Middle, Last, Suffix)
Anne Brown

1. B. Social Security Number
555-55-5555

1. C. Daytime Phone Number, including area code (include IDD and country codes if outside the U.S. or Canada)
303-555-5534

☐ Check this box if you do not have a phone number where we can leave a message.

1. D. Alternate Phone Number – another number where we may reach you, if any
None

1. E. Email Address (Optional)
Brown11@yahoo.com

❷ **SECTION 2 – CONTACTS**

Give the name of someone **(other than your doctors)** we can contact who knows about your medical conditions, and can help you with your claim. (e.g., friend or relative)

2. A. Name (First, Middle, Last)
Sam Brown

2. B. Relationship to Disabled Person
Husband

2. C. Mailing Address (Street or PO Box), include apartment number or unit if applicable.

City	State/Province	ZIP/Postal Code	Country (if not U.S.)
472 11th Street	CO	80299	

2. D. Daytime Phone Number, including area code (include IDD and country codes if outside the U.S. or Canada)
303-555-5534

2. E. Can this person speak and understand English?
☒ Yes   ☐ No

If no, what language does the contact person prefer? _____

2. F. Who is completing this form?
☐ The person who is applying for disability (Go to SECTION 3 - MEDICAL CONDITIONS).
☒ The person listed in 2.A. (Go to SECTION 3 - MEDICAL CONDITIONS).
☐ Someone else (Please complete the information below).

2. G. Name (First, Middle, Last)

2. H. Relationship to Disabled Person

2. I. Mailing Address (Street or PO Box) Include apartment number or unit if applicable.

City	State/Province	ZIP/Postal Code	Country (if not U.S.)

2. J. Daytime Phone Number, including area code (include IDD and country codes if outside the U.S. or Canada)

Form SSA-3441-BK, *Disability Report—Appeal* (Page 2)

Form **SSA-3441-BK** (04-2018) UF

❸   **SECTION 3 – MEDICAL CONDITIONS**

3. A. Since you last told us about your medical conditions, has there been any **CHANGE** (for better or worse) in your physical or mental conditions?

☒ Yes, approximate date change occurred: A month ago   ☐ No

If yes, please describe in detail: My wife has chronic schizophrenia. She is more

withdrawn and seems to be more out of touch with reality. Her auditory

hallucinations came back. Her psychiatrist had to increase her Clozaril.

3. B. Since you last told us about your medical conditions, do you have any **NEW** physical or mental conditions?

☒ Yes, approximate date of new conditions: 10-11-15   ☐ No

If yes, please describe in detail: Anne developed a new heart condition—an abnormal

heart rhythm that affects her ability to lift and carry (See Section 10 -

Remarks)

If you need more space, use SECTION 10 – REMARKS on the last page.

❹   **SECTION 4 – MEDICAL TREATMENT**

4. A. Have you used any other names on your medical or educational records? Examples are maiden name, other married name, or nickname.

☐ Yes   ☒ No

If yes, please list the other names used: _____

_____

4. B. Since you last told us about your medical treatment, have you seen a doctor or other health care provider, received treatment at a hospital or clinic, or **do you have a future appointment scheduled**?

☒ Yes   ☐ No (Go to SECTION 6 – MEDICINES)

4. C. What type(s) of condition(s) were you treated for, or will you be seen for?

☒ Physical   ☒ Mental (including emotional or learning problems)

If you answered "Yes" to 4.B., please tell us who may have **NEW** medical records about any of your **physical or mental** conditions (including emotional or learning problems).

Use the following pages to provide information for up to three (3) providers. **Complete one page for each provider**. If you have more than three providers, list them in SECTION 10 - REMARKS on the last page.

Please include:

- doctors' offices
- hospitals (including emergency room visits)
- clinics
- mental health center
- other health care facilities.

Only list the providers you have seen since you last told us about your medical treatment.

Form SSA-3441-BK, *Disability Report—Appeal* (Page 3)

Form **SSA-3441-BK** (04-2018) UF

SECTION 4 – MEDICAL TREATMENT (continued)
Provider 1

4. D. Name of facility or office	Name of health care provider who treated you
The Mental Health Group	Dr. Claudia Edwards

ALL OF THE QUESTIONS ON THIS PAGE REFER TO THE HEALTH CARE PROVIDER ABOVE.

Phone Number	Patient ID# (if known)
303-123-4567	

Address

10001 Forest View Drive

City	State/Province	ZIP/Postal Code	Country (If not U.S.)
Denver	CO	80255	

Dates of Treatment (approximate date, if exact date is unknown)

Office, Clinic or Outpatient visits at this facility	**Emergency Room visits at this facility**	**Overnight hospital stays at this facility**
First Visit Jan 1, 2000	Date _____	Date in _____ Date out _____
Last Visit Dec 1, 2019	Date _____	Date in _____ Date out _____
Next scheduled appointment	Date _____	Date in _____ Date out _____
(if any) March 2020	☒ None	☒ None

What medical conditions were treated or evaluated?

Schizophrenia.

What treatment did you receive for the above conditions? (Do not list medicines or tests in this box.)

Medication and psychotherapy.

Has this provider performed or sent you to any tests? Please include tests you are scheduled to have in the future.   ☒ Yes (Please complete the information below.)   ☐   No (Go to the next page.)

KIND OF TEST	DATES OF TESTS	KIND OF TEST	DATES OF TESTS
☐ Biopsy (list body part) _____		☐ MRI/CT Scan (list body part) _____	
☒ Blood Test (not HIV)	10/2019	☐ Speech/Language Test	
☐ Breathing Test		☐ Treadmill (exercise test)	
☐ Cardiac Catheterization		☐ Vision Test	
☐ EEG (brain wave test)		☐ X-ray (list body part) _____	
☐ EKG (heart test)			
☐ Hearing Test		☐ Other (please describe)	
☐ HIV Test		_____	
☐ IQ Testing			

If you need to list more tests, use SECTION 10 - REMARKS on the last page.

If you do not have any more providers to describe,

go to SECTION 5 – OTHER MEDICAL INFORMATION on page 6.

Form SSA-3441-BK, *Disability Report—Appeal* (Page 4)

Form **SSA-3441-BK** (04-2018) UF

SECTION 4 – MEDICAL TREATMENT (continued)
Provider 2

4. D. Name of facility or office	Name of health care provider who treated you
Cardiology Associates	Dr. Howard Stuckey

ALL OF THE QUESTIONS ON THIS PAGE REFER TO THE HEALTH CARE PROVIDER ABOVE.

Phone Number	Patient ID# (if known)
303-555 2222	

Address

Suite 200, 1201 Canyon Blvd.

City	State/Province	ZIP/Postal Code	Country (if not U.S.)
Denver	CO	80302	

Dates of Treatment (approximate date, if exact date is unknown)

Office, Clinic or Outpatient visits at this facility	**Emergency Room visits at this facility**	**Overnight hospital stays at this facility**
First Visit August 2019	Date _____	Date in _____ Date out _____
Last Visit October 2019	Date _____	Date in _____ Date out _____
Next scheduled appointment (if any) January 2020	Date _____	Date in _____ Date out _____
	☒ None	☒ None

What medical conditions were treated or evaluated?

What treatment did you receive for the above conditions? (Do not list medicines or tests in this box.)

Has this provider performed or sent you to any tests? Please include tests you are scheduled to have in the future. ☒ Yes (Please complete the information below.) ☐ No (Go to the next page.)

KIND OF TEST	DATES OF TESTS	KIND OF TEST	DATES OF TESTS
☐ Biopsy (list body part) _____		☐ MRI/CT Scan (list body part) _____	
☐ Blood Test (not HIV)		☐ Speech/Language Test	
☐ Breathing Test		☐ Treadmill (exercise test)	
☐ Cardiac Catheterization		☐ Vision Test	
☐ EEG (brain wave test)		☒ X-ray (list body part) Chest X-Ray	October 2019
☒ EKG (heart test)	October 2019	☒ Other (please describe) Echocardiogram	October 2019
☐ Hearing Test			
☐ HIV Test			
☐ IQ Testing			

If you need to list more tests, use SECTION 10 - REMARKS on the last page.

If you do not have any more providers to describe,

go to SECTION 5 – OTHER MEDICAL INFORMATION on page 6.

Form SSA-3441-BK, *Disability Report—Appeal* (Page 5)

Form **SSA-3441-BK** (04-2018) UF

SECTION 4 – MEDICAL TREATMENT (continued)
Provider 3

4. D. Name of facility or office | Name of health care provider who treated you

ALL OF THE QUESTIONS ON THIS PAGE REFER TO THE HEALTH CARE PROVIDER ABOVE.

Phone Number | Patient ID# (if known)

Address

City | State/Province | ZIP/Postal Code | Country (if not U.S.)

Dates of Treatment (approximate date, if exact date is unknown)

Office, Clinic or Outpatient visits at this facility | **Emergency Room visits at this facility** | **Overnight hospital stays at this facility**

First Visit _____ | Date _____ | Date in _____ Date out _____

Last Visit _____ | Date _____ | Date in _____ Date out _____

Next scheduled appointment | Date _____ | Date in _____ Date out _____

(if any) _____ | ☐ None | ☐ None

What medical conditions were treated or evaluated?

What treatment did you receive for the above conditions? (Do not list medicines or tests in this box.)

Has this provider performed or sent you to any tests? Please include tests you are scheduled to have in the future. ☐ Yes (Please complete the information below.) ☐ No (Go to the next page.)

KIND OF TEST	DATES OF TESTS	KIND OF TEST	DATES OF TESTS
☐ Biopsy (list body part) _____		☐ MRI/CT Scan (list body part) _____	
☐ Blood Test (not HIV)		☐ Speech/Language Test	
☐ Breathing Test		☐ Treadmill (exercise test)	
☐ Cardiac Catheterization		☐ Vision Test	
☐ EEG (brain wave test)		☐ X-ray (list body part) _____	
☐ EKG (heart test)			
☐ Hearing Test		☐ Other (please describe) _____	
☐ HIV Test			
☐ IQ Testing			

If you need to list more tests, use SECTION 10 - REMARKS on the last page.

If you have been treated by more providers, use section 10 - REMARKS on the last page.

Form SSA-3441-BK, *Disability Report—Appeal* (Page 6)

Form **SSA-3441-BK** (04-2018) UF

⑤   **SECTION 5 – OTHER MEDICAL INFORMATION**

5. **Since you last told us about your other medical information**, does anyone else have **medical information** about any of your **physical or mental** conditions (including emotional and learning problems) or are you scheduled to see anyone else?

This may include:

- workers' compensation
- vocational rehabilitation services
- insurance companies who have paid you disability benefits
- prisons and correctional facilities
- attorneys
- social service agencies
- welfare agencies
- school/education records

☐ Yes (Please complete the information below.)
☒ No (Go to SECTION 6 – MEDICINES)

Name of Organization	Claim or ID Number (if any)

Address

City	State/Province	ZIP/Postal Code	Country (if not U.S.)

Name of Contact Person	Phone Number

Date of First Contact	Date of Last Contact	Date of Next Contact (if any)

Reasons for Contacts

If you need to list more people or organizations, use SECTION 10 – REMARKS on the last page.

⑥   **SECTION 6 – MEDICINES**

6. Are you <u>currently</u> taking any medicines (prescription or non-prescription)?

☒ Yes (Please complete the information below. You may need to look at your medicine containers.)
☐ No (Go to SECTION 7 – ACTIVITIES)

NAME OF MEDICINE	IF PRESCRIBED, NAME OF DOCTOR	REASON FOR MEDICINE	SIDE EFFECTS YOU HAVE
Clozaril	Dr. Edwards	Schizophrenia	Sleepy, weak
Metoprolol	Dr. Stuckey	Atrial fibrillation	Lethargic, sleepy
Pradaxa	Dr. Stuckey	Atrial fibrillation	Bruise easily

If you need to list more medicines, use SECTION 10 – REMARKS on the last page.

Form SSA-3441-BK, *Disability Report—Appeal* (Page 7)

Form **SSA-3441-BK** (04-2018) UF

7 ### SECTION 7 - ACTIVITIES

7. Since you last told us about your activities, has there been any **change** (for better or worse) in your daily activities due to your **physical or mental** conditions? (Examples of daily activities are household tasks, personal care, getting around, hobbies and interests, social activities, etc.)

☒ Yes   ☐ No

If yes, please describe in detail: Anne is now less able to perform daily chores like cooking a meal and cleaning. She also has to be told to bathe and is less willing to socialize with family members or guests.

If you need more space, use SECTION 10 – REMARKS on the last page.

8 ### SECTION 8 – WORK AND EDUCATION

8. A. Since you last told us about your work, have you worked or has your work changed?

☐ Yes   ☒ No

If yes, you will be asked to provide additional information.

8. B. Since you last told us about your education, have you completed or are you enrolled in any type of specialized job training, trade school, or vocational school?

☐ Yes   ☒ No

If yes, what type? _____

Date(s) attended: _____

If you need more space, use SECTION 10 – REMARKS on the last page.

9 ### SECTION 9 – VOCATIONAL REHABILITATION, EMPLOYMENT, OR OTHER SUPPORT SERVICES

9. Since you last told us about your vocational rehabilitation, have you participated, or are you participating in:

- an individual work plan with an employment network under the Ticket to Work Program?
- an individualized plan for employment with a vocational rehabilitation agency or any other organization?
- a Plan to Achieve Self-Support (PASS)?
- an individualized education program (IEP) through an educational institution (if a student age 18-21)?
- any program providing vocational rehabilitation, employment services, or other support services to help you go to work?

☐ Yes (Please complete the information below.)
☒ No (Go to SECTION 10 – REMARKS)

Name of Organization or School

Name of Counselor, Instructor, or Job Coach	Phone Number

Address

City	State/Province	ZIP/Postal Code	Country (if not U.S.)

Date when you started participating in the plan or program:

If you need more space, use SECTION 10 – REMARKS on the last page.

Form SSA-3441-BK, *Disability Report—Appeal* (Page 8)

Form **SSA-3441-BK** (04-2018) UF

⑩ **SECTION 10 – REMARKS**

Use this space to provide any information you could not show in earlier sections of this form or any additional information you feel we should know about. Please be sure to include the number of the question you are answering (For example, 3A, 4D, etc.).

3A. Anne needs almost constant supervision and will wander off if I don't watch her and is increasingly depressed and suspicious of people's motives. She wears her clothes in bizarre ways. Anne has a severe chronic mental disorder. She can function minimally under the supervision and support of our family. Contrary to what the DDS stated when they denied her benefits, Anne's mental condition has not significantly improved and is even worse. Dr. Edwards emphasized we must provide a highly supportive home for Anne, or she will decompensate even more. I think she is clearly worse, and Dr. Edwards agrees. Anyway, she's certainly not better, and her benefits should not have stopped.

8. The DDS now says she can work. This is wrong, as shown by medical records and Dr. Edwards's opinion. I wonder if a real mental specialist reviewed her records and why they didn't contact Dr. Edwards for a statement.

7. Anne's heart condition limits her physically now, in addition to her mental condition and the fact her medications make her lethargic. Dr. Stuckey says he can't completely control her rhythm and that she's at risk for stroke. Anne can sometimes do simple things like making a sandwich or doing a little dusting, but our daughters do most of the cooking and cleaning. Anne often refuses to help, saying "I'm just not interested."

3B. I forgot to mention that Anne has a narrowed heart valve that causes her rhythm problem but also decreases her ability to do physical chores; she tires very easily. She certainly has not been able to work since her benefits were wrongly denied, in my opinion. Please contact her treating doctor!

Date Report Completed MM/DD/YYYY: November 11, 2019

iii. Form SSA-827, *Authorization for Source to Release Information to the SSA*

Use this form to authorize your medical sources—doctors, hospitals, clinics, nurses, social workers, family members, friends, governmental agencies, employers, and anyone else who has medical information about you—to release information to the SSA. It is important to understand that Form SSA-827 releases *all* of your medical records, including information pertaining to drug abuse, alcoholism, mental disorders (excluding psychotherapy notes), AIDS, and HIV. You cannot pick and choose what medical information is released under this form.

Here are instructions on how to fill out the form.

❶ This section reminds you to read the form (Page 1) and associated legal comments on Page 2 (not included below).

❷ **Information Being Disclosed.** You should read the top part of the form carefully to make sure you understand what information will be available to the SSA when you sign the form.

❸ **Signature.** The claimant, legal guardian of a child claimant, or legal representative must sign the form in the block indicated. If the claimant is not signing, specify the relationship of the person who is signing— such as parent or legal representative.

❹ **Date, Address, and Daytime Phone Number.** Enter the requested information.

❺ **Signature of Witness.** All forms must be witnessed. Many medical sources will not honor an authorization to release information unless it is witnessed. The witness can be any competent adult, including your spouse, neighbor, or a social worker. Include the witness's address.

iv. Forward Forms to the SSA

Once you have completed all the forms, attach copies of any evidence showing that the original determination was incorrect, such as medical records not included in the initial decision. Then fold all forms and documents in thirds, insert them in a standard business envelope, and mail to your local Social Security office. If you are not sure where that office is, call 800-772-1213. Keep a copy of each form and the originals of your attached evidence for your records. You may use a nonstandard envelope if your papers will not fit into a standard one.

b. Reconsideration Appeal Process

The reconsideration is a complete review of your claim. It takes place at the DDS, but is done by a medical consultant and an examiner who were not a part of the initial decision. This means that the claims examiner and medical consultant who had anything to do with the denial of your initial claim are barred from deciding your reconsideration claim.

The DDS reconsideration medical consultant and examiner team will look at all the evidence submitted for the original decision, plus any new evidence you include with your reconsideration request.

Form SSA-827, Authorization for Source to Release Information to the SSA

WHOSE *Records to be Disclosed*	Form Approved OMB No. 0960-0623
NAME *(First, Middle, Last, Suffix)* Myrtle A. Johnson	
SSN 987 65 4321	Birthday *(mm/dd/yy)* 04/22/52

AUTHORIZATION TO DISCLOSE INFORMATION TO THE SOCIAL SECURITY ADMINISTRATION (SSA)

** PLEASE READ THE ENTIRE FORM, BOTH PAGES, BEFORE SIGNING BELOW **

❶
❷ I voluntarily authorize and request disclosure (including paper, oral, and electronic interchange):
OF WHAT *All my medical records*; also education records and other information related to my ability to perform tasks. This includes specific permission to release:

1. All records and other information regarding my treatment, hospitalization, and outpatient care for my impairment(s) *including* , and not limited to :

   - Psychological, psychiatric or other mental impairment(s) (excludes "psychotherapy notes" as defined in 45 CFR 164.501)
   - Drug abuse, alcoholism, or other substance abuse
   - Sickle cell anemia
   - Records which may indicate the presence of a communicable or noncommunicable disease; and tests for or records of HIV/AIDS
   - Gene-related impairments (including genetic test results)

2. Information about how my impairment(s) affects my ability to complete tasks and activities of daily living, and affects my ability to work.

3. Copies of educational tests or evaluations, including Individualized Educational Programs, triennial assessments, psychological and speech evaluations, and any other records that can help evaluate function; also teachers' observations and evaluations.

4. Information created within 12 months after the date this authorization is signed, as well as past information.

FROM WHOM

	THIS BOX TO BE COMPLETED BY SSA/DDS (as needed) Additional information to identify the subject (e.g., other names used), the specific source, or the material to be disclosed:
• All medical sources (hospitals, clinics, labs, physicians, psychologists, etc.) including mental health, correctional, addiction treatment, and VA health care facilities • All educational sources (schools, teachers, records administrators, counselors, etc.) • Social workers/rehabilitation counselors • Consulting examiners used by SSA • Employers, insurance companies, workers' compensation programs • Others who may know about my condition (family, neighbors, friends, public officials)	

TO WHOM The Social Security Administration and to the State agency authorized to process my case (usually called "disability determination services"), including contract copy services, and doctors or other professionals consulted during the process. [Also, for international claims, to the U.S. Department of State Foreign Service Post.]

PURPOSE Determining my eligibility for benefits, including looking at the combined effect of any impairments that by themselves would not meet SSA's definition of disability; and whether I can manage such benefits.
  ☐ Determining whether I am capable of managing benefits ONLY (check only if this applies)

EXPIRES WHEN This authorization is good for 12 months from the date signed (below my signature).

- I authorize the use of a copy (including electronic copy) of this form for the disclosure of the information described above.
- I understand that there are some circumstances in which this information may be redisclosed to other parties (see page 2 for details).
- I may write to SSA and my sources to revoke this authorization at any time (see page 2 for details).
- SSA will give me a copy of this form if I ask; I may ask the source to allow me to inspect or get a copy of material to be disclosed.
- I have read both pages of this form and agree to the disclosures above from the types of sources listed.

❸ PLEASE SIGN USING BLUE OR BLACK INK ONLY | IF not signed by subject of disclosure, specify basis for authority to sign
INDIVIDUAL authorizing disclosure | ☐ Parent of minor ☐ Guardian ☐ Other personal representative (explain)

SIGN ▶ *Myrtle Johnson* | (Parent/guardian/personal representative sign here if two signatures required by State law) ▶

❹
Date Signed 10/02/15	Street Address 2300 Illiard Way		
Phone Number (with area code) (201) 472-0001	City Baltimore	State MD	ZIP 22212

WITNESS *I know the person signing this form or am satisfied of this person's identity:*

	IF needed, second witness sign here (e.g., if signed with "X" above)
❺ SIGN ▶	SIGN ▶
Phone Number (or Address)	Phone Number (or Address)

This general and special authorization to disclose was developed to comply with the provisions regarding disclosure of medical, educational, and other information under P.L. 104-191 ("HIPAA"); 45 CFR parts 160 and 164; 42 U.S. Code section 290dd-2; 42 CFR part 2; 38 U.S. Code section 7332; 38 CFR 1.475; 20 U.S. Code section 1232g ("FERPA"); 34 CFR parts 99 and 300; and State law.

Form **SSA-827** (11-2012) ef (11-2012) Use 4-2009 and Later Editions Until Supply is Exhausted   Page1 of 2

c. Review Your File Before the Reconsideration

Over the past few years, the SSA has transferred its files into a computer system that stores all of its information, including disability claims, in a format that all of the various parts of the agency can access. In the past, a paper file had to be shipped from one location to another—for example, from a Field Office to the DDS and many other potential destinations. This greatly slowed down the decision-making process. Now, every SSA component has instant access to data entered by any other component.

If you complete an application or other form online, that information goes into a highly secure and confidential "electronic folder" (EF) assigned to your name and SSN. When you are interviewed at an SSA Field Office, the official will scan the information into your EF, even if you complete a paper form. Also, medical evidence in the form of paperwork is scanned into your electronic folder either by the Field Office or the DDS.

Any physical records that you submitted are still retained, but the SSA no longer keeps its own decisional documents in the paper file. In the past, for example, you could find various medical consultant write-ups and administrative documents in the paper file. These are now in electronic form. So if you want to review the SSA's decision process, you must have access to your electronic disability records. Fortunately, the SSA recognizes your or your representative's rights to information.

The access and disclosure policies are no different for paper and electronic records. SSA officials have the authority to copy appropriate disability information in your EF to a CD-ROM. In some instances, you might even be able to persuade your local Field Office to mail you a copy. If you don't have a computer, you might have to pay a fee to have the information printed.

As you review your file, note all problems, including inaccurate and missing information. Ask to have pages copied, if necessary. You cannot write directly on records in your file. You can ask that information be added, such as new medical information, and even your own statements about your condition. Specifically, look at the following:

Your medical records. Make sure your important medical records are in the file. If your medical records contain comments by your treating doctor about your disability, note what they say. You or your representative might need to contact your treating doctor for clarification of a statement or to contest a comment you think is inaccurate.

EXAMPLE: Orris has heart disease and is being treated for heart failure. His treating doctor tells the SSA that he can do "light work." When Orris walks a half block, however, he gets short of breath, his heart rate races, he breaks out in a sweat, and he gets dizzy. He can't stand for more than ten minutes at a time. Orris takes several medications, and the side effects make him feel even worse. The SSA decided he could do light work and used his treating doctor's statement in support. Because of his age, education, and work experience, he would have been granted benefits if the SSA had not found that he could do light work.

Orris's treating doctor might not know the SSA's definition of light work, which requires lifting up to 20 pounds and standing or walking six to eight hours a day. Orris must talk with his treating doctor, explain the SSA definition of light work, explain that he cannot do it, and ask for a new letter accurately describing his limitations to be used in his reconsideration claim.

Sometimes, a treating doctor doesn't provide information the SSA needs, even if the doctor has it. For example, your doctor might have described one of your conditions but not another. Or a doctor might have provided unclear or inaccurate information. Ask your doctor to forward the necessary information to the DDS. If your treating doctor doesn't have it, the DDS must have you examined at the government's expense through a consultative examination (CE). (See Chapter 5, Section C, for more on CEs.)

It's also possible that your treating doctor provided accurate information, but not enough detail. Although medical judgment determines how much information is enough, sometimes the issues are not clear. For example, suppose your treating doctor said you have arthritis with some pain in certain joints. This isn't enough information to decide the severity of your arthritis. If your doctor can't say more, the DDS should have sent you for CEs to obtain X-rays, evaluate

the swelling around your joints, have blood tests done for rheumatoid arthritis, and consider how your arthritis limits your ability to carry out your daily activities. Be sure the reconsideration examiner at the DDS knows that your complaints were not adequately evaluated, and remind the examiner that you have a right to an adequate medical evaluation of all of your allegations.

Your work records. If the DDS made inaccurate statements about your previous work history, you will need to correct it. Compare your statements on any Form SSA-3369-F6, *Vocational Report*, or other forms, against those made by the SSA on your denial rationale. If necessary to correct your SSA file, ask your employer or coworkers to submit written information to the DDS.

Form SSA-831: *Disability Determination and Transmittal.* This form is the official disability determination document used by the DDS. One copy stays with your file. Other copies go to other SSA offices. No copy goes to you. Most of the information on the front of the form will be of little use to you because of the number of codes used by the SSA. But it should contain the name and signature of both the disability examiner and the DDS medical consultant who worked on your claim.

Attached to Form SSA-831 or on Form SSA-4268, *Explanation of Determination*, should be the technical rationale used in making your disability determination. Because the technical rationale contains a lot more detailed information than the personalized explanation rationale you were sent with your denial notice, it is in your interest to look it over, even though it might include bureaucratic language you do not understand. By reviewing the technical rationale, you can see the step-by-step reasoning that the SSA used to deny your claim. The DDS examiner handling your claim writes these rationales. (See Appendix B for examples of technical rationales.)

Note the name of the medical consultant who signed the SSA-831 and the number of the specialty code near his or her name. Such specialty code information can be very valuable in demonstrating that the wrong kind of doctor reviewed your claim. For instance, child or adult mental impairments should always be evaluated by a psychiatrist or psychologist, and children's claims about physical impairments should always be evaluated by a pediatrician.

Residual functional capacity (RFC) forms. RFC forms might not be in your file if your claim was denied because your impairments were considered not severe (mild or slight).

Your file might contain physical RFCs (Form SSA-4734-U8, *Residual Functional Capacity Assessment*), mental RFCs (Form SSA-4734-F4-SUP, *Mental Residual Functional Capacity Assessment*), or both.

Check the RFC forms to make sure that the information is actually true. Note the limitations and abilities the medical consultant (MC) gave you. Do you agree with them? Do they contradict your treating doctor? Did the MC say you have more exertional ability (such as lifting, carrying, walking) than your treating doctor says you

have? Did the MC fail to give you limitations suggested by your treating doctor, such as avoiding excessive fumes or restrictions on frequent bending of your back? Did the MC attribute to you mental abilities you do not have—such as the ability to complete tasks in a timely manner? If the MC's RFC does not agree with your treating doctor's evaluation, the MC must provide an explanation on the RFC form describing why your doctor's recommendations were not used. (See Chapter 8 for more on RFCs.)

Form SSA-2506-BK, *Psychiatric Review Technique Form* **(PRTF).** If you have a mental condition, this form should be in your file. It is supposed to ensure that the DDS psychiatrist or psychologist considers all of the important information about your mental impairment. The PRTF contains the following:

- Dates covered by the assessment, the MC's signature, and the date signed should be present.
- Section I should contain a medical summary.
- Section II should include the MC's record of pertinent signs, symptoms, findings, functional limitations, and effects of treatment that have a significant bearing on your case. This section should also include the MC's reasoning about why you received a particular medical determination.
- Section III should include the MC's record of signs, symptoms, and findings that show the presence of the categories of mental disorders in the Listing of Impairments.

DDS Medical Consultant Codes

Here is a list of the codes and the type of doctor each refers to.

1	Anesthesiology	29	Orthopedics
2	Ambulatory Medicine	30	Osteopathy
3	Audiology	31	Pathology
4	Cardiology	32	Pediatrics
5	Cardiopulmonary	33	Physiatry
6	Dermatology	34	Physical Medicine
7	E.E.N.T. (Eyes, Ears, Nose, & Throat)	35	Plastic Surgery
8	E.N.T. (Ear, Nose, & Throat)	36	Preventive Medicine
9	E.T. (Ear & Throat)	37	Psychiatry
10	Emergency Room Medicine	38	Psychology
11	Endocrinology	39	Public Health
12	Family or General Practice	40	Pulmonary
13	Gastroenterology	41	Radiology
14	Geriatrics	42	Rehabilitative Medicine
15	Gynecology	43	Rheumatology
16	Hematology	44	Special Senses
17	Industrial Medicine	45	Surgery
18	Infectious Diseases	46	Urology
19	Internal Medicine	47	Other
20	Neurology	48	Speech – Language Pathology
21	Neuro-ophthalmology	49	Child and Adolescent Psychiatry
22	Neuropsychiatry	50	Allergy and Immunology
23	Neonatology	51	Thoracic Surgery
24	Nephrology	52	Nuclear Medicine
25	Obstetrics	53	Neurosurgery
26	Occupational Medicine	54	Vascular Surgery
27	Oncology	55	Critical Care
28	Ophthalmology		

- Section IV should include the MC's rating of functional limitations that are relevant to your ability to work.

Look for errors on the PRTF, such as incorrect dates or incorrect diagnosis of your mental condition, or statements that contradict those of your treating psychiatrist or psychologist. Did the MC state that you have had no episodes of worsening in your mental condition affecting your ability to work when in fact you did—for example, did you have to leave work or were you unable to work for certain periods of time because of worsening symptoms?

Who made the medical determination? It is important for you to establish that an MC reviewed your file and made the medical determination about what you can and cannot do. Here's how to do that:

- **MC review notes.** A medical consultant's notes demonstrate the MC's thinking, interpretation of test results, recommendations on medical development, and statements about medical severity. Did the MC make erroneous statements? Does your file lack MC notes completely? If the DDS concluded that you do not have severe impairments, but your file lacks MC notes showing that an MC came to that conclusion by reviewing your file, the fact that an MC signed the disability determination form is no assurance that the MC performed a review of your file.

In such a situation, be highly suspicious. Your denial may have been made by the DDS examiner, not the MC. Insist on a review by an MC. (See Chapter 6 for suggestions on how to demand that an MC review your file.)

- **RFC forms.** Note the name of the MC who signed the RFC form. Is the handwriting the same as on the other parts of the form—that is, did the doctor actually complete the form? If not, the MC may have simply signed an RFC completed by the examiner. Legally, you have the right to have a medical determination by an MC. An MC's signature is supposed to assure that your file was medically reviewed. But, in reality, this is not always the case. Insist that an MC review your claim if there is any question that was not done. (See Chapter 6 for suggestions on how to demand that an MC review your file.)

d. Reconsideration Decision

If your claim is denied again, you will receive a denial notice and explanation very much like the one you received when your initial claim was denied. The only difference is that the DDS should have evaluated any new evidence and new allegations you presented. The next level of appeal, if you want to pursue it, would be to request a hearing before an administrative law judge. (See Section E3, below.)

CAUTION

Medical consultant involvement in reconsiderations. Legislation passed in 2015 requires a doctor (medical consultant) to be a part of every decision on the "initial claim" but did not make it clear whether the requirement extended to the reconsideration step in DDS applications. Some DDSs may try to let examiners who are not doctors make medical decisions at the reconsideration step. If so, this could be to your disadvantage if your case is denied. The SSA or the federal courts must eventually clarify this issue. Until then, if you apply for reconsideration of an initial denial at a DDS, you have the right to insist a doctor look at your medical evidence.

2. Request for Reconsideration of Continuing Disability Claim

Once you begin receiving disability benefits, your case is reexamined periodically through a continuing disability review (CDR). (See Chapter 14 for more on this subject.) The SSA can end your benefits for a variety of reasons, including:

- a determination that your condition has improved and you can now work, or
- your failure to cooperate in the CDR.

The decision to terminate your benefits is made by a DDS medical consultant and examiner team.

You will receive a notice and explanation from the SSA explaining why your benefits are being terminated. The language of the notice should include something similar to the following words:

We are writing to tell you that we have looked at your case to see if your health problems are still disabling. After looking at all of the information in your case carefully, we found that you are not disabled under our rules as of (*month/year*).

The notice will come with a brief explanation of your medical condition and of how the SSA reached its decision. If you want to appeal, you must request a reconsideration of a CDR at a hearing before a disability hearing officer (DHO). If you appeal, before your claim goes to the hearing officer, it will receive a second review by a different DDS medical consultant and examiner who could reverse the prior CDR decision to terminate your benefits (see Subsection b, below).

Reconsideration hearings to appeal a termination of benefits are heard by a disability hearing officer (DHO) instead of an administrative law judge (ALJ). Although the DHOs are not doctors or psychologists, they are allowed to form their own medical opinions about the severity of your physical or mental impairments. In fact, some DHOs reverse half the CDR denial (termination) cases they see, saving the claimants' benefits. They are often not hesitant to disregard the judgments of two different DDS medical consultant/examiner teams who thought your benefits should stop. So, there is a fairly good chance your benefits will be continued, and you have nothing to lose by trying.

Beware of Copycat Reconsiderations

When you appeal a claim to the DDS for reconsideration, the medical consultant and the examiner selected to review your file must be different from those who denied your initial claim. This doesn't mean the new DDS team will do a thorough examination. A few examiners and MCs are copycats who rubber-stamp claims— simply copy the initial denial determination instead of doing another review.

If your reconsideration is denied and you presented new evidence or had new issues you wanted considered, visit the DDS and look at your file. Check the technical rationale and MC review notes to make sure the DDS did not ignore the new information. If it looks like your claim was rubber-stamped by a copycat, demand that it be recalled and that the new medical and nonmedical evidence be considered. You have a right to request such a reopening (see Section F, below), which can be accomplished by a telephone call or letter to the DDS director. If the DDS refuses, you have an even stronger basis for appeal.

As you prepare for the DHO hearing, keep in mind that the SSA must have good evidence that you have had significant work-related medical improvement—except for certain exceptions discussed in Chapter 14. At your DHO hearing, this is the critical issue. And it is a matter of medical judgment, so the SSA has to consider your treating doctor's opinion. If your case is borderline, your benefits should continue.

a. Complete the Forms

To request a reconsideration determination by a disability hearing officer, you must file Form SSA-789-U4, *Request for Reconsideration—Disability Cessation*, with your local Social Security Field Office. If many months pass between when your CDR began and your hearing with a DHO, you can update the information you originally provided on the SSA Form 454-BK with Form SSA-3441-BK, which you must request from your local Social Security Field Office or get online. It is not available from the DDS.

i. Form SSA-789-U4, *Request for Reconsideration—Disability Cessation*

Form SSA-789-U4 is easy to complete, and your local Field Office will be happy to help with any questions you have. If you request reconsideration of disability cessation, the form is completed by the SSA representative in the Field Office. The form is a multicopy form separated by carbon paper. We include instructions and a sample form below.

The top of the form asks for the claimant's name and Social Security number (SSN). If the wage earner is different from the claimant, then the name of that person is required, along with their SSN. If your claim is an SSI case, there is a blank requiring your spouse's name and SSN. The blank space in the upper right-hand corner is called "For Social Security Office Use Only" but has

Form SSA-789-U4, *Request for Reconsideration*

Form **SSA-789** (01-2019) UF
Discontinue Prior Editions
Social Security Administration

OMB No. 0960-0349

REQUEST FOR RECONSIDERATION - DISABILITY CESSATION RIGHT TO APPEAR

(SEE REVERSE SIDE FOR PAPERWORK/PRIVACY ACT NOTICE)

FOR SOCIAL SECURITY OFFICE USE ONLY (DO NOT WRITE IN THIS SPACE)

NAME OF CLAIMANT Howard E. Walker	SOCIAL SECURITY NUMBER 888-88-8888

☐ FO Code _____

NAME OF WAGE EARNER OR SELF-EMPLOYED PERSON (if different from Claimant)

SOCIAL SECURITY NUMBER

☐ Benefit Continuation

SPOUSE'S NAME AND SOCIAL SECURITY NUMBER (COMPLETE ONLY IN SUPPLEMENTAL SECURITY INCOME CASE)
Helen Walker   SSN 777-77-7777

☐ Foreign Language Notice _____

TYPE OF BENEFIT	DISABILITY			SSI		
	☒ WORKER	☐ WIDOW	☐ CHILD	☒ DISABILITY	☐ BLIND	☐ CHILD

I DO NOT AGREE WITH THE DETERMINATION TO STOP DISABILITY BENEFITS AND I REQUEST RECONSIDERATION.

My reasons are (reasons should relate to the basis for stopping disability benefits and be as specific as possible):

NOTE: If the notice of the determination on your claim is dated more than 65 days ago, include your reason for not making this request earlier. Include the date on which you received the notice.

There has been no significant improvement in my impairments. Furthermore, the DDS ignored my treating doctor's opinion about my physical and mental abilities.

I AM SUBMITTING THE FOLLOWING ADDITIONAL INFORMATION (If "NONE" write "NONE")
(Attach additional page if needed):

Russell Crane, M.D.—see attached records

CHECK BLOCK 1 AND THE STATEMENTS THAT APPLY OR CHECK BLOCK 2

☒ 1. **I (and/or my representative) wish to appear** at a disability hearing. The disability hearing will be with a person called a disability hearing officer and it will let me explain why I do not agree with the decision to stop benefits.

☐ I need an interpreter at the disability hearing - Language _____
(If you need an interpreter, SSA will provide one at no cost to you.)

OR

☐ 2. **I do not wish to appear nor do I wish a representative to appear for me** at the disability hearing. I have been advised of my right to have a disability hearing. I understand that a disability hearing will give me a chance to present witnesses. It will also let me explain to the disability hearing officer why my disability benefits should not end. I understand that this chance to be seen and heard could help the disability hearing officer learn about the facts in my case. The disability hearing officer would give me a chance to have people who know about my condition give information and explain how my condition keeps me from working and restricts my activities. I have been told about my right to representation at the disability hearing, including representation by an attorney or other person of my choice. Although the above has been explained to me, I do not want to appear at a disability hearing, or have someone represent me at a disability hearing. I prefer to have the disability hearing officer decide my case on the evidence in my file, plus any evidence that I submit or that may be obtained by the Social Security Administration. I have been advised that if I change my mind, I can request a disability hearing prior to the writing of a decision in my case. In this case, I can make the request with any Social Security office.

Getting Benefits During an Appeal

If you want your benefits to continue during your appeals, you have only ten days from the time you receive the CDR benefit cessation notice to file your appeal. The CDR benefit termination notice (see Chapter 14) will remind you of this fact. Since the SSA allows five days for mailing time, a more accurate way to count the days you actually have is to add 15 days to the date on the cessation notice.

If you continue benefits through your appeals and lose, you may have to repay the SSA. In case you are asked to repay the benefits you were paid during appeals, you should also file Form SSA-632-BK, *Request for Waiver of Overpayment*, with your local Social Security Field Office. One of the exemptions for having to repay benefits is if you are unable to do so. Even if you eventually have to pay back some benefits, the amount can be as small as $10 per month.

Your benefits will usually stop if you lose your appeal before an ALJ. An exception to this rule concerns claims that are also under Appeals Council or federal court review, and which are sent back (remanded) to the ALJ for a new decision. If you are already receiving benefits during this time, the Appeals Council or the court may require the SSA to continue your benefits until a final ALJ decision. (This situation does not apply to most claimants.) Of course, if your claim is denied by an ALJ and later allowed by the Appeals Council or federal court, you might be able to collect back benefits, even if they were terminated.

some important little boxes in it. One box allows you to request notices in Spanish. Another is to be checked if you want your benefits to continue during your appeal. (See above, Section C2 for more information.)

Continuation of benefits only applies to appeals before the SSA; you cannot continue to receive benefits while appealing to a federal court.

The next set of blanks concerns the type of benefit involved in your claim. There are boxes under "Disability" (SSDI claims) and SSI. Those that apply must be checked.

Next, the form asks for the specific reasons you don't agree with the determination to stop your benefits. Remember, this is just a form to get your appeal started. You don't need to make long arguments here—just the basic facts. For example, you might say, "My arthritis has not improved, and the decision to stop my benefits ignored the opinion of my treating doctor that I have not gotten better. I have additional information from my doctor showing that I have not improved."

Then the next line lets you refer to any additional information, such as "New medical records and opinion from my treating doctor." Then give your doctor's name and address. If there is not enough room, the Social Security representative will enter it onto additional pages.

The form then has check boxes asking if you or your representative wish to appear at the disability hearing, and whether you need an interpreter.

You do not want to waive your right to attend a hearing unless it will be impossible for you to attend. The hearing gives you the chance to personally explain to the DHO why you believe you are still disabled. Also, the hearing officer may notice something about you that is not obvious from the medical file that supports your contention that you are still disabled.

As discussed above, Form SSA-789 lets you waive your right to personally appear at the hearing. Another SSA form is also used to waive the right to personally appear at the hearing (Form SSA-773). If you waive your right to appear, the DHO may ask you to sign Form SSA-773 to ensure that you understand what it means to waive your rights. Form SSA-773 contains the language (see excerpt below) that explains the nature and importance of the rights you waive when you sign Form SSA-773 or the waiver section of Form SSA-789.

On page 2 of the form (not included above), sign the form and enter your address and phone number. Make sure you provide an address where the SSA can reach you. Also enter the name and address of your representative, if you have one. Your representative may sign the form for you. Or, if you can only make an "X" for a signature, two witnesses who know you will also have to sign, as well as provide their addresses.

ii. Form SSA-3441-BK, *Disability Report—Appeal*

Use this form to update your disability information. This is the same form you may have used in filing for reconsideration of your original claim. (Instructions for completing this form are discussed in Section E1a, above.)

If you have already filed this form, you will need to file it again. But all you have to do is include only changes in your medical condition that were not included in your previous Form SSA-3441-BK. If you're not sure what has changed since the last time you completed an SSA-3441-BK, or if you have been receiving disability benefits for some time and completed a different form in the past, go ahead and complete the form as thoroughly as you can. It is better to repeat some facts than to leave out something important.

If you have not already filed a Form SSA-3441-BK, then complete the entire form.

b. DDS Review

Before the disability hearing officer considers your case, a new DDS team (consisting of a medical consultant and a DDS examiner) will review the decision to terminate your benefits. The purpose of the new review is to see if your benefits can continue without the inconvenience of a hearing. The second team might reverse the first team and grant you a continuation of your benefits, either because they think the first team is in error or if the DDS has received important additional information that influences the determination. In that case, the hearing is no longer necessary.

On the other hand, if the second team decides that the decision to terminate your benefits was correct, the second team will send an advisory rating decision to the DHO stating that you are to be considered medically improved and capable of performing some type of work.

c. Review Your File Before the Hearing

You want to review four categories of documents in your file.

Work activity records. Review Section E1c, above, for an explanation of what to look for.

Your medical records, including any letters sent to the DDS by your treating doctor. (See Section E1c.)

RFC forms. Section E1c contains an explanation of what to look for.

Technical rationale. Technical rationales are internal SSA forms containing long explanations of DDS decisions. Section E1c contains an explanation of them; examples are in Appendix B. The technical rationale will be on Form SSA-4268, *Explanation of Determination*, or on one of the following forms:

- Form SSA-833-U3, *Cessation or Continuance of Disability or Blindness Determination and Transmittal (SSDI)*, or
- Form SSA-834-U3, *Cessation or Continuance of Disability or Blindness Determination and Transmittal (SSI)*.

Look also for the SSA-831, *Disability Determination and Transmittal* and an associated rationale from your initial disability determination. This form helps you understand the DDS's reasoning in saying that you are no longer disabled.

d. Attend Hearing With a Disability Hearing Officer

Disability hearing officers (DHOs) are not medical doctors or psychologists, and do not need to have any formal medical training. Some DHOs are experienced disability examiners or examiner supervisors promoted into a DHO position and given administrative training on how to conduct hearings.

When the DHO receives your appeal, the DHO may allow your claim for continued benefits without requiring a hearing. If so, you will receive a notice to that effect. Otherwise, the DHO will send you a notice with the hearing date and location. If the DHO's office is far from your home, you can call that office to ask for a location closer to you. The notice will have the DHO's telephone number, which you can also obtain from your local Social Security office.

Before the hearing, the DHO will send you a notice asking for a list of the people you expect to attend the hearing with you, including witnesses or a representative, such as a lawyer. Witnesses, including your spouse, other relatives, and friends who are knowledgeable about your limitations, can testify that your activities continue to be severely limited. This would be very helpful to your claim. You cannot bring spectators to the hearing. If you bring people who have no legitimate reason to be present, the DHO has the authority to ask them to leave.

Excerpt From Form SSA-773, *Waiver of Right to Appear*

I have been advised of my right to have a disability hearing. I understand that a hearing will give me an opportunity to present witnesses and explain in detail to the disability hearing officer, who will decide my case, the reasons why my disability benefits should not end. I understand that this opportunity to be seen and heard could be effective in explaining the facts in my case, because the disability hearing officer would give me an opportunity to present and question witnesses and explain how my impairments prevent me from working and restrict my activities. I have been given an explanation of my right to representation, including representation at a hearing by an attorney or other person of my choice.

Although the above has been explained to me, I do not want to appear at a disability hearing, or have someone represent me at a disability hearing. I prefer to have the disability hearing officer decide my case on the evidence of record plus any evidence that I may submit or which may be obtained by the Social Security Administration. I have been advised that if I change my mind, I can request a hearing prior to the writing of a decision in my case. In this event, I can make the request with any Social Security office.

The DHO will make sure that your hearing takes place in privacy. A hearing with a DHO is informal. The room won't look anything like a courtroom. Chances are you will sit at a large table with the DHO and your representative or attorney, if any. There will be no one there arguing against your claim.

DHOs may vary somewhat in how they handle hearings. However, they all must deal with any new evidence you have regarding your jobs and work experience, your medical impairments, your treating doctor's opinions, and your statements on why you think the cessation determination was wrong. The DHO must make sure that all of your allegations have been adequately developed in your file.

The DHO should make introductions, ascertain that each person's name and purpose in being there is understood, and then briefly go over the way the hearing will proceed. You will undoubtedly be asked why you think your benefits should not be terminated.

You have the right to ask questions during the hearing, and you'll want to ask the DHO what significant medical improvement the SSA claims you have experienced that allows you to work and what level of work the SSA claims you can do. (Levels of work are explained in Chapters 8 and 9.)

If you or your representative reviewed your file before the hearing, show the DHO why the DDS documents are in error.

For example, can you demonstrate that your medical records show you've had no significant medical improvement or that your improvement doesn't mean you are well enough to return to the types of jobs recommended in the termination notice?

After the hearing, expect a written decision from the DHO within a few weeks. If you are again denied, you will receive a denial notice and explanation similar to those you received in your previous denials. If you disagree with it, you can appeal to an administrative law judge. (Your benefits can continue during appeal; see "Getting Benefits During an Appeal," above.)

3. Appeal to Administrative Law Judge

If your request for reconsideration (of an initial claim or continuing disability review termination) is denied and you want to appeal further, you must request a hearing before an administrative law judge (ALJ) within 60 days from receipt of your denial. Since the SSA adds five days for mailing time, you actually have 65 days from the date on your denial notice. The ALJ is likely to dismiss your case if you file your appeal notice later without good reason for doing so. (The ALJ can dismiss your case for other reasons as well, but these are not likely to be an issue in your case.)

Your benefits can continue through the ALJ hearing process, if you choose that option when submitting your hearing request. But if you lose your appeal, you will have to repay the benefits you received during that time (see "Getting Benefits During an Appeal" in Section E2, above).

ALJs are attorneys who work for the SSA's Office of Hearings Operations (OHO) (formerly known as the Office of Disability Adjudication and Review ODAR). OHO is entirely separate from the division that evaluates initial applications, continuing disability reviews, and reconsideration claims. ALJs are not like judges who work in the civil and criminal courts. ALJs' powers reside only within the SSA. Most of their work involves upholding or overturning DDS decisions to deny or terminate disability benefits; they also hold hearings on nondisability Social Security issues. There is no jury in an ALJ hearing; ALJ, alone, makes the decision to allow or deny you benefits.

You might think that an ALJ's decision would be very similar to that of the DDS or a hearing officer because they both work for the SSA. Nothing could be further from the truth. ALJs usually pay little attention to DDS determinations. Because ALJs are not physicians, however, it is sometimes difficult for them to evaluate medical information and decide which medical opinions in a claimant's file are the most accurate. Although ALJs can ask consulting medical experts to help them evaluate medical information, this is infrequently done. Some ALJs grant or continue benefits when a

DDS doctor has said that there is very little wrong with a claimant. Overall, ALJs grant about half of the claims that reach them.

a. Complete the Forms

To request an ALJ hearing, you need three forms:

- Form HA-501-U5: *Request for Hearing by Administrative Law Judge*
- Form SSA-3441-BK: *Disability Report —Appeal,* and
- Form SSA-827: *Authorization for Source to Release Information to the Social Security Administration* (see Section E1a).

> ⓘ CAUTION
>
> **You must use forms provided by the SSA.** You can obtain them at your local SSA Field Office or by calling the SSA hotline at 800-772-1213, Monday through Friday (except holidays), from 7 a.m. to 7 p.m. If you are deaf or hard of hearing, TTY service representatives are available at the same times at 800-325-0778. You can also download many necessary forms from the Social Security Administration website at www.ssa.gov. They are not available from the DDS.

i. Form HA-501, *Request for Hearing by Administrative Law Judge*

This is the form you use to request a hearing before an administrative law judge. Instructions and a completed sample follow.

❶ **Name of Claimant:** Enter your name or the name of another person on whose behalf this appeal is being filed.

❷ **Claimant SSN:** Enter your Social Security number or that of the person appealing.

❸ **Claim Number:** Enter the claim number if different from the Social Security number.

❹ **I Request a Hearing Before an Administrative Law Judge ... :** State the specific reasons why you feel the decision to terminate your benefits is incorrect. If you need additional space, use a blank sheet of paper and label it "Continuation Sheet."

❺ **Evidence:** If you have new evidence to submit, specify from whom you obtained the evidence. As the form notes, you have ten days from filing this form to submit the new evidence, but it's best if you submit it when you file this form.

❻ **Check whether you do or do not want to appear at the hearing.** Check the appropriate box. If you will not attend the hearing, you need also to complete Form HA-4608, which you can get from your local Social Security office.

If you have a representative and want that person to attend on your behalf (without you), the ALJ will make the decision based on the information in your file and your representative's presentation, unless the ALJ believes your presence is necessary. If you neither have a representative nor want to attend yourself, the ALJ can make a decision based on the written information in your file alone. If you check on this form that you do not want to attend and you file Form HA-4608, you can later change your mind and attend the hearing.

Form HA-501-U5, *Request for Hearing by Administrative Law Judge*

SOCIAL SECURITY ADMINISTRATION
OFFICE OF DISABILITY ADJUDICATION AND REVIEW

Form Approved
OMB No. 0960-0269

REQUEST FOR HEARING BY ADMINISTRATIVE LAW JUDGE

*(Take or mail the **completed original** to your local Social Security office, the Veterans Affairs Regional Office in Manila or any U.S. Foreign Service post and keep a copy for your records)*

See Privacy Act Notice

1. Claimant Name ❶ Myrtle Johnson	2. Claimant SSN ❷ 987-65-4321	3. Claim Number, if different ❸

4. I REQUEST A HEARING BEFORE AN ADMINISTRATIVE LAW JUDGE. I disagree with the determination because:

❹ The reviewer did not consider my doctor's statement that I met the listing and my illness is degenerative.

An Administrative Law Judge of the Social Security Administration's Office of Disability Adjudication and Review or the Department of Health and Human Services will be appointed to conduct the hearing or other proceedings in your case. You will receive notice of the time and place of a hearing at least 20 days before the date set for a hearing.

5. I have additional evidence to submit. ☑ Yes ☐ No	6. Do not complete if the appeal is a Medicare issue. Otherwise, check one of the blocks
Name and source of additional evidence, if not included. ❺ Dr. Paul Dogood, 455 Medical Way, Baltimore, MD 43407	☑ I wish to appear at a hearing.
Submit your evidence to the hearing office within 10 days. Your servicing Social Security office will provide the hearing office's address. Attach an additional sheet if you need more space.	☐ I do not wish to appear at a hearing and I request that a decision be made based on ❻ the evidence in my case. (Complete Waiver Form HA-4608)

Representation: <u>You have a right to be represented at the hearing.</u> If you are not represented, your Social Security office will give you a list of legal referral and service organizations. If you are represented, complete and submit form SSA-1696 (Appointment of Representative) unless you are appealing a Medicare issue.

7. CLAIMANT SIGNATURE (OPTIONAL) ❼ *Myrtle Johnson*	DATE 1/27/20	8. NAME OF REPRESENTATIVE (if any)	DATE
RESIDENCE ADDRESS 2300 Illard Way		ADDRESS ❽	

CITY Baltimore	STATE MD	ZIP CODE 43202	CITY	STATE	ZIP CODE
TELEPHONE NUMBER 555 555 5555	FAX NUMBER		TELEPHONE NUMBER	FAX NUMBER	

TO BE COMPLETED BY SOCIAL SECURITY ADMINISTRATION- ACKNOWLEDGMENT OF REQUEST FOR HEARING

9. Request received on _____ by: _____

(Date)   (Print Name)   (Title)

_____

(Address)   (Servicing FO Code)   (PC Code)

10. Was the request for hearing received within 65 days of the reconsidered determination? ☐ Yes   ☐ No
If no, attach claimant's explanation for delay and supporting documents if any.

11. If claimant is not represented, was a list of legal referral service organizations provided? ☐ Yes ☐ No	15. Check all claim types that apply:
	☐ Retirement and Survivors Insurance Only (RSI)
12. Interpreter needed ☐ Yes ☐ No	☐ Title II Disability - Worker or child only (DIWC)
Language (including sign language):	☐ Title II Disability - Widow(er) only (DIWW)
13. Check one: ☐ Initial Entitlement Case	☐ Title XVI (SSI) Aged only (SSIA)
☐ Disability Cessation Case or ☐ Other Postentitlement Case	☐ Title XVI Blind only (SSIB)
14. HO COPY SENT TO: HO on _____	☐ Title XVI Disability only (SSID)
☐ Claims Folder (CF) Attached: ☐ Title (T) II; ☐ T XVI;	☐ Title XVI/Title II Concurrent Aged Claim (SSAC)
☐ T VIII; ☐ T XVIII; ☐ T II CF held in FO ☐ Electronic Folder	☐ Title XVI/Title II Concurrent Blind (SSBC)
☐ CF requested ☐ T II; ☐ T XVI; ☐ T VIII; ☐ T XVIII	☐ Title XVI/Title II Concurrent Disability (SSDC)
(Copy of email or phone report attached)	☐ Title XVIII Hospital/Supplementary Insurance (HI/SMI)
16. CF COPY SENT TO: HO on _____	☐ Title VIII Only Special Veterans Benefits (SVB)
☐ CF Attached: ☐ Title (T) II; ☐ T XVI; ☐ T XVIII	☐ Title VIII/Title XVI (SVB/SSI)
☐ Other Attached:	☐ Other - Specify:

Form **HA-501-U5** (01-2015) ef (01-2015)
Use 08-2012 Edition Until Stock is Exhausted

TAKE OR SEND ORIGINAL TO SSA AND RETAIN A COPY FOR YOUR RECORDS

❼ Sign and date the form and enter your address, daytime phone number, and fax number (signing is optional).

❽ If a legal representative is handling your appeal (see Chapter 15), enter the relevant contact information here. (The SSA cannot discuss your case with your legal representative until it receives Form SSA-1696. If you have a representative, that person will do all the paperwork associated with SSA-1696.)

Leave the rest of the form blank. The SSA will complete it.

ii. Form SSA-3441-BK, *Disability Report—Appeal*

Use this form to update your disability information. This is the same form you may have used in filing for reconsideration of your original claim or termination of your benefits. (Instructions for completing this form are in Section E1a, above.)

If you have already filed this form, you will need to file it again. But you only need to include changes in your medical condition that were not included in your previous Form(s) SSA-3441-BK. If you're not sure what has changed since the last time you completed an SSA-3441-BK, or if you have been receiving disability benefits for some time and completed a different form in the past, go ahead and complete the form as thoroughly as you can. It is better to repeat some facts than to leave out something important.

If you have not already filed a Form SSA-3441-BK, then complete the entire form.

iii. Forward Forms to the SSA

Once you have completed all the forms, attach to them copies of any evidence showing that the original determination was incorrect, such as new medical records. Then fold all forms and documents in thirds, insert them in a standard business envelope, and mail to your local Social Security office. If you are not sure where that office is, call 800-772-1213. Keep a copy of each form and the originals of your attached evidence for your records. If you can't follow these SSA instructions for mailing because your documentation won't fit in a standard envelope, then use a larger one.

b. Prehearing Conference

The ALJ can decide to hold a prehearing conference to facilitate the hearing or the decision on your claim. You can also ask for such a conference, although the ALJ is not required to grant your request. A prehearing conference is normally held by telephone, unless the ALJ decides that a different format (such as an in-person conference) is desirable. You will be given reasonable notice of the time, place, and manner of the conference.

At the conference, the administrative law judge may consider matters such as simplifying or changing the issues; obtaining and submitting evidence, such as medical records; and any other matters that may speed up the hearing. The ALJ will make a record of the conference. If neither you nor your representative appear at the prehearing conference without a good reason, the SSA may dismiss your request for a hearing.

Good causes for missing the conference include:

- SSA actions somehow misled you (you should be able to explain how).
- You have physical, mental, educational, or language problems that prevented you from attending.
- Some other unusual, unexpected, or unavoidable circumstance beyond your control prevented you from attending.

Also, other circumstances may, if documented, establish good cause. For example:

- You were seriously ill, and your illness prevented you from contacting the SSA in person, in writing, or through a friend, relative, or other person.
- There was a death or serious illness in your immediate family.
- Important records were destroyed or damaged by fire or another accidental cause.
- You were trying very hard to find necessary information to support your claim but did not find the information within the stated time period.

c. Attorney Advisor Proceedings

A prehearing proceeding also may be held by an "Attorney Advisor," rather than an ALJ. (20 CFR 404.942.) The SSA has expanded the use of Attorney Advisor nationwide after several years of testing in a few states. The purpose of an Attorney Advisor is to take some of the workload off of ALJs. An Attorney Advisor has the full authority to exercise the functions of an administrative law judge. The Attorney Advisor may simply review your file when you appeal to an ALJ, or may contact you or your representative for more information or a conference regarding your case. Attorney Advisor might review your claim when:

- New and material evidence is submitted.
- There is an indication that additional evidence is available.
- There is a change in the law or regulations.
- There is an error in the file or some other indication that a fully favorable decision may be issued.

Note the last item. This provision of the regulation allows attorney advisors to review any claim, because they have the full authority to overrule the DDS on both medical and nonmedical issues and allow your claim.

If an Attorney Advisor approves your claim, the SSA will send you written notice, and you won't have to worry about an ALJ hearing. If you still want an ALJ hearing despite being allowed, you have 30 days to request that; otherwise, the ALJ hearing will be automatically dismissed. (It is not clear why you might want to have an ALJ hearing if an Attorney Advisor approves your claim for benefits, but that provision is available to you. An ALJ does not have the explicit regulatory authority to reverse an Attorney Advisor allowance into a denial. But the Appeals Council may review an Attorney Advisor's decision.)

An Attorney Advisor cannot deny your claim, but if the Attorney Advisor does not issue a fully favorable decision, then your ALJ hearing will proceed as scheduled. "Fully favorable" means you get everything you ask for, such as your alleged onset date. If an Attorney Advisor prehearing proceeding is not completed before a scheduled ALJ hearing, then the hearing with the ALJ will still occur at the scheduled date—unless you ask for a delay.

So, if an Attorney Advisor gets your claim, it's just one more chance of a favorable decision, with no downside. Importantly, it could mean a favorable decision much sooner than you could get with a scheduled ALJ hearing. Federal regulations do not say you cannot ask for an Attorney Advisor case review, but there is no method to do so.

d. Schedule the Hearing

If your case is not resolved in your favor during the prehearing case reviews, the ALJ will notify you or your representative of the time and place of the hearing at least 75 days before it is to take place. If you have any new evidence you want considered, you are required to submit it at least five business days before the hearing. Any new evidence you submit must be "without redaction"—meaning you must not edit or otherwise change the evidence in any way.

The ALJ can be flexible in changing the hearing date, which might be necessary if you or your representative has a conflict. To avoid a conflict, you or your representative can call the ALJ to discuss the hearing date before the ALJ sends out the notice. The ALJ's telephone number should be on all paperwork you receive. (You can also easily find any ALJ's telephone number by asking your local Field Office or looking online at the SSA's Office of Hearings Operations at www.ssa.gov/appeals/ho_locator.html.)

ALJs commonly have large backlogs of cases, so you may have to wait a year or more for a hearing. Although ALJs technically are part of the SSA, they have a lot of independence. Informally, the SSA assumes that an ALJ can do about 500 cases per year. In the past, ALJs have been solely responsible for scheduling their own hearings. However, the SSA became frustrated that some ALJs were not scheduling reasonable numbers of hearings. In some areas, some ALJs worked harder than others, and the SSA wanted to even out the workload.

In 2010, the SSA made new regulations allowing it to take a much more active role in scheduling hearings. The SSA is not taking over the responsibility of scheduling hearings completely but will work with an ALJ in an attempt to ensure a more timely hearing of your case. However, the backlog of ALJ hearing cases is largely due to the many people applying for disability benefits. Although the SSA continues to add new facilities for hearing cases, you should not expect a quick hearing. That's why it's always better to be allowed at the DDS level—your medical, cash, and other benefits will start much sooner.

e. Where Hearings Are Held

Hearings are held either in person or through video conference. Often, a video hearing can be scheduled sooner than an in-person appearance. When you request an appeal to an ALJ, the SSA will consider any preference you may have expressed for or against having a video hearing when setting the time and place of your hearing. You have an absolute right to decline a video hearing and have a hearing in person at a date and location determined by the ALJ, but you must object to the video hearing no less than 30 days from the scheduled date.

You can object to the time or location of the hearing no less than 5 days before the hearing, and the SSA will try to accommodate reasonable requests. You should state what location and time you want, along with the reason. Good causes for missing the above deadlines are acceptable, such as a serious injury or illness or if your representative must be at a different hearing. Using this information, the ALJ will decide what's appropriate, taking into account all factors involved, such as hearing schedules. (Also, in rare instances, the ALJ may decline a request for a video hearing and require a hearing in person.)

These rules were updated in 2014 to prevent claimants or their representatives from "manipulating [the] rules in order to obtain a hearing with an ALJ with a higher allowance rate." It is important that claimants or their representatives not try to "game the system" in any way to control which ALJ hears a case. The SSA is well aware of this problem and is on the lookout for those who try to try to manipulate the hearing process. The SSA has sanctioned some representatives for misrepresenting facts and using phony changes in a claimant's residence to get the ALJ changed.

i. Video Hearings

Video hearings are conducted over closed-circuit television; you and the other participants can see and hear one another through large color television screens. During the hearing, the judge remains in his or her office, and a technician will be with you at the video hearing location to make sure the video conferencing equipment works smoothly.

Except for the equipment, a video hearing is no different than a hearing at which you appear in person. The judge can see you and speak with you and anyone who comes to the hearing with you (such as your representative or witnesses). You can see the judge and anyone who is with the judge or anyone at another video conference site (such as a medical or vocational expert). The SSA ensures that the video hearing transmission is secure and that your privacy is protected. Your preparation for a video hearing should be no different than if you were attending a hearing in person.

All states have video hearing locations. The SSA does not videotape hearings but does make audio recordings, as it does for all hearings. The ALJ will instruct you on the date, time, and location of your video hearing.

ii. In-Person Hearings

Hearings are held throughout the United States, usually in a federal building in a major city that houses other federal offices—but separate from the DDS and SSA Field Offices. If you are assigned to an in-person hearing, it will usually be held as close to your home as possible.

iii. Telephone Hearings

The SSA recently changed its regulations to allow claimants or any other party, such as witnesses, to appear at an ALJ hearing by telephone. The ALJ, however, has the authority to determine in what way a person will appear and can deny you or a witness permission to testify by telephone. Telephone appearances are possible if the ALJ determines that there are "extraordinary circumstances" that prevent a claimant or witness from appearing in person or by video teleconferencing. Only the ALJ determines exactly what these extraordinary circumstances will be. Telephone conferencing does not remove your or your representative's right to question and be questioned, to cross-examine witnesses, or to object to a witness based on bias or inadequate qualifications.

iv. Expense Reimbursement for Hearings

The same travel reimbursement rules apply to video hearings and to hearings in person. If you accept a video hearing, you will probably be able to have your hearing sooner and won't have to travel as far.

If you must travel more than 45 miles to get to the hearing, the SSA may pay certain costs:

- The SSA may pay your transportation expenses, such as bus fare or gasoline and tolls.
- If you anticipate that you, your representative, or necessary witnesses will incur expenses for meals, lodging, or taxicabs, you must ask the ALJ to approve the expenses before the hearing.
- If you, your representative, or necessary witnesses incur unexpected and unavoidable expenses for meals, lodging, or taxicabs, you can ask the ALJ to approve the expenses at the hearing.

You must submit your reimbursement request in writing to the ALJ at the time of the hearing or as soon as possible after the hearing. List what you spent and attach receipts. If you requested a change in the scheduled location of the hearing to a location farther from your residence, the SSA will not pay for any additional travel expenses.

If you need money for travel costs in advance, tell the ALJ as far as possible before the hearing. The SSA can advance payment only if you show that without the money, you cannot travel to or from the hearing. If you receive travel money in advance, you must give the ALJ an itemized list of your actual travel costs and receipts within 20 days after your hearing. If the advance payment was for more than what you spent, the SSA will send you a notice of how much you owe the SSA, and you must pay it back within 20 days of receiving the notice.

f. Prepare for the Hearing

It is a good idea to have a representative (a disability lawyer or nonlawyer representative) at an ALJ hearing, unless you are certain you can represent yourself in a legal proceeding. While an ALJ hearing is far less formal than a regular court hearing (see Subsection g, below), it is still a legal proceeding. You can hire a representative after you file your hearing request, if you don't have one already (see Chapter 15).

As explained in Section E3a, above, when you file your request for a hearing, you must enclose new evidence you want the ALJ to consider. But between the time of filing the request and your hearing, you may obtain new medical evidence. If so, send it to the ALJ as soon as possible.

In addition, think of specific examples of your physical or mental limitations you can give to the ALJ. By preparing in advance to talk about your impairments and limitations, you not only lessen your anxieties about the hearing, but also increase your chance of convincing the judge of your position.

i. Review Your File

Sections E1c and E2c, above, explain how you can review your file. If you (or your representative) haven't yet done so, before the hearing you'll want to review the following:

- the technical rationales, to understand why the DDS or DHO denied your claim, and
- the reports of medical consultants (MCs), specifically their RFC ratings.

Before you review the MCs' reports, read about the impairment listing for your medical condition (in the Medical Listings that are on Nolo's website, Parts 1 through 14). Then look at the reports. Did the MCs make errors? Did they overstate your ability to work? Did they ignore symptoms and limitations for the type of mental disorder you have?

ii. Request Your Record and the Evidence

The SSA will generally give you a free copy of your record, if you say that it is for "program purposes." If your file is quite lengthy, however, the SSA may charge you a fee for printing it. Also, you or your representative may request to examine all evidence that is to be part of the hearing record before the hearing, in case you want to object to its admission or offer evidence to challenge it.

iii. Gather Your Medications

Gather together your bottles of medication so you can bring them to the hearing. If you'd rather not bring the medications themselves, make a list of the medications and doses you take.

iv. Figure Out Who All the Witnesses Will Be

If the ALJ plans to ask any expert witnesses to testify, you or your representative will receive a notice before the hearing. The ALJ might have a medical expert (ME) or vocational expert (VE) testify about your medical condition or work abilities. ALJs don't often use MEs; they use VEs more frequently. If you don't receive a witness notice from the ALJ at least a week before the hearing, call the ALJ's office and ask about experts. You should not attempt to personally contact any expert witnesses.

If you plan to bring witnesses, inform the ALJ about who your witnesses are as soon as possible after you've chosen them. The Field Office can send the ALJ a list of witnesses you want, but neither the ALJ nor the Field Office is responsible for contacting your witnesses and making sure they show up at the hearing. Your witnesses are your responsibility. Don't overload the ALJ with too many witnesses; two or three are best. It is quality, not quantity, that matters here. For example, your treating physician or a caregiver who sees you every day might know your condition better than anyone else. Many claimants have no witnesses.

g. Attend the Hearing

Hearing rooms and video hearing sites vary from location to location. Most likely, you'll be in a relatively small room with one or more tables. Remember, this is an informal hearing, not the kind of adversarial proceeding you might have in a court of law—there will be no government representatives arguing against you. If you don't have a lawyer or another representative, you should have received a letter from the SSA like the one shown below. (See Sample of Disability Review, below.)

If you have a representative, sit near that person and have your witnesses sit near you. In addition, follow these tips.

Arrive on time. If you are late, the ALJ may cancel your hearing. If you have a good cause for being late or not showing up—such as a medical emergency or severe weather conditions—the ALJ might reschedule the hearing, but don't count on it. You can lose your claim by not showing up for a hearing. Even if it is rescheduled, it might be several months before you can have another one.

If you don't know how to get to the hearing location, check the Office of Hearings Operations at www.ssa.gov/appeals/ho_locator.html. This page has detailed maps and instructions on finding the ALJ's hearing office that you can print out. You can also call the ALJ's office or your local Field Office for directions.

Ask for an interpreter. If English is not your first language and you requested an interpreter on your hearing request form, an interpreter should be at the hearing. If the interpreter is not there, ask that the hearing be rescheduled.

Sample Notice of Disability Review (Page 1)

Social Security Administration

Refer to:
(000-00-0000)

Addressee _____

Address _____

Dear _____ :

We have received your request for hearing. We will notify you in writing of the time and place of the hearing at least seventy-five (75) days before the date of the hearing. You have indicated that you are not represented.

YOU HAVE THE RIGHT TO BE REPRESENTED BY AN ATTORNEY OR OTHER REPRESENTATIVE OF YOUR CHOICE. A representative can help you obtain evidence and help you and your witnesses, if any, prepare for the hearing. Also, a representative can question witnesses and present statements in support of your claim. If you wish to be represented, you should obtain a representative AS SOON AS POSSIBLE so your representative can begin preparing your case. Please phone us at the number shown above if you decide to obtain a representative.

If there is an attorney or other person whom you wish to act as your representative, you should contact that person promptly to avoid any undue delay in scheduling your hearing. If you are unable to find a representative, we have enclosed a list of organizations which may be able to help you locate one. As indicated on the enclosed list, some private attorneys may be willing to represent you and not charge a fee unless your claim is allowed. Your representative must obtain approval from the Social Security Administration for any fee charged. Also, if you are not able to pay for representation, and you believe you might qualify for free representation, the list contains names of organizations which may be able to help you.

Sample Notice of Disability Review (Page 2)

If you have any evidence that you did not previously submit, please send it to this office immediately. If you are unable to send the evidence before the hearing, please bring it with you to the hearing.

You will be able to see all of the evidence in your file at the hearing. If you wish to see it sooner, or have any questions regarding your claim, please call this office at _____ .

Please have your Social Security number available whenever you call.

Sincerely,

Enclosures
(List of Representatives)
(Travel Expense Information)

Be aware that the hearing is recorded. ALJ hearings are tape recorded. At no charge to you, the proceedings will be transcribed to hard copy if you lose at the hearing and appeal further. The only part of the hearing that might not be recorded is discussion "off the record," but this should only relate to issues that are not relevant to the hearing. In any case, once the hearing goes back on the record, the judge must summarize what took place during the off-the-record discussion.

Don't bring spectators. Your hearing is not open to the general public. Of course, relatives or friends can come with you if you need assistance but they cannot answer questions for you. If you have any questions about bringing someone, contact the ALJ's hearing office before the hearing.

Be comfortable and be yourself. There's no need to dress up. Also, if you are in pain from sitting too long and need to stand, go ahead.

Be courteous and respectful to the ALJ and everyone else present. Do not curse or use other foul or threatening language, no matter how angry you are.

Pay attention to what is happening. Do not read, eat, chew tobacco or gum, use your cell phone, or do anything else that might be distracting. If you want to be taken seriously, you must take the hearing seriously. Also, you cannot answer questions properly if you don't know what's going on. If you have difficulty hearing, wear your hearing aid or let the ALJ know.

Be truthful. When asked questions, don't be vague or evasive. Vague and evasive answers are not clever; they leave a bad impression and force the ALJ to make a decision on factors other than what you say. At the same time, elaborate only to answer the question. Do not exaggerate your pain or other symptoms. Then again, don't be too proud to express how your condition has made your life difficult. If you don't know the answer to a question, just say so.

Don't stage emotional outbursts. ALJs have seen it all before, including crying and other acts of hysteria, and won't be swayed by it if they think it's an act.

On the other hand, if you find yourself in tears as you explain your condition, don't be embarrassed—again, the ALJ has seen it all and knows that this can be the natural response of someone under stress.

h. Follow the Hearing Procedure

ALJs conduct hearings in various ways—no law sets forth a specific sequence for a hearing. This section gives you some idea of what to expect, although the order of your hearing may be very different. If you have a representative, that person may be familiar with the procedures of your ALJ and can fill you in on what to expect.

At the beginning, the ALJ will introduce him- or herself and any witnesses or staff persons. Then, the ALJ may ask if you understand your right to have a representative (if you don't have one). The ALJ will also make a brief statement explaining how the hearing will be conducted, the procedural history of your case, and the issues involved. The ALJ will swear you in, that is, ask you to raise your right hand and swear that your testimony shall be "the truth and nothing but the truth." The appropriate response is, "I do." Any witnesses will also be sworn to tell the truth before they testify.

As the hearing progresses, the ALJ will need to establish your name, age, address, education, work experience, and some details on your medical history, medications, symptoms, medical disorders, and limitations on your activities of daily living. The judge might ask you questions or have your representative (if any) ask you some questions. As emphasized earlier, give clear and concise answers and concrete examples of how your physical or mental impairments limit your ability to function. To say, "I can't do anything," is not informative. Everyone does something during the day, even if it is just sitting on the couch.

i. Your Witnesses

Once some basics are established, the ALJ will move on to your witnesses, if any. Anyone with some specific knowledge of the limitations imposed by your impairments can be a witness. One or two credible witnesses should be sufficient to make the point to the judge; there is little point in having several people repeat the same thing over and over. As discussed in Section E3f, it is important that you review the chapters

in this book concerning your impairments. Those chapters will help you understand how witnesses can help your case.

The ALJ will often be the first to question any witnesses you bring to the hearing. You or your representative may also question the witnesses. This means that you or your representative will need to listen carefully during the judge's questioning and ask your witness only those questions that will bring to light whatever the judge left out. There's no need to bore the judge by going over the same territory. However, part of winning your case is making sure that the judge "gets" why you're disabled. If, for example, the judge asks your doctor about your condition, which is in remission, but fails to ask about the medication that keeps it in remission—and if that medication puts you to sleep—be sure to ask your doctor to talk about it during the hearing.

Physical disorders. The best witnesses are those who can testify to your inability to perform certain activities because of your impairments.

> EXAMPLE: Dwayne has chronic back pain related to degenerative arthritis and scarring around nerve roots associated with prior surgery for a herniated disk. Dwayne describes at his hearing the medications he takes for his pain, the doses, the other pain treatments he receives for the pain, and how the pain limits his sitting, standing, bending, lifting, and walking. The DDS said

that Dwayne could lift and carry up to 50 pounds, frequently bend his back, and stand six to eight hours daily. Dwayne tells the ALJ that he tried to lift 30 pounds and was in excruciating pain for a week and that he can't sit in one position or stand for more than an hour at a time. His wife testifies to these facts as well.

Mental disorders. Your witnesses should be able to testify as to how your mental disorders limit your activities. What can you do and not do? Exercise independent judgment? Plan and cook a meal? Shop alone and return home without getting lost? Remember things, people, or obligations? Relate to other people? Bathe and dress alone? Finish tasks in a timely manner, if at all? Do your own grooming and hygiene? Pay bills? An employer or coworker in a mental disorder claim might testify that you can't remember work procedures or are too irritable to work with other people.

EXAMPLE: Homer has progressive dementia of the Alzheimer's type, and his employer is a witness. The employer tells the ALJ that Homer has slowly lost his ability to do his job as a supervisor in a furniture manufacturing facility—he couldn't remember procedures, didn't seem motivated any more, and he was irritable and short-tempered with the employees he supervised. As examples, the employer stated that Homer had left dangerous machinery running unattended, hadn't

returned tools to their proper storage places, and had blamed other employees for his shortcomings. Sometimes, Homer would just start crying for no reason, which upset the other employees and disrupted the work schedule. On other occasions, Homer seemed to be unaware of dangers and walked right in front of a forklift carrying heavy boxes. The employer tried to give Homer simple jobs requiring minimal skill— such as counting boxes in the warehouse— but Homer still couldn't seem to do them without too many errors. The employer says he was sorry, but he had to lay Homer off work indefinitely.

Homer's wife then testifies that he has the same kinds of problems around the house as he had at work. He doesn't seem interested in anything but watching TV. His previous hobbies that he loved—fishing and playing his guitar—are no longer of interest to him. He did halfheartedly try to play his guitar once but angrily broke it against a wall when he couldn't remember even his favorite song. He eats and sleeps poorly and gets confused doing simple jobs around the house. For instance, he was trying to repair an old chair and stopped for lunch. When he returned to the chair he was confused about how to put it together and cried. He can't drive the car because he gets lost and almost had a wreck by running a red light. The saddest thing of all, Homer almost didn't recognize their daughter, who had come to visit from another city. Often, he doesn't remember to change his clothes or bathe unless his wife supervises him.

ii. Medical Experts

Medical experts (MEs) are doctors in private practice hired by the SSA to help the ALJ understand the medical issues involved in a case. The ME cannot be a doctor who has seen you in the past.

An ALJ can use an ME in several ways: to review your file and give the ALJ a medical opinion before the hearing, or to testify at the hearing itself. The ALJ cannot ask the ME for an opinion on vocational matters relating to your claim, even if the ME is also a vocational expert. If an ME will testify at your hearing or review your file, the ALJ must include the ME in the witness list and send you copies of any correspondence between the ALJ and ME.

At the hearing, you can cross-examine any ME involved in your case. Of course, before you can cross-examine the ME, you need to have understood what the person said. If the ME talks like a medical textbook, the ALJ is supposed to ask follow-up questions that require the ME to explain things in plain English. If the ALJ forgets to do this, be sure to offer a reminder. If the ME gave the ALJ advice affecting your claim and is not put on the witness list or brought to the hearing, you have been deprived of your right to cross-examine the ME. This can be the basis of an appeal to the Appeals Council, or later, federal court.

An ME may give a medical opinion as to whether or not you qualify for disability benefits, but such an opinion is not binding on the ALJ. MEs are paid only a small sum of money that is the same whether you win or lose, so they have little financial incentive for bias. Furthermore, MEs are not paid by the SSA to argue against your claim for benefits. In some instances, an ME might argue that your claim should be allowed.

In fact, you can actually request that the ALJ call an ME to testify, if you think it will help your case. Because MEs usually know far less about disability regulations than do medical consultants (MCs), an attorney knowledgeable about Social Security disability often can cross-examine an ME in a way so that the ME agrees to certain facts that point toward your disability. If the ME won't agree to such facts, then it is important to get the ME to admit that the ME has not examined you.

iii. Vocational Experts

Vocational experts (VEs) are people with vocational expertise who evaluate your residual functional capacity (RFC) rating (see Chapter 8) to determine if there are jobs in the national economy you can do. Like medical experts, some VEs are consultants for the SSA's Office of Hearings Operations. MEs are specialists in various medical disciplines and have medical licenses; a few MEs are also vocational experts.

The training and qualifications of a VE are not standardized; a vocational expert may claim a background in a variety of fields, such as psychology, vocational education, vocational counseling, or vocational rehabilitation. It's possible to call oneself

Medical Witnesses: Your Treating Doctor and SSA Medical Consultants

It's highly unusual for a claimant's treating doctor to attend an ALJ hearing. In the event your treating doctor will come, be sure to include the doctor on your witness list. If you don't, the ALJ can postpone the hearing. Even with the testimony of a medical expert, the ALJ must consider the opinion of your doctor—even if the ALJ has just the doctor's written opinions in your file. For example, suppose your treating doctor's opinion says you have greater functional limitations than what the medical consultant indicated during the initial determination of your claim. The medical consultant said you can lift 50 pounds and walk six to eight hours a day, but your medical doctor wrote that you can lift only 20 pounds and walk six to eight hours a day. The ALJ must consider how persuasive your treating doctor's opinion is regarding your functional limitations, including whether the doctor's opinion is supported by medical evidence and whether it is consistent with the other evidence in your file.

In accordance with federal regulations, if there is an opinion from your treating doctor and from a medical consultant and they are equally well-supported by the evidence and consistent with your file, the ALJ must consider the length of your relationship with the doctor, how frequently you visited the doctor, the extent of examinations and testing performed by the doctor, whether the doctor is a specialist, and whether the doctor examined you in person. The ALJ must explain in writing

how these factors were considered in determining the severity of your functional limitations and your RFC. It's important for you to point out that the MC did not examine you, lacks personal knowledge of what you can and cannot do physically and mentally, and is therefore less reliable than your treating doctor. In reality, this might not be true, but asserting this position is supported by the law.

The opinions of a consultative examination (CE) doctor cannot be so easily disposed of, given that that doctor did examine you. (See Subsection h, above.) But again, if your treating doctor's opinion is supported by the evidence and consistent with your file, the ALJ must consider the length and extent of your relationship with your treating doctor when considering which doctor's opinion is more persuasive.

If you have read this book, then you know far more about SSA medical policies than your average medical expert. This is an important point, because SSA policies are not the same as medical knowledge. For example, an ME might think that if you have had major epileptic seizures controlled for six months, then you have no environmental restrictions (such as not driving or working at unprotected heights). The ME is entitled to that opinion, but the SSA applies environmental restrictions for epilepsy for a period of 12 months. As this example shows, you and your representative need to be alert to instances where the ME's opinion contradicts SSA policy.

a vocational expert without even having a college degree, but some VEs have advanced university degrees in subjects such as vocational education. Various credential labels might appear after a vocational expert's name, such as certified vocational evaluator or expert (CVE), certified rehabilitation counselor (CRC), certified case manager (CCM), certified disability management specialist (CDMS), or federally certified rehabilitation counselor for the U.S. Department of Labor. So you might see something like this, John Doe, Ph.D., CVE, CRC, CCM. Although the legal standards for being a vocational expert are slim, there has been a private effort to create board certification requirements for being a vocational expert. For example, the American Board of Vocational Experts (www.abve.net), a nonprofit organization, has high standards for certification. (Note that vocational analysts used by a DDS are usually trained by the DDS and may have a much more limited vocational education and background than vocational experts in private practice.)

The ALJ might have a VE at your hearing—and you should have been told this when you received the ALJ's witness list. You should also have been sent copies of any correspondence between the judge and the VE. Because a VE reviews your file and offers an opinion about your job capabilities, the VE is subject to cross-examination by you just like a medical expert. And as with an ME, the judge is supposed to make sure that the VE speaks in plain English that you can understand. In addition to questions at the hearing, the ALJ might send a VE interrogatories (written questions) about vocational aspects of your claim, before or after the hearing. If the answers are obtained by the ALJ after a hearing and your claim is denied, you have a right to examine that evidence, and so you should be informed by the SSA that it exists.

The ALJ will ask the VE about the types of jobs you could do, given your impairments. You or your authorized representative will have the chance to question the VE as well. VEs refer to the federal government's *Dictionary of Occupational Titles* (DOT), which describes the physical and mental requirements of various kinds of work. When there is a disagreement between the VE's opinion and the DOT, courts have ruled that the DOT should be followed.

To counter the VE's testimony, you can bring your own vocational expert to the hearing, if you are willing to pay any fees. You can find numerous private vocational experts simply by putting "vocational expert" in your favorite Internet search engine. To get a good idea of the kind of credentials and experience a VE should have, visit the ABVE website, above, and review its criteria for certification. You can also call a local Field Office and ask if they have a list of local vocational experts in private practice, as well as try your telephone book under "vocational" and "rehabilitation." Another possibility is to call your state vocational rehabilitation

What the ALJ Might Ask the ME

Below is the Office of Hearing Operations' official list of suggested questions for ALJs to use when getting expert testimony from MEs. Studying these questions and the answers given by an ME can help you cross-examine the ME or respond to answers you think are not valid.

1. Please state your full name and address.

2. Is the attached curriculum vitae a correct summary of your professional qualifications?

3. Are you board certified in any medical field and, if so, which field?

4. Are you aware that your responses to these interrogatories are sought from you in the role of an impartial medical expert?

5. Has there been any prior communication between the Administrative Law Judge and you regarding the merits of this case?

6. Have you ever personally examined the claimant?

7. Have you read the medical data pertaining to the claimant that we furnished you?

8. Is there sufficient objective medical evidence of record to allow you to form an opinion of the claimant's medical status? If not, what additional evidence is required?

9. Please list the claimant's physical or mental impairments resulting from anatomical, physiological, or psychological abnormalities which are demonstrable by medically acceptable clinical and laboratory diagnostic techniques. In addition, please state your opinion as to the severity of each impairment, and the exhibits and objective findings which support your opinion.

10. Are there any conflicts in the medical evidence of record which affected your opinion and, if so, please state how you resolved them?

11. Have we furnished you with copies of the pertinent section of the Listing of Impairments, Appendix 1, Subpart P, Social Security Regulations No. 4?

12. In your opinion, do any of the claimant's impairments, when taken individually, meet the requirements of any of the listed impairments? Please fully explain this answer and cite the appropriate sections in the Listing. (Please specifically refer to Listing sections.)

13. In your opinion, do any of the claimant's impairments present medical findings which are at least equal in severity and duration to a listed impairment in Appendix 1?

14. In your opinion, if the impairment(s) is a listed impairment or the medical equivalent thereof, on what date did the impairment(s) attain that level of severity?

15. Is there any evidence that the claimant has not properly complied with prescribed treatment?

16. Has any treatment been prescribed which may improve the claimant's condition?

What the ALJ Might Ask the ME (continued)

17. List the specific functional (exertional) limitations, such as sitting, walking, standing, lifting, carrying, pushing, pulling, reaching, and handling imposed by these impairments.

18. List the specific functional (nonexertional) limitations, such as environmental restrictions (sensitivity to fumes, etc.), or visual limitations, such as inability to read small print or work with small objects, imposed by these impairments.

19. Please describe the claimant's visual acuity in terms of its effect on the claimant's ability to work safely.

20. Do you have any additional comments or information which may assist us in reaching a decision? If so, please state.

center and ask for the names of vocational experts they might know about. If you have a disability lawyer or an authorized representative, that person will know of available private vocational experts.

Medical doctors and psychologists—your own, DDS medical consultants, and SSA medical experts—are not usually vocational experts, and their opinion about whether you can do any job in the national economy carries little weight. Still, your treating doctor's opinion will be an important medical factor. Remember that the ALJ must consider your treating doctor's opinion about what you can do medically (lifting, walking, and so on), even when it conflicts with an MC's or ME's opinion. If the VE did not use your treating doctor's medical assessment, find out why. Ask what job recommendations the VE would make if using the doctor's assessment.

iv. Consultative Examinations

If the ALJ needs medical information to evaluate limitations you raise that are not covered in your medical records, you might be asked to undergo a consultative examination (CE) by a physician or psychologist who does work for the SSA (see Chapter 2, Section C2). The ALJ could request that you attend a CE before the hearing, or could decide on the need for more information during a hearing itself. In the latter instance, the ALJ would postpone the hearing until after the CE.

i. Await the ALJ's Decision

Don't expect the ALJ to give you a decision at the end of the hearing. The SSA will send you a copy of the ALJ's decision, which usually takes about two more months. If the ALJ denies your claim, you can appeal further to the Appeals Council.

What the ALJ Might Ask the VE

Below is the official list of suggested questions for ALJs to use when questioning a vocational expert. Use this to help prepare your own questions for the VE.

1. Please state your full name and address.

2. Is the attached curriculum vitae a correct summary of your professional qualifications?

3. Are you aware that your responses to these interrogatories are sought from you in the role of an impartial vocational expert?

4. Has there been any prior communication between the administrative law judge and you regarding the merits of this case?

5. Has there been any prior professional contact between you and the claimant?

6. Have you read the evidence pertaining to the claimant that we furnished you?

7. Is there sufficient objective evidence of record to allow you to form an opinion of the claimant's vocational status? If not, what additional evidence is required?

8. Please state the following:

   a. Claimant's age, in terms of the applicable age category described in Sections 404.1563 and 416.963 of federal regulations. (See Chapters 8 and 9.)

   b. Claimant's education, in terms of the applicable education category described in Sections 404.1564 and 416.964 of federal regulations. (See Chapters 8 and 9.)

   c. Claimant's "past relevant work" (PRW); i.e., the claimant's work experience during the last 15 years, in terms of the physical exertion and skill requirements described in Sections 404.1567, 404.1568, 416.967, and 416.968 of federal regulations, and the *Dictionary of Occupational Titles*. (See Chapters 8 and 9.)

   d. The extent that any job during the last 15 years required lifting, carrying, pushing, pulling, sitting, standing, walking, climbing, balancing, stooping, kneeling, crouching, crawling, reaching, handling, fingering, feeling, talking, hearing, and seeing, as well as any environmental or similar aspects of the job (indoors, outdoors, extremes of heat or cold, wetness, noise, vibration, and exposure to fumes, odors, or toxic conditions). (See Chapters 8 and 9.)

   e. If the claimant's past relevant work was either at a skilled or semiskilled level, describe the skills acquired by the claimant during the performance of the job(s), and furnish a complete explanation for your opinion(s).

9. Hypothetical questions:

   a. Assume that I find the claimant's testimony credible, that because of his impairment he can only sit for up to three hours and stand or walk for no more than three hours before experiencing severe pain, and can lift no more than ten pounds, and then he must lie down

What the ALJ Might Ask the VE (continued)

for at least two hours in any eight-hour period to relieve the pain. If I accept this description of his limitations, could the claimant, considering his age, education, and work experience, engage in his past relevant work? Or, if not, could he transfer acquired skills to the performance of other skilled or semiskilled work?

b. Assume that I find that the claimant can sit for up to three hours at a time, stand or walk for no more than three hours, and lift up to ten pounds. Can he engage in his past work? If not, can he transfer any skills to perform other skilled or semiskilled work?

c. Assume that I find that the claimant can stand and walk for approximately six hours, and lift no more than 20 pounds at a time with frequent lifting or carrying of objects weighing up to ten pounds. Can he engage in his past work or, if not, can he transfer his skills to perform other skilled or semiskilled work?

d. If the claimant can transfer his skills to perform other skilled or semiskilled work, please provide some examples of these jobs and the frequency with which they are found in the national economy.

CAUTION

Not all hearings end the day they begin. Various circumstances might cause you or the ALJ to suggest that the hearing be "continued" to another day. For example, the ALJ could decide that additional evidence is needed before making a decision on your case. You might have to gather and submit this evidence yourself, or the ALJ might order additional tests or opinions. If the ALJ gathers the additional evidence, you will be given an opportunity to look it over and request a supplemental hearing if you think you need one. These posthearing conferences follow the same rules as prehearing conferences (discussed in Section 3b, above).

4. Appeals Council Review

If you are denied benefits by the ALJ, the final step in your administrative appeals process is with the SSA's Appeals Council (AC).

a. How to Appeal to the Appeals Council

To appeal to the Appeals Council, you must complete and return to the SSA Form HA-520-U5: *Request for Review of Decision/Order* discussed in Section E4a, above. The SSA must receive this form within 60 days of when you receive your denial notice from the ALJ, or 65 days from the date on the ALJ's denial (five days are allowed for mailing).

> ⚠ **CAUTION**
>
> **You must use forms provided by the SSA.** You can obtain them at your local SSA field office or by calling the SSA hotline at 800-772-1213, Monday through Friday (except holidays), from 7 a.m. to 7 p.m. If you are deaf or hard of hearing, TTY service representatives are available at the same times at 800-325-0778. You can also download many necessary forms from the Social Security Administration website at www.ssa.gov. The form is not available from the DDS.

Your other option is to simply write a letter, but it's best to use the official form so you include all necessary information. If you decide to just write a letter, state: "I request that the Appeals Council review the Administrative Law Judge's action on my claim because [state a reason, such as one of the following]":

- My ALJ hearing only lasted 20 minutes, and I didn't have a chance to present my evidence.
- I think the ALJ made a mistake in not considering my treating doctor's opinion.
- I have new evidence showing that the ALJ was wrong in denying my claim.
- The ALJ did not consider my mental problems.

Once you have completed the form, attach to it copies of any evidence showing that the ALJ's decision was incorrect, such as, for example, new evidence showing your heart disease is more severe than thought by the ALJ. Then fold the documents in thirds, insert them in a standard business envelope, and mail them to your local Social Security Field Office. The Field Office will then mail your appeal papers to the Appeals Council, Office of Appellate Operations, 5107 Leesburg Pike, Falls Church, VA 22041-3255.

Keep a copy of your completed form and the originals of your attached evidence for your records. You may need a larger envelope if you have too many documents to follow the SSA's instructions about using a standard business envelope.

b. Will the Appeals Council Review Your Case?

The Appeals Council (AC) will examine your review request and notify you in writing of its intended action. It may grant, deny, or dismiss your request for review.

The AC can dismiss your case without review unless it finds any of the following:

- an abuse of discretion by the ALJ (something like the ALJ's deciding that ten minutes is enough for a hearing)
- an error of law (something like not permitting a claimant or an authorized representative to cross-examine a witness, or not considering the opinion of the treating doctor)
- the ALJ's decision not being supported by substantial evidence, or
- a broad policy or procedural issue raised by the case (such as the ALJ not notifying a claimant that an expert witness would be present at the hearing).

If you file late, request a dismissal, or die, the AC might also dismiss your claim without reviewing it. The AC usually looks for a flaw in the ALJ decision before granting a review. In those situations, your chance of winning is only 2%–3%. The AC is not a place where you are likely to find success. For most people, the only reason to file a request with the AC is to exhaust all the SSA administrative appeal avenues, which you must do before you sue the SSA in federal court. (See Section E5, below.)

Appeals Council Can Initiate Review

Even if you don't appeal to the AC, the AC can select ALJ decisions for review at random or if referred from other divisions of the SSA. This means that on its own, the AC could review and grant a claim that had been denied by an ALJ, but it also means that the AC could reverse an ALJ allowance of benefits and deny your claim. When the AC decides to review a case on its own, you will be notified of its proposed action (reversing or affirming) and given an opportunity to offer input. Although it is very unlikely that your case would fall into such a review sample, it does happen.

---

c. How the Appeals Council Conducts a Review

The Appeals Council judge will attempt to process your review request at the AC level. But if the AC feels the claim needs further factual development before it can issue a legally sufficient decision, it will return the case to the ALJ to gather the evidence, which provides the opportunity for you to have another hearing and for the ALJ to issue a new decision.

If the AC keeps your case for review at the AC level, it will look at the evidence of record (the evidence that was in your file when you asked for AC review), any additional evidence submitted by you, and the ALJ's findings and conclusions. Also, the AC can consult physicians (called Medical Support Staff, or MSS) and vocational experts on its staff. When the MSS recommends granting your claim and the AC relies on that recommendation to reach its decision, the AC must add the MSS comments to your record.

If the MSS recommendation is unfavorable and the AC intends to rely on that recommendation to make its decision, the AC must offer the MSS report to you for comment before entering it into the record. If the AC doesn't use the MSS opinion to reach a decision, the AC does not make the MSS analysis a part of your record.

The AC uses its MSS in only about a fifth of its decisions—but must use the MSS if it grants you benefits based on the fact that your impairments equal a listing. (See Chapter 7 for an explanation of listings.)

d. The Appeals Council's Decision

If the Appeals Council dismisses your case without reviewing it, it will send you a notice advising that it finds no basis to disturb the ALJ's decision. The ALJ's decision then becomes the final decision. This is usually the result of an AC review.

If the AC does review your case, remember that you aren't likely to win, and you'll be lucky to hear from the AC within a year. If you file a new application after requesting an Appeals Council review, Social Security will forward the application to the Appeals Council to be combined with your existing case. But if you have a new critical or disabling condition, you can tell the Appeals Council that you want to file a new application, and the Appeals Council might allow you to file a new application before it completes its review of your existing appeal.

5. Sue the SSA in Federal Court

If you disagree with the Appeals Council's decision or the AC refuses to review your case, you can pursue your case further by filing a lawsuit—that is, suing the SSA—in U.S. district court. You must file your complaint in a district court within 60 days after you receive notice of the AC's dismissal or 65 days from the date on the AC's decision. If you don't yet have an attorney representative, you will almost certainly need one now.

Federal judges hear disability cases without juries. The judge is only supposed to review the case for legal errors by the SSA, but in reality many judges rule on factual questions, too, substituting their judgment for that of the SSA. Of course, federal judges are not doctors. Nor do they have the training to interpret medical information, so they often base their decision on which doctor they believe. They most often believe treating doctors and may rely on the opinions of their clerks—attorneys working under their supervision in their office. District court judges reverse ALJs or the AC in at least a third of all cases, often saying that the SSA did not give sufficient weight to a treating doctor's opinion, did not consider pain and other symptoms, or should have asked for assessments of abilities from treating doctors.

The federal judge might allow your claim (approve benefits) or deny it (uphold the SSA's denial determination)—but these aren't the court's only options. The court might also send your claim back to the ALJ to reevaluate your claim according to some special legal instruction. For example, the court might find that the ALJ did not obtain important medical information or consider your treating doctor's opinion. The court might order the ALJ to do these things at a new hearing. Since the AC refuses to review most claims, most federal court reversals are of an ALJ's decision rather than the AC's decision.

Appealing to a Higher Court

If you lose a case in a federal district court, you can appeal to a circuit court of appeals. The U.S. federal court system is divided into circuits. Each circuit covers several states— for example, the 8th Circuit contains North Dakota, South Dakota, Nebraska, Minnesota, Iowa, Missouri, and Arkansas.

The decision of an individual circuit court is binding only on the district courts within its circuit. For instance, a decision by 8th Circuit Court of Appeals will not have to be followed in New York, and a decision by the 2nd Circuit Court of Appeals (which covers New York) isn't binding on federal district courts in Nebraska. This means that the outcome of your case could depend on where you live.

If you lose an appeal to a federal circuit court, you can theoretically take your case to the U.S. Supreme Court, but the Supreme Court only hears cases that it thinks warrant its special consideration. If your claim involves a broad legal or Constitutional issue that potentially affects the entire country, the Supreme Court might consider hearing your case.

Although you have a fair chance of winning an appeal in federal court, it is not an attractive option. Fewer than 1% of disability claimants actually take their cases to court. Suing the SSA is expensive and very time-consuming. Even if you win, it might take years to reach that level. Consequently, few attorneys are willing to file a disability case in federal court. Of course, you could represent yourself, but few nonattorneys have the skills, time, or money to do so, especially if they suffer from severe medical conditions.

RESOURCE
Should you choose to appeal on your own, you can refer to *Represent Yourself in Court: How to Prepare & Try a Winning Case*, by Paul Bergman and Sara Berman (Nolo), for guidance.

If you do file in federal court, you can file a new initial claim at the DDS while your case is pending, and the SSA will let the new claim proceed as long as your alleged onset date is after the date of the last administrative action (after the Appeals Council denial or dismissal) on the claim.

F. Reopening of Decisions

An alternative to appealing your case is requesting a reopening of your claim— asking for a second look by whichever administrative level of the SSA has your claim. Here are the rules governing when you can reopen your case:

- If you make your request within 12 months of the date of the notice of the initial determination by the DDS, ALJ, or AC, you can ask for a reopening for any reason.
- If you believe that the determination to deny you or terminate your benefits was based on fraud or a similar fault, you can request a reopening at any time.
- If you make your request within four years, for SSDI applicants, or two years, for SSI applicants, of the date of the notice of the initial determination, the SSA may reopen the case if it finds good cause. "Good cause" is defined as follows:
  - new, important (called "material") evidence
  - a clerical error in the computation of your benefits, or
  - evidence of a clear error.

Good cause does not include a change of legal interpretation or administrative ruling upon which the determination or decision was made.

If the SSA agrees to reopen your case and issues a revised determination, that new determination is binding unless one of the following is true:

- You file a request for reconsideration or a hearing.
- You file a request for review by the Appeals Council.
- The Appeals Council reviews the revised decision.
- The revised determination is further revised.

G. Refiling an Initial Claim

If you lose your appeal (no matter at what level), you have the option to file another initial claim. Just go to your local Social Security Field Office (or online, for SSDI claims) and start the process over again. Your chance of being granted benefits will improve if a change in your condition—such as a worsening of impairments or new impairments—warrants a different disability decision.

However, a possible legal barrier to filing a subsequent claim is called "res judicata," which means "the thing has been decided." The DDS can use res judicata to avoid deciding a claim that has previously been determined if all the facts, issues, conditions, and evidence are the same.

If you file a new disability application with the same issues and no new facts or evidence, your application may be denied on the basis of res judicata. But the SSA may give you the benefit of the doubt and treat your new claim as a request for reopening (see Section F, above).

If anything has changed—including the law or regulations, or you offer new evidence—res judicata won't apply.

> **EXAMPLE—RES JUDICATA APPLIES:**
> You are denied on your first application on 1/30/16 and do not appeal. You file a second application, claim the same alleged onset date, submit no new evidence, and show that you were last insured for benefits before 1/30/16. The SSA denies your claim on the basis of res judicata.

EXAMPLE 2—RES JUDICATA DOES NOT APPLY: The same example, except that you submit new evidence with your claim. The new evidence could describe more about how your condition has been all along, or show a new development in your illness. The SSA would not apply res judicata to your claim.

Also, if you are still insured for SSDI disability benefits (in other words, you are still eligible for benefits based on your work earnings) after the date of your last determination, res judicata cannot be applied to the time after that determination. This is true even if you allege the same onset date, same impairment, and same condition.

Once You Are Approved

A. Disability Benefit Payments

Once you are awarded disability benefits, you will receive a Certificate of Award containing answers to many questions about Social Security payments. If any of your relatives are eligible for dependents benefits due to your disability (SSDI only), they will receive a separate notice and a booklet about what they need to know.

1. When Benefits Start

For SSDI, you will be paid SSDI benefits starting five months after the time you are declared disabled (your established onset date). Your first payment might include some retroactive benefits going back to your established onset date, even if it was before you applied for SSDI. (However, you can't receive more than 12 months of retroactive benefits. How your retroactive benefits are calculated is covered in Chapter 10, Section C.)

SSI benefits begin the month following the month in which you qualify for disability benefits. You cannot get retroactive SSI benefits going back to your date of disability. However, since it takes a while to get approved for SSI, you will probably be owed some back payments going back to the month after which you applied for SSI. (See Chapter 10, Section C, for more details.)

2. How Much Benefits Will Be

How much your benefits will be depends first on whether you have an SSDI claim or an SSI claim, because each program uses different formulas to determine benefits. SSDI benefits are usually higher than SSI benefits.

a. SSDI Benefits

The SSA will tell you the amount of your benefits when it sends you notice that your claim has been allowed. Your SSDI benefits are calculated using a complicated formula. The SSA first calculates your average earnings over a period of many years, known as your "average indexed monthly earnings" (AIME).

Your AIME is then used to calculate your "primary insurance amount" (PIA)—the basic figure the SSA uses in finding the actual benefit amount. The PIA is a total of fixed percentages of predetermined dollar amounts of your AIME. The dollar amounts increase yearly, but the percentages stay the same. For 2020, for example, the monthly PIA benefit for a disabled worker is as follows:

Percentage of Amount in Right Column	Amount of AIME
90%	$0–$960
32%	$960–$5,785
15%	$5,785

EXAMPLE: Horace's AIME is $6,000. The SSA calculates his PIA as follows:

$$\$ \quad 960 \times 90\% = \$ \quad 864.00$$

Plus

$$
\begin{array}{r}
5,785 \\
- \quad 864 \\
\hline
\$ \quad 4,921 \times 32\% = \$ \quad 1,574.72
\end{array}
$$

Plus

$$
\begin{array}{r}
\$ \quad 6,000 \\
- \quad 5,785 \\
\hline
\$ \quad 215 \times 15\% = \$ \quad 32.25
\end{array}
$$

$$\text{TOTAL} = \$ \quad 2,471^*$$

* rounded to nearest $0.10 as required

Family members who were dependent on your income may also be eligible for benefits. For example, a child eligible to receive benefits on your record while you are alive is entitled to 50% of your PIA; if you die, the percentage increases to 75% of your PIA.

The "maximum family benefit" (MFB) is the total monthly benefit that can be paid to you (the wage earner) and any family members entitled to benefits on your record. The MFB does not affect the amount of your benefit. Instead, added to your PIA are different amounts for each family member based on a percentage of your PIA.

These amounts will be reduced if the total of your benefits and your dependents' benefits exceeds the MFB limit, which is 85% of your AIME, as long as the amount doesn't fall below your PIA. At the same time, the total MFB amount cannot exceed 150% of your PIA.

There is a formula used to compute the family maximum, consisting of four separate portions of the worker's PIA. The dollar amounts increase yearly, but the percentages stay the same. For 2020, for example, the MFB benefit for a disabled worker is as follows:

150% of the first $1,226 of PIA, plus
272% of PIA over $1,226 through $1,770, plus
134% of PIA over $1,770 through $2,309, plus
175% of PIA over $2,309.

This basic summary doesn't consider other factors that can influence the actual amount. It is not practical for you to try to calculate your own monthly benefit. It makes more sense to let the SSA do the calculations. Of course, the SSA could make a mistake.

The following table can give you an idea of the approximate monthly amount of SSDI benefits paid to disabled recipients and qualified family members. The table also shows some types of Social Security nondisability benefits for comparison. Once you reach full retirement age, you will receive retirement benefits rather than disability benefits. Be aware that these amounts can vary with individual eligibility circumstances.

The following table represents estimated average monthly Social Security benefits payable in 2020.

Type of Beneficiary	Award
Aged couple both receiving benefits	$2,531
Widowed mother and two children	$2,935
Aged widow(er) alone	$1,421
Disabled worker, spouse, and one or more children	$2,178
Disabled worker	$1,258
Retired worker	$1,503

The maximum a disabled worker can receive in 2020 is $3,011 per month (for high earners). (Also see Chapter 2 regarding how your benefit can be reduced by workers' compensation and other public disability or pension payments.)

b. SSI Benefits

Although your entitlement to SSI benefits depends on both your income and resources, only your income influences the amount of your monthly payment.

In 2020, the maximum SSI payment for a disabled adult is $783 per month and $1,175 for a couple. Some states supplement SSI payments with more money (called a state supplemental payment; see Chapter 1).

Your SSI check might not be the same every month. Each monthly amount depends on your other income and living arrangements. The SSA will tell you whenever it plans to change the amount of your check. See Chapter 1 for information on how your income and resources affect the amount of your SSI benefits.

3. When and How Payments Are Made

When and how benefits are paid depends on the type of benefit and whether the payment is by check or direct deposit to a bank account. If you don't have a bank account, your local SSA Field Office can help you find banks that offer low- or no-cost accounts to receive your SSDI or SSI benefits.

a. Check by Mail

SSI checks and combined SSI/SSDI checks should arrive on the first day of the month. If the first falls on a weekend or legal holiday, you should receive your check on the business day before. For example, if your payment date would fall on a Sunday, you should receive your check on the prior Friday instead.

SSDI recipients who started receiving benefits before 1997 get their payments on the third day of the month or the business day preceding it, if the third is a weekend or holiday. If you were awarded benefits after 1997, your SSDI payment will arrive on a day as dictated by your birthday:

Birthday Day of Month	Day SSDI Arrives
1st – 10th	Second Wednesday
11th – 20th	Third Wednesday
21st – 31st	Fourth Wednesday

The SSA's site (www.ssa.gov) has a colorful calendar showing the exact dates you will receive your payments if you live in the United States.

If you are living outside the United States, your checks may arrive later than the due date. Delivery time varies from country to country, and your check may not arrive the same day each month.

b. Direct Deposits

The SSA prefers that you have a bank (or savings and loan association or credit union) account so that your check can be deposited directly. If your deposit doesn't take place on the date scheduled, call the SSA at once, so they can put a trace on the payment. The deposit should always be in your account on the correct date.

If you don't have a bank account for direct deposit, the U.S. Department of the Treasury automatically will send your benefits via the Direct Express® card program. Detailed information about the Direct Express program can be found at www.USDirectExpress.com.

c. Overpayments (Erroneous Payments)

If you receive a check or direct deposit payment to which you are not entitled— for example, for your spouse who died before the date the check was issued—you must return it to the SSA. If you return a check by mail, enclose a note telling why you are sending the payment back.

4. Paying Taxes on Disability Benefits

Social Security recipients must pay taxes on their benefits if they have substantial additional income. If you file an individual tax return and your combined income— your adjusted gross income plus nontaxable interest plus one half of your Social Security benefits—is between $25,000 and $34,000, you may owe taxes on 50% of your Social Security benefits. If your combined income is above $34,000, up to 85% of your Social Security benefits is subject to income tax.

If you file a joint return, you may owe taxes on 50% of your benefits if you and your spouse have a combined income between $32,000 and $44,000. If your combined income is more than $44,000, up to 85% of your Social Security benefits is subject to income tax.

If part of your benefits are taxed, they'll be taxed at your marginal income tax rate.

Most claimants don't make enough money to worry about paying taxes on their disability benefits. But situations vary; if you have substantial additional income, consult a knowledgeable tax preparer. SSI recipients are particularly unlikely to have a tax problem, because if they are liable for taxes, they probably make too much to get SSI.

5. How Long Payments Continue

Your disability benefits generally continue as long as your impairment has not improved and you cannot work.

But because of advances in medical science and rehabilitation techniques, increasing numbers of people with disabilities recover from serious accidents and illnesses. Some people recover enough to return to work. Your case will be reviewed periodically to make sure you're still disabled (see Chapter 14).

Your benefits may be reduced or terminated if you marry, receive certain other disability benefits, or move to certain countries where payments are prohibited (see Section B5, below). Also, if you are receiving SSDI when you turn 66, your benefits automatically will be changed to retirement benefits, generally for the same amount. If you are receiving benefits as a disabled widow or widower when you turn 60, your benefits will be changed to regular widow or widower benefits.

For a broad discussion of Social Security issues, see *Social Security, Medicare & Government Pensions*, by Attorney Joseph Matthews (Nolo).

6. Eligibility for Medicare and Medicaid

Medicare is a health insurance program for eligible people who are age 65 or older or disabled. To be eligible for Medicare, you have to have worked and paid Social Security and Medicare (FICA) taxes for a certain number of years.

Medicare coverage does not start right away for SSDI recipients. Instead, you become eligible after you have been entitled to receive SSDI benefits for 24 months. If you have chronic kidney disease requiring regular dialysis, amyotrophic lateral sclerosis (ALS), or a transplant, however, you may qualify for Medicare almost immediately.

Medicare protection includes hospital insurance (Part A) and medical insurance (Part B). The hospital insurance part of Medicare pays hospital bills and certain follow-up care after you leave the hospital. Medical insurance helps pay doctor bills and other medical services.

There is no cost for the hospital insurance. If you want the medical insurance, you must enroll and pay a monthly premium, by having it withheld from your SSDI payment. If you choose not to enroll when first eligible and then sign up later, your premiums will be 10% more for each 12-month period you could have been enrolled but were not (unless you receive health care insurance through an employer or your spouse's employer).

If you receive Medicare and have low income and few resources, your state may pay your Medicare premiums and, in some cases, other out-of-pocket Medicare expenses, such as deductibles and coinsurance. Contact a local welfare office or Medicaid agency to see if you qualify.

Once you are covered by Medicare's medical insurance, if you want to cancel it, notify the SSA. Medical insurance and premiums will continue for one more month after the month you notify the SSA that you wish to cancel. For example, because Medicare generally does not cover health services you get outside the United States, you might want to either not sign up for coverage or cancel coverage if you plan to be abroad for a long period of time. There is little reason to pay the premium until you return.

SSI recipients are eligible for Medicaid in most states. There is no Medicaid waiting period.

B. Reporting Changes— SSDI Recipients

Promptly report to the SSA any changes that may affect you or your family members' SSDI benefits. To let the SSA know the new information, you can call 800-772-1213 (voice) or 800-325-0778 (TTY), visit any SSA office (a clerk will help you), or complete and mail in the reporting form you received when you applied for benefits.

If you send a report by mail, be sure to include the following:

- your name or the name of the person on whose account you get benefits
- your Social Security number or the Social Security number of the person on whose account you get benefits
- name of the person about whom the report is being made, if not you
- nature of the change
- date of the change, and
- your signature, address, and phone number, and the date.

If you don't report a change, you might miss out on money to which you are entitled or have to pay back money to which you were not entitled. Even if the

SSA has no way to force you to repay an overpayment right now, the SSA will wait and deduct it from your retirement benefits when you turn 65.

In extreme situations—for instance, if you lie to the SSA to keep getting benefits—you could be prosecuted for Social Security fraud and fined, imprisoned, or both. The SSA has ways of finding out about true income and other factors affecting your eligibility for certain kinds of benefits—such as obtaining information from your employers and the Internal Revenue Service.

The events that must be reported follow.

1. You Move

As soon as you know your new address and phone number—even if it's before you move—let the SSA know. Include the names of any family members who also should receive their Social Security information at the new address.

Even if your benefits are deposited directly, the SSA must have your correct address to send you letters and other important information. Your benefits will end if the SSA is unable to contact you.

2. You Change or Establish Bank Accounts

If you receive your check by direct deposit and you change banks—that is, close one account and open another—you must report that to the SSA so your direct deposits continue. If you've been receiving your payments by Direct Express and you open a bank account, let the SSA know so it can set up direct deposit.

3. Your Condition Changes

If your medical condition improves or you believe you can work, you are responsible for promptly notifying the SSA. Failure to do so could mean that you would get payments you aren't entitled to receive— and might have to repay the SSA.

4. You Go to Work

Notify the SSA if you take a job or become self-employed, no matter how little you earn. You must tell the SSA if you start receiving wages that you have not previously reported. The SSA has made this reporting easier by letting you report wage changes online by using the "My Profile Tab" after you set up a "My Social Security" account on the SSA website. If you have a representative payee, he or she can also report your wages through their own Social Security account. (So far, this service is for SSDI only.)

If you are still disabled, you will be eligible for a trial work period and can continue receiving benefits for up to nine months, even if you make over the SGA limit (see Section D, below).

If you return to work and incur any special expenses because of your disability, such as specialized equipment, a wheelchair, or some prescription drugs, let the SSA know. In some cases, the SSA will pay your expenses.

5. You Leave the United States

If you move abroad, the reporting requirements are the same as for other types of reportable changes as described in the introduction to this section.

If you leave the United States and have questions about your SSDI while you are out of the country, you have several places to turn to get assistance:

- SSA Federal Benefits Units at U.S. consulates and embassies or at the American Institute in Taiwan
- SSA representatives stationed at consulates and embassies in London, Athens, Rome, Mexico City, Guadalajara, Manila, and Frankfurt, or
- SSA Field Offices located in the British Virgin Islands, Canada, and Western Samoa.

a. Your Right to Payments When You Are Outside the United States

Thousands of SSDI beneficiaries (and family members receiving benefits based on their work record) receive disability benefits while residing outside of the United States. If you are not in one of the 50 states, the District of Columbia, Puerto Rico, the U.S. Virgin Islands, Guam, the Northern Mariana Islands, or American Samoa, you are considered to be outside the United States.

If you are a U.S. citizen and receive SSDI, you can continue to receive payments outside of the United States, as long as you are eligible for them, without having to return to the United States periodically. You do not have to notify the SSA of temporary trips outside of the United States, regardless of the length. But you must be able to receive mail from the SSA. If no one will keep track of your U.S. mail and you will be outside of the United States for more than one or two months, give your local Social Security Field Office an overseas address. If you move permanently to another country, definitely tell the SSA, as you are required to keep the SSA informed of your residence address.

Much more complicated rules apply to noncitizens receiving benefits. If you are outside the United States for at least 30 days in a row, you are considered outside the country until you return and stay in the United States for at least 30 days in a row. In addition, if you are not a U.S. citizen, you may be required to establish lawful presence in the United States for that 30-day period before you can receive disability benefits. "Lawful presence" means you are in the United States legally. (More specific requirements for lawful presence are given in Chapter 1, Section A1.)

Because of the large numbers of international treaties and agreements, there are different rules for receiving benefits in different countries. With some exceptions, an alien beneficiary who leaves the United States must either return to the United States at least every 30 days, or for 30 consecutive days during each six-month period, in order to continue to draw benefits. (See "Benefits When Living Abroad," below, for countries where noncitizens can continue to receive benefits.)

Once your payments stop, they cannot be started again until you come back and stay in the United States for an entire calendar month. This means you have to be in the United States on the first minute of the first day of a month and stay through the last minute of the last day of that month. For example, if you move back on July 2, you won't be eligible again for SSDI until September 1, after you have been in the United States the full month of August. In addition, you might be required to establish lawful presence in the United States for that full calendar month period. The SSA will not give you back payments for the months you missed.

b. Additional Residency Requirements for Dependents and Survivors

If you receive benefits as a dependent or survivor of an SSDI recipient, special require-ments might affect your right to receive SSDI payments while you are outside the United States. If you are not a U.S. citizen, you must have lived in the United States for at least five years, during which time the family relationship on which benefits are based must have existed. For example, if you are receiving benefits as a spouse, you must have been married to the worker and living in the United States for at least five years.

Benefits When Living Abroad

Category 1

If you are a citizen of one of the following countries, payments will continue no matter how long you are outside the United States, as long as you remain eligible.

Austria	Japan
Belgium	Korea (South)
Brazil	Luxembourg
Canada	Netherlands
Chile	Norway
Czech Republic	Poland
Finland	Portugal
France	Slovak Republic
Germany	Slovenia
Greece	Spain
Hungary	Sweden
Ireland	Switzerland
Israel	United Kingdom
Italy	Uruguay

Category 2

If you are a citizen of one of the following countries, payments will continue no matter how long you are outside the United States, as long as you remain eligible, unless you receive payments as a dependent or survivor.

Albania	Bulgaria
Antigua and Barbuda	Burkina Faso
Argentina	Colombia
Bahamas	Costa Rica
Barbados	Côte d'Ivoire
Belize	Croatia
Bolivia	Cyprus
Bosnia-Herzegovina	Denmark
Brazil	Dominica

Dominican Republic	Montenegro
Ecuador	North Macedonia
El Salvador	Nicaragua
Gabon Grenada	Palau
Guatemala	Panama
Guyana	Peru
Iceland	Philippines
Jamaica	St. Kitts and Nevis
Jordan	St. Lucia
Latvia	St. Vincent and the Grenadines
Liechtenstein	
Lithuania	Samoa
Malta	San Marino
Marshall Islands	Serbia
Mexico	Trinidad-Tobago
Micronesia	Turkey
Monaco	Venezuela

Category 3

If you are not a citizen of a country listed in one of the two charts above, your SSDI payments will stop after you have been outside the United States for six calendar months, unless one of the following is true:

- You were eligible for monthly Social Security benefits in December 1956.
- You are in the active military service of the United States.
- The worker on whose record your benefits are based had done railroad work qualifying as employment covered by the Social Security program (see Chapter 2, Section D, regarding the Railroad Retirement Act and the Social Security program).

Benefits When Living Abroad (continued)

- The worker on whose record your benefits are based died while in U.S. military service or as a result of a service-connected disability and was not dishonorably discharged.
- You are a resident of a country listed below with which the United States has a Social Security agreement. Note that the agreements with Austria, Belgium, Germany, Sweden, and Switzerland permit you to receive benefits as a dependent or survivor of a worker while you reside in the foreign country only if the worker is a U.S. citizen or a citizen of the foreign country.

Australia	Japan
Austria	Korea (South)
Belgium	Luxembourg
Canada	Netherlands
Chile	Norway
Czech Republic	Poland
Denmark	Portugal
Finland	Slovak Republic
France	Slovenia
Germany	Spain
Greece	Sweden
Hungary	Switzerland
Ireland	United Kingdom
Italy	Uruguay

- The worker on whose record your benefits are based lived in the United States for at least ten years or earned at least 40 earnings credits under the U.S. Social Security system, and you are a citizen of one of the following countries:

Afghanistan	Madagascar
Bangladesh	Malawi
Bhutan	Malaysia
Botswana	Mali
Burma	Mauritania
Burundi	Mauritius
Cameroon	Morocco
Cape (Cabo) Verde	Nepal
Central African Republic	Nigeria
Chad	Pakistan
China	Senegal
Congo	Sierra Leone
Eritrea	Singapore
Ethiopia	Solomon Islands
Fiji	Somalia
Gambia	South Africa
Ghana	South Sudan
Haiti	Sri Lanka
Honduras	Sudan
India	Taiwan
Indonesia	Tanzania
Kenya	Thailand
Laos	Togo
Lebanon	Tonga
Lesotho	Tunisia
Liberia	Uganda
	Yemen

Children who cannot meet the residency requirement on their own might be considered to meet it if the SSDI recipient and other parent (if any) meet the requirement. Children adopted outside the United States will not be paid outside the United States, however, even if the SSDI recipient meets the residency requirement.

The residency requirement will not apply to you if one of the following applies:

- You were initially eligible for monthly benefits before January 1, 1985.
- You are a citizen of Israel or Japan.
- You are a resident of a country listed below with which the United States has a Social Security agreement:

Australia	Japan
Austria	Luxembourg
Belgium	Netherlands
Canada	Norway
Chile	Poland
Czech Republic	Portugal
Denmark	Slovak Republic
Finland	Slovenia
France	South Korea
Germany	Spain
Greece	Sweden
Hungary	Switzerland
Ireland	United Kingdom
Italy	Uruguay

- You are entitled to benefits based on the record of a worker who died while in the U.S. military service or as a result of a service-connected disease or injury.

c. How Payments Are Made When You Live Outside the United States

Normally, Social Security benefits can be paid to qualifying U.S. citizens and noncitizens who move outside of the United States. Unless you are a U.S. citizen who never plans to reside in another country, it is important that you understand the basics of how international payments are made. Banking technology permits the SSA to establish direct deposit to pay beneficiaries who reside in certain countries through International Direct Deposit (IDD) or Electronic Benefits Transfer (EBT). IDD and EBT will eventually be expanded to cover many countries.

IDD involves the assistance of a sponsoring or processing bank—either the central bank of the foreign country or a large commercial bank in that country. Payments are deposited directly into your account at the financial institution in that country, in that country's currency. The benefits are calculated in U.S. dollars. They are not increased or decreased because of changes in international exchange rates. IDD is available in Albania, Anguilla, Antigua and Barbuda, Argentina, Australia, Austria, Bahama Islands, Bahrain, Bangladesh, Barbados, Belgium, Belize, Bermuda, Bolivia, Bonaire, Bosnia & Herzegovina, Brazil, British Virgin Islands, Bulgaria, Cambodia, Canada, Cape (Cabo) Verde, Cayman Islands, Chile, China, Colombia, Costa Rica, Croatia, Curacao, Cyprus,

Czech Republic, Denmark, Dominica, Dominican Republic, Ecuador, Egypt, Eritrea, Estonia, Ethiopia, Finland, France, Gambia, Georgia, Germany, Ghana, Greece, Grenada, Guatemala, Haiti, Honduras, Hong Kong, Hungary, Iceland, India, Indonesia, Ireland, Israel, Italy, Jamaica, Japan, Jordan, Kenya, Laos, Latvia, Lebanon, Liberia, Lithuania, Luxembourg, Macao, Malaysia, Malta, Marshall Islands, Martinique, Mexico, Micronesia, Monaco, Montserrat, Nauru, Netherlands, New Zealand, Nicaragua, Nigeria, Norway, North Macedonia, Pakistan, Palau, Palestinian Territories, Panama, Paraguay, Peru, Philippines, Poland, Portugal, Qatar, Romania, Russia, Samoa, San Marino, Singapore, St. Kitts and Nevis, St. Lucia, St. Vincent and the Grenadines, Samoa, San Marino, Saudi Arabia, Senegal, Sierra Leone, Singapore, St. Maarten, Slovakia, Slovenia, South Africa, South Korea, Spain, Sri Lanka, Sudan, Suriname, Sweden, Switzerland, Taiwan, Tanzania, Trinidad and Tobago, Tunisia, Turkey, Uganda, United Arab Emirates, United Kingdom, Uruguay, and Vietnam.

Electronic Benefits Transfer (EBT) allows you to have payments deposited in a special account in a U.S. bank. You can withdraw the benefits by using a bank card at an automated teller machine (ATM) in the country in which you reside. You can't write checks on the account, nor can you add funds to the account. EBT is only currently available in Argentina. SSI payments are available through EBT, but not IDD.

When you move from one country to another, the way your benefits will be paid depends on the countries involved.

If You Move to a Prohibited Country

U.S. Treasury Department regulations prohibit sending payments to you if you are in Cuba or North Korea. In addition, Social Security restrictions prohibit sending payments to you if you are in Azerbaijan, Belarus, , Kazakhstan, Kyrgyzstan, Moldova, Tajikistan, Turkmenistan, or Uzbekistan. Not only can't the SSA normally send payments to these countries, federal regulations bar you from receiving payments even by direct deposit or through a representative. Exceptions are possible for receiving payments to all of the above countries other than Cuba and North Korea. Exceptions are not automatically granted, and specific conditions must apply. If you desire the SSA send you benefits in the above countries, you should contact an SSA Field Office for help.

If the SSA does learn that you are in Cuba or North Korea and stops payments, when you return, the SSA will send you the money it withheld while you were away, but only if you are a U.S. citizen. If you are not a U.S. citizen, generally you cannot receive payments for the months you lived in Cuba or North Korea.

You move from the United States to an IDD country. If you move to an IDD country, the SSA will encourage you to open an account in the new country and receive payments in the new account. Until you open your new account, the SSA will make deposits to your old account. If you close your old account before you open your new one, the SSA will pay you by check until you open the new account. In either event, contact the Federal Benefits Unit at the U.S. embassy in the country to which you move to get enrolled in IDD. Although you don't have to open an account (see Section A3, above), it is in your best interest to receive your benefits by IDD rather than by check.

When you return from the IDD country, the IDD cannot continue while you have a U.S. address. As soon as you return, open up a U.S. bank account and let the SSA know so it can arrange direct deposit into that account.

You move from the United States to a non-IDD country. If you move from the United States to a non-IDD country, the SSA will encourage you to keep your bank account in the United States open (or to open one in an IDD country) to receive direct deposits. You can then access your U.S. account from overseas with an ATM card. If you don't have a bank account, the SSA will send you a check—unless you live in a prohibited country. (See "If You Move to a Prohibited Country," above.)

Payment dates and amounts are a frequent source of confusion for overseas beneficiaries. Regular IDD SSDI payments generally are made on the third of the month. If that date is a nonbusiness day in the foreign country, payments generally are made the next business day.

PMA "prior monthly accrual" SSDI payments are made on either the 12th or the 26th of the month. The PMA is a combined payment for all benefits due to you at the time your award is processed, and is paid immediately, subject to any delays by the U.S. processing partner, the Federal Reserve Bank of New York. The cutoff date for figuring out the PMA is about a week before the PMA payment date. PMA payments that arrive after the cutoff are scheduled for the next PMA payment date. Because the PMA payment includes the prior months' benefits, it could erroneously appear that these benefits are being paid incorrectly—especially because the check could arrive or be deposited after your first full monthly benefit check.

d. Reporting Changes While Living Outside the United States

When you live outside the United States, you do not avoid the SSA's continuing disability reviews—a periodic process to determine whether you are still eligible for benefits. The SSA will send you a questionnaire to fill out and return. You must return it to the office that sent it to you as soon as possible; if you do not, your payments will stop. (See Chapter 14.)

In addition to responding to the questionnaire, you are responsible for notifying the SSA promptly about changes that could affect your payments. If you fail to report something or deliberately make a false statement, you could be penalized by a fine or imprisonment. You might also lose some of your payments if you do not report changes promptly.

To report changes, contact the SSA in person, by mail, or by telephone. If you choose mail and you live in Canada, send your report to the nearest U.S. Social Security office. In Mexico, send your report to the nearest U.S. Social Security office, embassy, or consulate. In the Philippines, send your report to Veterans' Affairs Regional Office, SSA Division, 1131 Roxas Boulevard, Manila, Philippines.

In all other countries, you can contact the nearest U.S. embassy or consulate. If you'd rather send your report to the SSA in the United States, ship it via airmail to Social Security Administration, Office of International Operations, P.O. Box 17769, Baltimore, MD 21235-7769, USA.

In reporting a change, include all of the following information:

- name of person or persons about whom the report is being made
- what is being reported and the date it happened, and
- the claim number on the Social Security check (the nine-digit Social Security number followed by a letter, or a letter and a number).

6. You Receive Other Disability Benefits

If you are disabled and younger than 65, Social Security benefits for you and your family may be reduced if you receive workers' compensation or black lung payments or disability benefits from certain government programs. Let the SSA know if any of the following are true:

- You apply for another type of disability benefit.
- You begin receiving another disability benefit or a lump sum settlement.
- You already receive another disability benefit and the amount changes or stops.

7. You Get a Pension From Work Not Covered by Social Security

Let the SSA know if you start receiving a pension from a job where you did not pay Social Security taxes. For example, state workers covered under a state or local retirement system may receive pension benefits related to work that did not require the payment of Social Security taxes. Whether a particular state employee is covered under Social Security can vary from state to state and the type of agreements the particular state has entered into with the federal government. If you are not sure about your own situation, contact the official who manages your retirement plan.

Also, if you receive U.S. Social Security disability benefits and start to receive a monthly pension that is based in whole or in part on work that the U.S. Social

Security system doesn't cover (such as a foreign social security pension), then your U.S. Social Security benefit may be smaller, because the SSA may use a secondary formula to figure your U.S. Social Security benefit. For more information, ask at any U.S. embassy or Social Security office.

8. You Are a Spouse or Surviving Spouse Who Receives a Government Pension

If you are a disabled widow or widower or the spouse of someone getting disability benefits, your Social Security payments may be reduced if you worked for a government agency where you did not pay Social Security taxes and you receive a pension from that agency. Notify the SSA if you begin to receive such a pension or if the amount of that pension changes.

9. You Get Married

Marriage might affect your disability benefits. Be sure to notify the SSA in the following situations:

- **You are an adult who was disabled before age 22 and receive benefits on the Social Security record of a parent or grandparent.** Payments generally will end when you get married unless you marry a person who receives certain Social Security benefits. (Specifically, your benefits will not end if you are age 18 or older and disabled, and you marry a person

entitled to child's benefits based on disability or a person entitled to old age, divorced wife's, divorced husband's, widow's, widower's, mother's, father's, parent's, or disability benefits.) Once your benefits end, they cannot start again unless the marriage is declared void. A void marriage is one that was illegal from the outset, such as if you marry someone who is already married. If your marriage ends in a divorce or your spouse dies, you won't be eligible to have the benefits restart.

- **You receive benefits as the child of a disability recipient.** Your benefits will end when you marry.
- **You receive benefits on your own earnings record.** Your payments will continue, and you don't need to report the marriage. But report any name change, so it will appear on your future mailings.
- **You receive benefits as a disabled widow or widower.** Payments will continue, but remember to report any name change. If your current spouse dies, you may be eligible for higher benefits on that partner's work record.

10. You Get a Divorce or an Annulment

Notify the SSA if your marriage is annulled or you get divorced. Divorce or annulment does not necessarily mean that your SSDI payments will stop. It depends on the circumstances.

If you are receiving payments based on your own work record, divorce or annulment of your marriage will not affect your payments. If you are an ex-spouse age 62 or older and you were married to an SSDI recipient for ten years or more, your SSDI auxiliary payments will continue even if you divorce. But still contact the SSA if your name is changed as a result of the divorce, so that the SSA can put your new name on your payments.

11. You Cannot Manage Your Funds

If you become unable to manage your funds, you must appoint a person or an organization, called a "representative payee," to receive and use the benefits on your behalf. The payee is responsible for the following:

- properly using the benefits on your behalf
- reporting to the SSA any events that might affect your payments, and
- completing any reports the SSA requires.

If you appoint a representative payee because you have a drug or alcohol addiction, the SSA may refer you to a state substance abuse agency for treatment.

Note that if you have appointed someone to manage your finances or health care under a power of attorney, that person will not be qualified as representative payee simply because of the power of attorney. You must separately notify the SSA. Also, a representative payee is not the same as an attorney or other representative who might help you pursue your claim.

The SSA prefers to appoint friends or family as payees, but if they are not available, the SSA may appoint a qualified organization, such as a social services agency, to be a representative payee. The SSA permits qualified organizations to subtract a fee from your benefits to cover the cost of services provided as your representative payee. This fee cannot be more than 10% of the monthly benefit or $42 per month, whichever is less. However, if the SSA assigns a representative payee due to a claimant's drug or alcoholism condition, the fee can be up to $80 per month. These maximum fees are adjusted yearly based on the SSA's cost-of-living adjustment (COLA).

12. You Are Convicted of a Crime

When you are convicted of a crime, the SSA should be notified if you are imprisoned or confined to an institution. Benefits generally are not paid while you are imprisoned or institutionalized, although any family members eligible on your record may continue to receive benefits.

Confinement to an institution without conviction does not result in a suspension of benefits if it results from a court or jury finding that you are one of the following:

- guilty by reason of insanity or similar factors (such as mental defect or incompetence), or
- incompetent to stand trial.

(Also see Section E4, below, regarding other law applicable to prisoners.)

If Your Representative Payee Misuses Your Funds

What happens if your representative payee steals or otherwise misuses your benefit money? The SSA may provide replacement benefits. Until recently, in order to receive replacement benefits, you had to prove that the SSA was "fully negligent" in following its own procedures for authorizing your representative payee. Under that policy, you had little chance of getting replacement benefits from the SSA. Fortunately, the SSA has made an improvement in this area.

Now, if a representative payee misuses your benefits, the SSA must repay you, provided that the representative payee handles the accounts of 15 or more beneficiaries. Otherwise, you will still need to prove that the SSA was "fully negligent." The SSA does not have any discretion in this rule—it is clearly specified by law. In other words, it is not an issue that can be negotiated or argued.

However, representative payees are liable for both civil and criminal penalties if they misuse your benefits and can be required to pay back misused or lost benefits. (Details can be found on Social Security's website at www.ssa.gov/payee.)

13. Recipient Dies

You must notify the SSA when an SSDI recipient dies. The deceased's survivors are not entitled to keep the payment for the month in which the death occurred. For example, if Herman died in June, even June 30, Herman's survivors must return the July payment, which is actually the June benefit. If Herman and his wife Eloise receive a joint monthly payment, however, Eloise should contact the SSA before returning the payment, as she's entitled to a portion of it.

If the SSA was depositing the benefit directly into the recipient's bank account, be sure to notify the bank, so it can return any payments received after death.

If the deceased's family members received benefits on the deceased's record, those payments will change to survivors benefits. If an SSDI recipient also received benefits on behalf of his or her children, the family will have to appoint a new representative payee for the children. The survivors will need to provide a death certificate or another proof of death to the SSA.

14. Child Reaches Age 18

Payments to a child will stop when the child reaches age 18 unless the child is unmarried and either disabled or a full-time student at an elementary or secondary school.

Twice a year, the SSA sends each student a form to be filled out and returned. If the form is not sent back, the student's payments will stop.

If a child age 18 or older receives payments as a student, be sure immediately to notify the SSA if the student:

- drops out of school
- changes schools

- changes attendance from full time to part time
- is expelled or suspended
- is paid by an employer for attending school
- marries, or
- begins working.

If a child whose payments were stopped at age 18 either becomes disabled before age 22 or is unmarried and enters elementary or secondary school full time before age 19, the SSA can resume sending payments to the child. Also, a disabled child who recovers from a disability can have payments started again upon becoming disabled again within seven years.

15. Changes in Parental or Marital Status

If you adopt a child, let the SSA know the child's name and the date of the adoption. The child may be entitled to auxiliary benefits.

Also, payments to a child who is not a U.S. citizen could stop or start if the child's natural or adoptive parent or stepparent dies, marries, or gets a divorce (or an annulment), even if the parent does not receive SSDI payments.

16. Child Leaves Your Care

If you receive benefits as a wife, husband, widow, or widower caring for a child who is younger than 16 or who was disabled before age 22, notify the SSA as soon as the child leaves your care. Failure to report this could result in a penalty, an overpayment, or an additional loss of benefits. A temporary separation does not affect your benefits as long as you retain parental control over the child. Also, let the SSA know if the child returns to your care.

17. Deportation or Removal From the United States

If you are not a U.S. citizen and are deported or removed from the United States for certain reasons, your Social Security benefits are stopped and cannot be started again unless you are lawfully admitted to the United States for permanent residence. Even if you are deported or removed, your dependents can receive benefits if they are U.S. citizens.

If your dependents are not U.S. citizens, they can still receive benefits if they stay in the United States for the entire month. But they cannot receive benefits for any month if they spend any part of it outside the United States.

C. Reporting Changes— SSI Recipients

Your obligation to report any changes that may affect your SSI benefits is similar to the requirements described for SSDI recipients, with a few differences. For example, residents of California, Hawaii, Massachusetts, Michigan, New York, or Vermont have special reporting requirements described in Section C10, below.

You must report any required change within ten days after the end of the month in which it happens. For example, if you move on November 5, you must let the SSA know by December 10. Make sure you notify the SSA of any address change as soon as you can.

The SSI law has specific penalties for failing to make timely reports. These penalties can be deducted from your benefits—and you'll still have to return any overpayments. The penalty is $25 for the first failure to timely report, $50 for the second time, and $100 for each subsequent failure. Penalties will not be assessed if you were without fault or had good cause for the failure to report.

This section describes only the situations in which reporting changes are different for SSI recipients than for SSDI recipients. Be sure to read Section B, above, first, before you read the following additional requirements.

1. You Change the Number of People With Whom You Live

The SSA insists on knowing the number of people who live with you. This means that you must tell the SSA if someone moves into or out of your home, if someone you live with dies, or, if you or someone you live with has or adopts a baby.

2. Your Income Changes

If you had a source of income other than your SSI when you applied for benefits and

the amount of that other income changes after you begin receiving SSI, tell the SSA. Similarly, if you start receiving income from another source while you are on SSI, you must tell the SSA. If you are married, you must notify the SSA if your spouse's income changes.

TIP

Reporting wages from work. To report wages, you can use the automated toll-free SSI Telephone Wage Reporting system or the free SSI Mobile Wage Reporting smartphone app. Contact your local Social Security office to get set up.

If your child younger than 18 lives with you and receives SSI, notify the SSA of any of the following:

- changes in the child's income
- changes in your income
- changes in your spouse's income
- changes in the income of a child who lives with you but does not get SSI
- the marriage of a child who lives with you but does not get SSI, and
- changes in the student status (starts or stops attending school full time) of a child who is working or is age 18 to 20 and lives with you.

Changes in household income generally mean that your SSI benefit will be recalculated; the new amount will affect your SSI check two months later.

If you also receive Social Security (SSDI) benefits or retirement benefits, you don't have to notify the SSA of changes in those benefits. (It already knows.) But if your spouse gets Social Security disability or retirement benefits, you do have to tell the SSA about benefit changes.

For SSI purposes, income includes cash, checks, and the equivalent that can be used for food, clothing, or shelter. It even includes items you wouldn't have to report for federal, state, or local income taxes. The following are examples of income:

- wages from a job
- net earnings from your own business
- value of any food, shelter, or clothing that someone provides for you ("in-kind support and maintenance")
- money for food, shelter, or clothing (excluding food stamps and housing allowances)
- annuity or pension payments
- veterans benefits, railroad retirement, and railroad unemployment benefits
- workers' compensation, unemployment, black lung, or SSDI benefits
- prizes, settlements, and awards, including court awards
- life insurance proceeds
- gifts and contributions
- child support and alimony
- inheritances
- interest and dividends earned on deposit accounts and investments
- rental income, and
- strike pay and other benefits from unions.

The following items are not considered income by the SSA:

- medical care
- social services
- cash from selling, exchanging, or replacing items you own
- income tax refunds
- earned income tax credit payments
- payments from life or disability insurance on charge accounts or other credit accounts
- bills paid by someone else for things other than food, clothing, or shelter
- proceeds of a loan
- replacement of lost or stolen items
- weatherization assistance (for example, insulation, storm doors, windows)
- credit life and credit disability insurance policies issued to or on behalf of borrowers to cover payments on loans in the event of death or disability
- income interest or dividends
- gifts used to pay tuition, fees, or other necessary educational expenses at any educational institution, including vocational and technical institutions, and
- income and interest on resources excluded under other federal statutes.

EXAMPLE: Frank Fritz, an SSI recipient, purchased credit disability insurance when he bought his home. Subsequently, Mr. Fritz was in a car accident and became totally disabled. Because of his disability, the insurance company paid off the home mortgage. Neither the payment nor the increased equity in the home is considered income to Mr. Fritz.

Some things the SSA normally counts as income are not counted as income under certain conditions—such as food, clothing, shelter, or home energy assistance provided free or at a reduced rate by private nonprofit organizations. But you still must tell the SSA about income that you think falls in the "not counted" category; the SSA makes that judgment.

3. You Obtain Assets

To qualify for SSI, a single person can own up to $2,000 of property, and a married couple can own as much as $3,000 worth. If you (or your spouse, if you are married, or your child if your child receives SSI) acquire property and the total value of what you own exceeds these limits, you must tell the SSA. You don't have to include property not counted toward these limits, such as your home. (See Chapter 1, Section A2.)

If you receive back pay checks from the SSA to cover periods you were eligible for but did not receive SSI or SSDI (past-due benefits going back to the month after your application date), those payments won't be counted for the nine months after the month you get the money. However, if you have any money left over after the nine-month period, it will count as resources. For example, Jillian starts receiving SSI on March 3; her first payment includes an extra $2,000 in back payments to cover the time she qualified for SSI before her payments began. If she has any of this money left over after December 3, she must tell the SSA. The SSA will consider it

resources and count it toward her eligibility for future SSI benefits. If your past-due SSI benefits are paid in installments, you have nine months to spend each installment.

If you agreed to sell property to qualify for SSI, notify the SSA when you sell it. If you don't sell the property, you may not be eligible for SSI and you may have to return checks already sent to you.

If your name gets added to a bank account with another person, the SSA will probably consider all the money yours even if it isn't. If someone wants to add your name to an account, check with the SSA first. If the money is not yours or is for a special purpose such as paying your medical expenses, the SSA can tell you how to set up the account so it will not affect your SSI.

4. You Enter or Leave an Institution

You must tell the SSA if you enter or leave a residential institution, hospital, skilled nursing facility, nursing home, intermediate care facility, halfway house, jail, prison, public emergency shelter, or similar kind of institution. The SSA needs the name of the institution and the date you enter or leave. If you can't contact the SSA, ask someone in the institution's office to help you.

In most cases, you cannot get SSI while you are in an institution, or your SSI payment will be greatly reduced. If you enter a medical institution, however, your SSI can probably continue if your stay is for 90 days or less. Your doctor must sign a statement about how long you will stay, and you must sign a statement that you need to pay expenses for your home while you're in the institution. The SSA must receive both statements by the 90th day you are in the institution or the day you leave, if that's earlier.

5. You Marry, Separate, or Divorce

You must let the SSA know of any change in your marital status—that is, you marry, divorce, separate, or get back together after a separation. These changes can affect your income and, therefore, possibly the amount of your SSI benefits.

6. You Leave the United States

If you leave the United States for 30 days or more, you usually can no longer get SSI. Before you leave, you are obligated to notify the SSA of the dates you will be gone. Once you return, your checks can't start again until you have been back in the United States for at least 30 continuous days.

Dependent children of military personnel who leave the United States may continue to get SSI while overseas if they were receiving SSI in the month before the parent reported for overseas duty.

7. You Are a Sponsored Immigrant

If you qualified for SSI as an immigrant sponsored by a U.S. resident, then when deciding whether you qualified for SSI, the SSA considered the income and assets of the following people:

- you (including items you own in your homeland)
- your spouse
- your parents if you are under 18
- your sponsor, and
- your sponsor's spouse.

For five years after you enter the United States, you must report any changes in the income and assets of these people. After the five-year period, you have to report only changes in the income and assets of you, your spouse, and your parents if you are under 18.

This rule doesn't apply if you are a refugee or have been granted asylum. The rule also does not apply if you become blind or disabled after being lawfully admitted for permanent residence in the United States. Note that if you are not a citizen, the date you physically entered the United States is not necessarily the same as the date in which you technically became "lawfully admitted" as a permanent resident.

8. You Are Younger than 22 and Start or Stop Attending School

If you are younger than 22, notify the SSA of any date you start or stop attending school on a full-time basis.

9. You Become Addicted to Drugs or Alcohol

If you receive SSI based on disability and you become addicted to drugs or alcohol, the SSA may refer you to a state substance abuse agency for treatment. (Also, see Section E4, below, regarding the law affecting DAA cases.)

10. 10. You Live in California, Hawaii, Michigan, or Vermont

Residents of California, Hawaii, Michigan, and Vermont have additional reporting requirements that can affect the state supplement portion of your SSI benefits.

California. You must let the SSA know if you were regularly eating your meals away from home and you now eat at home, or you were regularly eating at home and you now eat out. (Additional state payments may be available to people who cannot cook or store food where they live or who are unable to cook for themselves.) "Regularly" means where you must eat, not how often you eat in one place or another. If you are able to prepare meals at home but eat out frequently, you are considered to regularly eat at home and you would not qualify for extra benefits because where you eat is a matter of choice, not necessity. The actual rules are extremely complex; report any change affecting your ability to prepare meals at home—including broken appliances.

Hawaii, Michigan, and Vermont. You must notify the SSA if you live in a facility that provides different levels of care, and the level of care you receive changes. For example, Bernadette lives in a home that provides both assisted living and skilled nursing. Her health has deteriorated and she has been moved from the assisted living unit to the skilled nursing section. She must notify the SSA. Generally, if you are in a nursing home or another medical facility where Medicaid pays for more than half of the cost of your care, your federal SSI payment is limited to $30 a month. But some states' supplemental payment rules differ depending on the type of facility in which you live. If your level of health care changes, contact the SSA. You could be entitled to considerably more than $30 per month. (See also Chapter 3 regarding children in such facilities.)

D. Returning to Work

After you start receiving SSDI or SSI, you might want to try to return to work. The decision, of course, is yours. But if you think you can work, you probably feel like most people, who see working as more than just an opportunity for extra cash. They cite satisfaction from overcoming a disability through their skills, connecting with people, and getting back into the mainstream.

But returning to work is a big step for a person with a disability. Questions and concerns might be swirling around in your head: "How will my benefits be affected?" "Will I lose my Medicare or Medicaid?" "What if I need special equipment at work?"

Special rules called "work incentives" can help you ease back into the workforce. These work incentives include:

- cash benefits while you work
- medical coverage while you work
- help with expenses your employer incurs because of your disability, and
- help with education, training, and rehabilitation.

1. SSDI Work Incentives

The SSDI work incentives are fairly extensive.

Trial work period. If you return to work, during the first nine months you will continue to receive your SSDI benefits. At the end of nine months of work, the SSA will decide if you are doing substantial gainful activity (SGA)—earning an average of at least $1,260 per month (in 2020). If you are self-employed, your income may not be the best measure of whether you are doing SGA. Often, more consideration is given to the amount of time you spend in your business than to the amount of your income. Either way, if the SSA determines that you are doing SGA, you will receive benefits for three more months, and then they will stop.

Not all work counts toward the nine-month period. Generally, a month will count only if you earn more than $910 (2020) in gross wages (regardless of amount of time worked) or spend 80 hours in your own business (regardless of the amount of earnings). In addition, for the SSA to consider stopping your benefits because you have worked for nine months, the nine months do not need to be in a row, but they must take place within a 60-month period. Note that these rules are different, and more lenient, from those the SSA used to determine whether you were doing SGA when you first applied for benefits. Issues involving the trial work period or SGA can be confusing and complex. If you have any questions, do not hesitate to call your local SSA Field Office.

Extended period of eligibility or reentitlement period. If you are still disabled but you continue to work after the nine-month trial work period, you still receive a special protection for the next 36 months. To avoid confusion, it is important to remember that this 36-month period, also known as the "extended period of eligibility" (EPE), begins only after the trial work period ends. (As explained in the preceding paragraph, the trial work period could end anywhere from nine to 60 months after your first returning to work.)

During the extended period of eligibility (the 36-month period that follows the trial work period), the SSA will pay you your SSDI benefit in any month you earn below the SGA level, even if you stop working for a reason unrelated to your disability—for instance, you get laid off. You do not have to file a new application; you simply notify the SSA. If you stop working again because of your disability, your benefits will resume without your having to reapply. (See Section E1, below.)

EXAMPLE: Pamela, age 24, was receiving disability benefits of $750 a month based on a childhood condition that made it difficult for her to walk. She wanted to work but was afraid of losing her benefits and Medicare. After learning about the disability work incentives, Pamela started working in a local laundry earning $1,200 a month. Here's how her income changed.

First nine months of work—no change

Gross earnings		$ 1,200
Social Security check	+	750
Total monthly income		$ 1,950

Next three months of work

At the end of the nine months of work, the SSA determined that Pamela's work was SGA—it averaged more than $1,260 per month. Her benefits continued for three more months and then stopped. (However, note that because Pamela is still considered disabled, her benefits could be reinstated anytime during the next 36 months if her earnings drop below $1,260.)

Following the first year of work

During the first year after her trial work period, Pamela's company relocated to a town not accessible by mass transit. She hired a neighbor to drive her to work and paid a coworker to bring her home. Her transportation expenses totaled $100 a month. In addition, Pamela purchased a special motorized wheelchair so she could get around the new suburban plant. This cost $75 a month.

Gross earnings		$ 1,200
Transportation expenses	–	100
Wheelchair cost	–	75
Countable earnings		$ 1,025

Because Pamela's countable earnings were less than $1,260 a month, the SSA reinstated her checks. Her total income changed as follows:

Countable earnings		$ 1,025
Social Security check	+	750
Total income		$ 1,775

Following the second year of work

After another year, Pamela paid off the motorized chair and received a raise to $1,500 a month.

Gross earnings		$ 1,500
Transportation expenses	–	100
Countable earnings		$ 1,400

Because her countable earnings exceed $1,260, her SSDI stopped. Her Medicare continued another 93 months past her trial work period.

The point of this example is to show that at each point in her working life, Pamela's total income was greater than it would have been had she not worked and simply relied on disability benefits.

Resumption of benefits if you become disabled again. If you return to work and become disabled again within five years after your benefits were stopped, they can begin again following the first full month you become disabled again. Although the SSA does not have to redetermine your eligibility, you do have to complete a new application. During this five-year period, you can apply for an expedited reinstatement of benefits. (See Section E1b, below, to learn more.)

Continuation of Medicare. If you are still disabled but you return to work for more than nine months and your benefits stop, your Medicare coverage can continue for at least eight-and-a-half years. During this period, your hospital insurance coverage is free. After the eight and a half years, you can buy Medicare coverage by paying a monthly premium. (See Section E3, below.) Of course, if you are covered by your employer's medical insurance at that time, there will be no reason to buy the Medicare coverage.

In addition, if you get Medicare and have a low income and few resources, your state might pay your Medicare premiums and, in some cases, other out-of-pocket Medicare expenses, such as deductibles and coinsurance. Only your state can decide if you qualify. To find out if you do, contact your local welfare office or Medicaid agency. Having the federal government pay for these additional medical expenses makes it easier to become self-supporting when attempting to leave the disability rolls.

Impairment-related work expenses. If you need certain equipment or services to help you work, the money you pay for them might be deducted from your monthly wages in calculating whether you are earning more than the SGA level. Generally included are the costs of equipment (such as a wheelchair or specialized work equipment), attendant care services (such as a personal attendant, job coach, or guide dog), prostheses, prescription drugs, and transportation to and from work. Remember that expenses you pay are deductible from your income as work expenses to determine whether you are making more than the SGA amount; expenses paid by your employer would not be deducted from your monthly wages to determine whether you are earning more than the SGA level. If the deduction brings your monthly income to less than $1,260, you'll receive your SSDI benefit, and the month won't count toward your nine-month trial period, if you are still in your trial work period.

Recovery during vocational rehabilitation. If you participate in a vocational rehabilitation program that is meant to result in your becoming self-supporting and your disability ends while you are in the program, your disability benefits generally will continue until the program ends.

Special rules for blind persons. If you are blind and return to work and earn above the SGA level for blind people (above $2,110 per month for the year 2020), you are still eligible for a disability "freeze." This means that the years in which you have low or no earnings because of your disability will not be counted in figuring your future benefits, which are based on your average earnings over your work life.

If you are 55 or older and you are blind, the SSA figures your ability to perform

SGA differently. After age 55, even if your earnings exceed the SGA level, benefits are only suspended, not terminated, if your work requires a lower level of skill and ability than work you did before age 55. The SSA assumes that your ability to do SGA is low and that you sometimes might be unable to work because of your disability. Thus, your eligibility for Social Security benefits might continue indefinitely, and the SSA will pay benefits for any month your earnings fall below the SGA level.

If you're blind and self-employed, the SGA level becomes the only measure of SGA. The SSA does not make a separate evaluation of the time you spend in your business, as it does for nonblind benefi-ciaries. This means you can be doing a lot of work for your business but still receive disability benefits, as long as your net profit does not exceed the SGA level.

2. SSI Work Incentives

Like the SSDI work incentives, the SSI work incentives are quite extensive.

Continuation of SSI. If you return to work, you can continue to receive payments until your income exceeds the SSI income limits.

Continuation of Medicaid. If you return to work, your Medicaid coverage will likely continue until your income reaches a certain level. The level varies from state to state and reflects the cost of health care in your state. If your actual health care costs are higher than the average for your state, you might be able to keep your Medicaid. Be aware, however,

that for Medicaid to continue after you go back to work, you must:

- need it in order to work
- be unable to afford similar health insurance coverage
- have a disabling condition, and
- meet the nonincome SSI disability requirements.

In addition, if you have low income and few resources, your state may pay your Medicaid premiums and, in some cases, other out-of-pocket Medicaid expenses, such as deductibles and coinsurance. (See Section E3, below, to learn about Medicaid expenses for disabled workers.)

Work expenses related to your disability. If you need certain equipment or services to help you work (impairment-related work expenses, or IRWE), the money you pay for them may be deducted from your monthly wages to determine your income level. Generally included are the costs of equipment (such as a wheelchair or specialized work equipment), attendant care services (such as a personal attendant, job coach, or guide dog), prostheses, prescription drugs, or transportation to and from work. Only expenses you pay are deductible from your income as a work expense; expenses your employer pays are not deducted from your monthly wages in determining whether you are earning more than the SGA level. If you are blind, the work expenses need not be related to the impairment. Special rules for blind persons (see below) are even more favorable.

Plan for Achieving Self-Support. A special SSA rule called a "Plan for Achieving Self-Support," or PASS, lets you put aside money and assets toward a plan designed to help you support yourself.

The money won't be counted toward your SSI eligibility and won't reduce your SSI payment. The goal of your plan might be to start a business or get a job.

If you go back to work and your income exceeds the SSI eligibility level, a PASS might help you qualify. You can set aside income and assets you need to accomplish a work goal and reduce the money counted by the SSA toward your SSI eligibility or benefit amount.

Your vocational rehabilitation worker, your employer, an SSA staff person, or anyone else can help you write up a PASS. In general, the PASS must:

- **be in writing,** preferably on form SSA-545, *Plan to Achieve Self-Support* and signed by you, and, if applicable, the representative payee

- **state a specific work goal,** one that you have a reasonable chance of achieving given your strength and abilities (for example, "becoming a carpenter" or a "computer programmer")

- **show a reasonable time frame,** including your projected beginning and ending dates, milestones along the way, and a last step that indicates how you'll get a job, and

- **specify the amount and sources of income or resources to be set aside,** including a description of expenses

---

How Working Reduces Your SSI Amount

If you receive income from a job, the SSA doesn't count the first $85 in earnings you get each month. One half of what you earn over $85 is deducted from your SSI check.

If you have income in addition to job earnings and SSI, the SSA doesn't count the first $65 in job earnings you get each month. One half of what you make over $65 is deducted from your SSI payment. So is your other income, less $20.

If you have no income other than job earnings and SSI, you could earn over $1,650 a month before your SSI will stop (depending on your state—whether your state has a supplement matters in this calculation). If you have income in addition to job earnings and SSI, the amount you can earn before losing your SSI payment may be lower.

If you lose your job while you are still getting SSI, your SSI payments will increase. If you lose your job within 60 months of when your SSI payments stopped because of excess income, but you are still disabled, you can request your benefits to be started again without your having to reapply. (This is called expedited reinstatement.) If you lose your job after working more than 12 months from when your SSI has stopped for other reasons, you may have to reapply. (See Section E1, below.)

(reasonably priced) that are necessary to achieve the work goal.

EXAMPLE: Delano receives SSI payments of $750 each month. It is his only income. He is offered a job in a local fast food restaurant at $215 per month and contacts his local SSA office to see how this would affect his SSI payment. He is told that Social Security would not count the first $85 of earnings and half of the earnings over $85.

Gross monthly earnings		$ 215
First $85	–	85
Earnings over $85		$ 130
SSI payment		$ 750
Half of earnings over $85		
($130 ÷ 2)	–	65
New SSI award		$ 685
Gross monthly earnings	+	215
Total monthly income		$ 900

After working 18 months, Delano gets a raise to $367 a month. He also purchases an electric wheelchair to help him get around at work, which he pays off at $52 a month.

Gross monthly earnings		$ 367
First $85	–	85
Earnings over $85		282
Wheelchair cost	–	52
Balance		$ 230
SSI payment		$ 750
Half of balance ($230 ÷ 2)	–	115
New SSI award		$ 635
Gross monthly earnings	+	367
Total monthly income		$ 1,002

Even though Delano's earnings went up by $152, his SSI payment was reduced by only $50 because of the work expense deduction for the wheelchair. And his total income now is $1,002, substantially more than the $750 he had before he started working.

After a few more months, Delano decides that he wants to get a college degree. His sister helps him write a PASS describing his plans to work and save money for school. He wants to save $75 each month for school.

Gross monthly earnings:		$ 367
First $85	–	85
Earnings over $85		282
Work expenses (wheelchair)	–	52
Balance		$ 230
Half of balance ($230 ÷ 2)		$ 115
PASS savings plan	–	75
Remainder after PASS deduction		$ 40
SSI payment		$ 750
Remainder after PASS deduction	–	40
New SSI award		$ 710
Gross monthly earnings	+	367
Total monthly income		$ 1,077

Even though Delano's job earnings didn't change, his SSI checks increased because of the PASS.

Recovery during vocational rehabilitation. If you participate in a vocational rehabilitation program that is meant to result in your becoming self-supporting and your disability ends while you are in the program, your SSI benefits generally will continue until the program ends.

Sheltered workshop payments. If you work in a "sheltered workshop," a company that employs primarily disabled people, special rules allow the SSA to exclude some of your earnings when figuring your SSI payment.

Grants to disabled students. Most scholarships or grants used to pay for tuition, books, and other expenses directly related to getting an education will not be counted as income if you go to school or enroll in a training program. Students may also exclude up to $1,900 of earnings a month, up to $7,670 a year, in 2020. This amount is usually increased yearly.

Rules for blind persons. If you meet the medical definition of blind, SGA is not a factor for your SSI eligibility either at the application stage or while you're receiving benefits. Your SSI eligibility continues until you medically recover or the SSA ends your eligibility because of a nondisability-related reason (for instance, you go over the SSI income or resource limits).

Also, most of your work expenses—not just those related to your disability—are deducted from your income when the SSA decides you are eligible for SSI and decides how much of your income should be deducted from your SSI payment. For example, the cost of special clothes needed on the job can be deducted.

Some other examples of "blind work expenses" (BWE) are:

- guide dog expenses
- transportation to and from work
- federal, state, and local income taxes
- Social Security taxes

- attendant care services
- visual and sensory aids
- translation of materials into Braille
- professional association fees, and
- union dues.

EXAMPLE: Ahmed is 20 years old and receives SSI payments because he is blind. He receives $750 each month and has Medicaid coverage.

In January, Ahmed begins working part-time during the evenings and on weekends for the veterinarian who cares for his guide dog. Ahmed is paid $425 a month to answer the phone, make appointments, and help with the care and feeding of animals boarded at the kennel.

Ahmed reports his work and earnings to his local Social Security office and reports the following blind work expenses:

Transportation to/from work	$ 50.00
Care/feeding of his guide dog	+ 35.00
Taxes	+ 40.50
Total blind work expenses	$ 125.50

Here is how SSA calculates Ahmed's SSI amount, based on his earnings and his blind work expenses:

Gross monthly earnings	$ 425.00
First $85	– 85.00
Earnings over $85	$ 340.00
Half of earnings over $85	$ 170.00
Blind work expenses	– 125.50
Countable income	$ 44.50
SSI payment	750.00
Countable income	– 44.50
	$ 705.50

This means that, even though Ahmed is earning $425 per month, he loses only $44.50 in SSI payments, and his Medicaid coverage continues. Ahmed's total monthly income becomes $1,130.50 ($705.50 SSI + $425 monthly earnings = $1130.50).

In late March, Ahmed reports to the SSA that his employer has asked him to work longer hours and also is giving him a raise. Ahmed begins earning $700 per month in April. He tells SSA that he likes working with animals so much that he would like to go to school to learn to be a dog trainer and groomer. He plans to save $225 per month from his increased earnings so that he will have $1,125 saved to pay for books and tuition by September when the course begins at a local vocational school. The SSA helps Ahmed to write a PASS so that $225 per month is excluded from the income used to figure his SSI payment for the months from April through August.

Additionally, Ahmed reports that working longer hours and earning more will increase his transportation costs and his taxes. He reports the following blind work expenses beginning with April:

Transportation to/from work	$	65.00
Care/feeding of his guide dog	+	35.00
Taxes	+	75.50
Total blind work expenses	$	175.50

Here is how SSA computes Ahmed's SSI payment beginning with April:

Gross monthly earnings		$ 700.00
First $85	–	85.00
Earnings over $85		615.00
Half of earnings over $85		$ 307.50
Blind work expenses	–	175.50
Countable income		32.00
PASS adjustment		225.00
Countable income		$ 0.00

Because SSA was able to deduct so many of his work expenses, none of Ahmed's income is subtracted. He receives $750, the maximum SSI payment in his state. Even though Ahmed is earning $275 more each month than he did in January, February, or March, his SSI check will increase from $705.50 to $750 because of his PASS. His Medicaid coverage continues. Ahmed's total monthly income beginning in April is $1,450 ($700 monthly earnings + $750 SSI).

Ahmed begins a four-month course to learn to be a dog groomer and trainer in September. His PASS ended in August because he had saved the $1,125 to pay for books and tuition. But now he is an unmarried student under age 22 and he can use the student-earned income exclusion to reduce his countable income. He can exclude earnings of $1,900 per month up to a maximum of $7,670 annually. Because he will be in school for only four months in the calendar year, he can use the exclusion for each of these months without exceeding the $7,670 annual maximum.

Ahmed continues to work for the veterinarian and receives another pay raise, which increases his earnings to $800 per month beginning in September. His blind work expenses for transportation and care and feeding of his guide dog are unchanged, but his increased wages cause his taxes to go up $12. His total blind work expenses, beginning in September, rise from $175.50 to $187.50 per month, including the $12 additional taxes.

Here is how SSA figures Ahmed's countable income while he is a student from September through December:

Ahmed's earnings	$ 800
Student earned inc. exclusion	– 1,900
Countable income	$ 0

Ahmed continues to receive $750 per month from SSI in addition to his monthly earnings of $800, and his Medicaid coverage continues. Ahmed's total monthly income becomes $1,550 ($750 SSI + $800 earnings = $1550).

E. Passage of the Ticket to Work and Work Incentives Improvement Act

A law called the Ticket to Work and Work Incentives Improvement Act (TWWIIA; Public Law 106-170) contains some provisions that affect how the SSA handles work incentives. The intention of the TWWIIA is to:

- increase the amount of choice that disability recipients have in obtaining rehabilitation and vocational services

to help them go to work and attain their employment goals

- remove the barriers that required people with disabilities to choose between health care coverage and work, and
- assure that more people with disabilities can participate in the workforce and lessen their dependence on public benefits.

Some of the more important highlights directly affecting disability recipients are described in this section. The SSA has issued regulations interpreting the law, at 20 CFR Part 411.

1. Elimination of Work Disincentives

Although the SSA already offered work incentives, as discussed previously, Congress's intent in passing the TWWIIA was to further encourage those receiving Social Security disability benefits to return to the workforce by eliminating additional financial obstacles.

a. Work Activity as a Basis for Review

One of the obstacles for you, a disabled person returning to work, is termination of SSDI if you perform substantial gainful activities (SGA). The revisions don't take that away entirely, but they prohibit the SSA from using SGA as a means of triggering a continuing disability review (CDR) if a claimant has been receiving benefits for at least two years. Regular, scheduled CDRs will still take place, however. This law:

- prohibits the use of SGA as a basis for review if you are entitled to disability insurance benefits under Section 223 of the Social Security Act (42 U.S.C.A. § 423) or monthly retirement or survivors insurance benefits under Section 202 of the Social Security Act (42 U.S.C.A. § 402) and you have received such benefits for at least 24 months, and
- allows for regular CDRs and for the termination of benefits if you are earning more than the SGA.

b. Expedited Reinstatement of Benefits

By speeding up reinstatement of benefits in the event that people need to get back on disability benefits quickly, these provisions might make claimants less reluctant to try working. Provisions of this law and associated regulations include:

- **Applying for benefits.** If your SSDI or SSI is terminated because you are doing SGA or because of medical improvement, you may request a reinstatement of benefits without filing a new application if you are not able to work on account of your medical condition and you file the reinstatement request within 60 months of when your benefits ended. You must apply for expedited reinstatement of benefits in writing. You are permitted to apply for expedited reinstatement of benefits the same month you became unable

to do SGA, so that you can obtain provisional benefits the very next month (see below). To obtain specific instructions, call your local SSA Field Office (you can get your Field Office number from the SSA at 800-772-1213). You'll need to complete Forms SSA-371 (SSDI), SSA-372 (SSI), or SSA-373 (SSI, Disabled Spouse). These are simple forms, mainly requiring addresses and Social Security numbers.

- **Medical standard of review.** Unlike a new disability application, when you request an expedited reinstatement of benefits, the SSA will consider only the impairments you had the last time you received benefits. The SSA will consider your request using the "medical improvement review standard" (MIRS) as used in continuing disability reviews (see Chapter 14). Using this standard, it is likely that you'll be found disabled again—because the MIRS requires that in order to deny benefits, the SSA must find significant medical improvement in your condition. The SSA's regulations acknowledge this fact, stating "Under the medical improvement review standard, we will generally find that you are disabled." (20 CFR Parts 404.1592b and 416.999.)

- **Unsuccessful work attempt.** The SSA considers that you have had an "unsuccessful work attempt" (UWA) if you tried to work and your work attempt lasted no more than 6 months before you had to stop working or before your income fell below SGA levels. You don't apply for a UWA determination; it is something the SSA does internally, but it can affect your reinstatement because earnings in a UWA period will not be applied to SGA determinations. That can affect when your benefits can begin again. For SSDI, UWA determinations by the SSA can apply either to claimants (applicants) seeking expedited reinstatement of benefits previously received or to new claimants. For SSI, UWA determinations apply only to new claimants.

- **Provisional benefits.** While the SSA is deciding your reinstatement request, you can receive provisional benefits for up to six months. Provisional benefits begin the month you file your request, and the amount will be based on the amount you received in the month immediately before your benefits were terminated. If you were entitled to more than one type of benefit (SSDI and SSI), the SSA is supposed to pay you the higher one. Of course, you can fail to qualify for provisional benefits for a variety of reasons, such as being a prisoner, still working, or not having previously received disability benefits.

- **Repayment of provisional benefits.** Generally, you do not have to repay any provisional benefits if your reinstatement request is denied. There

are, however, some exceptions for fraud or mistake. For example, if you obtained provisional benefits that you knew you were unqualified to receive (such as by fraud), the SSA could demand the money back. If the SSA made a mistake (such as sending you a payment after deciding you couldn't have one, sending you a payment as a prisoner, or sending you a payment while you were doing substantial gainful activity), the SSA can demand repayment. Also, the SSA can deduct any Medicare premiums you owe from your provisional benefits.

- **Concurrent application for disability.** Applying for expedited reinstatement of benefits does not prevent you from filing a new application for disability. In the unlikely event your application for reinstated benefits is denied, the SSA will automatically consider that you have filed a new initial application and begin reviewing all of your medical conditions to see if you are disabled.

- **What if your request Is denied?** Technically, denials for expedited reinstatement cannot be appealed either to the SSA or federal courts. Nor can you reapply for denied expedited benefits. You can, however, make an informal protest, and the SSA will generally reexamine its denial decision. If you want to make such a protest, call or visit your local Field Office and ask what you should do. Ask the representative to make a record of your protest and put it in your file.

- **24-month reinstatement period.** During the 24 months following the date your reinstatement request is granted, you will not receive benefits for any months in which you perform substantial gainful activity (SSDI) or your income and resources are too high (SSI). Following this 24-month period, your status will return to where it was when you originally received disability benefits. For example, you can again apply for work incentives, such as in the Ticket to Work program (see Section F, below), and can even reapply for expedited reinstatement of benefits at some point in the future.

2. Creation of New Work Incentives: Planning, Assistance, and Outreach

These provisions direct the SSA to establish a community-based planning and assistance program for work incentives to provide disabled beneficiaries with accurate information related to work incentives. Specifically, the SSA must:

- establish a program to provide benefits planning and assistance, including information on the availability of protection and advocacy services, to disabled beneficiaries
- conduct ongoing outreach efforts to disabled beneficiaries, and
- establish a corps of work incentive specialists within the SSA to provide information to disabled beneficiaries.

(For information on how to reach such organizations in your state or U.S. territory, go to the SSA website at http://choosework.net/resource/jsp/searchByState.jsp. This page gives current contact information for service providers.)

3. Expansion of Health Care Services

Loss of vital health care coverage is one of the biggest problems for disabled people trying to return to work. These provisions give additional assistance in decreasing health-cost barriers to working.

a. State Options Under Medicaid

For beneficiaries between 16 and 64, the law expands the states' options and funding for Medicaid for workers with disabilities by liberalizing the limits on resources and income and giving working people who have impairments the right to buy Medicaid, even though they are no longer eligible for SSDI or SSI. The states can require individuals to contribute to the cost on a sliding scale based on income.

b. Continuation of Medicare Coverage

Congress extended premium-free Medicare Part A coverage for SSDI beneficiaries who return to work for eight and one-half years (the prior length was four years).

c. Election to Suspend Medigap Insurance

The law allows workers with disabilities who have Medicare coverage and a Medigap policy to suspend the premiums and benefits of the Medigap policy if they have employer-sponsored health coverage.

4. Additional Amendments

Congress also added several technical amendments involving the SSA's handling of claims involving drug addicts and alcoholics, as well as prisoners.

a. Drug Addicts and Alcoholics

Congress expanded the law that authorizes the SSA to determine if a representative payee would be in the best interest of a disabled beneficiary who is incapable and has a "drug addiction or alcohol condition" (DAA). The SSA was also given expanded powers to determine whether such person should be referred to a state agency for substance abuse treatment services.

b. Prisoners

Several provisions under this law provide for incentive payments to institutions to report SSDI and SSI inmates to the SSA, shorten the length of confinement making an inmate ineligible for benefits, and address the issue of sexual predator confinement:

- The law extends the incentive payment provisions that were already in effect for SSI prisoners to SSDI recipients, and authorizes the SSA to report this information to any agency administering a federal or federally assisted cash, food, or medical assistance program for pur-poses of determining program eligibility. These provisions—which already applied to SSI claimants—allow the SSA to pay $200 to $400 as a reward incentive for information that leads to a suspension of prisoner benefits.

- The law eliminates the requirement that benefits end if confinement stems from a crime punishable by imprisonment for more than one year. Instead, benefits would be suspended for any full month during which the person was confined because of a crime or a finding of not guilty by reason of insanity.

EXAMPLE: An SSDI beneficiary is arrested and confined in jail on March 21. He is not granted bail and is sent to trial. The court convicts the beneficiary on April 15. He is not released from jail once convicted and is sent to prison on April 16. Under benefit suspension provisions, the beneficiary is considered convicted and confined on April 15. He must serve over 30 continuous days in a penal institution before the SSA will suspend his benefits. The period of time in jail prior to conviction is not considered when determining what date to suspend benefits.

Certain provisions apply only to prisoners whose confinement began on or after April 1, 2000. The law prohibits the payment of benefits to any SSDI beneficiary who, upon completion of a prison term, remains confined by court order to a public institution based on a finding that the person is sexually dangerous or a sexual predator.

Promoting Opportunity Demonstration Project (POD)

Congress amended the Social Security Act in 2015 in an attempt to help SSDI recipients return to work or increase their earnings. SSI beneficiaries are not affected. The law requires the Social Security Administration (SSA) to conduct a demonstration project during a five-year period; it's called the promoting opportunity demonstration project (POD). It's only available in some states and participation is voluntary.

Here are its main features:

- SSDI recipients will receive a reduction of $1 in monthly benefits for every $2 in earnings that exceed a person's impairment-related work expenses (IRWEs) for that month.
- No SSDI benefits will be paid in any month in which benefits are reduced to $0 due to earnings. During any month that benefits are reduced due to earnings but still payable, there will be no termination of benefits due to work, and the trial work period or extended period of eligibility won't apply. (Under one test group, however, recipients whose benefit is reduced to $0 for 12 consecutive months will have their SSDI entitlement terminated.)
- If benefits are terminated because they are reduced to $0 due to earnings, a person eligible for Medicare remains eligible for Medicare for 93 additional months, provided the physical or mental impairment continues.

- For the purposes of this demonstration project, a person's impairment-related work expenses will be deemed to be set at a threshold amount set by the SSA, with the SSA having the authority to test different threshold amounts. If IRWEs are greater than the threshold amount, they will be set at the actual amount of the person's IRWEs. In no case will a person's impairment-related work expenses exceed the substantial gainful activity level.

In the example below, the SSA shows how the agency will calculate the amount by which monthly SSDI benefit payments will be reduced for a recipient whose earnings exceed the POD threshold. (The POD threshold is the same as the threshold for trial work periods—$910 in 2020.)

EXAMPLE: An SSDI recipient reports monthly earnings of $1,050. The POD threshold is $910, so the recipient's monthly earnings exceed the threshold by $140. The SSA will reduce the beneficiary's SSDI benefit payment by $70 ($140 ÷ 2).

The SSA considers monthly IRWEs in the calculation only when the total is greater than the POD threshold. Here's where it gets complicated. If the total monthly amount of itemized IRWEs is greater than the POD threshold, the SSA will use the total monthly amount of itemized IRWEs as the monthly POD threshold for the offset.

Promoting Opportunity Demonstration Project (POD) (continued)

However, if the total monthly amount of itemized IRWEs equals or exceeds the SGA amount ($1,260 in 2020), the SSA will use the SGA amount as the monthly POD threshold for the offset. In other words, the SSA will not penalize you if your IRWEs exceed the POD for a month.

In the example below, the SSA shows how the agency will calculate the amount by which monthly SSDI benefit payments will be reduced under the offset for a beneficiary whose earnings and itemized IRWEs exceed the POD threshold.

EXAMPLE: An SSDI recipient reports monthly earnings of $1,050. The beneficiary also reports monthly itemized IRWEs of $950 (and all are approved). Since the total monthly amount of itemized IRWEs is greater than $910, the SSA will use the IRWE amount ($950) as the POD threshold. The recipient's monthly earnings therefore exceed the threshold by $100. The SSA will reduce the recipient's SSDI benefit payment by $50 ($100 ÷ 2).

It's important to understand that the demonstration project is voluntary; you can withdraw at any time. In addition, POD will be tested only in the following areas:

- Alabama (all counties)
- California (Los Angeles, Orange, and San Diego counties)
- Connecticut (all counties)
- Maryland (Anne Arundel, Baltimore, Harford, Howard, Montgomery, and Prince George's counties; Baltimore City)
- Michigan (Barry, Berrien, Branch, Calhoun, Cass, Kalamazoo, Kent, St. Joseph, and Van Buren counties)
- Nebraska (Adams, Buffalo, Douglas, Hall, Lancaster, and Sarpy counties)
- Texas (Bexar, Dallas, and Tarrant counties), and
- Vermont (all counties).

If you are eligible for this POD demonstration project study, the SSA may contact you with more details, and then you can decide if you want to participate. Note: The POD demonstration project ends in June 2021.

F. Participation in the Ticket to Work Program

You might be eligible to participate in the Ticket to Work program, which can lead to new training and opportunities that empower you to return to work and enjoy the rewards that personal achievement and satisfaction can bring.

1. Can You Participate in the Ticket to Work Program?

You are eligible to participate in the Ticket to Work program if you are either a Title 2 (SSDI) or Title 16 (SSI) beneficiary between 18 and 64 years of age. There are no other qualifications.

2. Should You Participate?

The Ticket to Work program offers great benefits to those who may be able to perform some type of work. It's another way that you can receive vocational rehabilitation services that may allow you to ultimately earn more money than you are able to receive in disability benefits.

Many people receiving disability benefits could perform less physically demanding jobs if they had the training. Some beneficiaries worry, however, that if they try to return to work before they are ready, they may risk losing their disability benefits or their medical coverage under Medicare or Medicaid. The Ticket to Work program offers numerous safety net features to prevent loss of disability benefits.

It is important to understand that the program is entirely voluntary. Its purpose is to offer you greater choice when it comes to finding work or earning more money—not to force you into working. If you decide that you are not interested in the program or are not able to work, you do not have to take part. Your decision will have no effect on your disability benefits.

Also, when you enroll in the program, continuing disability reviews on your claim will stop, you will have access to free legal assistance, you'll get free planning and assistance in evaluating your work alternatives, and you'll receive free training. The Ticket to Work law provides extensive training assistance and protection of

benefits for those beneficiaries who are interested. It is certainly a program worthy of your consideration and a program that the SSA can point to with pride.

The SSA sends out letters along with what they call "tickets," which you can use to access services.

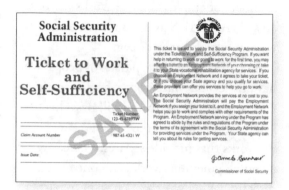

You should receive only one ticket. However, it is also possible that you could receive a new ticket, or even multiple tickets over your lifetime, if your benefits are stopped and then restarted.

TIP

Don't toss your ticket. Even if you don't think you want to take part in this program now, keep any ticket the SSA sends to you in a safe place. Having this ticket will make things easier if you decide later to take part in the program.

3. Getting a Ticket

If you are interested in taking part in the Ticket to Work program but haven't yet received a ticket and think you should have, call MAXIMUS, Inc., at 866-968-7842 (TTY 866-833-2967). MAXIMUS is a private company that is working with the SSA to help manage the program. MAXIMUS can answer most of your questions about the Ticket to Work program and can give you the names, addresses, and telephone numbers of employment networks in your area. MAXIMUS also has a website at www.yourtickettowork.com.

MAXIMUS will keep track of people who have tickets but have not yet begun participating in the program and will pass this information along to the employment networks that provide services. Therefore, an employment network may contact you directly, asking whether you want to participate. Of course, you can always say "no."

4. Where You'll Go for Services

Unlike previous SSA programs, you will no longer be referred directly to state vocational rehabilitation agencies for rehabilitation services. Instead, you'll be able to use your ticket to go to an approved service provider of your choice, called an "employment network" (EN). The EN can be a private organization or a public agency (such as a state vocational rehabilitation agency) that has agreed to work with the SSA to provide vocational rehabilitation, employment, and other support services to assist beneficiaries in going to work and remaining on the job.

TIP

Shop around before you assign your ticket to a provider. You don't need to sign up with the first EN whose door you enter. If there are more than one of them in your area, talk with their staff members about the services they provide and about your goals. Make sure you've found an EN with which you're comfortable before you hand over your ticket.

5. What to Expect From the Employment Network

At your first formal appointment with the EN you've chosen, remember to take your ticket with you—they're serious about treating these things like actual tickets. Expect to be asked a number of questions about your disability, your work history, and other subjects. Although the EN may already have received information about you from the SSA, these questions are necessary so the EN can consider whether and how it can help you. Feel free to ask any questions of the EN about its role in assisting you to reach your employment goal.

After you've met with an EN staff person, the two of you will develop and sign an individual work plan (IWP). The SSA regulations require that your completed IWP include statements of:

- your vocational goal, including goals for earnings and job advancement
- the services and support you need to achieve your vocational goal

- any terms and conditions related to the provision of these services and supports
- the EN's acknowledgment that it cannot receive any compensation directly from you for the cost of services and support
- the conditions under which the EN can modify your IWP or terminate its relationship with you
- your rights under the Ticket to Work program, including your right to take back your ticket if at any time you are dissatisfied with the EN
- the remedies available to you, including the availability of the protection and advocacy system (discussed in Section F8, below) for the resolution of disputes
- your right to amend your IWP, if the EN is also in agreement
- your right to privacy and confidentiality, and
- your right to have a copy of your IWP, in an accessible format chosen by you.

You'll notice that you have a number of important rights under the IWP, including the right to change your plan and the right to move to a different EN. If you do decide to switch ENs, however, make sure to get your ticket back—you'll need it at the next EN office.

6. How the EN Gets Paid— And How This Affects You

An EN can choose between two primary methods of payment for providing services under the Ticket to Work program:

- the "outcome payment system," or
- the "outcome milestone system."

> ### You Can Still Receive Vocational Rehab Services Without a Ticket
>
> State "vocational rehabilitation" (VR) agencies will continue to exist, and you don't need a ticket to use their services. Don't be confused by the fact that they must also participate in the Ticket to Work program. Each state VR agency can decide whether its participation will be as an EN or as a state VR agency. If your agency is functioning as a state VR agency, your plan for returning to work will be called an "individualized plan for employment" (IPE). The IPE has requirements similar to the individual work plan (IWP). To you as a disability beneficiary, whether a VR agency also functions as an EN is probably of little significance.

Under the outcome payment system, the EN can choose to be paid for each month (up to a maximum of 36 months for SSDI and 60 months for SSI beneficiaries) during which you don't collect federal disability benefits because of your work and earnings. By contrast, if the EN selects the outcome milestone system, it will get paid only when you achieve one or more milestones toward permanent employment, with a limit of 60 months of outcome payments. Overall, the EN stands to make more on you if it chooses the outcome payment rather than the outcome milestone system. In special cases, the EN has other payment options, such as to be reimbursed for the exact costs of rehabilitating you.

Why should you care about this? Because it may help explain the EN's behavior and what sort of plan or activities it is steering you toward. However, note that the EN, not you, has the power to choose its payment option. Much more detailed information is available at www.yourtickettowork.com.

7. Your Progress Toward Self-Supporting Employment

The purpose of the Ticket to Work program is to provide you with the services and support you need to work—with the ultimate goal of reducing or eliminating your dependence on SSDI or SSI benefits. That means that the SSA will keep an eye on you (through MAXIMUS, the central program manager) to determine whether you are, in fact, making timely progress on your work plan. At a certain point, the SSA will expect you to start working. To better understand what will be required, you need to first understand what the SSA means by timely progress and what it will count as work.

a. Definition of Timely Progress

What is timely progress? In general, the SSA asks you to show an increasing ability, year by year, to work at levels that will reduce or eliminate your dependence on disability benefits. However, the SSA also has a very specific calendar of what it considers timely progress.

The SSA's regulations (20 CFR § 411.180) define "timely progress" as follows:

1. 12-month review requires three months' work at Trial Work level ($910/month in 2020) or 60% of full-time college credits for one year earned.

2. 24-month review requires six months' work at Trial Work level or 75% of full-time college credits for one year earned.

3. 36-month review requires nine months' work earning more than SGA-level income, or completion of a two-year program or an additional one year of full-time college credit earned.

4. 48-month review requires nine months' work earning more than SGA-level income, or an additional one year of full-time college credit earned.

5. 60-month review requires six months at $0 payment level from the SSA or an additional one year of full-time college credit earned.

6. 72-month review requires six months at $0 payment level from the SSA or completion of four-year college program.

7. Successive reviews at 12 months require six months at $0 payment level from the SSA.

b. Definition of Work

Whether you are said to be working under the Ticket to Work program depends on the type of benefits you are receiving and various other individual factors.

SSDI nonblind beneficiaries. If you are receiving SSDI for a disability other than blindness, then during your first and second 12-month progress reviews, the SSA will consider you to be working during any month in which your earnings from employment or self-employment are at or above the SGA level for nonblind beneficiaries.

During your third 12-month progress review period, and during later 12-month progress review periods, the SSA will consider you to be working during any month for which Social Security disability benefits are not payable to you because of your work or earnings.

SSDI blind beneficiaries or beneficiaries in trial work period. If you are receiving SSDI and are blind, or are in a trial work period, then during your first and second 12-month progress reviews, the SSA will consider you to be working during any month in which your earnings are at the SGA level for nonblind beneficiaries, if either of the following is true:

- Your gross earnings from employment are at the SGA level for nonblind beneficiaries, before deductions for impairment-related work expenses.
- Your net earnings from self-employment are at the SGA level for nonblind beneficiaries, before deductions for impairment-related work expenses.

During your third 12-month progress review period, and during later 12-month progress review periods, the SSA will consider you to be working during any month for which SSDI is not payable to you because of your work or earnings.

SSI beneficiaries. If you receive SSI, then during your first and second 12-month progress reviews, the SSA will consider you to be working during any month in which your:

- gross earnings from employment are at the SGA level for nonblind beneficiaries, before any SSI income exclusions, or
- net earnings from self-employment are at the SGA level for nonblind beneficiaries, before any SSI income exclusions.

During your third 12-month progress review period, and during later 12-month progress review periods, the SSA will consider you to be working during any month in which your earnings from employment or self-employment are sufficient to preclude the payment of SSI cash benefits for one month.

Concurrent SSDI and SSI nonblind beneficiaries. If you are receiving SSDI and SSI at the same time for something other than blindness, then during your first and second 12-month progress reviews, you will be considered working during any month in which your earnings from employment or self-employment are at the SGA level for nonblind beneficiaries.

Concurrent SSDI and SSI blind beneficiaries or beneficiaries in trial work period. If you are receiving SSDI and SSI concurrently and are blind or are in a trial work period, then during your first and second 12-month progress reviews, you will be considered working during any month in which your:

- gross earnings from employment, before any SSI income exclusions or deductions for impairment-related work expenses, are at the SGA level for nonblind beneficiaries, or

- net earnings from self-employment, before any SSI income exclusions or deductions for impairment-related work expenses, are at the SGA level for nonblind beneficiaries.

During your third 12-month progress review period, and during later 12-month progress review periods, the SSA will consider you to be working during any month in which your earnings from employment or self-employment are enough so that you don't need SSDI or SSI cash benefits for the month.

c. If You Fail to Make Timely Progress

If, after reviewing your EN or state VR agency reports, the program manager (MAXIMUS) decides that you are not making timely progress toward self-supporting employment, it will conclude that you are no longer using your ticket. MAXIMUS will deactivate your ticket, and you will once again be subject to continuing disability reviews (CDRs).

Nevertheless, you can reenter the Ticket to Work program under certain conditions, depending on how far you had gotten in your work plan when the failure occurred. The various reinstatement rules are discussed below. For further help in understanding how these rules apply in your case, contact your EN or the program manager.

i. Reinstatement During First 24-Month Period

If you failed to make timely progress during the initial 24-month period, no matter what the reason, you can be reinstated by showing three consecutive months of active participation in your work plan. The program manager will be responsible for sending you a notice of reinstatement. After reinstatement, your next review would be the 24-month progress review.

ii. Reinstatement After Initial 24-Month Review

If, at the time of your initial 24-month review, the program manager decides that you have failed to make timely progress, the rules for reinstatement are somewhat complex. To be reinstated, you'll need to work for three months after the program manager's decision, and to work at the SGA level. You'll also need to satisfy the timely progress guideline requirements of the second 12-month progress review, as they pertain to anticipated work levels for the next progress review period. This means that you must expect to be able to work six months out of a 12-month period at the SGA level for nonblind beneficiaries. The reinstatement will be effective on the date the program manager sends you the favorable decision notice. With your reinstatement, your second 12-month progress review period will begin.

iii. Reinstatement After First 12-Month Review

If, at the time of your first 12-month review, the program manager decides that you have failed to make timely progress, your reinstatement will depend on your working for a subsequent three months at the SGA level. You must also satisfy the timely progress guideline requirements of the second 12-month progress review as they pertain to anticipated work levels for the next progress review period. This means that you must expect to be able to work for six months out of a 12-month period at the SGA level for nonblind beneficiaries. The reinstatement will be effective on the date the program manager sends you the favorable decision notice.

After reinstatement, your second 12-month progress review period will begin. Then you will be required to work at least six months at the SGA level for nonblind beneficiaries. At your 12-month progress review, the program manager will determine whether you have met this requirement. If so, you'll go back to a normal schedule—and the program manager will conduct 12-month progress reviews in the usual manner.

iv. Reinstatement After Second 12-Month Review

If, at the end of your second 12-month review period, the program manager decides that you failed to make timely progress, you can be reinstated by completing six months of work at the SGA level within the next 12-month period. You must also meet the requirements for timely progress for the next 12-month progress review (anticipated work level) by showing that you can expect

to work at the required levels for the third 12-month progress review period (six out of 12 months, with earnings sufficient to preclude payment of SSDI or SSI cash benefits).

After you are reinstated, your third 12-month progress review period will begin. During this 12-month period you will be required to work at least six months with earnings high enough that you don't need cash benefits. At your review, the program manager will determine if you have met this requirement. After this, the program manager will conduct 12-month progress reviews in the usual manner.

v. Reinstatement After Third 12-Month Review or Later

If, after any progress review beyond your second one, the program manager decides that you have failed to make timely progress, you may be reinstated by completing six months of work within the next 12-month period. Your earnings during those six months will need to be high enough to preclude payment to you of SSDI or SSI cash benefits.

You must also satisfy the anticipated work level requirement, by showing that you can expect to meet the work level requirements for the next 12-month progress review period—again, six out of the 12 months with earnings sufficient to preclude payment of cash benefits.

After you are reinstated, your next 12-month progress review will begin. At the end of this period, the program manager will determine whether you met the work level and other requirements. After this review, the program manager will conduct 12-month progress reviews in the usual manner.

d. Reinstatement Procedures and Appeals

When you have satisfied the requirements for reinstatement, you'll need to submit a written request to the program manager. If you are approved, you will receive a written decision reinstating you to "in-use status" for your Ticket to Work. If the program manager denies your request, you can appeal to the SSA within 30 days. (You'll receive instructions with the denial letter.) If the SSA agrees with you, then the SSA will send you a notice and inform the program manager. In that event, you will be reinstated as of the date of the SSA's decision.

8. Dissatisfaction With Your Employment Network

The transition from receiving disability benefits to supporting yourself through employment is bound to involve difficulties and frustrations—it's no easy task. With any luck, you'll receive the assistance you need from the EN, but the EN itself may also frustrate you through errors, decisions you don't agree with, or bureaucratic hassles.

a. Internal Grievance Procedures

There are several internal steps you can take if you are having a problem with your employment network. Your EN is required to have

a grievance process through which unhappy clients can voice their dissatisfaction and receive a reply. If you don't get a satisfactory reply, you can call the program manager (MAXIMUS) and ask it to resolve your grievance informally. If MAXIMUS cannot help, it will pass the matter on to the SSA.

You also can request an agency in the protection and advocacy system in your state to help you if you are unhappy with an employment network. You can ask your state agency to help you at any stage of the grievance process.

If your EN happens to be a state vocational rehabilitation agency, the agency must give you a description of the services available through the client assistance program. It also must give you the opportunity to resolve your grievance through mediation or an impartial hearing.

> **TIP**
> **Remember, you don't have to stay with your EN.** You can take your ticket out of assignment with any EN (including a state vocational rehab agency) for any reason. However, be sure to notify MAXIMUS, so that it can update the SSA database to show that your ticket is no longer assigned.

b. For Outside Help: Your State Protection and Advocacy System

In every state, various organizations have been designated to help you navigate the Ticket to Work system. Collectively, they are referred to as the protection and advocacy system, but the particular organization you contact will no doubt go by a different name. See the state-by-state list of organizations at http://choosework. net/resource/jsp/searchByState.jsp. Or for more information about this program, call MAXIMUS toll-free at 866-968-7842 (TTY 866-833-2967).

Your state protection and advocacy agency can give you help and personal representation on matters like:

- information and advice about vocational rehabilitation and employment services
- specific advice about selecting an EN
- information about special rules called "work incentives," which are designed to support your efforts to work
- assistance in resolving any complaints against your EN or other associated provider, and
- assistance with any problems that arise with the work plan you develop with your EN.

The protection and advocacy agencies are mainly concerned with advocacy and advice about work incentives, rehabilitation opportunities, and dispute resolution from a legal perspective. For example, you might wish to dispute the legality of an EN's terminating your Ticket to Work for reasons you think are unfair. In that event, you would contact the appropriate protection and advocacy agency in your state. Or you might just have a question about the difference in the way the SSA evaluates income earned under the Ticket to Work program compared to income earned by a person not in the program.

c. Help From Work Incentives Planning and Assistance Projects

Social Security's Work Incentives Planning and Assistance (WIPA) program can help you answer questions about the SSA's work incentives and decide whether you're ready to start working. It's run through local community organizations, which are paid by the SSA. Each WIPA agency will have benefits specialists on its staff. The specialists should be able to deal with complex issues, such as how working will affect your benefits payments and what additional federal, state, and local supports are available to help you in your effort to work.

In contrast to the legal guidance and advocacy a protection and advocacy agency offers, the major purpose of the WIPA program is to provide planning information and assistance regarding work incentives that may be appropriate for you personally. For example, you might want expert advice on the kind of rehabilitation and work goals that would be most appropriate in view of your impairments and limitations. Go to the SSA's list of service providers, at www.chooseworkttw.net/findhelp, for a list of WIPA organizations and their contact information. Or for more information about this program, call MAXIMUS toll-free at 866-968-7842 (TTY 866-833-2967).

9. Working Shouldn't Affect Your Disability Finding

Ordinarily, the SSA would review your case from time to time to see if you are still disabled—and would stop your benefits if it thought you could work. However, if you choose to participate in the Ticket to Work program, the SSA will not conduct its usual medical reviews, which should protect you from any suspicion or finding that you're no longer disabled.

To avoid these medical reviews, however, you must be actively using your ticket—that is, engaging in activities outlined in your employment plan on a regular basis and in the approximate time frames set forth in the plan.

10. Advising the SSA When You Go Back to Work

If you go back to work, or you begin to earn more money, you must notify your local Social Security office. The Ticket to Work program does not replace the special rules, called "work incentives," that help serve as a bridge between Social Security and SSI disability benefits and financial independence. These work incentives include:

- cash benefits while you work
- Medicare or Medicaid while you work, and
- help with any extra work expenses you may have as a result of your disability.

(See Section D, above, for more information about work incentives.)

11. When Your Ticket Can Be Terminated

You've already read about one of the reasons that your participation in the Ticket to Work program can be cancelled, namely your inability to make timely progress on your work plan (Subsection 7, above). However, the SSA has set forth a number of other bases on which it can stop your participation (or, in their language, "terminate your ticket"). These are summarized below; to read the list in full, see 20 CFR § 411.155.

a. Ticket Termination for Reasons Other Than Work or Earnings

Your ticket can be terminated for any of the following reasons as early as the first month involving one of them:

- Your entitlement to SSDI benefits based on disability has ended for reasons other than your work activity or earnings (such as death, reaching retirement age, or medical improvement); or your eligibility for benefits under SSI based on disability or blindness has ended for reasons other than your work activity or earnings (such as death, reaching retirement age, medical improvement, or excess resources), whichever happens later. Note that although the SSA will not review your condition for medical improvement while in the Ticket to Work program, you might declare your own improvement to SSA and return to regular work. That is why medical improvement is mentioned here as a possible reason for ticket termination.

- If, while you are entitled to widow's or widower's insurance benefits based on disability, you reach age 66.
- If, while you are eligible for benefits under SSI based on disability or blindness, you reached age 66 the month before.

b. Ticket Termination Because of Work or Earnings

Your ticket can also be terminated for reasons having to do with your work and earnings. Remember that the purpose of the program is to help you return to work full time. When you have successfully completed the Ticket to Work program, subject to the work incentives discussed in Section D,

---

Summary of Ticket to Work Program

Here's a summary of the important features of the Ticket to Work program:

- The program is designed to help both SSDI and SSI Social Security disability beneficiaries make a transition to work.
- The program is entirely voluntary, and you can stop at will. There is no expense to you.
- An employment network of your choosing will help you develop an individual employment plan, and your progress will be evaluated on a regular basis.
- While participating in the program, you will not be subject to continuing disability reviews (CDRs) for purposes of determining whether your medical condition has improved. Nor will your earnings trigger a CDR—even if they're over the SGA maximum.
- Free legal assistance will be available to you through a protection and advocacy agency for disputes or other legal questions you may have with your employment network.
- Free planning and knowledge assistance regarding rehabilitation and vocational alternatives will be available to you through the Work Incentives Planning and Assistance (WIPA) agencies available in each state. For a list of such agencies and their contact information, see the SSA's list at www.choosework.net/resource/jsp/searchByState.jsp.
- Participation in or successful completion of the program and return to full-time work does not eliminate your entitlement to work-incentive provisions, as discussed in Sections D1 or D2. For example, you will still have prolonged access to Medicare or Medicaid health care coverage and other privileges, even when you return to full-time work.

above, you will be performing SGA, and your disability benefits will cease. This is the type of ticket termination you are hoping to achieve if you are in the program.

The relationship of your work and income to your receipt of benefits can be difficult to puzzle out, so if you have any questions, the protection and advocacy agencies and WIPA agencies are there to help. The SSA Field Offices can also help you clear up any questions. There is plenty of expert advice available—all you have to do is ask.

G. The Ticket to Hire Program

The SSA has begun a national referral service to assist employers in hiring motivated, qualified workers with disabilities from the Ticket to Work program. The "Ticket to Hire" system works like this:

1. An employer contacts Ticket to Hire and provides information on a job vacancy.
2. The SSA contacts the employment networks (ENs) and state vocational rehabilitation agencies (SVRAs) that service the employer's local area to ask which ones have one or more qualified candidates for the position.
3. Ticket to Hire then gives the employer a referral list of the ENs and SVRAs with candidates and states how many qualified candidates each one can offer.

4. Any follow-up is in the employer's hands—the employer's identity is not given out to anyone.

If you have the skills an employer needs, your EN or SVRA will enter your name into this program—you don't have to contact Ticket to Hire directly. And your EN will give you ongoing support after you are hired to ensure your success. You can discuss the specific nature of this support with your EN while you're being considered for the job. The discussion will focus on the nature and severity of your impairments. For example, do you need special transportation to get to work? A prosthesis? Everyone's case is different. But don't be shy about asserting your needs. They'll lead to your success later—and bear in mind that the employer isn't suffering by hiring you. The employer gains various advantages through hiring you via referral from an EN or SVRA, such as tax credits, shortened employee-recruiting time, and decreased cost of health insurance, because you will have extended Medicaid or Medicare coverage for many years, even after your disability benefits stop.

The SSA has many publications on the above topics and more. These publications are available on the SSA's website at www. ssa.gov/pubs or by calling 800-772-1213 or 800-325-0778 (TTY).

Continuing Disability Review

Your case will be reviewed from time to time to see if you still qualify for benefits. If you have experienced significant medical improvement and are capable of working, you may lose your benefits. This review process is called "continuing disability review" (CDR). If you receive benefits for many years, expect to go through many CDRs. (See Section A, below, for more on how often reviews are performed.)

When it is time for your CDR, you will receive a notice in the mail, or someone from your Social Security office will contact you to explain the process and your appeal rights (see Section B, below).

The CDR process is complex, and improperly trained reviewers are prone to making errors. So be sure to study this chapter closely before you undergo a CDR.

CDRs are initially done by a team from the Disability Determination Services (DDS)—the state agency that reviews files for the SSA—including a disability examiner and a doctor known as a medical consultant (MC). First, they review your file; next, they will ask you to provide information about any medical treatment you've received and any work you've done; then the DDS team will gather information about you. They will ask your doctors, hospitals, and clinics for reports about your health, including the results of medical tests and the medical treatments you have received and how your health problems limit your activities.

The DDS is concerned not only with improvements since your last review or initial disability award, but also with any new health problems. If the DDS medical consultant needs more medical information, you might be asked to undergo a special examination or test, known as a "consultative examination" (CE), paid for by the SSA.

If your health has improved, the DDS will want to know if you can work. The CDR evaluation measures whether your overall health affects the kind of work you can do—both the work you did in the past and any other kind of work. (See Chapters 8 and 9 for the elements considered in evaluating your ability to work.)

If you are appealing a CDR decision, whoever is hearing the appeal—whether an administrative law judge or federal court judge—should obey the CDR principles set forth in this chapter. (See Chapter 12 for a comprehensive discussion of the appeals process.)

Child CDRs are evaluated in essentially the same way as CDRs for adults. (The minor differences are covered in Section D, below.)

A. Frequency of Reviews

How often your case is reviewed depends on the severity of your condition and the likelihood of improvement. The frequency can range from six months to seven years. The certificate of award of benefits you received when the SSA approved your claim shows when you can expect your first review. Exactly when that review will occur, and the times of subsequent reviews, is left to the SSA's judgment, depending on which of the following categories you fall into.

Medical improvement expected (MIE). If, when your benefits first start, the SSA expects your medical condition to improve, your first review is likely to be six to 18 months later.

> **EXAMPLE:** Betty was in an automobile wreck and suffered severe fractures in her leg and arm, along with other injuries. Six months after her injury, her fractures had not healed properly, and she developed an infection in her bone. She cannot walk without help. Her orthopedic surgeon plans several more operations to restore function and predicts that she will need at least six more months to heal. Because of the high probability that she will improve, the SSA would schedule a CDR as soon as six months after she was granted benefits.

Your age can affect whether you will be put into this category. If you will be at least 54½ years old at the scheduled review date, the SSA will generally not use this category, unless either of the following is true:

- You have an impairment that is almost certain to result in great improvement, or even full recovery, such as sprains and fractures, as well as cancers with a high cure rate like certain lymphomas and types of leukemia. You could get an MIE review up to age 59½. After age 59½, It's unlikely you'll get another review.
- You receive SSI and are legally blind but are expected to improve. You could get an MIE review up to age 64½.

Medical improvement possible (MIP). If, when your benefits first start, the SSA believes it is possible for your medical condition to improve, but the SSA cannot predict when that improvement might happen, your case will be reviewed about every three years. Examples of disorders in which improvement is possible would be conditions such as increased thyroid gland activity (hyperthyroidism) and inflammatory intestinal diseases like regional enteritis or ulcerative colitis.

> **EXAMPLE 1:** After several weeks of having dull, aching pains in the center of his chest, especially when he exerted himself or got excited, Livan woke up one morning with a smothering chest pain like an elephant on his chest. Livan was rushed to the nearest hospital in the middle of a life-threatening heart attack. Treatment stabilized his condition, but he has severe blockages in multiple major arteries supplying his heart muscle. Despite optimum medical treatment, his heart disease is crippling, and his symptoms of chest pain, shortness of breath, weakness, and fatigue are so severe that the SSA considers him disabled. Livan has refused heart surgery because he is scared—his uncle died on the operating table during a similar procedure. Livan is

relatively young at age 50, and medical improvement with surgery could make a big difference in his ability to work. The SSA knows that medical improvement is possible if Livan has surgery and that there's a good chance Livan will change his mind about the operation. His case will be reviewed within a few years of his being allowed benefits.

EXAMPLE 2: Sharon has had high blood pressure for years, as well as diabetes. She tried to treat herself with various herbal remedies. Her kidneys were progressively ravaged by disease, and complete kidney failure qualified her for disability benefits. The SSA knows that a kidney transplant could result in marked medical improvement, and so her case is put in the MIP category. If, during Sharon's application for benefits, her doctor reported that she was soon going to have a kidney transplant, the SSA might put her in the MIE category.

Medical improvement not expected (MINE). If the SSA does not expect your medical condition to improve, your case will be reviewed about every five to seven years. You are most likely to fall into this category if any of the following apply:

- You will be older than 54½ years when the CDR is scheduled.
- You already have had several CDRs.
- You have multiple severe impairments or an irreversible condition with no known treatment.

Some disorders that the SSA puts into a MINE category include the following:

- amputation
- ankylosing spondylitis of the spine
- autism
- blindness or glaucoma
- cerebral palsy
- chronic myelogenous leukemia
- deafness
- degenerative nervous system diseases
- diabetic eye disease
- diabetic nerve damage
- Down syndrome
- major mood disorders, such as major depression
- mental disorders caused by organic brain disease
- intellectual disability
- multiple sclerosis
- Parkinson's disease
- peripheral vascular disease (arteries or veins)
- polio with permanent residuals
- psychotic mental disorders, such as schizophrenia
- rheumatoid arthritis
- stroke, or
- traumatic spinal cord or brain injuries.

EXAMPLE 1: Doug is 55 years old, has degenerative arthritis throughout his lower spine, and suffers pain and stiffness. Surgery would not relieve his symptoms, and other forms of treatment have been only moderately effective. Doug has a limited education and has worked only in jobs lifting and carrying 50 pounds or more. In his condition, he can't lift more than 20 pounds and he is not qualified for jobs with that kind of light work. He's already had two CDRs, and his disability benefits were continued each time. The SSA will put him in the MINE category.

EXAMPLE 2: Sally is 52 years old and was diagnosed with severe depression at age 40. Following an initial recovery, Sally's medical record shows years of only partially successful treatment with a variety of medications and six hospitalizations. She continues to live with her elderly parents but doesn't help much with chores; she spends much of her day watching television but has poor recall of the programs. Her parents manage her disability benefits, and she cannot function outside of the protective environment of her parents' home without her condition worsening. She continues to show serious signs of depression, such as lack of pleasure, weight loss, feelings of hopelessness, poor sleep, lack of general interests, and some continuing suicidal thoughts. She has had two CDRs and is seen weekly at a community mental health center, with only marginal improvement.

Don't be surprised if you are not notified for a CDR when you are expecting it, based on the MIE, MIP, or MINE time limits. When the SSA runs short of operating money, it typically stops performing CDRs rather than cut back on vital operations. The result is that your CDR might come later than would otherwise be the case—sometimes years later.

B. How the SSA Contacts You

A CDR begins when you receive a notice stating that the SSA is reviewing your disability claim. The important thing is to remain calm, understand that this is a regular part of the process, and know that you have not been singled out. Don't assume that you will be automatically terminated from the program.

1. Form SSA-455, *Disability Update Report*

Accompanying the CDR notice will be Form SSA-455, *Disability Update Report*. A sample copy of the form follows. Be sure to read the SSA's instructions before filling out the form. You must return the completed form within 30 days.

> CAUTION
> **You must use forms provided by the SSA.** You can obtain them at your local SSA Field Office or by calling the SSA hotline at 800-772-1213, Monday through Friday (except holidays), from 7 a.m. to 7 p.m. If you are deaf or hard of hearing, TTY service representatives are available at the same times at 800-325-0778. You can also download many necessary forms from the Social Security Administration website at www.ssa.gov.

Sample Notice of Continuing Disability Review (Page 1)

Office of Disability Operations
1500 Woodlawn Drive
Baltimore, Maryland 21241

Date: June 14, 2020

Claim Number: 000-00-0000

We must regularly review the cases of people getting disability benefits to make sure they are still disabled under our rules. It is time for us to review your case. This letter explains how we plan to start our review of your case.

What You Should Do
Please complete the form enclosed with this letter. Answer all the questions on the form because they are very important. They ask about your health problems and any work you did within the last two years.

We have enclosed an envelope for you to use. If there is no envelope with this letter, please send the signed form to us at the address shown above.

If We Do Not Hear From You
You should return the form within 10 days after you receive it. If we do not hear from you in that time, we will contact you again.

If you don't give us the information we need or tell us why you cannot give us the information, we may stop your benefits. Before we stop your benefits, we will send you another letter to tell you what we plan to do.

When We Receive the Completed Form
- If we need more information, we will call you. If you do not have a telephone, please give a number where we can leave a message for you.
- The information you give us now will help us decide when we should do a full medical review of your case. We will let you know within 90 days after we receive the completed form whether or not we need to do a full medical review now.

Sample Notice of Continuing Disability Review (Page 2)

Important Information

If we decide to do a full medical review of your case:

- You can give us any information which you believe shows that you are still disabled, such as medical reports and letters from your doctors about your health.
- We will look at all the information in your case, including the new information you give us.
- We may find that you are no longer disabled under our rules, and your payments will stop. If this happens, you can appeal our decision. You can also ask us to continue to pay benefits while you appeal.

Things to Remember

Do you want to work but worry about losing your payments or Medicare before you can support yourself? We want to help you go to work when you are ready. But work and earnings can affect your benefits. Your local Social Security office can tell you more about how work and earnings can affect your benefits.

If You Have Any Questions

If you have any questions, you may call us at 800-772-1213 or call your Social Security Office at 000-000-0000. We can answer most questions over the phone. You can also write or visit any Social Security office. The office that serves your area is located at:

12345 Main Street
New York, NY 10000

If you do call or visit an office, please have this letter with you. It will help us answer your questions. Also, if you plan to visit an office, you should call ahead to make an appointment. This will help us serve you more quickly.

Janice L. Warden
Janice L. Warden

Deputy Commissioner for Operations
Enclosures:
Form SSA-455, *Disability Update Report*
Return envelope

Form SSA-455, *Disability Update Report* (Page 1)

✱

Disability Update Report

DATE: June 30, 2020

Social Security Administration, P.O. Box   , Wilkes-Barre. PA 18767-

FORM APPROVED
OMB NO. 0960-0511

PAYEE'S NAME AND ADDRESS	REPORT PERIOD
John Smith 123 4th Street Baltimore, MD 21241 PSC:	From: 12-31-19 To The Present

BENEFICIARY
John Smith

TELEPHONE NUMBER	CLAIM NUMBER
201-123-6789	

Please be sure to **use black ink or a #2 pencil to print your answers.** Also, **read the enclosed instructions** before completing the form. Finally, remember that when answering the questions, **the "REPORT PERIOD" for which we need information about you is from** 12-31-19 **to the present.** If you have any questions, call 1-800-772-1213 or TTY for the hearing impaired at 1-800-325-0778.

1. a. Since 12-31-19 have you worked for someone or been self-employed? ⟶   YES ☐   NO ☒

     b. If you answered "YES" to 1.a., please complete the information below.

	WORK BEGAN		WORK ENDED		MONTHLY EARNINGS
	Month	Year	Month	Year	Dollars Only, No Cents
Most Recent Work 1.	☐	☐	☐	☐	$ ☐,☐
2.	☐	☐	☐	☐	$ ☐,☐
3.	☐	☐	☐	☐	$ ☐,☐

2. Have you attended any school or work training program(s) since 12-31-19 ?   YES ☐   NO ☒

3. Since 12-31-19 to the present...*(Please place an 'X' in one box only):*

☐ my doctor and I have not discussed whether I can work.   ☒ my doctor told me I cannot work.   ☐ my doctor told me I can work.

4. Place an "X" in only one box which best describes your health now as compared to 12-31-19 .

☐ BETTER   ☐ SAME   ☒ WORSE

Form SSA-455-OCR-SM (10-2013)   Continued on the Reverse ⟶

Form SSA-455, *Disability Update Report* (Page 2)

FOR SSA USE ONLY			
AC?			

5. a. Have you gone to a doctor or clinic for treatment (including evaluations, checkups, counseling, prescriptions, or medicine) since 12-31-19 ? ⟶ YES [X] NO [ ]

b. If you answered "YES" to 5.a., please list:

Reason For Visit:

		Reason For Visit	Month	Year
Most Recent Visit	1.	C H E S T P A I N	0 1	2 0
	2.	S H O R T B R E A T H	0 1	2 0
	3.	A R T H R I T I S	0 2	2 0

6. a. Have you been hospitalized or had surgery since 12-31-19 ? ⟶ YES [X] NO [ ]

b. If you answered "YES" to 6.a., please list:

Reason For Hospitalization or Surgery:

		Reason For Hospitalization or Surgery	Month	Year
Most Recent	1.	H N P	0 3	2 0
	2.			
	3.			

REMARKS: If you use this space to further answer questions 1. through 6., place an "X" in the box to the right and print on the lines below. [X]

Back pain from HNP surgery persists. I can't lift over 10 lbs. and carry it very far without both chest and back pain. My heart doctor says I may need more testing to see if I have heart artery blockages. Please contact my doctors for more information.

I declare under penalty of perjury that I have examined all the information on this form, and on any accompanying statements or forms, and it is true and correct to the best of my knowledge. I understand that anyone who knowingly gives a false or misleading statement about a material fact in this information, or causes someone else to do so, commits a crime and may be sent to prison, or may face other penalties, or both.

SIGN HERE ➤ *John Smith*

TODAY'S DATE
6-30-20

TELEPHONE NUMBER *(include Area Code)*
201-123-6789

Form SSA-455-OCR-SM (10-2013)

Once the SSA Field Office receives your Form SSA-455, the SSA will decide whether your benefits should simply continue—in which case the CDR process ends—or whether a full medical review of your claim is necessary. You have no other participation in this screening procedure. In either event, you will be notified in writing by another notice. If a full medical review of your claim occurs, when it's complete, you'll receive notice of whether your benefits will continue or end.

2. Form SSA-454-BK: *Continuing Disability Review Report*

If the SSA chooses a full CDR, you will be sent SSA-454-BK: *Continuing Disability Review Report* to complete.

Along with the form will be a notice inviting you to contact a Social Security representative at your local Field Office. Such contact is meant to protect your rights and assure that you fully understand the questions on the form. It will also give you the opportunity to ask questions that you might have about your CDR. You can complete the form and mail it back to your local Field Office. If you need help filling out the form, the SSA prefers face-to-face contact, but you can do it by telephone if you wish. It is also possible for you to waive personal contact under certain conditions, such as:

- The relationship between you and your representative payee is an official one (for example, it is an institution or a government agency).
- You or your representative payee agrees or requests that the CDR be conducted by mail.
- Contact must be made but is not practical at the present time (for example, because of weather or travel considerations), and you or your representative payee agrees to waive the personal contact and have the CDR conducted by mail instead.
- You reside in a foreign country, unless you are in a country that has a U.S. district office.

Form SSA-454-BK is 13 pages long, but filling it out is more time-consuming than difficult. In addition to the help available at the SSA Field Office, an attorney or other representative can fill out much of the form for you. A copy of the form and instructions on how to complete it are below. For all questions, the SSA wants to know what has happened since the time you filed your original disability application or had your last CDR.

Don't worry about the little code boxes asking for the "types of entitlement." The SSA Field Office representative can complete that information.

❶ Provide your name, address, contact information, and so on.

❷ Provide contact information for a person (other than your doctors) whom the SSA can contact and who knows about your medical conditions and can assist with your claim. A spouse is a good example, but it could be a friend or relative. If there's no one you can put down, enter n/a.

❸ List the physical or mental disorders that you feel limit your ability to work, along with your height and weight. Do not provide additional details or the medications you take. For example, you could just name "heart disease, emphysema, hearing problem, and arthritis."

❹ This section asks for information about visits to doctor's offices and hospitals in the last year. List contact information, diagnoses, hospitalizations, clinic visits, tests given, treatment, and so on, for only the prior year. The SSA does not want earlier information, which they probably already have. In the examples given, the claimant has a cardiologist, pulmonary specialist, and orthopedist. The SSA only wants general information, not a lot of detail. It's okay to say you received medication as a part of treatment, but the SSA doesn't want specific drug names or the outcome of tests in this section. If you had tests that are not listed on the form, describe them under the Remarks section of the form (Section 11).

❺ List your medications, what they were prescribed for, and who prescribed them.

Again, the SSA only wants information for the previous year. Do not provide any additional details. The SSA only wants to get an overview of your condition. If there is not enough room for all your drugs, or you want to say more about them, use the Remarks section, page 13 of the form.

❻ This section asks for other medical information, but only for adults. (For disability recipients younger than 18, you are instructed to skip ahead to the Remarks section.) Here the SSA wants to know if there are any organizations— like vocational rehab facilities, attorneys, workers' compensation, or social welfare services—that have any information about your medical condition. Simply provide the contact information if your answer to the first question is "yes." Otherwise, check "no" and go to the next section. This section wants only information about the prior year; do not provide earlier information, as it is likely to only duplicate what the SSA already knows. If the SSA needs earlier information, the agency will ask for it.

❼ The SSA wants to know about any additional adult education or training you've had since your last disability decision. This information could be from before the past year.

❽ List any adult services you've had since your last disability decision that involve vocational rehab, employment, or anything else that might relate to helping you return to work, such as the Ticket to Work program or a "Plan to Achieve Self Support" (PASS). As for the other questions, you'll need names, dates, addresses, and phone numbers. If you've had physical exams, vision or hearing tests, work evaluations, psychological tests, or other medically related tests, the SSA wants to know that. Do not worry about describing the results—the SSA will obtain the tests and their outcome and will reach its own conclusion about their meaning.

❾ Section 9 gives you an opportunity to describe in detail the effect of your medical disorders on your ability to function during a typical day. This section is one of the most important on the form. It is your chance to describe to the SSA in your own words the difficulties you have in performing "activities of daily living" (ADLs). Take your time and write something in every section. Tell the SSA what activity is limited, to what degree that activity is limited, and how the limitation is caused by your medical condition. If you need more room, use the Remarks section and add more pages if you want. Examples are given on the sample form in Remarks Section 11, but here are some specific suggestions:

❾A, Personal mobility. Write down the specific things you have difficulty doing— such as walking, getting out of a chair, or moving about in some other way. Next, describe the symptom or problem that specifically limits you—such as weakness or paralysis, numbness, pain, poor balance, dizziness, or lack of coordination. Finally, describe the degree of severity of your symptoms—such as inability to stand for more than 30 minutes because of back pain, inability to walk more than two blocks due to leg pain, or shortness of breath.

❾B, Recreational activities and hobbies. This information helps the SSA learn important things about your physical and mental abilities. For example, hunting requires a certain amount of physical stamina, but the amount depends on the type of hunting you do. There is a big difference between a hunter who can hunt only by riding down a dirt road on a four-wheeler looking for a deer and one who can walk miles through the woods for hours.

Similarly, the ability to play musical instruments implies an ability to use the fingers in a coordinated way, especially regarding fine movements. Reading newspapers shows the ability to read small print and to concentrate. The lack of interest in various recreational activities can be a sign of depression and withdrawal.

❾C, Daily activities. The SSA has a long list of specific questions about your ability to perform daily activities. Check "yes" or "no" for each and briefly describe any difficulty. You can always explain in more detail using the Remarks section. Some examples are given on the sample form how to do this, and below there are some additional issues you might want to consider.

Form SSA-454-BK, *Continuing Disability Review Report* (Page 1)

SOCIAL SECURITY ADMINISTRATION

Form Approved
OMB No. 0960-0072

CONTINUING DISABILITY REVIEW REPORT

For SSA Use Only - Do not write in this box.

Date of your last medical disability decision: _____

Claim Number: _____ Number Holder: _____

Type(s) of Case(s): TITLE II ☐ DIB ☐ DWB ☐ CDB ☐ FZ ☐ ESRD ☐ HIB

(Check all that apply.) TITLE XVI ☐ DI ☐ DS ☐ DC ☐ BI ☐ BS ☐ BC

If you are filling out this report for the disabled person, please provide information about him or her. When a question refers to "you", "your", or the "disabled person", it refers to the person receiving disability benefits

SECTION 1 - INFORMATION ABOUT THE DISABLED PERSON

1.A. NAME (First, Middle Initial, Last)
❶ Jesse Chang

1.B. SOCIAL SECURITY NUMBER
111-11-1111

1.C. MAILING ADDRESS (Street or PO Box) Include apartment number if applicable
1234 Pasadena Way

CITY	STATE/Province	ZIP/Postal Code	COUNTRY (if not USA)
Dallas	TX	82221	

1.D. DAYTIME PHONE NUMBER, including area code, and the IDD and country codes if you live outside the USA or Canada.

Phone Number: (901) 555-5555

☑ Check this box if you have a phone or a number where we can leave a message

1.E. ALTERNATE PHONE NUMBER, including area code where we may reach you, if any.

Alternate Phone Number: (901) 556-5555

1.F. Can you speak and understand English? ☑ YES ☐ NO

If NO, what language do you prefer? _____

If you cannot speak and understand English, we will provide an interpreter free of charge.

1.G. Have you used any other names on your medical or educational records in the last 12 months? Examples are maiden name, other married names, or nickname. ☐ YES ☑ NO

If YES, please list _____

SECTION 2 - CONTACTS

Give the name of a friend or relative (other than your doctors) we can contact who knows about your medical conditions, and can help you with your case.

2.A. NAME (First, Middle Initial, Last)
❷ Sue Chang

2.B. Relationship to Disabled Person
wife

2.C. MAILING ADDRESS (Street or PO Box) Include apartment number if applicable
1234 Pasadena Way

CITY	STATE/Province	ZIP/Postal Code	COUNTRY (if not USA)
Dallas	TX	82221	

Sample Form SSA-454-BK, *Continuing Disability Review Report* (Page 2)

SECTION 2 - CONTACTS (Continued)

2.D. DAYTIME PHONE NUMBER (as described in 1.D. above)
(901) 555-5555

2.E. Can this person speak and understand English? ☑ YES ☐ NO
If NO, what language is preferred?

2.F. Who is completing this report?

☑ The disabled person listed in 1.A. (Go to **Section 3 - Medical Condition(s)**)

☐ The person listed in 2.A. (Go to **Section 3 - Medical Condition(s)**)

☐ Someone else (Complete the rest of Section 2 below)

2.G. NAME (First, Middle Initial, Last)	**2.H.** Relationship to Disabled Person

2.I. DAYTIME PHONE NUMBER (as described in 1.D. above)

2.J. MAILING ADDRESS (Street or PO Box) Include apartment number if applicable

CITY	STATE/Province	ZIP/Postal Code	COUNTRY (if not USA)

❸ SECTION 3 - MEDICAL CONDITION(S)

3.A. If you are an adult (age 18 or older), list the physical and/or mental condition(s) (including emotional or learning problems) that limit your ability to work. If you are completing this report for a child (under age 18), list the physical and/or mental condition(s) (including emotional and learning problems) that limit the child's ability to do the same things as other children the same age. **List each physical and/or mental condition separately.**

1. Heart disease; coronary arteries blocked. Bypass surgery in 2013
2. Emphysema
3. Hearing problem
4. Arthritis in hands

If you need more space go to Section 11 - Remarks

3.B. What is your height without shoes? ____5____ ____8____ OR _____
feet / inches / centimeters (if outside USA)

3.C. What is your weight without shoes? ___155___ OR _____
pounds / kilograms (if outside USA)

3.D. Do you use an assistive device (for example: eye glasses, hearing aids, braces, canes, crutch(es), walker, wheelchair, service animal)?

☐ Always ☐ Sometimes ☑ Never

If ALWAYS OR SOMETIMES, please describe what kind, when, and how you use it.

If you need more space, use SECTION 11 - Remarks

Sample Form SSA-454-BK, *Continuing Disability Review Report* (Page 3)

④   **SECTION 4 - MEDICAL TREATMENT**

Within the last 12 months, have you seen a doctor or other health care professional, or received treatment at a hospital or clinic, or do you have a future appointment scheduled:

4.A. For any **physical** conditions?

     ☑ Yes   ☐ No

4.B. For any **mental** condition(s) (including emotional or learning problems)

     ☐ Yes   ☑ No

If you answered "No" to both 4.A. and 4.B., go to Section 5 - Other medical Information on page 9

4.C. Tell us who may have medical records covering **the last 12 months** about any of your physical or mental condition(s) (including emotional or learning problems). This includes doctors' offices, hospitals (including emergency room visits), clinics, and other health care facilities. Tell us about your next appointment, if you have one scheduled.

NAME OF FACILITY OR OFFICE	NAME OF HEALTHCARE PROFESSIONAL THAT TREATED YOU
Stanley Crowe, M.D.P.A	Dr. Stanley Crowe (cardiologist)

ALL OF THE QUESTIONS ON THIS PAGE REFER TO THE HEALTH CARE PROFESSIONAL ABOVE

PHONE NUMBER	PATIENT ID# (if known)
(214) 555-5555	124322

MAILING ADDRESS
412 11th Street

CITY	STATE/Province	ZIP/Postal Code	COUNTRY (if not USA)
Dallas	TX	93870	

Dates of Treatment (within the last 12 months)

1. Office, Clinic or Outpatient visits	2. Emergency Room Visits List the most recent date first	3. Overnight Hospitals Stays	
First visit 6-6-15	A.	A. Date in	Date out
Last visit 6-6-16			
Next Scheduled Appointment (if any) 12-6-16	B.	B. Date in	Date out
	C.	C. Date in	Date out

What medical conditions were treated or evaluated?

Heart disease

What treatment did you receive for the above conditions? (Do not describe medicines or tests in this box.)

Check-ups on heart

Form SSA-454-BK, *Continuing Disability Review Report* (Page 4)

SECTION 4 - MEDICAL TREATMENT (continued)

Check the boxes below for any tests this provider performed or sent you to **within the last 12 months,** or has scheduled you to take. Please give the dates for past and future tests. If you need to list more tests, use **Section 11 - Remarks.**

☐ **Check this box if no tests by this provider or at this facility.**

KIND OF TEST	DATES OF TEST(S)	KIND OF TEST	DATES OF TEST(S)
☑ EKG (heart test)	June 2016	☐ EEG (brain wave test)	
☑ Treadmill (exercise test)	June 2016	☐ HIV Test	
☐ Cardiac Catheterization		☑ Blood Test (not HIV)	June 2016
☐ Biopsy (list body part)		☑ X-Ray (list body part) Chest	June 2016
☐ Hearing Test		☐ MRI/CT Scan (list body part)	
☐ Speech/Language Test			
☐ Vision Test		☐ Other	
☐ Breathing test			

**If you do not have any more doctors or hospitals to describe, go to
Section 5 - Medicines on page 9.**

4.D. Tell us who may have medical records covering **the last 12 months** about any of your physical or mental condition(s) (including emotional or learning problems). This includes doctors' offices, hospitals (including emergency room visits), clinics, and other health care facilities. Tell us about your next appointment, if you have one scheduled.

NAME OF FACILITY OR OFFICE	NAME OF HEALTHCARE PROFESSIONAL THAT TREATED YOU
The Pulmonary Clinic	Dr. Glen Rose

**ALL OF THE QUESTIONS ON THIS PAGE REFER TO THE HEALTH CARE
PROFESSIONAL ABOVE**

PHONE NUMBER (214) 555-6666	PATIENT ID# (if known)

MAILING ADDRESS

82 Oak Cove

CITY Dallas	STATE/Province TX	ZIP/Postal Code 93872	COUNTRY (if not USA)

Dates of Treatment (within the last 12 months)

1. Office, Clinic or Outpatient visits	2. Emergency Room Visits List the most recent date first	3. Overnight Hospitals Stays	
First visit 5-5-2016	A.	A. Date in	Date out
Last visit 8-2-2016			
Next Scheduled Appointment (if any) 1-3-2017	B.	B. Date in	Date out
	C.	C. Date in	Date out

Form SSA-454-BK, *Continuing Disability Review Report* (Page 5)

SECTION 4 - MEDICAL TREATMENT (continued)

What medical conditions were treated or evaluated?

Emphysema and bronchitis

What treatment did you receive for the above conditions? (Do not describe medicines or tests in this box.)

Drugs, advice how to breathe

Check the boxes below for any tests this provider performed or sent you to **within the last 12 months,** or has scheduled you to take. Please give the dates for past and future tests. If you need to list more tests, use **Section 11 - Remarks**.

☐ **Check this box if no tests by this provider or at this facility.**

KIND OF TEST	DATES OF TEST(S)	KIND OF TEST	DATES OF TEST(S)
☑ EKG (heart test)	5-5-2016	☐ EEG (brain wave test)	
☐ Treadmill (exercise test)		☐ HIV Test	
☐ Cardiac Catheterization		☑ Blood Test (not HIV)	5-5-2016
☐ Biopsy (list body part)		☑ X-Ray (list body part) Chest	5-5-2016
☐ Hearing Test		☐ MRI/CT Scan (list body part)	
☐ Speech/Language Test			
☐ Vision Test		☐ Other	
☑ Breathing test	5-5-2016		

If you do not have any more doctors or hospitals to describe, go to Section 5 - Medicines on page 9.

4.E. Tell us who may have medical records covering **the last 12 months** about any of your physical or mental condition(s) (including emotional or learning problems). This includes doctors' offices, hospitals (including emergency room visits), clinics, and other health care facilities. Tell us about your next appointment, if you have one scheduled.

NAME OF FACILITY OR OFFICE	NAME OF HEALTHCARE PROFESSIONAL THAT TREATED YOU
The Orthopedic Specialists	Dr. Jane Barr

ALL OF THE QUESTIONS ON THIS PAGE REFER TO THE HEALTH CARE PROFESSIONAL ABOVE

PHONE NUMBER (215) 555-5555	PATIENT ID# (if known) 22345

MAILING ADDRESS

920 Freeway Drive

CITY Dallas	STATE/Province TX	ZIP/Postal Code 93875	COUNTRY (if not USA)

Form SSA-454-BK, *Continuing Disability Review Report* (Page 6)

SECTION 4 - MEDICAL TREATMENT (continued)

Dates of Treatment (within the last 12 months)

1. Office, Clinic or Outpatient visits		2. Emergency Room Visits List the most recent date first	3. Overnight Hospitals Stays	
First visit	7-2016	A.	A. Date in	Date out
Last visit	7-2016			
Next Scheduled Appointment (if any)		B.	B. Date in	Date out
	None	C.	C. Date in	Date out

What medical conditions were treated or evaluated?

Back pain

What treatment did you receive for the above conditions? (Do not describe medicines or tests in this box.)

Medication and how to avoid back pain as much as possible.

Check the boxes below for any tests this provider performed or sent you to **within the last 12 months,** or has scheduled you to take. Please give the dates for past and future tests. If you need to list more tests, use **Section 11 - Remarks**.

☐ **Check this box if no tests by this provider or at this facility.**

KIND OF TEST	DATES OF TEST(S)	KIND OF TEST	DATES OF TEST(S)
☐ EKG (heart test)		☐ EEG (brain wave test)	
☐ Treadmill (exercise test)		☐ HIV Test	
☐ Cardiac Catheterization		☐ Blood Test (not HIV)	
☐ Biopsy (list body part)		☑ X-Ray (list body part) Low back	7-2016
☐ Hearing Test		☐ MRI/CT Scan (list body part)	
☐ Speech/Language Test			
☐ Vision Test		☐ Other	
☐ Breathing test			

If you do not have any more doctors or hospitals to describe, go to
Section 5 - Medicines on page 9.

4.F. Tell us who may have medical records covering **the last 12 months** about any of your physical or mental condition(s) (including emotional or learning problems). This includes doctors' offices, hospitals (including emergency room visits), clinics, and other health care facilities. Tell us about your next appointment, if you have one scheduled.

NAME OF FACILITY OR OFFICE	NAME OF HEALTHCARE PROFESSIONAL THAT TREATED YOU

Form SSA-454-BK, *Continuing Disability Review Report* (Page 7)

SECTION 4 - MEDICAL TREATMENT (continued)

ALL OF THE QUESTIONS ON THIS PAGE REFER TO THE HEALTH CARE PROFESSIONAL ABOVE

PHONE NUMBER	PATIENT ID# (if known)

MAILING ADDRESS

CITY	STATE/Province	ZIP/Postal Code	COUNTRY (if not USA)

Dates of Treatment (within the last 12 months)

1. Office, Clinic or Outpatient visits	2. Emergency Room Visits List the most recent date first		3. Overnight Hospitals Stays	
First visit	A.		A. Date in	Date out
Last visit				
Next Scheduled Appointment (if any)	B.		B. Date in	Date out
	C.		C. Date in	Date out

What medical conditions were treated or evaluated?

What treatment did you receive for the above conditions? (Do not describe medicines or tests in this box.)

Check the boxes below for any tests this provider performed or sent you to **within the last 12 months,** or has scheduled you to take. Please give the dates for past and future tests. If you need to list more tests, use **Section 11 - Remarks.**

☐ **Check this box if no tests by this provider or at this facility.**

KIND OF TEST	DATES OF TEST(S)	KIND OF TEST	DATES OF TEST(S)
☐ EKG (heart test)		☐ EEG (brain wave test)	
☐ Treadmill (exercise test)		☐ HIV Test	
☐ Cardiac Catheterization		☐ Blood Test (not HIV)	
☐ Biopsy (list body part)		☐ X-Ray (list body part)	
☐ Hearing Test		☐ MRI/CT Scan (list body part)	
☐ Speech/Language Test			
☐ Vision Test		☐ Other	
☐ Breathing test			

If you do not have any more doctors or hospitals to describe, go to Section 5 - Medicines on page 9.

Form SSA-454-BK, *Continuing Disability Review Report* (Page 8)

SECTION 4 - MEDICAL TREATMENT (continued)

4.G. Tell us who may have medical records covering **the last 12 months** about any of your physical or mental condition(s) (including emotional or learning problems). This includes doctors' offices, hospitals (including emergency room visits), clinics, and other health care facilities. Tell us about your next appointment, if you have one scheduled.

NAME OF FACILITY OR OFFICE	NAME OF HEALTHCARE PROFESSIONAL THAT TREATED YOU

ALL OF THE QUESTIONS ON THIS PAGE REFER TO THE HEALTH CARE PROFESSIONAL ABOVE

PHONE NUMBER	PATIENT ID# (if known)

MAILING ADDRESS

CITY	STATE/Province	ZIP/Postal Code	COUNTRY (if not USA)

Dates of Treatment (within the last 12 months)

1. Office, Clinic or Outpatient visits	2. Emergency Room Visits List the most recent date first	3. Overnight Hospitals Stays	
First visit	A.	A. Date in	Date out
Last visit			
Next Scheduled Appointment (if any)	B.	B. Date in	Date out
	C.	C. Date in	Date out

What medical conditions were treated or evaluated?

What treatment did you receive for the above conditions? (Do not describe medicines or tests in this box.)

Check the boxes below for any tests this provider performed or sent you to **within the last 12 months,** or has scheduled you to take. Please give the dates for past and future tests. If you need to list more tests, use **Section 11 - Remarks**.

☐ **Check this box if no tests by this provider or at this facility.**

Form SSA-454-BK, *Continuing Disability Review Report* (Page 9)

SECTION 4 - MEDICAL TREATMENT (continued)

KIND OF TEST	DATES OF TEST(S)	KIND OF TEST	DATES OF TEST(S)
☐ EKG (heart test)		☐ EEG (brain wave test)	
☐ Treadmill (exercise test)		☐ HIV Test	
☐ Cardiac Catheterization		☐ Blood Test (not HIV)	
☐ Biopsy (list body part)		☐ X-Ray (list body part)	
☐ Hearing Test		☐ MRI/CT Scan (list body part)	
☐ Speech/Language Test			
☐ Vision Test		☐ Other	
☐ Breathing test			

If you need to list more doctors or hospitals use Section 11 - Remarks and give the same detailed information as above for each one you list.

❺ **SECTION 5 - MEDICINES**

5. Are you now taking, or have you taken in the last 12 months, any prescription or non-prescription medicines?

☑ Yes (Complete the following information. Look at your medicine containers, if necessary.)

☐ No (Go to section 6 - Other Medical Information on page 10.)

NAME OF MEDICINE	IF PRESCRIBED, GIVE NAME OF DOCTOR	REASON FOR MEDICINE
Theophylline	Dr. Rose	Bronchitis
Ibuprofen	Dr. Barr	Back pain

If you need to list other medicines use Section 11 - Remarks.
If you are under age 18, Skip to Section 11 - Remarks.

Form SSA-454-BK, *Continuing Disability Review Report* (Page 10)

⑥ **SECTION 6 - OTHER MEDICAL INFORMATION**
Complete only if you are age 18 years or older

6. Does anyone else have medical information about your physical or mental condition(s) (including emotional and learning problems) covering the last 12 months, or are you scheduled to see anyone else? (This may include places such as workers' compensation, vocational rehabilitation, insurance companies who have paid you disability benefits, prisons, attorneys, social service agencies and welfare agencies.)

☐ Yes (Complete the following information.)

☑ No   (Go to **SECTION 7 - Education and Training**.)

NAME OR ORGANIZATION	PHONE NUMBER

MAILING ADDRESS

CITY	STATE/Province	ZIP/Postal Code	COUNTRY (if not USA)

NAME OF CONTACT PERSON	CLAIM NUMBER (if any)

Date First Contact (in last 12 months)	Date Last Contact (in last 12 months)	Date Next Contact (if any)

Reason(s) for Contacts

If you need to list other people or organizations use Section 11 - Remarks and give the same detailed information as above for each one you list.

❼ **SECTION 7 - EDUCATION AND TRAINING**
Complete only if you are age 18 years or older

7.A. Have you received any education since your last disability decision? (See date at top of Page1.)

☐ YES (Complete the information below.)   ☑ NO, go to question **7.B** below

If YES, what year did you last attend any school?

Please describe the education you received.

7.B. Have you received any type of specialized job, trade, or vocational training since your last disability decision? (See date at top of Page 1.)

☐ YES (Complete the information below.)   ☑ NO

NAME OF TRAINING FACILITY	PHONE

MAILING ADDRESS

CITY	STATE/Province	ZIP/Postal Code	COUNTRY (if not USA)

TYPE OF PROGRAM	Date Completed (or scheduled to be completed)

If you need to list other education information or training facilities use Section 11 - Remarks and give the same detailed information as above

Form **SSA-454-BK** (04-2014) ef(04-2014)   Page 10

Form SSA-454-BK, *Continuing Disability Review Report* (Page 11)

⑧   **SECTION 8 - VOCATIONAL REHABILITATION, EMPLOYMENT, OR OTHER SUPPORT SERVICES**
Complete only if you are age 18 years or older

8.A. Since the date of your last medical disability decision (see date on top of Page 1), have you participated, or are you participating, in:

- an individualized work plan with an employment network under the Ticket to Work Program;
- an individualized plan for employment with a vocational rehabilitation agency or any other organization;
- a Plan to Achieve Self-Support (PASS);
- an Individualized Education Program (IEP) through a school (if a student age 18-21); or
- any program providing vocational rehabilitation, employment services, or other support services to help you go to work?

☐ YES (Complete the information below.)   ☑ NO (Go to **Section 9 - Daily Activities**)

If YES, what year did you last attend any school?

NAME OF ORGANIZATION OR SCHOOL

NAME OF COUNSELOR, INSTRUCTOR OR JOB COACH	PHONE NUMBER

MAILING ADDRESS

CITY	STATE/Province	ZIP/Postal Code	COUNTRY (if not USA)

8.B. When did you start participating in the plan or program?

8.C. Are you still participating in the plan or program?

    ☐ YES, I am scheduled to complete the plan or program on: _____
                                      (date to be completed)

    ☐ NO, I completed the plan or program on: _____
                                    (date completed)

    ☐ NO, I stopped participating in the plan before completing it because.

8.D. What types of services, tests, or evaluations were provided (for example: intelligence or psychological testing, vision or hearing tests, physical exam, work evaluations, or classes?)

If you need to list another plan or program use Section 11 - Remarks and give the same detailed information as above

Form SSA-454-BK, *Continuing Disability Review Report* (Page 12)

⑨   **SECTION 9 - DAILY ACTIVITIES**
Complete only if you are at age 18 years old or older

9.A. Describe what you do in a typical day (for example: I get up around 7 A.M., take a shower, eat breakfast, etc.).

I get up, take a shower, then eat breakfast. I can't sleep too long because of back pain. After breakfast, I take the dog for a walk but can't do over about 3 blocks, and that takes 15 minutes because I get short of breath and my back starts hurting more. Then I come back and sit on the front porch in a recliner to keep my back from hurting. I talk to neighbors if they walk by and watch the neighbor's kid cut my lawn, as I can't do it anymore. In the afternoon, I take a nap or go with my wife to the store. I don't lift anything heavy. If it's cold, I stay inside. At night, I read or watch TV but have to stand up frequently because of back pain.

If you need more space, go to Section 11 - Remarks

9.B. Do you have hobbies or interests?

☐ YES   ☑ NO

If YES, please describe what they are and how much time you spend doing them.

9.C. Do you ever have difficulty doing any of the following? (Please explain any "Yes" answers.)

Dressing	☑ YES	☐ NO	Hurts back to bend to step into and pull pants up
Bathing	☑ YES	☐ NO	Can't get in and out of tub. Take showers OK.
Caring for hair	☐ YES	☑ NO	
Taking medicines	☐ YES	☑ NO	
Preparing meals	☐ YES	☑ NO	
Feeding self	☐ YES	☑ NO	
Doing chores (inside/outside house)	☑ YES	☐ NO	Can't do things like mow or house repair;
Driving or using public transportation	☐ YES	☑ NO	can pick up small objects using extension tool so no bending
Shopping	☐ YES	☑ NO	
Managing money	☐ YES	☑ NO	
Walking	☑ YES	☐ NO	Not over 3 blocks on flat
Standing	☑ YES	☐ NO	Back pain if over 30 min
Lifting objects	☑ YES	☐ NO	Can't lift over 10 lbs because of back and can't
Using arms	☐ YES	☑ NO	carry over 20 lbs because of back and lungs.
Using hands or fingers	☐ YES	☑ NO	
Sitting	☑ YES	☐ NO	Back hurts if I sit over 2 hrs at a time
Seeing, hearing, or speaking	☐ YES	☑ NO	
Concentrating	☐ YES	☑ NO	
Remembering	☐ YES	☑ NO	
Understanding or following directions	☐ YES	☑ NO	
Completing tasks	☑ YES	☐ NO	If too much physical effort involved; no mental problem doing things
Getting along with people	☐ YES	☑ NO	

Form **SSA-454-BK** (04-2014) ef(04-2014)   Page 12

Form SSA-454-BK, *Continuing Disability Review Report* (Page 13)

---

⑩   **SECTION 10 - WORK**
                Complete only if you are age 14 years old or older

10. Since the date of your last medical disability decision have you worked? (see date at top of Page1)   ☐ YES (If yes, we may contact you for additional information)   ☑ NO

---

⑪   **SECTION 11 - REMARKS**

Please write any additional information you did not give in earlier parts of this report. If you did not have enough space in the sections of this report to write the requested information, please use this space to tell us the additional requested in those sections. Be sure to show the section to which you are referring.

3A. Every year my breathing test results get worse and so does my back pain. My doctors say they can't do anything else to help. Back surgery would be an option but can't be done because of my lung problem. My doctors say I'm getting slowly worse and will provide the lung tests and x-rays to show it, if SSA asks for them. Dr. Rose said I should avoid dust and fumes like I was exposed to during 25 years of farm work. He also said to avoid very hot or cold environments because of stress to my lungs. If it's very hot or cold outside, or if there's much ozone pollution, I get more short of breath.

Dr. Barr has always said I have severe arthritis in my spine as well as degenerative discs. She said I should never lift over 20 lbs and should avoid excessive bending of my back. She said I should avoid activities that jar my back, like riding heavy equipment like tractors.

Date Report Completed (month, day, year)
10-11-2016

Personal needs and grooming. Describe any difficulties you have. Don't underestimate the importance of these everyday activities that many people take for granted. For example, if you have had a stroke, you may be unable to button your shirt with one hand. Inability to button a shirt or pick up coins tells the SSA that you have difficulty with fine movements of your fingers, movements that are critical in some kinds of work.

A claimant with a profound mental disorder, such as severe dementia like Alzheimer's disease, might require help in even basic personal needs. Be sure to note if a caregiver provides help. And if you are completing the form for a recipient with a mental disorder, ask the caregiver for insight into what the recipient can and cannot do.

Household maintenance. The SSA is not so much interested in whether you actually do things around the house—the SSA wants to know if you *can* do these things. For example, the fact that you don't cook is not an argument that you cannot cook. It is more significant that you could previously cook but no longer are able to because you can't stand for very long and your kitchen isn't wheelchair accessible; you can't use your fingers; you are inattentive and burn food; or your anxieties keep you from going out to shop.

With a physical disorder, you might have difficulty standing or using your hands to perform routine household activities—for instance, the pain in your hands is so severe you cannot turn a wrench or hold a paintbrush, or your loss of coordination means you can't hit a nail to do repairs around the house. Maybe you can't vacuum because of shortness of breath.

Whatever the limitation, be specific and give the reason for the limitation. For example, you might write, "I can rake leaves slowly for 30 minutes before I get so exhausted I have to rest for the same length of time."

Social contacts. The SSA is looking at your ability to interact with other people. That you don't engage in any of these activities does not necessarily mean you can't. Social skills are important in determining the type of work you can do, especially in evaluating the severity of a mental disorder.

What is particularly revealing to the SSA is a change in which social activities previously of interest to you are no longer, and what symptoms you have that prevent your socialization. For example, the SSA will want to know if you previously enjoyed going to church but no longer do because of depression, paranoia, or fear of leaving home—but the SSA does not care that you've never been interested in going to church.

Social contacts need not be limited solely because of mental disorders. For example, advanced lung disease, muscle weakness, or pain can limit your desire and ability to interact socially.

❿ Check "yes" or "no" to answer whether you have worked since your last disability decision. If "yes," the SSA will contact you for additional details—the agency does not want you to enter that information here.

⓫ In the remarks section, describe any other problems not previously discussed, such as epilepsy that restricts your driving a car, difficulties with balance that prevent you from riding a motorcycle, fear or confusion that prevent you from traveling alone on a bus or subway, or memory problems that keep you from going out alone without getting lost.

Some example text is written on the form, but it is just for general guidance. Write what you think is best for a realistic picture of your problems.

Remember to date the form at the end.

C. Medical Improvement Review Standard

The SSA evaluates your case using what it calls the "medical improvement review standard" (MIRS). The MIRS governs how the SSA evaluates CDRs. Congress created the MIRS in the early 1980s when many disability recipients claimed that their benefits were being terminated despite the fact that they were still disabled.

You need to understand the MIRS because some medical consultants, examiners, and others who conduct CDRs are inadequately trained in the MIRS. Someone could incorrectly terminate your benefits.

The MIRS isn't applied under certain circumstances (see Section C2, below).

> **CAUTION**
>
> **Insist on a medical review.** If the DDS terminates your benefits, ask to review your file. If necessary, insist that a DDS medical consultant review your claim. Otherwise, a disability examiner who is not a doctor may be responsible for stopping your benefits. (See Chapter 6, Section G. Also see Chapter 12 on how to review your file and file an appeal.)

Under the MIRS, your CDR will be evaluated quite differently from your original application for disability benefits. During your initial application, the burden of proof to show that you were disabled was on you. But in a CDR, the burden shifts to the SSA. This means that your benefits will continue unless the SSA can clearly show that you have medically improved to the extent you can work. The MIRS requires two different showings before the SSA can terminate your benefits. The SSA must show both of the following:

- You have significant medical improvement related to your ability to work, as determined by a DDS medical consultant (see Subsection a, below).
- You can actually perform substantial gainful activity, as determined by a DDS claims examiner or vocational specialist (see Subsection b, below).

1. Medical Improvement Related to Your Ability to Work

"Medical improvement" means there has been some lessening in the severity of your impairments since your last CDR. It is important to understand that medical improvement is sometimes only minor. In these instances, it would be unfair for the SSA to say your condition has gotten better in any meaningful sense. (See the example regarding trivial impairments, below.) Therefore, federal regulations require that there be "significant" medical improvement.

Disorders Showing Temporary Improvement

If the severity of your disorder fluctuates, the SSA is supposed to take this into consideration when considering medical improvement. For example, let's say your rheumatoid arthritis flares up every three or four months and then is better for several months. The severity of your impairment should be stable for six months to a year before the SSA decides you have improved enough to have your benefits terminated. Multiple sclerosis and systemic lupus erythematosus (SLE) are examples of other physical conditions that can act in this way.

Mental disorders can also show a lot of variation in severity—such as manic-depressive psychosis. The SSA must look at all of your medical history "longitudinally"—that is, to evaluate how your impairments affect you over a period of at least 12 months, before making a decision to stop your benefits.

In most instances, any significant improvements will be "related to your

ability to work." However, this is not always true, and "related to the ability to do work" is important legal language used by the SSA. For example, if you have a marked improvement in the medical severity of one of your various disorders that has nothing to do with your ability to work (such as a hair transplant for alopecia or a hysterectomy for uterine fibroids), the SSA should not say you have had significant medical improvement related to your ability to work. No matter how much some things improve, they might have little to do with the ability to work. To exclude impairments that are irrelevant or trivial from application of MIRS is the reason federal regulations use the phrase "related to your ability to work."

a. Comparison Point

The date that your claim was last reviewed and benefits allowed or continued is called the "comparison point decision" (CPD). Depending on the history of your claim, the CPD could be the date of your initial allowance, the date you were allowed at some appeal level, or the date of a previous CDR.

The DDS medical consultant should not be concerned with how or why you were placed on disability or reapproved after your previous CDR, or who made the decision, subject to the exceptions discussed in Subsection 2b, below. The MIRS applies only to the medical severity of your impairments at the CPD date as compared to those same impairments at your current CDR.

If you do not have significant medical improvement in your impairments, then your benefits will continue.

b. New Impairments

If you do have significant medical improvement, this does not necessarily mean that your overall medical condition has significantly improved. If you suffer new impairments that began after the last CPD date, the medical consultant will consider the impact of the new impairments on your ability to work. (New impairments are further discussed in Subsection 2d, below.) Of course, if you don't have significant medical improvement in the impairments that got you disability, then your benefits will continue, and there will be no point in reviewing your new impairments.

c. Evaluating Evidence

The SSA evaluates "symptoms," "signs," and "laboratory abnormalities" to determine the medical severity of your impairments and whether they have improved:

- **Symptoms** are your own description of your physical or mental impairment. Common examples include, "My back hurts," "My abdomen hurts," "I have chest pain," "I'm cold," "I'm tired," "I'm dizzy," "I'm short of breath," "I'm scared," and "I feel worthless." For children who cannot describe their symptoms, the SSA will accept the statements of parents or guardians who know the child best.

- **Signs** are physical or psychological abnormalities that can be observed apart from your statements (symptoms). A sign could be a missing limb, a skin rash, an abnormal reflex, a fast pulse, sweating, struggling to breathe, bleeding, a tremor, an epileptic seizure, decreased emotional expression, agitation, paranoid delusions, or many other things.

- **Laboratory findings** are physical or psychological facts that can be shown by use of diagnostic techniques such as chemical tests, X-rays or other imaging studies, EKGs, or psychological tests. The SSA evaluates signs and laboratory findings using methods generally acceptable to the scientific medical community. For example, the SSA would not accept reports claiming to diagnose disease or severity of disease from examination of the colored part of the eye (iridology) or as a result of "therapeutic touch," because these types of reports are not acceptable to the scientific medical community.

d. When Improvement Might Be Found

How the MIRS is applied to physical disorders, mental disorders, and a combination of the two can be found in the following examples.

Physical disorders. Chapters 7 and 8 explain the Listing of Impairments and residual functional capacity (RFC), and how they affect whether or not you qualify for disability benefits. If you move up at least one exertional level of severity, such as from sedentary work to light work, or from light work to medium work, or from medium work to heavy work, or from meeting or equaling a listing to an RFC for sedentary work, then you clearly have experienced a significant medical improvement.

> **EXAMPLE:** Two years ago, after Kota's diseased heart valve resulted in heart failure, she was granted disability benefits. She was restricted to nothing more than sedentary work in her RFC rating. Subsequently, she had heart surgery with placement of a new valve. During the CDR, the DDS medical consultant found her capable of performing light work—and therefore found significant medical improvement.

Medical improvement that remains within a physical RFC exertional level may or may not be significant. In the following example, improvement is significant even though the exertional level remains at light work.

> **EXAMPLE:** At Rick's previous CDR, he was given an RFC for light work because of asthma and arthritis in his spine. Since then, Rick has had treatment for the asthma and breathes much better, according to both his symptoms and objective pulmonary function tests. He's had significant medical improvement because of his improved breathing. His arthritis still restricts his lifting to light work, however.

Mental disorders. If you move up at least one mental skill level of severity, such as from unskilled work to semiskilled work, or from semiskilled to skilled work, or from meeting or equaling a listing level to a mental RFC rating for unskilled work, then you clearly have experienced a significant medical improvement.

> **EXAMPLE:** Julie is a 35-year-old college-educated CPA with a ten-year history of successful skilled work who suffered a major depression. She was initially granted benefits a year before the current CDR by meeting the listing for major depression. That was her first episode of major depression, and her prognosis was favorable. Julie has received ongoing treatment, and while she still has some signs of depression, she has significantly improved to the extent that she now has a mental RFC for unskilled work. Although Julie is not fully recovered from her depression, her ability to do unskilled work represents significant medical improvement.

Medical improvement that remains within a mental RFC skill level may or may not be significant. As discussed in Chapter 9, claimants with mental impairments alone who are restricted to semiskilled or skilled work are never granted benefits. Even those with the ability to do unskilled work are rarely granted benefits. In the rare instances in which those with the ability to do unskilled work are approved for benefits because of their age, education, and work experience (vocational factors), these same factors would probably result in a continuance of benefits on review.

Combined physical and mental disorders. Significant improvement in either a physical or mental impairment alone can be sufficient to establish significant medical improvement.

EXAMPLE 1: Paul is a 34-year-old worker who fell off a roof and suffered a severe fracture of his spine. Even after maximum healing, he was capable of only sedentary work, and no further improvement could be expected. His fifth grade education and work experience limit him to unskilled types of work. He also suffered significant anxiety that was worsened by his accident. Although neither his physical or mental impairment alone could satisfy the Listing of Impairments, he was awarded disability two years ago based on having multiple conditions equivalent in severity to the requirements of a combination of physical and mental disorder listings. Following treatment of his anxieties with psychotherapy and medication, his mental impairment has become not severe, and he has experienced significant improvement in his mental condition.

EXAMPLE 2: Cindy is 50 years old with 25 years' experience as a laundry worker. She has subaverage intelligence, with an IQ of 68, which limits her to unskilled work. She does not meet the listing for severe intellectual disability. She has no other mental impairment. She has always been outgoing, friendly, and capable of taking care of her own personal needs. Two years prior, she had suffered a fractured tibia that

was somewhat slow in healing, and she was granted benefits based on her subaverage intellect and the fracture. Her fracture is now completely healed without any significant residual problem, and the SSA determines that there has been significant medical improvement.

Trivial impairments. If you experience great improvement in a trivial impairment, the DDS team should not find a significant medical improvement.

EXAMPLE: Maria was originally granted disability because of a heart disease; at the same time, she also had a minor case of athlete's foot. At her CDR, the MC determined that her athlete's foot was cured and her heart disease was the same. Maria has not had significant medical improvement. If the heart disease had improved significantly, significant medical improvement would be obvious.

2. Your Ability to Work

If the medical consultant finds that you have experienced significant medical improvement, your benefits will not be automatically terminated. A DDS examiner or vocational analyst must also show that you are capable of performing some work "available in the national economy." The DDS examiner must take into account your original impairments and any new impairments you might have. (See Subsection 4d, below, regarding new impairments.)

EXAMPLE: Max is 55 years old, has a third-grade education, and has always done heavy work. He was originally allowed benefits because of multiple unhealed fractures and arthritis in his spine. By the time of his CDR, his fractures had healed, and the DDS finds significant medical improvement. But Max's spinal arthritis still restricts him to an RFC for light work. He will continue to receive benefits because the SSA will not be able to show there is any job that he can perform with his RFC, age, education, and work experience.

Either a mental impairment or your vocational factors can influence the skill level of work that you can perform. When the SSA considers whether there are jobs you can perform, the SSA must use your lower skill level, whether your lower skill level is due to your vocational factors or your mental impairment. In other words, you can be mentally healthy but you are still not going to be able to work at levels of skill higher than those supported by your education and work experience. Similarly, you could have education or work experience that would support skilled work, yet be capable of only unskilled work due to a mental impairment.

3. Age and Time Receiving Disability

The SSA does not usually consider your age in deciding your physical capacity on an RFC. CDRs are an exception, however. The SSA knows that older recipients may be affected by aging and long periods of inactivity from not working. Aging and inactivity are often associated with decreased heart and lung function, weakening of muscles, degenerative joint changes, and decreased general exercise capacity. How severe the changes are and when they appear varies greatly among people.

The SSA considers age and inactivity if you are over age 50 and have been receiving disability benefits for at least seven years. These factors enter in when the DDS considers your current RFC rating and whether you've had significant work-related medical improvement. Age and time on the disability rolls can result in continuation of benefits when the decision is a close call.

The SSA might have you undergo tests if the available evidence does not indicate how much physical work you can do based on your age and time receiving disability benefits.

4. When the MIRS Doesn't Apply

Under certain conditions, the SSA doesn't have to apply the MIRS to your CDR evaluation. In these cases, you might be able to keep your benefits without a DDS review for medical improvement. On the other hand, it is possible that without the protections of the MIRS, you could lose your benefits.

a. Your Impairment Meets or Equals a Listing

If you are an adult and your impairment continues to meet or equal the same listing in the Listing of Impairments (see Chapter 7, Step 3) as it did at the time you obtained

The Lesser the Disability, the Less Room There Is for Improvement

One of the amazing things about the MIRS is that if you were granted benefits in a situation in which you really weren't entitled to them, they can't be taken away except in limited situations (discussed in Section 4, below). Through errors in judgment by someone working in the SSA, it is possible for people who actually have mild impairments to be initially allowed by being judged as much worse than they actually are. For example, you might have a mild or slight disability, rather than a severe one, but you were wrongly allowed under a rating for less-than-sedentary work. Because the law does not allow the judgment of past decision makers to be questioned, you can be in benefit status the rest of your life (as long as you are not working above the SGA level).

How can this happen? Once you get to the ALJ level of appeal, your claim, in many instances, will be treated with leniency. For example, an ALJ might allow your claim under a less-than-sedentary rating after a DDS medical consultant (MC) gave you a higher RFC rating (say for medium work).

Now look at what happens when your claim later comes up for CDR evaluation. The ALJ has given you a rating for less-than-sedentary work, which would allow benefits for any claimant with any age, education, or work experience. The DDS MC who looks at your claim on CDR might think, "There's nothing really seriously wrong with this person medically." But remember, medical evidence between the CPD and current CDR must be compared to determine if there is any medical improve-

ment. If there's nothing much wrong with someone at the CPD and still nothing much wrong with them at their CDR, there is no room for significant medical improvement—there is no significant impairment present that can undergo improvement.

In such a situation, and there are many, the DDS MC cannot legally find that significant medical improvement took place, and you will be entitled to benefits indefinitely, because no matter how many CDRs you have in the future, there will never be significant improvement, since you were not significantly disabled to begin with.

In reality, there is no question that medical doctors know more about medicine than ALJs or other nondoctors deciding appeal cases. Knowing this to be true, a DDS MC might try to say there has been medical improvement when there really is none, and the ALJ may believe the MC. MCs might do this because they think it is wrong for a person they know is not disabled to stay on the disability rolls. However, it is not legal to ignore the medical improvement requirement in such instances.

Watch out for this kind of intentional ignoring of the MIRS if you feel you're disabled even though a doctor doesn't think there's much wrong with you. You still get the protection of the law, no matter who is right, if at one point an ALJ gave you a less-than-sedentary RFC. In that case, a medical consultant can't say that medical improvement can be demonstrated if your condition hasn't changed.

disability benefits or at your last CPD, then the SSA can simply continue your benefits without having to consider the MIRS.

You will continue to receive your benefits, even if the requirements of the listing have been changed and you do not meet these new listing requirements. This is extremely important to know; many disability recipients, especially those with heart or other cardiovascular disease, were granted benefits under lenient listings that are now out of date. An inexperienced or poorly trained DDS medical consultant might overlook this "grandfathering" clause and terminate your benefits.

Similarly, if you qualify as an adult under any newer listings in effect at the time of your CDR—even if you originally qualified under older, different listings—your benefits will continue without a medical improvement evaluation. Moreover, meeting or equaling the listings in effect at the time of the CDR can also include any new impairments you have acquired since your CPD and also would not require a medical improvement evaluation.

In children, the rules are a little different in that qualification under a listing is decided only after a determination that there has been significant medical improvement. (See Section D, below.)

b. You Are No Longer Disabled or Never Were

If the DDS finds that you are no longer disabled at all, or never were disabled, the SSA can terminate your benefits without applying the MIRS if you are performing substantial gainful activity (SGA) (see Chapter 1, Section B) or are capable of doing so. Group I exceptions to the MIRS rule, include the following.

You have undergone vocational therapy related to your ability to work. If you are no longer disabled and can engage in SGA, your benefits can be terminated without going through the MIRS. This exception does not apply to SSI recipients.

EXAMPLE 1: Tanya was found to be disabled when her impairment allowed her only to do work with a sedentary level of exertion. Her prior work experience was in work that required a medium level of exertion, and her age and education at the time she was awarded benefits would not have qualified her for work below the medium level. Since then, Tanya has completed a specialized training course that qualifies her for a job as a computer programmer. During her CDR, the DDS concluded that Tanya has had no medical improvement and can still do only sedentary work. Because a computer programmer's work is sedentary in nature, however, Tanya is now able to engage in SGA and is no longer eligible for Social Security disability.

EXAMPLE 2: Jacques qualified for disability because the medical evidence and RFC showed he could do only light work. Jacques' prior work was heavy, and his age, education, and prior work qualified him for only medium or light in exertion. The current evidence and RFC show no medical improvement and that he can still do only light work. Since Jacques was originally awarded benefits, his vocational rehabilitation agency successfully enrolled him in a trade school course, and he can now do small appliance repair. This is considered light work. With these new skills, Jacques is now able to engage in SGA even though his RFC has not changed.

Based on new or improved diagnostic or evaluative techniques, your impairment is not considered to be as disabling as it was considered to be at the CPD. If your condition is no longer considered disabling, your benefits can be terminated without going through the MIRS. For this exception to apply, the new or improved techniques must have become generally available for medical use after the last CPD.

EXAMPLE: Ginger has heart disease. At the time of her last CPD, her heart function was measured with the Master's Two-Step Test. Since then, the EKG Exercise Test has replaced the Master's Two-Step Test as a measurement of heart function. Using the EKG Exercise Test, Ginger's condition is not considered as disabling as was previously thought. If Ginger is able to engage in SGA, she would no longer be considered disabled even though she's had no medical improvement.

A prior disability decision was erroneous. If a prior decision is found to be in error, your benefits can be terminated without going through the MIRS, under certain conditions. The DDS must find clear evidence that a prior decision granting you disability was in error. A difference in judgment between the past and current reviewers is not sufficient. The DDS can make this determination in one of three ways:

- Clear evidence (not open to judgment) already documented in your file shows that the decision in question should not have been made.

EXAMPLE: Rory was granted benefits when the SSA determined that his epilepsy met Listing 11.02 in the Listing of Impairments. Listing 11.02 requires a finding of major motor seizures more frequently than once a month. On a review of Rory's original SSA file, the DDS team finds a history of seizure frequency once or twice a year. The prior decision was erroneous, and whether Rory now will be considered disabled will depend on whether he can engage in SGA.

- At the time of the CPD, required material evidence of the severity of your impairment was missing. That evidence is now available. Had it been present at the time of the CPD, you would not have been found disabled.

EXAMPLE: Lance was originally found disabled on the basis of chronic obstructive lung disease. The severity of his breathing impairment was documented primarily by a pulmonary function test. Spirometric tracings of this test, although required by SSA regulations, were not obtained at the time of the CPD. A review of the tracings later obtained during the CDR shows that the test was invalid. Lance's current pulmonary function test, supported by spirometric tracings, reveals that his impairment does not limit his ability to perform basic work activities in any way. Lance is no longer entitled to disability.

• New evidence related to the prior determination of an allowance or continuation of benefits refutes the conclusions that were based on the prior evidence. Had the new evidence been present at the time of the CPD, you would not have been found disabled.

> EXAMPLE: K'ia was originally allowed benefits because of a lung tumor thought to be cancer. Because she had other health problems at the time, the doctors did not do a biopsy of the tumor. After K'ia began receiving benefits, she had a biopsy, and the tumor proved to be benign. K'ia is no longer entitled to disability.

Remember that difference in judgment between the past and current reviewers is not sufficient to find error, as illustrated by the following example.

> EXAMPLE: Tim was previously granted disability benefits on the basis of diabetes mellitus, which the prior DDS medical consultant (MC) believed was equivalent to the level of severity contemplated in the Listing of Impairments. At the time of the CPD, Tim had hard-to-control ("brittle") diabetes, for which he was taking insulin. Tim was spilling extra sugar into his urine and claimed occasional low blood sugar (hypoglycemic) attacks caused by exertion. During the CDR, the current MC finds no change in Tim's symptoms, signs, and laboratory results. The current MC believes, however, that Tim's impairment does not equal the severity contemplated by the Listings. Nevertheless, Tim continues to receive disability, because one SSA decision maker's judgment cannot be substituted for another.

You currently engage in SGA. If you are currently working above the SGA level, your benefits can be terminated without going through the MIRS. This exception does not apply to SSI recipients. It also does not apply if you receive SSI or SSDI during a trial work period or reentitlement period. (See Chapter 13 for a discussion of these terms.)

You are the beneficiary of advances in medical or vocational therapy or technology related to your ability to work. Because such advances usually result in significant medical improvement, rarely would this exception have any practical application. This exception does not apply to SSI recipients eligible to receive special SSI cash benefits.

c. Something Other Than Disability Disqualifies You

In a few rare situations, you may automatically lose your entitlement to SSI or SSDI for reasons unrelated to your disability. These are called the "group II exceptions." The SSA can apply these exceptions without considering your medical improvement or ability to work. The Group II exceptions are as follows.

The SSA is unable to find you. If the SSA can't find you, the SSA will find that your disability has ended (see Chapter 11, Section C).

You do not cooperate with the SSA. If the SSA asks for medical evidence, for other evidence, or for you to undergo an examination by a certain date and you refuse without good reason, the SSA will find that your disability has ended (see Chapter 11, Section D).

You fail to follow a prescribed treatment that is expected to restore your ability to engage in SGA. If you can't show a good reason for not following treatment, the SSA will find that your disability has ended (see Chapter 11, Section E).

You committed fraud. Committing fraud means you gave the SSA false or misleading information during any prior decision about your benefits (see Chapter 11, Section H).

d. New Impairments

The SSA does not consider any new impairments you develop after the CPD date as part of the medical improvement decision. In adults, new impairments either are evaluated after the issue of significant medical improvement is decided (see Section 1, above) or after they meet or equal a listing (see Section 4a, above).

In children, new impairments are evaluated only after a determination of whether there is significant improvement (see Section D, below).

But what if you develop a significant new impairment during or near the time you are having your CDR? In this case, your medical condition could be unstable, making the disability determination more difficult. The following example illustrates the procedure that should be followed.

EXAMPLE: Paul was originally allowed disability for lung cancer. Three years ago, he underwent successful surgery to remove a lung, and there has been no sign of recurrence. The current severity of his breathing problem will need to be determined. The SSA sends him a notice that it intends to do a CDR on his claim. Two weeks later, Paul is hospitalized with a heart attack and may also require heart surgery within the next month. The DDS medical consultant can postpone or carry out the CDR. If the MC believes Paul's disability from his lung disease is enough to approve continuing his benefits, the CDR could be held. If it is unclear how Paul's recovery from his lung disease or heart attack will affect the ultimate outcome of his claim, the CDR should be postponed.

D. Children and CDRs

SKIP AHEAD

Children younger than 18 who receive benefits as dependents of an SSDI recipient do not undergo continuing disability reviews because these benefits do not depend on the child's health. This section applies only to CDR evaluations for child SSI recipients.

CDR evaluations for children receiving SSI differ in some ways from the CDR evaluations of adult SSDI or SSI claims. First, the medical improvement determination in SSI children never involves changes in RFCs because children don't receive RFCs. Second, the order of CDR steps is a little different: the issue of medical improvement is considered before a decision is made whether the child meets or equals a listing. Third, the SSA doesn't consider the issue of "related to the ability to work."

Still, the main question is whether the child has experienced significant improvement in impairments. The SSA uses the following analysis:

Step 1. Has the child experienced significant medical improvement in the impairments present at the CPD? If "no" and none of the exceptions apply, benefits will continue. If "yes," proceed to Step 2.

Step 2. Do the impairments still meet or equal the severity of the listing that was met or equaled at the time of CPD? If "yes" and none of the exceptions apply, as described in Sections C4b and c, above, then benefits will continue. If "no," proceed to Step 3.

Step 3. Considering all of the child's current impairments—both those present at the CPD and new ones —do the impairments meet or equal a current listing? If "yes," then benefits will continue. If "no," benefits will end.

E. Appealing a CDR Decision

Once the SSA makes its CDR decision, you will receive a notice. If the SSA decides you are still disabled, your benefits will continue.

If the SSA determines that you are not still disabled, the SSA will send you a personalized explanation explaining how it reached its determination. If you don't appeal, you will receive benefits for the remainder of the month in which your disability ended, plus two more months. In no case, however, can your benefits be taken away earlier than the date it was decided to terminate your benefits.

This prevents the SSA from demanding back benefit repayment from you by saying that your disability ended before the agency even conducted your CDR. For example, suppose you were significantly improved and able to work a year before the SSA did a CDR evaluation of your claim. That is the SSA's fault, not yours, and you won't have to repay the money you received during this year. The only exception would be if you had committed fraud to obtain benefits; in that case the SSA could demand repayment of all paid benefits.

What if the SSA decided that your disability ended on the same day the SSA gives you notice that your benefits are ceased? In that case, your benefits would continue for three more months and then be stopped. (See Chapter 12 for information on appealing denied claims.)

Your Right to Representation

You do not need to represent yourself in a disability claim. You can appoint someone in writing to be your "authorized representative" to deal with the SSA on your behalf. (42 U.S.C. § 406; 20 CFR §§ 404.1700, 416.1500.) SSA personnel will work with your representative, just as they would work with you. Your authorized representative's primary role is to pursue your claim for benefits under SSDI or SSI.

> **TIP**
> **An authorized representative is different from a "designated representative,"** who is a person you can appoint to look at your medical records. An authorized representative is also different from a "representative payee," who is a person you can appoint to handle your benefit checks. Of course, you could name the same person to be your authorized representative, designated representative, and representative payee. (Designated representatives are discussed in Chapter 2, and representative payees are discussed in Chapter 13.)

A. When Do You Need an Authorized Representative?

Many people are perfectly capable of applying for disability benefits themselves, and most claimants do just that. They have the time and ability to complete the paperwork, meet with the claims examiner, contact their treating doctors and hospitals for their medical records, and follow up on any requests from the claims examiner, medical examiner, or medical consultant.

Other people appoint authorized representatives to handle their applications for benefits. Typical reasons for appointing such a person include the following:

- You just don't want to handle your own claim.
- Your medical condition prevents you from effectively representing yourself.
- You don't have the time to represent yourself.
- You have limited education or English skills and want someone to help with the paperwork.

Many people decide to appoint authorized representatives only if their initial claims for benefits (and perhaps reconsideration) have been denied and they want to appeal. Mind you, not everyone has an authorized representative for an appeal—a few claimants handle their appeals on their own, particularly at the administrative level. (Chapter 12 has complete information on appealing.)

On the other hand, a formal appeal means arguing your case before an administrative law judge (ALJ), an attorney who works for the SSA and reviews Disability Determination Service decisions. And if you lose your case before the ALJ, you can appeal to a federal district court. At that point, it is almost always in your best interest to hire an attorney as your authorized representative. (See Section D, below.)

Ultimately, the decision of whether or not to hire a representative requires judgment on your part—a judgment that often relates to money. If, after reading this book, you conclude that there is a really good chance you will be granted benefits, then there is little reason to spend money on hiring someone—usually a lawyer—to submit your application and let the SSA make its decision. But if you are uncertain, or you've been denied benefits and want to appeal, then hiring an authorized representative may make sense. You need to balance the fee you'll have to pay the representative against the amount of money you potentially could recover if you are awarded benefits. (Fees are discussed in Section F, below.)

B. What Can an Authorized Representative Do?

An authorized representative can act for you in most Social Security matters, including the following:

- accompanying you—or attending on your behalf—any interview, conference, or hearing with the SSA or DDS
- helping get medical records or information from your treating sources to support your claim
- obtaining information from your Social Security file
- requesting reconsideration of your claim, a hearing, or an Appeals Council review
- helping you and your witnesses prepare for a hearing

- presenting your case at a hearing and questioning any witnesses, or
- filing an appeal beyond the Appeals Council—that is, in court—if the representative is an attorney.

All correspondence will be sent to you and your representative. However, it is a good idea for you to inform your representative of any communications from the SSA in case, by some error, the representative doesn't get a copy. Even though you have appointed a representative, you (through your representative) remain legally obligated to provide Social Security with accurate information.

A representative usually might not sign an application for disability benefits on behalf of a claimant, but there is nothing to prevent a representative from helping the claimant fill out the forms. If there is a good reason why the claimant cannot sign the application, however, the SSA may accept an application signed by someone other than the claimant—such as a representative.

> **EXAMPLE:** Joe is a 55-year-old widower who had a heart attack a few days before the end of the month and was unable to file an application for SSI disability benefits. However, he hired authorized representative Sinclair to help him with his claim. The Social Security office accepted an application for Joe signed by Sinclair, because it would not be possible to have Joe sign and file the application until the next calendar month—which would mean that Joe would lose one month's benefits.

C. Who Can Be an Authorized Representative?

Authorized representatives generally fall into two categories—attorneys and nonattorneys. Your Social Security office has a list of organizations that can help you find an authorized representative.

1. Attorney Representatives

Any attorney in good standing, licensed to practice in the United States, can serve as your representative in dealing with the SSA. The only exceptions are if the attorney has been disqualified or suspended from acting as a representative in dealing with the SSA (see Section 3, below) or is otherwise prohibited by law from acting as a representative.

If the attorney you hire is a member of a law firm or organization, you can appoint a second or third person within the firm (corporation, LLC, or partnership) or organization as additional representatives to handle your case if your first representative is unavailable. Note that Social Security rules bar you from appointing a firm, corporation, LLC, partnership, or organization itself. You must name a specific person to be your authorized representative.

2. Nonattorney Representatives

You can appoint anyone you want to be your representative in dealing with the SSA as long as that person has a good character and reputation, can give you valuable help with your claim, has not been disqualified or suspended from acting as a representative in dealing with the SSA (see Section 3, below), and is not otherwise prohibited by law from acting as a representative. The law does not define what good character is, but it most likely means the person has not been convicted of any serious crimes.

3. Suspended or Disqualified Representatives

On occasion, the SSA suspends or disqualifies people from serving as authorized representatives. The reasons for doing so include such activities as knowingly and willingly providing false information to the SSA or charging an unauthorized fee for services. If you attempt to name someone as your authorized representative who has been suspended or disqualified, the person's name will pop up in the SSA's computers as suspended or disqualified. If you want to check beforehand, call the SSA hotline (800-772-1213). Tell the person who answers that you want to find out if the person you are considering appointing to be your authorized representative has been suspended or disqualified by the SSA.

D. Should Your Authorized Representative Be an Attorney?

If you want to appoint an authorized representative, you must decide between an attorney and a nonattorney. The same general analysis suggested at the end of Section A, above, applies here: If you are at the application stage and don't foresee too many problems, then a nonlawyer representative might serve you fine. There are undoubtedly very capable and highly experienced nonattorney representatives who can represent your claim before an administrative law judge.

If your case is questionable from the outset or you've been denied benefits and are filing a reconsideration claim or an administrative appeal, then it will probably be to your advantage to have your representative be an attorney knowledgeable in disability rights. An attorney doesn't charge any more than a nonattorney (see the discussion on fees below), but often has more knowledge of Social Security law.

Attorneys with extensive disability rights experience should be well equipped to handle the legal issues that arise in your claim. They know a lot about the SSA and its regulations. They can make sure that you do not miss deadlines, can help you obtain medical records that hospitals or treating doctors won't give the SSA, and can call the examiner handling your file and ask questions on your behalf. Of course, if you know of a capable nonattorney whom you trust and want to represent you, then you can use that person. You could always change to an attorney later, if necessary. (Using an attorney as your representative is necessary if you appeal your claim to a federal court. No one else can serve as your representative there.)

Attorneys vary in their competence, skill, and experience. Some attorneys are new to the field of Social Security disability representation of claimants. Disability law is an extremely specialized area. Attorneys cannot quickly review a few law books and capably represent your claim.

You should be cautious in retaining attorneys who only take occasional disability cases, while most of their time is spent in another kind of law practice. Some attorneys not only have extensive disability case experience representing claimants but a history of working in some other capacity that gives them additional valuable insights —former jobs, such as being a former SSA attorney, a former administrative law judge, or a former DDS supervisor or examiner. You can call an attorney's office and find out the answers to these questions before making an appointment.

E. How to Find a Disability Attorney

How do you find a competent disability attorney? You can find a local disability lawyer in a variety of ways: through a personal recommendation, in a directory, or through a referral service. If you use a referral service, make sure it guarantees its lawyers are active members of its state's bar in good standing.

Nolo offers a directory of disability lawyers on our website that provides a comprehensive profile for each attorney that tells you about the lawyer's disability experience, education, and fees. Nolo has confirmed that every listed attorney has a valid license and is in good standing with the bar association.

When considering whether to hire an attorney, you should ask yourself whether the attorney:

- is easy to relate to
- listens to what you have to say
- seems genuinely concerned with your disability problem
- is friendly—or aloof, and
- is willing to answer your questions in a way you can understand.

Many attorneys use paralegal assistants to help them with disability claims. This should be acceptable to you only as long as the attorney adequately supervises the paralegal, keeps up with what is happening in your claim, and personally handles any significant legal events, such as hearings. After all, you're supposed to be paying for attorney representation.

It is also important to find out what the attorneys think about working with the DDS. If they bad-mouth the DDS medical consultants and examiners, it is not likely they have good working relationships with the DDS staff. For example, some attorneys proudly proclaim how they have no interest in the opinions of DDS medical consultants or DDS job specialists (vocational analysts). This arrogant attitude cannot work to your advantage, since the SSA uses the opinions of such personnel to make disability determinations.

If the attorney says that the DDS denies everyone and that your only chance is at the administrative law judge appeal level above the DDS, don't believe it! This statement is not true. DDSs allow more claims than any other level of the SSA disability system. And appeals above the DDS can require one or more years. If your case drags on and you are eventually allowed benefits, you will get more past-due benefits (and the lawyer's share will also be higher), but can you withstand the hardship of being without your benefits that long?

Attorneys do not accept all cases that come to them. And because they usually take payment only if you win benefits (see Section F, below), they spend considerable time judging whether or not you have a reasonable chance of being awarded benefits. For example, if you're 25 years old and in good health, except for an artificial leg on which you walk well, an attorney is not likely to take your case, because anyone experienced in the Social Security system knows that your chance for benefits is small. On the other hand, if your case is fairly complex and you're older than 55, the whole picture changes. In that instance, if an attorney says you don't have a chance, visit another attorney for a second opinion.

F. Notifying the SSA of Your Choice for Representative

Once you choose a representative, you must tell the SSA in writing by completing Form SSA-1696, *Appointment of Representative*.

CAUTION

You must use forms provided by the SSA. You can obtain them at your local SSA Field Office or by calling the SSA hotline at 800-772-1213, Monday through Friday (except holidays), from 7 a.m. to 7 p.m. If you are deaf or hard of hearing, TTY service representatives are available at the same times at 800-325-0778. You can also download many necessary forms from the Social Security Administration website at www.ssa.gov.

The location of your claim determines where you should send the form. If it is at a DDS office, send the form to a Social Security Field Office. If you have filed an administrative appeal of your claim, file the form with the SSA administrative office. If you are appealing an administrative law judge's decision to the Appeals Council, send the form to the Appeals Council. An attorney or another professional representative chosen as the representative should take care of these details for you.

On the form, you give the name and address of the person who is your representative. If your representative is not an attorney, the form must show the representative's name and state that the representative accepts the appointment. Both you and the representative must sign the form, and you provide your address, Social Security number, and telephone number. If the claimant is not the same person as the wage earner (for SSDI claims), such as a parent signing for a child, the Social Security numbers of both are needed.

G. When and How Your Representative Is Paid

In both SSDI and SSI claims, attorneys and nonattorneys who represent disability applicants know that their clients don't have a lot of money to spend and will work for payment subtracted from your past-due benefits if your claim is allowed. This means that, in most instances, if you lose your claim, you don't have to pay your authorized representative, this is called a "contingency" arrangement. To avoid any misunderstanding, be clear on the nature of the fee arrangement offered before you hire someone as your representative. However, you should understand that, win or lose, your representative might expect you to pay any out-of-pocket office costs associated with handling your claim. These might include long distance telephone calls, copying birth and death certificates, travel expenses, or postage.

1. SSA Approval of Fee Agreements

The SSA must approve in writing all fee agreements between claimants and their authorized representatives.

To request approval of a fee agreement from the SSA, your authorized representative must file a copy of the agreement with your Social Security Field Office before a decision has been reached on your claim.

The SSA usually approves a fee agreement (following a decision on your claim) as long as all of the following are true:

- You and your representative both signed the agreement.
- The fee you agreed to pay your representative is no more than 25% of your past-due benefits or $6,000, whichever is less (past-due benefits are those that you have yet to receive, dating back to the date the SSA determines you were eligible for benefits).
- Your claim was approved and you were awarded past-due benefits.

Your representative must provide you with a copy of the fee agreement sent to the SSA. The SSA will consider the fee agreement and let you and your representative know of its decision.

> **EXAMPLE:** If it took 17 months from your onset date to get your claim approved, the SSA would owe you a year's worth of benefits. If that amount was more than $24,000, your representative could only get $6,000.

Fee agreements can be used by both attorney and nonattorney representatives, and for both SSDI and SSI claims. However, the actual way the representative gets paid depends on several factors (see Section 3, below). Also, remember that you can be charged additional amounts for representation by a lawyer before a federal court (see Section 4, below), as well as a representative's out-of-pocket expenses at any level.

It is important to understand that your fee agreement applies to your total SSDI and SSI benefits for the part of your fee

that is for representation before the SSA. In other words, under your fee agreement for the SSA representation, your attorney can only collect a total maximum payment of $6,000 from your past-due benefits—not a $6,000 maximum for your SSDI claim and another $6,000 maximum from your SSI past-due benefits.

If the SSA does not approve the fee agreement, it will notify you and your representative that your representative must file a fee petition. (See Section 2, below.) A representative who forgets to request approval of a fee agreement must use the fee petition process (see Section 2, below). Most representatives prefer fee agreements.

> **RESOURCE**
> **To read more about fee agreements and see sample language that the SSA suggests for these agreements,** visit the SSA's website at www.ssa.gov/representation.

2. SSA Approval of Fee Petitions

Your authorized representative might not want to make a fee agreement with you, preferring the fee petition process as a means of collecting the money. Also, if the representative forgets to do a fee agreement or the SSA fails to approve the fee agreement, the representative must file a fee petition. The SSA will not accept a fee petition until a final decision has been made on your claim.

In the petition, your representative must state in detail the amount of time spent on each service provided to you. The representative must give you a copy of the fee petition. If you disagree with the information shown, you must contact the SSA within 20 days. You should contact your SSA Field Office in writing and follow up with a telephone call a few days later to make sure it has your letter.

In evaluating a fee petition, the SSA looks to the reasonable value of the services provided. The SSA may approve your representative's request to charge you but not the amount in the petition. In that case, the SSA will tell you and your representative the approved amount. Your representative cannot charge you more than the approved amount, except for out-of-pocket expenses—such as the cost of getting your doctor's or hospital records. If you or your representative disagree with the approved amount, the person who objects can ask the SSA to look at the petition again.

A representative who charges or collects a fee without the SSA's approval, or who charges or collects more than the approved amount, may be suspended or disqualified from representing anyone before the SSA and may face criminal prosecution.

3. How Your Representative Is Paid

If your representative is an attorney, the SSA usually withholds 25% of your past-due benefits to put toward your attorneys' fee and sends you anything left over after the lawyer is paid. If the SSA fails to withhold the attorneys' fees, you must pay the attorney out of your benefit amount. If you do not pay, the SSA can withhold the amount you owe your attorney from future benefits.

You must pay the representative directly if:

- Your representative is not an attorney or appointed representative (registered with Social Security).
- Your attorney did not request fee approval or did not request it on time.
- The fee is for more than the amount the SSA withheld, in which case you must pay the balance.

In certain cases, including where you agree to pay your representative directly, your representative can accept money from you to be placed in an escrow account. The basic reason a representative would want to do this is to ensure that you pay the fees or costs. However, this is no longer much of an issue in hiring an attorney or another representative. In the past, the SSA did not withhold a representative's share of benefits in SSI claims, so it presented a particular problem for the representative to ensure receipt of fees. But most disability representatives offer services on a contingency basis, so you don't have to offer any money for an escrow account because the SSA will usually pay the attorney if you win your claim—and there is no cost to you if you lose your claim. Such a fee contingency offer is less likely, however, if you have an appeal above the SSA—in federal court.

4. Attorney Representation in Federal Court

It is possible to appeal your case to federal court if the SSA denies your claim and any administrative appeals. A federal court can order the SSA to allow your claim, or it can instruct the SSA to obtain more information or re-hear the case. To get your claim into federal court, you must file a formal appeal using an attorney.

If you appeal to federal court, the court can allow reasonable attorneys' fees for the part of your representation that involves the court proceedings. This fee is in addition to any fee allowed by a fee agreement you and your attorney might have with the SSA. Remember that the courts and the SSA are two different organizations; when you enter the federal court system, you have left the SSA behind. Whether or not you have to pay your attorney for representing your claim in federal court depends on the type of payment arrangement you have with your attorney. The SSA has no authority to approve or disapprove attorney charges for court representation.

Many attorneys, however, use "two-tier fee agreements" that allow the attorney to petition for fees if the case is appealed to federal district court. A two-tier agreement allows for the lawyer to be paid the usual maximum fee of 25% of your back pay, capped at $6,000, if you are approved at the initial application, reconsideration, or ALJ hearing stage; the attorney is free, however, to petition for fees beyond the $6,000 cap if the case goes further.

It costs money to go to federal court, and claimants frequently don't have the means to pay for such representation. Therefore, an attorney will not take your case to federal court unless he or she thinks there is a reasonable chance of winning, because if you lose, the attorney might have to pay court costs in addition to not getting paid for representing you.

On the other hand, if the payment arrangement you have with your attorney says you will have to pay for federal court representation, then the attorney's fee could be your burden—the arrangement might be that you only pay if you win, or you might have to pay whether you win or lose.

Assuming your claim is approved, the court will order the SSA to consider you disabled and start paying you benefits. Based on when the federal judge decides the onset date of your disability was, you will also be entitled to some past-due benefits from the SSA. If you have an SSDI claim, your past-due benefits could extend back to a time before you even applied for disability; if you have an SSI claim, the earliest onset would be the month after you applies for benefits (see Chapter 10). If you have both SSDI and SSI claims (concurrent claims), you can receive past-due benefits for both. Note that the judge can order the SSA to take the attorneys' fee out of your past-due benefits provided there is enough money there.

Otherwise, you and your attorney will have to work something out regarding payment for court representation.

Remember that when a federal court approves a claim, there are two payment issues that come up at the same time: the fee for your attorney for previously representing you before the SSA, and the fee your attorney will charge you for federal court representation. It is not likely that an attorney is going to represent you in court unless you have enough past-due benefits to make it worth while or can make other arrangements for payment. Most attorneys, however, will file a claim under the Equal Access to Justice Act, which will pay part of the attorneys' fees if you win your claim— see below.

It is also important for you to understand that attorney payment issues can be extremely complex and in some instances, controversial or without precedent. The comments in this section are meant to guide you in the most important general principles. They are not a substitute for expert legal advice. You should discuss payment issues in detail with your attorney until you feel comfortable with what to expect to pay.

a. Attorney Payment for SSDI Claims Allowed or Denied in Federal Court

i. Payment for SSA Representation

To receive payment by the SSA from your past-due benefits in an SSDI claim, your attorney must file a request for direct payment and submit this request to a Social Security office within 60 days of when you are notified of being granted benefits. Remember, this is only for the SSA part of your representation. If your attorney does not meet the 60-day deadline, the SSA will send you and your attorney written notice that the SSA will send you all past-due benefits unless the lawyer asks for the fee within another 20 days. If your attorney still does not file the request on time, the SSA will send you all of your past-due benefits and the attorney must seek payment from you independently.

ii. Payment for Federal Court Representation

What about the amount of fees you might owe your attorney if you win in federal court? As a requirement of federal law 42 U.S.C.A § 406(b), the court part of your charges cannot exceed 25% of your total past-due SSDI benefits.

Payment for federal court representation differs from payment for representing you solely within the SSA. Within the SSA, your representative is generally limited to 25% of your past-due benefits, up to $6,000. At the federal court level, however, the U.S. Supreme Court decided in 2019 that attorneys representing SSDI claimants who win are not limited by the same 25% of back benefits, up to a maximum of $6,000, that applies to the agency representation (*Culbertson v. Berryhill Acting Commissioner of Social Security*). In other words, payments for representation before the SSA and the federal courts are separate: unless you have a fee agreement regarding the cost of federal court representation, an attorney can charge you up to 25% of your back benefits for the SSA representation and 25% for the federal court representation, and can even charge you if you lose your case in federal court.

The judge who hears your disability case must approve the amount of the attorney's fee for the court representation. Your attorney can then ask the SSA to take this money out of your back benefits.

If you lose your case in federal court, the SSA will not pay your attorney out of your past-due benefits, because you won't have any money coming.

b. Attorney Payment for SSI Claims Allowed or Denied in Federal Court

i. Payment for SSA Representation

If you win SSI benefits in federal court, the SSA must approve the fee agreement concerning the part of your representation before the SSA. As mentioned previously, the SSA has no authority over attorneys' fees for court representation.

ii. Payment for Federal Court Representation

What about the amount of fees you might owe your attorney if you win in federal court? Again, payments for representation before the SSA and the federal courts are separate: an attorney can charge you up to 25% of your back benefits for the federal court representation in addition to the 25% of your back benefits for representation at the SSA.

The judge who hears your disability case must approve the amount of the attorneys' fee. Your attorney can then ask the SSA to take this money out of your back benefits.

5. If Someone Else Pays Your Fee

If someone will pay your attorneys' fee for you—for example, a long-term disability insurance company—the SSA still must approve the fee, except in the following cases:

- A nonprofit organization or government agency will pay the fee.
- Your representative provides the SSA with a written statement that you will not have to pay any fee or expenses.

6. The Equal Access to Justice Act

The Equal Access to Justice Act (EAJA, found at 5 U.S.C. 504, 28 U.S.C. 2412), is an additional way attorneys can collect fees ($125 per hour) for representing you before a federal court, thereby decreasing your own costs. Whatever your lawyer can collect under EAJA is that much less of your back pay benefits that you would have to pay the attorney. EAJA fees are paid directly to you, not to your attorney, and then you pay the attorney from that money.

If you are planning on appealing to a federal court, you can ask your attorney to file an application for EAJA fees in order to pay legal bills. Application for EAJA assistance can be made within 30 days of the court's judgment, but in actual practice, applications may work 61–90 days after the court's judgment.

You will get paid EAJA expenses only if you win your case; that is, if the court reverses your prior SSA disability denial into an allowance. If you lose your appeal as a federal court denial, then you could owe your attorney money, depending on the type of payment agreement you have.

If the court remands your claim to an administrative law judge instead of reaching a decision, you can still collect EAJA fees. Generally, unless the court finds that the SSA was substantially justified in denying you benefits (had a good reason to do so), you will be awarded EAJA fees.

Note that court filing and administrative fees can cost hundreds of dollars, and EAJA will not cover these expenses, unless you ask and the court believes you are financially unable to pay them yourself.

Note that an attorney cannot collect fees from your back pay and from EAJA for the same federal court representation. (An attorney who is known or suspected to have collected fees under both statutes without refunding the smaller fee to you may be in violation of federal law.)

TIP

More information. If you have any questions about your right to representation, call the SSA at 800-772-1213.

H. Keeping Up on the Law Yourself

With or without a lawyer, you should realize that the material in this book can change between printings. The U.S. Congress and the Social Security Administration are constantly updating and revising the rules that affect you. To assist you, Nolo prints updates to all of its books on its website at www.nolo.com (search for the name of this book, and if there are any updates, they'll appear in the "Updates" tab).

Glossary of Bureaucratic Terms

Adjudication. The process of determining a disability claim.

Adjudicator. A person officially involved in making the disability determination.

Administrative law judge (ALJ). An SSA employee and attorney who holds hearings at the first level of appeals above the state agency (DDS).

Allegations. The medical problems that a claimant puts forth as the basis for wanting disability benefits.

Alleged onset date (AOD). The date a claimant states that he or she became unable to work due to impairments.

Claimant. The person who applies for disability benefits.

Closed period. If an impairment does not qualify as severe enough for benefits at the time of adjudication, benefits can still be given for prior periods of at least 12 months during which there was sufficient severity.

Concurrent claims. Two claims filed at the same time, under different aspects of the law. Usually, concurrent claims are SSDI Title 2 and SSI/Title 16 claims filed at the same time.

Consultative examination (CE). Physical or mental examination of a claimant at the expense of the SSA.

Consultative examination (CE) doctor. A doctor or another health professional paid by the SSA to perform a consultative examination. See "consultative examination."

Continuing disability review (CDR). The process by which the SSA reevaluates the severity of a claimant's impairments to determine whether there has been significant medical improvement.

Diary. A term that has two meanings:
- the interval of time until a claim is reevaluated after benefits are allowed, and
- the interval of time a state agency holds a claim to determine the outcome of some medical problem or treatment, before a final determination is made. When a claim is held to determine an outcome, the state agency will send the claimant a letter saying that a final decision has been delayed for a specified amount of time, usually not more than three months.

Disability determination. The determination that an adult is unable to work and qualifies for benefits or that a child qualifies for benefits.

Disability Determination for Social Security Administration (DDS-SSA) or Disability Determination Services (DDS). A state agency. See "state agency."

Disability hearing officer (DHO). An experienced disability examiner who interviews claimants receiving disability payments to determine if benefits should continue. Claimants appear before a DHO to appeal the termination of disability benefits when they are about to lose them.

Duration. How long a claimant has had an impairment severe enough to qualify for Social Security disability benefits.

Equal. Allowance term meaning that a claimant has an impairment as severe as required by the listings, although no specific listing exactly applies to his or her claim. The equal concept can be applied to single or multiple listings, as well as single or multiple impairments, as appropriate to a particular claim.

Examiner. The DDS examiner is specially trained to make initial, reconsideration, and continuing disability review determinations regarding nonmedical evidence from a claimant's file. Examiners physically control individual claimant files that are assigned to them, as well as communicate with claimants or their representatives. (See Chapter 5.)

Impairments. The medical problems that a claimant has, either mental or physical.

Initial claim. The first application for disability benefits.

Listings. Lists of rules giving the medical criteria that must be fulfilled for benefits to be granted without consideration of age, education, or work experience. Separate listings exist for adults and children. Listings are found in the Listing of Impairments in federal regulations (Code of Federal Regulations, Title 20, Part 404, Subpart P, Appendix 1, and reinterpreted in this book's online Medical Listings in Parts 1 through 14).

Medical consultant (MC). A medical doctor, osteopath, or psychologist who works under contract or as an employee of a state agency (DDS), or who works in some similar role in some other level of the SSA. The SSA may refer to those who evaluate mental disorders as "psychological consultants." The MC is specially trained by the SSA and other MCs to make the "overall determination of impairment severity" in initial, reconsideration, and continuing disability review determinations. This determination must be done according to federal rules, regulations, and other written guidelines based on the medical and nonmedical evidence. All medical evidence used in these determinations is obtained from medical and other sources outside of the state agency. MC determinations should not be biased, and, therefore, the MCs do not meet, talk to, or treat claimants concerning their individual claims. Medical consultants are not the same as doctors who do consultative examinations. Consultative examination doctors examine claimants for a fee paid by the SSA. Unlike medical consultants, they do not make disability determinations.

Medical-vocational allowance. Allowance of disability benefits based on a combination of RFC, age, education, and work experience.

Meet. Allowance term meaning that a claimant's impairment exactly fulfills the requirements of a listing.

Not severe (nonsevere). Term that means all impairments considered together are still not sufficient to produce any significant restriction in the functional capacity of a claimant. A mild or slight impairment.

Onset. The date at which a claimant's impairments are sufficiently severe to qualify for disability. This is not necessarily the same as the date when the impairment first arose.

Presumptive disability. A privilege of SSI/Title 16 claimants in which they can receive benefits (and sometimes Medicaid) for up to six months before a final decision is made on their claim by a state agency. SSDI/Title 2 claimants cannot have presumptive disability.

Projected rating. The opinion of the SSA about the level of residual impairment severity that is expected to exist 12 months after the onset of allowance-level severity. Allowance-level severity must persist 12 months before benefits are granted. Such a projected rating could result in either allowance or denial, depending on medical or vocational factors. If a projected rating is a denial, it is a way of saying that while an impairment may be severe enough to be disabling at the present time, it is expected to improve to nonallowance severity in less than 12 months.

Reconsideration claim. A denial of benefits or an unfavorable decision made by a DDS that is being reconsidered at the request of the claimant. Reconsideration is not automatic; a claimant must request it.

Residual functional capacity (RFC). A claimant's maximum mental or physical capabilities as determined by a DDS medical consultant in instances in which the impairment does not meet or equal a listing but is more than "not severe" (slight). See "medical consultant."

State agency. One of the agencies in each state funded by the Social Security Administration to make decisions on disability claims. The examiners and other administrative personnel are state employees, even though they're funded with federal dollars. Also known as Disability Determination Service (DDS).

Substantial gainful activity (SGA). The standard for determining a claimant is making too much money through work to be eligible for disability benefits. Blind claimants can make more than nonblind claimants. The amount that you can earn without losing benefits is increased yearly.

Treating doctor. Any medical doctor or psychologist who treats a claimant at the claimant's own request and is not paid by the SSA. A treating doctor can also be the claimant's CE doctor, if the treating doctor has agreed with the SSA to do such exams. See "consultative examination." According to federal regulations, your treating doctor is not involved in making disability determinations.

Trial work period (TWP). An interval of time for claimants already on the disability rolls in which they can work and continue to draw benefits until it is clear they can actually perform jobs well enough to take care of themselves.

Vocational analyst. In the DDS, an experienced disability examiner with special training in evaluating the combination of RFC, age, education, and work experience regarding a claimant's ability to perform various jobs.

Examples of Technical Rationales for Denials

We have included this appendix of technical rationales for denials to give you added insight into how and why the Social Security Administration issues denials in specific cases. In the following examples, the doctor and hospital names and dates have been removed or changed. Names and dates must, however, be listed in actual notice rationales. If the DDS fails to list some of your important medical sources, you can assume that they were not used in your disability determination. This can be the basis for an appeal. Explanations of abbreviations and medical terms have been added in brackets so the rationales are a little easier to follow.

Form SSA-4268, *Denials From Initial Application*

Example 1: Impairment(s) Not Severe

The only source of medical evidence provided by the claimant was the Mercy Hospital outpatient treatment report. Since this report was incidental to the claimant's alleged impairments and no other medical evidence existed, two consultative examinations (CEs) were arranged: one to evaluate the claimant's general health, the other to assess the possibility of organic brain damage due to apparent alcohol abuse. The claimant alleges disability since January 2, 20xx, due to "bad lungs, high blood pressure, and forgetfulness." There is no

indication that the claimant has worked since that date.

A review of the Mercy Hospital report indicates the claimant was treated for a bruised arm. An X-ray was taken due to complaints of pain in her arm. The X-ray was negative. She was treated for abrasions and released within hours of admittance.

The general CE was done by Dr. Meyer. Dr. Meyer's report notes the claimant alleged constant fatigue and an inability to remember recent events. She admitted to drinking about two six-packs of beer every day and to smoking one to two packs of cigarettes daily for at least three years. Medical examination shows the claimant's height as 66 inches and her weight as 140 pounds. Her blood pressure is 124/85 repeated; pulse 76 and regular. Some increased A/P [anterior-posterior or front to back] diameter of the chest, distant breath sounds, and scattered rhonchi [a type of abnormal breathing sound, heard through a stethoscope] are noted. The chest X-ray is consistent with chronic obstructive pulmonary disease (COPD) with somewhat flattened diaphragms. No infiltrates are noted. PFTs [pulmonary function tests] were obtained and show FEV1 [forced expiratory volume in 1 second] of 1.6 liters and MVV [maximum voluntary ventilation] of 75 L/min, both recorded after inhaled bronchodilators. The EKG [electrocardiogram] is normal, as is the neurologic examination. Extremities show no muscle wasting or weakness. Slight hepatomegaly [enlarged liver] is noted; however, LFTs [liver function tests] are normal with the exception of an elevated SGOT [a liver enzyme] of 75 units. The CBC [complete blood count] is normal with the exception of an MCV [mean corpuscular volume] of 110.

Analysis of findings based on the above medical summation shows the claimant's breathing capacity, as evidenced by PFT values, is not significantly diminished. In addition, despite some liver enlargement and elevated SGOT, other liver studies were normal. The neurological system was essentially intact, and blood pressure was within normal limits. Consequently, no impairment related to these findings exists, because they are essentially normal.

To assess the possibility of organic brain syndrome, the claimant was referred to Dr. Johnson. His assessment includes use of a WAIS [Wechsler Adult Intelligence Scale], the Wechsler Memory Scale, and the Bender-Gestalt. No indication of memory loss or psychosis is shown to exist. The claimant tested to be above average intellectually with a full-scale IQ of 110.

Dr. Johnson's report indicates the claimant admitted to drinking to steady her nerves, but she did not report any disorder of thought or constriction of interest. She appeared to have good personal habits. According to Dr. Johnson's report and the report by the DO [district office, same as Field Office], her daily activities are not restricted. She does not appear withdrawn or isolated. She helps her mother take care of the house and does the shopping.

The above medical summary indicates the claimant's mental functional restrictions are present only during acute intoxication. The claimant has above-normal intellect and normal memory and thought processes. She does not behave bizarrely. There is no indication she cannot understand and follow directions. Appropriate daily activities show there is no significant restriction of work-related functions. There is no evidence that the individual cannot perform basic work-related functions on a sustained, longitudinal basis.

For an impairment to be considered severe, it must significantly limit the individual's physical or mental abilities to do basic work activities. Medical evidence does not demonstrate an impairment that is severe, nor does the combined impact of respiratory, liver, and psychiatric impairments produce a severe impairment. Accordingly, the claimant is found not disabled because she has no severe impairment or any combination of impairments that is severe.

Example 2: Can Perform Past Work

The claimant has said that he became unable to work as of 6/15/2015 due to "a heart condition." He was in the hospital when he applied and was to have bypass surgery. There is no work issue.

The medical evidence documents the presence of coronary artery disease. The claimant was hospitalized 6/15/2015 due to chest pain, with EKG changes suggestive of ischemia. Cardiac catheterization showed 75% obstruction of the left main coronary artery. He was discharged to await bypass surgery. Triple bypass surgery was performed 6/30/2015. Three months after surgery, the treating physician reported that there was no chest pain. No treadmill test had been done and none was planned. The doctor said the claimant should limit lifting to 10–20 pounds.

The evidence documents the presence of a severe cardiovascular impairment. However, the findings do not meet or equal the severity of any of the listed impairments. While Listing 4.04C1.b was met at the time of the angiogram, the bypass surgery improved the condition, and there is no longer any chest pain. The claimant would be restricted from lifting more than ten pounds frequently or more than 20 pounds occasionally due to his heart condition. There are no other medically imposed limitations or restrictions. The individual is capable of performing light work.

After a military career that ended in 2005, the claimant did no work until 1/2008 when he was employed as a cashier in a discount liquor house. This was full-time work at SGA [substantial gainful activity] levels until 1/2010. From 1/2010 until AOD [alleged onset date], 6/15/2015, he worked on weekends only, and that work was not SGA. The period 1/2008–1/2010 lies within the relevant 15-year period and was of sufficient duration

for him to gain the job experience necessary for average job performance. Therefore, his job as cashier has current relevance.

Demands of the job included sitting most of the day while operating a cash register, observing the merchandise being purchased, taking the customers' money, and making change. These duties entailed the abilities to sit, see, talk, reach, handle, finger, and feel. He also demonstrated an elementary knowledge of mathematics and cash register function. It was occasionally necessary for him to stand and walk a few feet to secure a register tape and then insert the tape into the machine.

With the exertional capacity to do light work, and in the absence of any nonexertional limitations, this individual is able to do his past relevant work as he described it. Therefore, he is not disabled.

Example 3: Can Perform Other Work

The claimant has alleged disability since 5/1/2020 due to "diabetic, hearing, heart." When he has diabetic attacks, he has cold sweats, shakes, and acts drunk. He has no chest pain. The DO claims representative noted that he had a hearing aid and occasionally needed questions repeated. The claimant is not engaging in any work activity.

Medical evidence reveals the presence of insulin-dependent diabetes. There are allegations of frequent diabetic attacks, but there are no medical records to support this. A general consultative examination was obtained, as there was insufficient evidence from the treating source to evaluate severity. This revealed the following abnormal findings: Corrected vision was 20/25 with grade one over four diabetic changes of the fundi [retinas]. He wore a hearing aid and had difficulty hearing a tuning fork. Pulses were two plus over four. The lower extremities showed some mild chronic venous insufficiency but no varicose veins. There was no evidence of diabetic neuropathy. No heart problem was documented. There is X-ray evidence of an abdominal aortic aneurysm. This is asymptomatic, and surgery is not anticipated. There is no complaint of chest pain. A consultative hearing evaluation was done because further documentation of severity was needed. The audiogram showed bilateral hearing loss between 65 and 85 decibels. Speech discrimination is 88 percent, and a hearing aid is recommended and used by the claimant. He can hear loud conversational speech and can hear over the phone.

None of the above impairments is of the severity described in the Listing of Impairments. The combination of impairments also does not meet or equal the listed impairments.

The evidence reveals the presence of diabetes, aortic aneurysm, and a hearing deficit. Per SSA-4734-F4, dated September 10, 2014, heavy lifting would be precluded due to the aneurysm. The claimant can lift and carry 25 pounds frequently and up to 50 pounds oc-

casionally. The hearing deficit and alleged insulin reactions would preclude work around dangerous machinery or at heights.

The claimant is 60 years old and has completed nine years of school, which is considered to be limited education. He has worked for 34 years as a wire drawer for a wire company.

This heavy, semiskilled work performed in a noisy and hazardous work setting required him to be on his feet all day, frequently lift 50-pound coils of wire, and occasionally lift coils that weigh 100 pounds. It also required frequent pushing, pulling, stooping, crouching, reaching, handling, and fingering for purposes of situating the coils on the wire-drawing machine and drawing the desired finished product. The claimant set up the machine, demonstrated knowledge of the characteristics of various metals, and assessed conformance to specifications. Demands of his past relevant work correlate to those of Wire Drawer (wire), DOT 614.382-010 [job description in the *Dictionary of Occupational Titles*].

The claimant's exertional limitations in themselves as translated into a maximum sustained RFC for medium work would prevent him from doing his past relevant work. The special medical-vocational characteristics pertaining to those cases that feature arduous, unskilled work, or no work are not present. The exertional capability to do medium work presents a potential occupational base of approximately 2,500 unskilled sedentary, light, and medium occupations, which represent a significant vocational opportunity. This individual's hearing impairment and the medical restriction to avoid working around dangerous machinery and at heights would only minimally narrow that potential occupational base; age, education, and past work experience under the framework provided by [Medical-Vocational] Rule 203.04, he is expected to effectuate a vocational accommodation to other work.

Some examples of unskilled occupations that are within his RFC include: Bagger (ret. tr.), DOT 920.687-014, Turner (can. & preserv.), DOT 522.687-038, and Crate Liner (furn.), DOT 920.687-078. According to data shown in County Business Patterns for 1982, Harris County, Texas, had over 230,000 employees working in the retail trade industry, over 30,000 of which were employed in grocery stores. Both the furniture manufacturing and wholesale furniture industries combined employed over 5,000 individuals. Another 200–500 worked at canning and preserving fruits and vegetables. Based on these figures, which pertain only to one county, it can be inferred reasonably that the cited occupations exist as individual jobs in significant numbers not only in the region in which the individual resides, but also throughout the national economy. Therefore, since he has the capacity to do other work, disability is not established.

> **TIP**
> **More technical rationales from real Forms SSA-4268 are below.** These are from decisions to end benefits following a continuing disability review (CDR) and illustrate the many reasons benefits may be terminated. Again, explanations of abbreviations and medical terms have been added in brackets so the rationales are a little easier to follow.

Form SSA-4268, *Denials From Continuing Disability Review (CDR)*

Example 1: Not Severe, Medical Improvement (MI) Occurred

The beneficiary was found to be disabled beginning 8/10/2014, because of a fractured left femur with slow healing. The impairment met the requirements of Listing 1.06. Current evaluation is necessary because medical improvement was expected. He indicates that he is still unable to perform work activity due to a left leg problem. He has not engaged in any substantial gainful activity since onset.

Current medical evidence reveals that the disabled individual had full weight-bearing status at an examination in February 2016. X-rays interpreted at that time revealed that the fracture was well healed. A consultative orthopedic evaluation was secured because range-of-motion data were needed. The consulting orthopedic surgeon reported that the individual had good range of motion of both lower extremities. He walked with a normal gait and experienced no difficulty in getting on and off the examining table. His impairment does not meet or equal listing severity.

At the CPD [comparison point decision] the individual was unable to walk without crutches, and X-rays did not show the expected amount of healing. His impairment has decreased in severity because he is fully weight bearing, and an X-ray shows solid union; therefore, medical improvement has occurred. Since the beneficiary met a listing at the CPD but currently no longer meets that listing, the medical improvement is related to the ability to work. Although he alleges a left leg problem, his current impairment is not severe, as he now has no significant restrictions on standing, walking, lifting, or other work activities.

As medical improvement has occurred and the individual is able to engage in SGA, disability ceases April 2016, and benefits will terminate in June 2016.

Example 2: MI Occurred, Can Perform Past Work

This individual was found to be disabled beginning 8/17/2013 because of coronary artery disease. The impairment equaled Listing 4.04A1. The beneficiary has completed a nine-month trial work period. She continues to work as a telephone solicitor, with earnings indicative of SGA. Benefits have been stopped as indicated on SSA-833-U5 on 11/13/2015. She feels she still has a severe heart condition that limits activity. A current medical decision is needed to determine "impairment severity" and thus, entitlement for an extended period of eligibility.

Medical evidence indicates that the beneficiary underwent bypass surgery in June 2014. Although she initially progressed well, she subsequently began to complain of chest pain and shortness of breath. She underwent a second bypass surgery in April 2015. Current examination revealed normal heart sounds with only occasional premature ventricular contractions. The beneficiary experiences chest pain infrequently with heavy exertion. The pain is relieved with nitroglycerin or rest. The doctor stated that the patient would not be able to return to work activity. The treating cardiologist reported in March 2016 that the beneficiary performed a stress test to 7 METS [metabolic equivalents]. A chest X-ray revealed only mild cardiomegaly. The treating doctor assessed that because of the beneficiary's history of heart disorder, she should avoid lifting in excess of 25 pounds.

The record reveals that the patient underwent two bypass surgeries for her heart disorder. Chest pain of cardiac origin is experienced infrequently, but a treadmill exercise test was negative at 5 METS. It showed abnormalities at 7 METS. Therefore, the evidence does not show current findings that meet or equal the listed impairments. The second bypass surgery improved circulation to the heart, and symptoms have decreased. Therefore, medical improvement has occurred.

At the time of the CPD, a listing was equaled. Since the impairment no longer meets or equals that listing, the medical improvement is related to the ability to work.

The record reveals that the beneficiary continues to have a severe cardiovascular impairment that limits her ability to perform basic work activities. There is a current capacity to lift a maximum of 20 pounds occasionally and 10 pounds frequently.

The beneficiary is limited to light work activity. Her past work from 3/2005 to 8/2010 was that of a laundry marker, which involved such activities as sorting laundry, putting names on articles, etc. This is a light, nonstressful job. Accordingly, she can return to her past relevant work, as she has the functional capacity to do light work.

Although the beneficiary's treating physician stated she would not be able to return to work, the weight to be given such statements depends upon the extent to which they are supported by specific and complete clinical findings and are consistent with other evidence in the beneficiary's case. The clinical findings and other evidence do not support the conclusion that the beneficiary is disabled for any gainful work.

Because medical improvement has been demonstrated by a decrease in medical severity related to the ability to work, and because the beneficiary is able to engage in SGA, impairment severity ceases in 3/2016.

Example 3: MI Occurred, Can Do Other Work

The beneficiary has been disabled since 2/6/2012 because of musculoskeletal injuries sustained in a motorcycle accident. He was found to be limited to sedentary work and [Medical-]Vocational Rule 201.09 directed a finding of disabled. He has not worked since his established onset date. The beneficiary alleges he remains unable to return to any work activity because he still has knee pain. Current evaluation is needed because medical improvement was expected.

The treating physician reported that he continued treating the beneficiary for complaints of pain to the lower extremities. He states that he treated the beneficiary with medication and advised him to exercise. X-rays taken at the examination on 1/8/2015 revealed only spurring in the right knee, in addition to old healed fractures. A consultative examination was arranged to obtain range of motion. Evidence from the consulting orthopedist dated 3/1/2015 reveals that the beneficiary continues to walk with an abnormal gait. Flexion of the right knee is limited to 120 degrees. The left can be fully flexed. Range of motion of the hips and ankles is normal. The impairment does not meet or equal the requirements of the listings.

At the comparison point, the beneficiary was unable to ambulate for short distances as a result of his right knee impairment. X-rays revealed that all other injuries were healed except the right knee, which did not have complete healing. Current medical evidence demonstrates a decrease in severity since an X-ray revealed that the right knee fracture is well healed with minimal spurring and there is only mild limitation of motion. Therefore, medical improvement has occurred, as there is a decrease in medical severity. He now has the ability to stand and walk six out of eight hours and to lift 20 pounds occasionally and ten pounds frequently, which is a wide range of light work. The medical improvement that has occurred is related to his ability to work, because he could only do sedentary work activity at the CPD. The beneficiary's impairment imposes significant restrictions on his ability to perform basic work activities and is severe.

Although the beneficiary alleges pain in the right knee, the fracture is well healed, with minimal spurring and mild limitation of motion. He is restricted to light work, but the clinical findings do not establish an impairment that produces pain of such severity as to prevent the beneficiary from performing any gainful activity.

The disabled individual is 53 years of age, has a limited education, and has a 20-year work history as a general laborer in a foundry, which is unskilled work involving heavy lifting and carrying. Since the beneficiary is limited to light work, he would be unable to perform his past work due to the exertional demands involved. The special medical-vocational characteristics pertaining to those cases

that feature arduous, unskilled work or no work are not present. The facts in this case correspond exactly with the criteria of [Medical-]Vocational Rule 202.10, which directs a finding of not disabled. Since there is medical improvement and the individual has the ability to do SGA, disability is ceased in 2/2015, and benefits will be terminated as of 4/2015.

Example 4: MI Occurred; Multiple Not Severe Impairments; Combined Effect Is Severe, but One Impairment Is a Subsequent Impairment; Can Perform Other Work

The beneficiary has been under a disability since 10/19/2013 due to rheumatic heart disease with mitral stenosis [narrowing of the mitral heart valve] and peptic ulcer [of intestine], which led to an allowance in the framework of [Medical-] Vocational Rule 202.10. The case is being evaluated now because medical improvement is possible. The beneficiary believes he is still disabled because of his heart condition, plus recent pulmonary disease. He attempted working a few years ago but had to stop after three weeks. There is no SGA issue.

Medical evidence reveals a history of rheumatic heart disease that required hospitalization for congestive heart failure. This has responded to treatment, and currently there is no chest pain and no evidence of pulmonary or peripheral edema, according to his physician. There are no symptoms related to peptic ulcer disease, since diet has been adjusted. Recently, shortness of breath has been increasing. He had been smoking two packs of cigarettes a day for 20 years but has stopped because of respiratory problems. A consultative examination was scheduled for evaluation of his respiratory impairment with pulmonary function testing.

On physical examination, height was 69 inches and weight was 180 pounds. Breath sounds were diminished, with prolonged expiration and an expiratory wheeze. The chest was otherwise clear. On examination of the heart, a diastolic rumble [abnormal heart sound] at the apex. An EKG showed a prominent wide P-wave suggestive of left atrial enlargement, which was confirmed on the chest X-ray. The heart size otherwise was within normal limits. The lung fields were hyperaerated [over-expanded] and diaphragms were somewhat flattened [signs of emphysema]. Ventilatory function [breathing test] studies done by the consultant revealed post-bronchodilator [drugs] FEV1 was 1.9 liters and MVV 76 liters per minute [abnormally low results indicate emphysema, but not at listing-level severity].

Current medical findings do not meet or equal the findings described in any listed impairment. There is no current evidence of congestive heart failure and no active ulcer. This shows medical improvement, as there is a decrease in the medical severity of impairments present at the CPD. At that time, the functional capacity was for light work activity. The current RFC, considering only the rheumatic heart disease and peptic ulcer, shows full capacity to do all work activities, and these impairments are now not severe. Therefore, medical improvement related to ability to do work is demonstrated.

Although the heart and digestive impairments are not severe when considered alone, considering their effect on ability to perform work activities in combination with a respiratory impairment, the beneficiary would be restricted to lifting up to 50 pounds occasionally and 25 pounds frequently. The beneficiary now has the capacity to perform a full range of medium work. He cannot perform his prior work as baker helper (heavy, unskilled work). It involved much lifting of things, such as bags of flour (up to 100 pounds), racks of baked items, and piles of unfolded boxes. Although his most recent work was arduous and unskilled, it lasted only 17 years, and he previously did semiskilled work. Therefore, the special medical-vocational characteristics pertaining to those cases, which feature arduous, unskilled work or no work, are not present. He is of advanced age (56) with limited education (grade 6) and meets [Medical-] Vocational Rule 203.11, which indicates the ability to do SGA. Because there is medical improvement, demonstrated by decreased medical severity and related to the ability to work, and the individual has the ability to do SGA, disability is ceased on 4/2015. Benefits will be terminated 6/2015.

Example 5: MI Occurred; It Is Obvious That the Vocational Exception Also Applies; Can Perform Other Work

The beneficiary was initially allowed disability benefits from 12/7/2013, because of injuries received in a motorcycle accident. At the time of the CPD, he had a traumatic left above-the-knee amputation with persistent stump complications, inability to use a prosthesis, and a right recurrent shoulder dislocation. The impairment was found to meet Listing 1.05B. The current evaluation is necessary because medical improvement was expected. The beneficiary states that he is still disabled because of the left leg amputation and difficulty walking with his prosthesis. He has not worked since the onset date.

The medical evidence reveals that following his left above-the-knee amputation in 12/2013, the beneficiary experienced persistent pain and tenderness about the stump and underwent three stump revisions. The most recent revision was 2/1/2015 for excision of a bony spur and painful scar. Office notes from the beneficiary's treating physician show that following the latest stump revision, the beneficiary was able to wear his prosthesis over an extended period of time without much discomfort. Recent examination of the stump revealed that there were no neuromas [painful nerve tangles] or other abnormalities. An X-ray did not demonstrate any bony spurs or complications. Furthermore, the beneficiary

has had no recent problems with right shoulder dislocation. He had full range of motion of his shoulder without pain or instability. The beneficiary no longer has an impairment that meets or equals the level of severity described in the listings.

The beneficiary was unable to use his prosthesis at the time of the comparison point decision because of repeated stump complications. Current medical findings show that these complications have resolved, and the beneficiary is able to ambulate with his prosthesis over an extended period of time without discomfort. Therefore, medical improvement has occurred. Although he alleges difficulty walking with his prosthesis, the beneficiary has the residual functional capacity to stand and walk for two hours and to sit for six hours with no further restrictions. Since his current condition no longer meets or equals Listing 1.05B, his medical improvement is related to the ability to work.

The beneficiary received evaluation and counseling through the Department of Vocational Rehabilitation. He obtained funds to attend a two-year program at Central University. In December 2015, he received an associate degree in computer science. The combination of education and counseling constitute vocational therapy.

The beneficiary has a severe impairment that limits him to the performance of sedentary work. The beneficiary is 30 years old, with 16 years of education. He has four years of relevant work experience as a painter.

This job involved standing and walking at least six out of eight hours. The beneficiary is unable to perform his past work because of limitations on standing and walking. The special medical-vocational characteristics pertaining to those cases that feature arduous, unskilled work or no work are not present. Additionally, his ability to perform sedentary work has been enhanced by vocational therapy; therefore, the vocational therapy exception applies. The beneficiary meets [Medical-]Vocational Rule 201.28, which directs a decision of not disabled. Medical improvement is established, the vocational therapy exception applies, and the beneficiary is able to engage in SGA. Therefore, the beneficiary can no longer be considered disabled under the provisions of the Social Security Act as of May 2016, and benefits are terminated as of July 2016.

Example 6: MI Is Not Related to Ability to Do Work, but Vocational Therapy Exception Applies; Can Perform Other Work

The beneficiary was found to be disabled beginning 8/3/2013 as a result of a crush injury with fracture of his left ankle. He was restricted to the performance of light work and thereby met the requirements of [Medical-]Vocational Rule 202.06, which directed a decision of disabled. Current medical evidence was obtained because medical improvement was expected. The beneficiary states that he continues to be disabled because of left ankle pain and difficulty standing and walking. He has not worked since onset of his disability.

Recent medical information from the beneficiary's physician shows that the beneficiary continues to have pain and numbness in his left foot. An ankle fusion was done 9/2014 to provide a stable joint and to permit weight bearing. He is fully weight bearing now but walks with a prominent limp. In order to further document severity and obtain a current X-ray, the beneficiary was examined by a consulting orthopedic physician. Clinical examination of the left ankle revealed some thickening of the heel, but the fusion appeared to be stable. Ankle movements are limited to 10 degrees dorsiflexion [upward movement] and 20 degrees plantar-flexion [downward movement]. An X-ray was consistent with a healed subtalar arthrodesis [surgical ankle fusion] and moderate traumatic degenerative changes. Neurological evaluation revealed an absent left ankle jerk and inability to walk on heels and toes. There was decreased sensation over the lateral and dorsal [upper] aspects of the left foot and decreased strength of the left extensor hallucis longus [muscle that moves the great toe upward].

The beneficiary's impairments do not meet or equal the level of severity described in the listings. An X-ray shows that arthritis has developed at the fracture site. The beneficiary continues to experience left ankle pain. Further, he has an abnormal gait and limitation of motion of his ankle.

However, since the ankle fusion, the beneficiary has full weight bearing, which is medical improvement since the CPD. His left ankle impairment continues to restrict his ability to stand and walk to six hours during an eight-hour day. The beneficiary remains limited to the performance of a wide range of light work, lifting 20 lbs. occasionally and ten pounds frequently. This is the same RFC as that at the CPD. Therefore, the medical improvement is not related to his ability to work.

Since the comparison point decision, the beneficiary underwent vocational counseling through the Department of Rehabilitation Services and enrolled in an 18-month training program on small appliance repair. He completed the course on 11/30/2015, after working on appliances such as radios, electrical tools, and a variety of small household appliances.

The recent completion of this specialized training course, in conjunction with counseling, constitutes vocational therapy. This therapy has enhanced the beneficiary's ability to perform work because he has acquired a skill that provides for direct entry into light work.

Although the beneficiary continues to experience left ankle pain, he is fully weight bearing and is able to perform light work. The clinical findings do not establish an impairment that results in pain of such severity as to preclude him from engaging in any substantial gainful activity.

The beneficiary has a severe impairment that restricts him to light work. He is 57 years old with 12 years of education. He has six years of relevant work experience as a truck driver, which is a medium semi-skilled job. The beneficiary is unable to perform work as a truck driver because of the exertional demands of the job, and there are no transferable skills. The special medical-vocational characteristics pertaining to those cases which feature arduous, unskilled work or no work are not present. However, as a result of vocational therapy since the comparison point decision, the beneficiary has obtained job skills that are useful in the performance of light work and, therefore, meets [Medical-]Vocational Rule 202.08, which directs a decision of not disabled. He can do such occupations as an Electrical-Appliance Repairer (DOT 723.381-010), a Radio Repairer (DOT 720.281-010), or an Electrical Tool Repairer (DOT 729.281-022), all skilled light work in the electrical equipment industry. According to the Labor Market Trends Bulletin and the Virginia Department of Labor and Industry, over 30,000 individuals are employed in the electrical equipment industry in Virginia, and the cited occupations are well represented throughout that industry. It can be inferred that the occupations exist as individual jobs in significant numbers in the region where the individual lives and throughout the national economy.

Although there has been no medical improvement in the beneficiary's impairment related to the ability to work, the vocational therapy exception to medical improvement applies, and the beneficiary is able to engage in SGA. The beneficiary is no longer disabled as of 3/2016, and benefits are terminated as of 5/2016.

Example 7: No MI; Not Severe Impairment(s), but Error Exception Applies

The beneficiary was initially allowed disability benefits from 6/21/2016 because of chronic obstructive pulmonary disease and asthma. She was restricted to light work and [Medical-]Vocational Rule 202.09 was applied. Current findings were obtained because medical improvement is possible. The beneficiary alleges that she is still unable to work because of emphysema and has not worked since her onset.

A report from the beneficiary's treating physician states that the beneficiary has chronic obstructive pulmonary disease and complains of shortness of breath. She also has been diagnosed as having asthma, allergic sinusitis, and hay fever. These conditions are controlled with medications. A consultative exam was necessary to obtain ventilatory studies. A chest X-ray revealed mild chronic obstructive pulmonary disease. Pulmonary function studies [4/2/2016] showed FEV1 of 1.7 and MVV of 75. A physical exam showed a height of 5 feet 2 inches and weight of 120 pounds. There were decreased breath sounds; otherwise, the chest was clear [normal] to percussion

[thumping] and auscultation [listening]. The impairment does not meet or equal the level of severity described in the listings.

The beneficiary was receiving treatment for asthma and COPD at the comparison point. She was hospitalized in October 2016 for an asthma attack. Ventilatory studies done during the admission showed a functional restriction to light work, and the claim was allowed using a [Medical-] Vocational rule. Review of the records demonstrates that the studies were done while the beneficiary was in an acute phase of asthma. Wheezes and rales [abnormal breath sounds] were noted, and no broncho-dilator [drug] was administered prior to testing. Documentation guidelines in effect at the CPD prohibit the use of ventilatory studies performed in the presence of bronchospasm [narrowed airways]. Outpatient records sent later reveal that ventilatory testing was repeated in December 2016. These studies show an FEV1 of 1.9 and MVV of 84. Medical improvement has not occurred [because there is no significant difference between the 4/2016 and 12/2016 breathing test results]. However, the error exception applies because the beneficiary was allowed ventilatory studies performed in the presence of bronchospasm without the administration of bronchodilators, and additional evidence that relates to the CPD shows that if that evidence had been considered in making the CPD, disability would not have been established.

The beneficiary does not have any restrictions on standing, walking, or lifting as a result of her breathing impairment, and her impairment is not severe. Therefore, the beneficiary retains the capacity to do SGA.

The error exception of the Medical Improvement Review Standard (MIRS) applies, and the beneficiary has the ability to perform SGA. Disability ceases April 2016, and benefits will terminate as of June 2016.

Example 8: Failure to Cooperate

The beneficiary has been under a disability since 4/13/2010 due to histiocytic lymphoma of the ileum [lymph node cancer affecting the third part of the small intestine] that equaled the listing. Current evaluation is necessary because medical improvement is possible. There has been no work since onset. The beneficiary says he is still disabled because of stomach problems. He had chemotherapy and radiation therapy after his operation. Because he has ulcers, he must avoid certain foods.

The only treatment source given by the beneficiary was Wadsworth Memorial Hospital. The Oncology [cancer] Clinic notes indicate he had completed chemotherapy. He was last seen 12/8/2015, at which time he was progressing satisfactorily. He weighed 170 pounds with height of 6 feet. Lymph nodes were shotty [small and hard, like shot], and the liver was enlarged. Since no current medical evidence was available, a consultative examination was scheduled for February 10, 2016.

The beneficiary failed to keep the consultative examination. He was contacted, and another appointment was scheduled, which he again failed to keep. On 3/1/2016 personal contact was made by the District Office at the beneficiary's home. The need for current medical evidence and for his cooperation in going for a CE was explained. There was no indication of any mental impairment or other condition that would make him unable to cooperate. Since he agreed to keep a CE, another appointment was scheduled for 3/9/2016. The beneficiary did not keep the CE, and the DDS was unable to contact him by telephone. On 3/15/2016, written notice that failure to cooperate could result in termination was sent to the beneficiary. He did not respond.

At the CPD, the beneficiary had malignant lymphoma of the ileum with metastasis. The most recent available evidence from 12/8/2015 indicates satisfactory progress. There is no current medical evidence available to determine if medical improvement has occurred, and the beneficiary has repeatedly failed to cooperate in efforts to obtain current medical evidence. Therefore, since there is failure to cooperate, a group II exception to medical improvement, disability is ceased 3/2016, the month the beneficiary was notified that failure to cooperate could result in termination of benefits. Disability will terminate 5/2016.

Medical-Vocational Rules

If you are not eligible for disability based solely on your illness or injury, the Social Security Administration looks at other issues to determine if you meet eligibility requirements in some other way.

The SSA uses the following tables of medical-vocational rules to decide whether physical impairment claims should be allowed or denied based on a combination of how much work you can do (called residual functional capacity, or RFC), age, education, and work experience. These rules are literally applied only in claims where the RFC is for sedentary, light, or medium work without other restrictions. If the RFC has additional special restrictions, then a vocational analyst may need to look at the claim. Other restrictions can include almost anything, such as the claimant's inability to work around excessive dust and fumes, inability to do fine movements with the fingers, inability to bend the back frequently, or inability to use leg controls.

In the Disability Determination Service (DDS), a vocational analyst is an experienced disability examiner with special training to evaluate the combination of RFC, age, education, and work experience in relation to a claimant's ability to perform various jobs.

Claimants capable of heavy work can do such high levels of physical exertion that the SSA considers them to have "not severe" (mild or slight) impairments, and so they do not actually receive RFCs for heavy work.

If your physical impairments are significant but not severe enough to meet any listing, the medical-vocational rules will give you a good idea whether you are eligible for benefits at all. You already know your age, education, and work experience. You would have to either estimate the RFC yourself or find out from the SSA after a determination has been made on your claim.

The medical-vocational rules in these tables are only applied when the RFC is so physically restrictive that you cannot return to your prior work, if you had any. The medical-vocational rules help determine whether you could do any other kind of work. The rules are a consistent way for the SSA to determine disability. There are no similar medical-vocational rule tables for mental impairments.

If you *can* return to your prior work based on your RFC, there would be little point in looking at the medical-vocational rules—the SSA would simply deny your claim, stating that you can return to your prior work.

If you are less than six months away from your next birthday, your age will be counted as if you have reached that day. For example, if you are 49½ years old, the SSA will consider you 50 years old.

(Review Chapter 8, "Whether You Can Do Some Work: Your RFC," and Chapter 9, "How Age, Education, and Work Experience Matter," for information that will help you use these tables.)

> **TIP**
> **Medical-vocational rules are** sometimes simply referred to as "vocational rules," but this is inaccurate because each rule involves both medical and vocational factors.

Abbreviations	
AA	Advanced age (55 and older)
CAAA	Closely approaching advanced age (50–54 years old)
CARA	Closely approaching retirement age (60 and older)
YI	Younger individual (less than 50 years old)
M	Marginal education (6th grade or less)
LL	Limited or less education (grades 7–11)
HSG	High school graduate or more (high school graduate, college graduate, or equivalent special training)
US	Unskilled
SS	Semiskilled
S	Skilled
N	None
I	Illiterate or unable to communicate in English

Table No. 1: Sedentary RFC

Rule	Age	Education	Previous Work Experience	Decision
201.01	AA (55 and older)	LL	US or N	Disabled
201.02	AA (55 and older)	LL	S or SS—skills not transferable	Disabled
201.03	AA (55 and older)	LL	S or SS—skills transferable	Not disabled
201.04	AA (55 and older)	HSG—education does not provide for direct entry into skilled work.	US or N	Disabled
201.05	AA (55 and older)	HSG—education provides for direct entry into skilled work.	US or N	Not disabled
201.06	AA (55 and older)	HSG—education does not provide for direct entry into skilled work.	S or SS—skills not transferable	Disabled
201.07	AA (55 and older)	HSG—education does not provide for direct entry into skilled work.	S or SS—skills transferable	Not disabled
201.08	AA (55 and older)	HSG—education provides for direct entry into skilled work.	S or SS—skills not transferable	Not disabled
201.09	CAAA (50–54)	LL	US or N	Disabled
201.10	CAAA (50–54)	LL	S or SS—skills not transferable	Disabled
201.11	CAAA (50–54)	LL	S or SS—skills transferable	Not disabled
201.12	CAAA (50–54)	HSG—education does not provide for direct entry into skilled work.	US or N	Disabled
201.13	CAAA (50–54)	HSG—education provides for direct entry into skilled work.	US or N	Not disabled
201.14	CAAA (50–54)	HSG—education does not provide for direct entry into skilled work.	S or SS—skills not transferable	Disabled
201.15	CAAA (50–54)	HSG—education does not provide for direct entry into skilled work.	S or SS—skills transferable	Not disabled
201.16	CAAA (50–54)	HSG—education provides for direct entry into skilled work	S or SS—skills not transferable	Not disabled

Rule	Age	Education	Previous Work Experience	Decision
		Table No. 1: Sedentary RFC (continued)		
201.17	YI (45–49)	I	US or N	Disabled
201.18	YI (45–49)	LL	US or N	Not disabled
201.19	YI (45–49)	LL	S or SS—skills not transferable	Not disabled
201.20	YI (45–49)	LL	S or SS—skills transferable	Not disabled
201.21	YI (45–49)	HSG	S or SS—skills not transferable	Not disabled
201.22	YI (45–49)	HSG	S or SS—skills transferable	Not disabled
201.23	YI (18–44)	I	US or N	Not disabled
201.24	YI (18–44)	LL	US or N	Not disabled
201.25	YI (18–44)	LL	S or SS—skills not transferable	Not disabled
201.26	YI (18–44)	LL	S or SS—skills transferable	Not disabled
201.27	YI (18–44)	HSG	US or N	Not disabled
201.28	YI (18–44)	HSG	S or SS—skills not transferable	Not disabled
201.29	YI (18–44)	HSG	S or SS—skills transferable	Not disabled

Table No. 2: Light RFC				
Rule	Age	Education	Previous Work Experience	Decision
202.01	AA (55 and older)	LL	US or N	Disabled
202.02	AA (55 and older)	LL	S or SS—skills not transferable	Disabled
202.03	AA (55 and older)	LL	S or SS—skills transferable	Not disabled
202.04	AA (55 and older)	HSG—education does not provide for direct entry into skilled work.	US or N	Disabled
202.05	AA (55 and older)	HSG—education provides for direct entry into skilled work.	US or N	Not disabled
202.06	AA (55 and older)	HSG—education does not provide for direct entry into skilled work.	S or SS—skills not transferable	Disabled
202.07	AA (55 and older)	HSG—education does not provide for direct entry into skilled work.	S or SS—skills transferable	Not disabled
202.08	AA (55 and older)	HSG—education provides for direct entry into skilled work.	S or SS—skills not transferable	Not disabled
202.09	CAAA (50–54)	I	US or N	Disabled
202.10	CAAA (50–54)	LL	US or N	Not disabled
202.11	CAAA (50–54)	LL	S or SS—skills not transferable	Not disabled
202.12	CAAA (50–54)	LL	S or SS—skills transferable	Not disabled
202.13	CAAA (50–54)	HSG	US or N	Not disabled
202.14	CAAA (50–54)	HSG	S or SS—skills not transferable	Not disabled
202.15	CAAA (50–54)	HSG	S or SS—skills transferable	Not disabled
202.16	YI (18–49)	I	US or N	Not disabled
202.17	YI (18–49)	LL	US or N	Not disabled
202.18	YI (18–49)	LL	S or SS—skills not transferable	Not disabled
202.19	YI (18–49)	LL	S or SS—skills transferable	Not disabled
202.20	YI (18–49)	HSG	US or N	Not disabled
202.21	YI (18–49)	HSG	S or SS—skills not transferable	Not disabled
202.22	YI (18–49)	HSG	S or SS—skills transferable	Not disabled

Table No. 3: Medium RFC				
Rule	**Age**	**Education**	**Previous Work Experience**	**Decision**
203.01	CARA (60–64)	M or N	US or N	Disabled
203.02	CARA (60–64)	LL	N	Disabled
203.03	CARA (60–64)	LL	US	Not disabled
203.04	CARA (60–64)	LL	S or SS—skills not transferable	Not disabled
203.05	CARA (60–64)	LL	S or SS—skills transferable	Not disabled
203.06	CARA (60–64)	HSG	US or N	Not disabled
203.07	CARA (60–64)	HSG—education does not provide for direct entry into skilled work.	S or SS—skills not transferable	Not disabled
203.08	CARA (60–64)	HSG—education does not provide for direct entry into skilled work.	S or SS—skills transferable	Not disabled
203.09	CARA (60–64)	HSG—education provides for direct entry into skilled work.	S or SS—skills not transferable	Not disabled
203.10	AA (55–59)	LL	N	Disabled
203.11	AA (55–59)	LL	US	Not disabled
203.12	AA (55–59)	LL	S or SS—skills not transferable	Not disabled
203.13	AA (55–59)	LL	S or SS—skills transferable	Not disabled
203.14	AA (55–59)	HSG	US or N	Not disabled
203.15	AA (55–59)	HSG—education does not provide for direct entry into skilled work.	S or SS—skills not transferable	Not disabled
203.16	AA (55–59)	HSG—education does not provide for direct entry into skilled work.	S or SS—skills transferable	Not disabled
203.17	AA (55–59)	HSG—education provides for direct entry into skilled work.	S or SS–skills not transferable	Not disabled
203.18	CAAA (50–54)	LL	US or N	Not disabled
203.19	CAAA (50–54)	LL	S or SS—skills not transferable	Not disabled

Rule	Age	Education	Previous Work Experience	Decision
		Table No. 3: Medium RFC (continued)		
203.20	CAAA (50–54)	LL	S or SS—skills transferable	Not disabled
203.21	CAAA (50–54)	HSG	US or N	Not disabled
203.22	CAAA (50–54)	HSG—education does not provide for direct entry into skilled work.	S or SS—skills not transferable	Not disabled
203.23	CAAA (50–54)	HSG—education does not provide for direct entry into skilled work.	S or SS—skills transferable	Not disabled
203.24	CAAA (50–54)	HSG—education provides for direct entry into skilled work.	S or SS—skills not transferable	Not disabled
203.25	YI (18–49)	LL	US or N	Not disabled
203.26	YI (18–49)	LL	S or SS—skills not transferable	Not disabled
203.27	YI (18–49)	LL	S or SS—skills transferable	Not disabled
203.28	YI (18–49)	HSG	US or N	Not disabled
203.29	YI (18–49)	HSG—education does not provide for direct entry into skilled work.	S or SS—skills not transferable	Not disabled
203.30	YI (18–49)	HSG—education does not provide for direct entry into skilled work.	S or SS—skills transferable	Not disabled
203.31	YI (18–49)	HSG—education provides for direct entry into skilled work.	S or SS—skills not transferable	Not disabled

How to Use the Medical Listings on Nolo.com

This book comes with PDF files containing the SSA's disability listings that you can download here: **www.nolo.com/back-of-book/QSS.html**

To use the files, your computer must have Adobe *Reader* (free software available from Adobe.com).

List of Files on Nolo.com

To download the following Medical Listings, go to: **www.nolo.com/back-of-book/QSS.html**

Part Name	File Name
Musculoskeletal Disorders and Growth Impairments	Part1.pdf
Vision, Balance, Hearing, and Speech	Part2.pdf
Breathing Disorders	Part3.pdf
Heart and Blood Vessel Diseases	Part4.pdf
Digestive System Disease	Part5.pdf
Kidney Disease	Part6.pdf
Blood Diseases	Part7.pdf
Skin Diseases	Part8.pdf
Hormone Disorders	Part9.pdf
Multiple Body System Disorders	Part10.pdf
Nervous System Disorders	Part11.pdf
Mental Disorders	Part12.pdf
Cancer	Part13.pdf
Immune System Disorders	Part14.pdf

Index

W